A COLD WAR STATE OF MIND

A VOLUME IN THE SERIES

Culture, Politics, and the Cold War

edited by
Christian G. Appy

OTHER TITLES IN THE SERIES

James T. Fisher, *Dr. America: The Lives of Thomas A. Dooley, 1927–1961*

Daniel Horowitz, *Betty Friedan and the Making of "The Feminine Mystique": The American Left, the Cold War, and Modern Feminism*

Tom Engelhardt, *The End of Victory Culture: Cold War America and the Disillusioning of a Generation*

Christian G. Appy, ed., *Cold War Constructions: The Political Culture of United States Imperialism, 1945–1966*

H. Bruce Franklin, *Vietnam and Other American Fantasies*

Robert D. Dean, *Imperial Brotherhood: Gender and the Making of Cold War Foreign Policy*

Lee Bernstein, *The Greatest Menace: Organized Crime in Cold War America*

David C. Engerman, Nils Gilman, Mark H. Haefele, and Michael E. Latham, eds., *Staging Growth: Modernization, Development, and the Global Cold War*

Jonathan Nashel, *Edward Lansdale's Cold War*

James Peck, *Washington's China: The National Security World, the Cold War, and the Origins of Globalism*

Edwin A. Martini, *Invisible Enemies: The American War on Vietnam, 1975–2000*

Tony Shaw, *Hollywood's Cold War*

Maureen Ryan, *The Other Side of Grief: The Home Front and the Aftermath in American Narratives of the Vietnam War*

David Hunt, *Vietnam's Southern Revolution: From Peasant Insurrection to Total War*

Patrick Hagopian, *The Vietnam War in American Memory: Veterans, Memorials, and the Politics of Healing*

Jeremy Kuzmarov, *The Myth of the Addicted Army: Vietnam and the Modern War on Drugs*

Robert Surbrug Jr., *Beyond Vietnam: The Politics of Protest in Massachusetts, 1974–1990*

Larry Grubbs, *Secular Missionaries: Americans and African Development in the 1960s*

Robert A. Jacobs, *The Dragon's Tail: Americans Face the Atomic Age*

Andrew J. Falk, *Upstaging the Cold War: American Dissent and Cultural Diplomacy, 1940–1960*

Jerry Lembcke, *Hanoi Jane: War, Sex, and Fantasies of Betrayal*

Anna G. Creadick, *Perfectly Average: The Pursuit of Normality in Postwar America*

Kathleen Donohue, ed., *Liberty and Justice for All? Rethinking Politics in Cold War America*

Jeremy Kuzmarov, *Modernizing Repression: Police Training and Nation Building in the American Century*

Roger Peace, *A Call to Conscience: The Anti–Contra War Campaign*

Edwin A. Martini, *Agent Orange: History, Science, and the Politics of Uncertainty*

Patrick Hagopian, *American Immunity: War Crimes and the Limits of International Law*

A COLD WAR STATE OF MIND

★ ★ ★

BRAINWASHING AND POSTWAR AMERICAN SOCIETY

Matthew W. Dunne

University of Massachusetts Press

Amherst & Boston

Printed in the United States of America

ISBN 978-1-62534-041-2 (paper); 040-5 (hardcover)

Designed by Jack Harrison
Set in Trump Mediaeval
Printed and bound by IBT/Hamilton, Inc.

Library of Congress Cataloging-in-Publication Data
Dunne, Matthew W., 1980–
A Cold War state of mind : brainwashing and postwar American society /
Matthew W. Dunne.
pages cm. — (Culture, politics, and the Cold War)
Includes bibliographical references and index.
ISBN 978-1-62534-041-2 (pbk. : alk. paper) —
ISBN 978-1-62534-040-5 (hardcover : alk. paper)
1. Popular culture—United States—History—20th century.
2. Politics and culture—United States—History—20th century.
3. Cold War—Influence. 4. Cold War—Social aspects—United States.
5. Brainwashing—United States—History—20th century. 6. United States—Civilization—1945–
7. Political culture—United States—History—20th century. I. Title.
E169.12.D859 2013
973.91—dc23
2013031732

British Library Cataloguing-in-Publication Data
A catalogue record for this book is available from the British Library.

Cover: Illustration by Larry Kritcher, in Sidney Herschel Small,
"The Brainwashed Pilot," *Saturday Evening Post,* 227, no. 38 (19 March 1955), 31.

publication of this book
is supported by a grant from

FIGURE FOUNDATION

FOR

Lily Mae, Julia Rose, and Evie Marie

Contents

Acknowledgments

The journey to finishing this book has proven to be an all-consuming one for the better part of four years, and in my time working on the project I have become indebted to many people. All of this help has been humbling, and ultimately this book and my experience writing it would have been lesser without it. I am deeply grateful to Howard Chudacoff at Brown University for his tireless support and invaluable comments on early versions of the manuscript. Feedback and encouragement from Robert O. Self and Elliott Gorn assisted in broadening my research and my approach to the topic of brainwashing. Their intellectual generosity helped me get this project off the ground and left an immeasurable imprint on the final version. I also benefited from many formal and informal discussions with members of my graduate cohort at Brown, who consistently challenged and inspired me during my years in Providence.

Research support for this project was initially provided by Brown University and the Eisenhower Foundation. This support funded my archival research at the Dwight D. Eisenhower Library, whose staff helped guide me through their massive collection and assisted me in pinpointing material that made a significant contribution to my study of postwar America. Generous faculty funding at Stonehill College also greatly contributed to this project and provided me with opportunities to expand the research I conducted in the later years.

While I was at Stonehill my colleague Shane Maddock generously read my manuscript and provided critical feedback and advice that influenced much of my thinking on the 1960s and the Vietnam era. In April 2012 I presented research related to this book at the spring conference of the New England Historical Association, where I received valuable comments on the physical fitness craze of the early postwar period from the audience and the session chair, Jennifer Tebbe-Grossman. A special thanks as well to the external reviewers for the University of Massachusetts Press, whose expertise and insight helped make this a much more nuanced final product.

For the past twenty-four months Chris Appy and Clark Dougan at the University of Massachusetts Press have helped guide me through every step of the publication process. They saw potential in this project in its fledgling stage and showed great faith and patience as I worked to bring it to maturity. I can't thank them enough. I am also deeply indebted to my copyeditor, Lawrence Kenney, and to Carol Betsch, Jack Harrison, and their colleagues at the University of Massachusetts Press for their attention to detail and tireless support.

Finally, I want to thank my family for their love and support. I have been fascinated with the past since I was a child, when conversations with my grandfather inspired me to see history as exciting and important. He had an innate talent for making a child see the wonder in the world. I like to think he would appreciate this book. I also want to thank my parents, who have been loving and supportive throughout this process and have spent countless hours talking about and reading this manuscript. Their suggestions and thoughts were always insightful, and they have been a constant source of encouragement. Above all, I want to thank my wonderful wife and partner, Teri. I have been consumed by brainwashing and by this project for the duration of our married life. Each and every day you inspired me to move forward and were patient and supportive when I was bogged down by this book. Between the time I embarked on it and its publication, we also started a family, which has been thoroughly life changing and entirely life affirming. You and our three little ladies are my inspiration.

A COLD WAR STATE OF MIND

Introduction

When the director Jonathan Demme remade *The Manchurian Candidate* in 2004 he updated several aspects of John Frankenheimer's classic psychological thriller from the 1960s for a contemporary audience. Among the more noteworthy changes, Demme shifted the setting from the Cold War to the war on terror, completely abandoned the McCarthy-esque character Senator Johnny Iselin, and transformed the Communist enemy from the original into America's own corporate allies. As one critic observed, "What was a thriller set in the deepest, darkest paranoid waters of the Cold War has become a sort of post–Gulf War Halliburton-dunit."[1] But notably the original film's central plot device was left essentially unaltered, and the protagonist in both films, Raymond Shaw, was brainwashed and controlled by external forces. The science behind this process had become more sophisticated in the new film, exchanging Communist hypnosis for microchips, but when Demme's Ben Marco (Denzel Washington) tried to persuade Raymond Shaw (Liev Schreiber) that a conspiracy was afoot, the dialogue echoed the same themes of psychological invasion and manipulation as the original: "Somebody got into our heads with big steel-toe boots or cable cutters and a chainsaw, and they went to town. Neurons got exposed and circuits got rewired. Our brain cells got obliterated." The film's markedly different politics, gender dynamics, and visions of American democracy speak to the profound changes the United States underwent in the four decades since the original had first played in theaters. However, at its core Demme's *The Manchurian Candidate,* like Frankenheimer's version before it, is a film about Americans' anxieties over individuality in the postwar world.[2]

Concerns about the state of modern individuality and personal autonomy have been recurring themes in American life, but during the early Cold War they took on a new poignancy when the concept of brainwashing ushered anxieties over Communist psychological warfare into the center of the national discourse. Since the birth of the nation, the belief that human beings have the ability to reason as free and rational subjects has been perhaps the central guiding principle of American political culture, but brainwashing threw many of the underlying assumptions about America's grand experiment in democracy into a state of flux. Do American citizens, who live in a nation that glorifies independent thinkers and individual rights, really have complete control over their actions and beliefs? Or are they more like Raymond Shaw, innocent victims who can be exposed to forces that have developed the psychological tools to get into their heads and "[go] to town"? The public discourse surrounding brainwashing in the 1950s and 1960s indicated that, to varying degrees, we are all Raymond Shaws.

Although the Cold War is over, the mind-set about individuality it fostered remains an integral part of our culture. Since the start of the war on terror many of these anxieties have been reborn, although, like the remake of *The Manchurian Candidate,* their original links to the Cold War have tended to be obscured. Contemporary concerns about the link between violent films and video games and the national epidemic of school shootings, the popular construction of radical Muslim terrorists, widespread media reports about the supposed use of propaganda by the administration of George W. Bush, the so-called enhanced interrogation techniques employed by the Central Intelligence Agency (CIA), and cultural products like the Emmy award–winning Showtime drama *Homeland* are all indebted to ideas and anxieties first produced by brainwashing nearly sixty years ago. Today, however, many Americans are unaware of the links between contemporary anxieties about individuality and the rhetoric, logic, and original Cold War framework of the brainwashing scare of the 1950s.

The purpose of *A Cold War State of Mind* is to reexamine the history of postwar America through the prism of brainwashing and analyze the mind-set that the concept produced. In the pages that follow, I attempt to recapture what the concept conveyed to audiences during the postwar era and explore the discursive reach of the concept well beyond those years. The fact that brainwashing is so frequently dismissed today as a pseudoscientific reminder of the irrationality and paranoid style of Cold War America has obscured the concept's true legacy. As this book will demonstrate, the history of brainwashing reveals something more important about American society in the postwar years than a paranoid streak in the body politic, and it had much wider currency and significance in the early 1950s and beyond than historians have traditionally acknowledged. Studying brainwashing from the perspective of the American public in particular reveals a hidden history of the Cold War and illustrates how central the concept was to the rise of new models of behavior, new ideas about the mind and anxieties about the potential for domestic and foreign institutions to misuse psychology in order to manipulate human beings, and the breakdown of a postwar consensus based on the notion that the United States was a beacon of freedom in a world threatened by authoritarian and Communist forces. In focusing on brainwashing and related concepts I also shed new light on a number of broad national trends that have typically been associated with the late 1960s and 1970s, including a widespread decline in Americans' trust of politicians, the appearance of increasingly sophisticated consumer identities, a waning sense of community nationwide, and an emphasis on self-fulfillment that has led baby boomers to become known pejoratively as the Me Generation.

This book does not delve into questions related to the actual legitimacy of brainwashing as a technique of mind control, a topic better suited to neuroscience or psychology. Nor does the book explore the CIA's mind control experiments in the fifties and sixties in detail, which have been addressed in several other books.[3] Instead, my research primarily focuses on brainwashing as an idea rather than as a technique and investigates not only why brainwashing attained such widespread acceptance and explanatory power during the Cold War but also how it influenced several generations of Americans to believe that their individuality was under attack and that conformity, groupthink, and other-directedness were threats aimed at the destruction of the very fabric of the United States of America.

When brainwashing first entered the American Cold War lexicon in 1950, the future impact of the concept would have been nearly impossible to imagine. The brainchild of a relatively obscure journalist named Edward Hunter who had ties to the Office of Strategic Services and the CIA, the term first appeared in the print media in a *Miami News* article by Hunter in 1950 and only grew in credibility and profile during the Korean War. After it became associated with the mysterious behavior of American soldiers behind enemy lines in Korea, brainwashing became front-page fodder for months and was widely deemed a legitimate new threat to the free world that could potentially produce a form of psychological slavery that had no precedent in human history. As material prepared for Department of Defense officials contended, "In the old days, thumb screws were used. The methods employed today are more subtle. Devices of psychology and neurology. The baffling word-play of courtroom forensics. The trickery of stagecraft. Third-degree tactics modernized."[4] This, indeed, was the frightening next step in the "battle for men's minds."

The publicity surrounding brainwashing would eventually transform the battle for human minds from the abstract to the literal, forcing Americans to redefine the Communist threat and conceptualize the Cold War within an increasingly individualistic, rather than geopolitical, framework. As the specter of nuclear war threatened the safety of Americans' physical bodies, brainwashing threatened the sanctity of their minds. However, while Americans could unite in civil defense or underground shelters to combat the threat of nuclear war, brainwashing allowed no such community. In a profound sense this new peril alluded to the ultimate war without boundaries and a Cold World future that pitted the lone individual against the Communist enemy. As a result, brainwashing helped produce a dual front: the physical front that existed along the borders of the Iron and Bamboo Curtains and a mental front that existed in the minds of every American citizen. Hunter chillingly outlined this new battlefield when he claimed, "There is no 'behind the lines' any longer."[5]

The popular understanding of the concept would eventually mirror the murky contours of the vague and sinister Communist enemy. Described by one Cold War expert as "the total psychological weapon by means of which . . . Soviet Russia firmly expects to conquer the rest of the world," brainwashing was defined as a sinister new form of Communist mind control that could potentially turn the most patriotic American into an unwitting pawn of the Communist enemy.[6] Appearing as a logical next step in the evolution of preexisting methods of manipulation and psychological warfare, brainwashing harmonized with the popular perception of the Communist enemy and their totalitarian aims. As a result, brainwashing was widely accepted as a new Communist weapon, and by the middle of the 1950s it had stirred pervasive fears of mind control as the latest alien threat in the United States.

By the conclusion of the Korean War brainwashing had already left an indelible imprint upon the American imagination and produced vivid new fears that Americans' brains were under attack. Linking the individual American psyche to national security, the threat of Communist brainwashing indicated that Americans' memories, their beliefs, their freedom, even their very souls might be at risk. Over time the concept would evolve and stray from its original cultural terrain and become one of the most ubiquitous and malleable concepts of the entire postwar era. In the midfifties, journalists, contemporary observers, and Cold War experts argued that the success of Communist brainwashing was due to a new softness in American men, which they attributed variously to flaws in the nation's child-rearing practices, the American education system, and widespread generational and social decay. As the logic of brainwashing became an accepted part of the intellectual and cultural Cold War landscape, contemporary observers began to see a pattern of psychological machinations within American society as well. They identified "hidden persuaders" who attempted to subliminally shape Americans' economic decisions; manipulative political ad campaigns that subtly influenced Americans' decisions at the polls; violent television programs and comic books that turned innocent American children into juvenile delinquents; and a corporate and suburban culture that encouraged conformity and dulled the minds of the middle class.[7] By the end of the 1950s brainwashing was no longer perceived as a uniquely Communist threat but had emerged as an internal enemy linked to capitalism and a decadent America. Americans had imported brainwashing from the communist other, but they quickly turned it on themselves, creating an elastic tool of self-examination employed equally by the political right and left in a two-decade culture war.

During the early fifties the American Cold War consensus had rested on the assumption that Communism represented mental slavery and American consumerism and capitalistic democracy represented freedom. When Vice President Richard Nixon took part in the Kitchen Debates with Nikita Khrushchev in July 1959 at the opening of the American National Exhibition in Moscow, the link between consumer goods and American society was on proud display. The American exhibition was almost singularly focused on American consumer products and prominently featured a model suburban home. The debate crystallized the perception that the freedom to buy and live in a suburban home, complete with all the gadgets, was not only the birthright of all free Americans but also a cornerstone of democratic society.[8] Yet by the end of the decade intellectuals and the public alike were increasingly beginning to question the underlying assumptions that had made such assertions possible. If suburbanization and the corporate world sapped Americans of their individuality, were Americans truly free? If television, comic books, and American mass media could turn children into juvenile delinquents, drug addicts, and perverts, were American children really autonomous? If big business was employing subliminal ads and hidden persuasion that manipulated Americans' subconscious minds, was capitalistic society any less authoritarian than Communist society?

As Americans struggled with these questions, the cultural and intellectual assumptions that had supported the status quo during America's second Red Scare slowly began to dissolve. Since government and military figures had already prominently used the specter of Communist brainwashing to criticize the Communist state and publicly labeled brainwashing a crime against humanity, when similar practices were identified in domestic American society it opened a cultural space that presented Americans with an opportunity to safely criticize the United States during a period when to do so was fraught with danger. Taking a page out of the McCarthyite playbook, Americans and public intellectuals on the left and right discredited the mainstream media, big business, and American politics by linking their use of practices associated with psychological manipulation to Communism. By calling into question the Americanness of institutions that lay at the heart of domestic American society, the application of the brainwashing narrative to postwar America promoted a significant breakdown of the Cold War consensus.

As the lines between Communism and capitalism became more and more nebulous, the modern American personality archetype was born. Because brainwashing encouraged Americans to focus on threats to their individuality, they became increasingly sensitive to any perceived intrusions on their psyche and began reinterpreting aspects of postwar culture that had traditionally been viewed as relatively innocuous. Influencing policymakers as well as ordinary Americans, the concept helped transform the few remaining comforts of Cold War America into increasingly dubious vehicles for external domination. Politicians who had enjoyed the public's trust in more carefree times were now deemed potentially devious actors bent on molding public opinion to suit their own agendas. The American capitalist system, once defined as the most fair and balanced economic system in the world, was viewed from a more cynical perspective because of the possibility that hidden persuaders were peering into the public's subconscious minds and controlling their desires. And members of American's local communities—their neighbors and even members of their own families—were regarded with new suspicion because they could potentially be brainwashed Communist saboteurs. Who was there left to trust in Cold War America? As Americans emerged from the era of brainwashing, they were encouraged to think for themselves and taught to distrust traditional sources of external authority. Ironically, in what some critics saw as an age of creeping conformity, brainwashing helped create new ideals for Americans that were loaded with subversive potential. In response to assorted threats to the national psyche, American culture began to stress character traits that combated the ills of conformity and emphasized individuality, and a new generation of Americans was encouraged to think for itself and taught to be as suspicious of a Marlboro advertisement as they were of *Pravda*.

Brainwashing was a central concept of the postwar period not simply because it was ubiquitous but also because it affected the way Americans saw the world outside the United States as well as how they perceived themselves. As a transient but potent idea, brainwashing forced Americans to reevaluate the nature of modern identity and the limits of personal autonomy in a new postwar world controlled by Big Brother and big business. Although a pattern of government-sponsored psychological manipulation, indoctrination, and propaganda emanating from the Soviet Union and China was clearly visible by the early 1950s, the evidence for overt mind control was never as strong as some alarmists proclaimed. Yet despite the questionable authenticity of brainwashing the concept colored postwar Americans' perception of reality and influenced their behavior, subtly encouraging nonconformity and individuality at the height of a domestic Red Scare. Shaping the cultural terrain on which both communism and capitalism came to be understood in the postwar years, the beliefs and tensions spurred on by brainwashing assisted in the creation of a new perspective of the world that focused on the precariousness of freedom in the modern era. It was a Cold War state of mind.

Thematically, this book is based on a loose chronological format and is divided into two parts. Part 1 focuses on the anxieties surrounding brainwashing when it first emerged in the national discourse and was predominantly linked to the nation's apprehensions over Communist psychological warfare. In part 2 I trace the evolution of these anxieties as they shifted from the external threat of the Communist enemy to internal concerns about the state of American society and the manipulative tendencies of American consumer culture.

During the early stages of this project I envisioned writing a very different book on brainwashing and Cold War American society, a book much more centrally focused on military and government sources and the people and institutions that had produced them. After making a research trip to the Dwight D. Eisenhower Presidential Library in Kansas, however, I realized that the larger story of brainwashing was not limited to government archives or the declassified records of executive agencies. As I read through hundreds of documents related to the practice during Eisenhower's administration, I kept returning to editorials, magazine articles, films, and television shows. In large part this was because they were recurring topics in the archives. The Eisenhower administration, it turned out, had been acutely aware of the public discussion of brainwashing. As I dug through this material it dawned on me that the reason members of the government had become so concerned about the public narrative of brainwashing was that they had lost control of it. By the midfifties the government, military, and medical and scientific authorities repeatedly attempted to downplay the severity of brainwashing, but by that point it was too late—the concept had become a cultural phenomenon, defined and disseminated by public intellectuals, journalists, and popular culture.

Although the manner in which elite members of the government, military, and national security apparatus addressed brainwashing is a significant part of postwar history and promoted "the rapid creation of a massive new intelligence infrastructure and . . . new frameworks of discourse, knowledge, and terminology," how select policymakers addressed the concept tells only a fraction of a much broader history.[9] This book represents an attempt to shift the focus on brainwashing from the intellectual and policymaking elite to ordinary citizens and is centrally concerned with the lived experience of Communist mind control and its capitalist variations and how they were portrayed and conceptualized outside the halls of power. In the long run, how ordinary Americans internalized and acted upon the brainwashing narrative cast a much larger shadow on postwar American history than the development of CIA programs such as Project MKUltra.

By the end of the 1950s brainwashing was nearly omnipresent, simultaneously influencing the popular portrayal of the Communist enemy while also routinely surfacing in Americans' debates and anxieties about their own society. Since concerns over mind control and psychological manipulation touched on so many diverse arenas of American life, this book draws on a wide range of sources, from government documents and congressional hearings to film and literature. In order to effectively tap into this public discourse I have made a conscious effort to use sources that were reflective of public opinion and eminently available to Americans during the postwar era. I have also opted to use media coverage of speeches, academic conferences, and congressional hearings when possible to accurately convey how official narratives on brainwashing were disseminated to the public. When appropriate, I have also utilized archival material from the Eisenhower Presidential Library to document how policymakers attempted to shape public opinion and how they reacted to it. In addition to focusing on material that reveals what Americans were told about brainwashing, I have addressed sources that illustrate how Americans reacted to these narratives, including letters to the editor, quotes from ordinary citizens in the mainstream media, and candid comments from government and cultural figures. Taken together, these documents illustrate how the brainwashing narrative was articulated by different governmental and cultural figures, how it was received by the public, and what impact it had on people's behavior and beliefs.

As Andreas Killen and Stefan Andriopoulos recently noted, brainwashing "has remained largely neglected by most professional historians, quarantined from the 'real' history of the Cold War."[10] This oversight is finally starting to be rectified, and brainwashing has emerged as the focus of serious scholarly analysis in a small but growing secondary literature.[11] Although this scholarship is invaluable, it has primarily focused on how specific governmental and cultural institutions conceptualized, portrayed, and in some cases even mimicked the Communist technique of brainwashing, while predominantly ignoring its impact on ordinary Americans' behavior and their perceptions of the postwar world. As a result, brainwashing's broader impact on postwar Americans' beliefs and anxieties about modern identity remain ill understood. This book builds on and moves beyond the existing scholarship by stressing the relationship between brainwashing and the development of a new postwar discourse and mind-set that influenced many Americans to believe, in the words of the public intellectual William H. Whyte, that they were "more acted upon than acting."[12]

Long after the anxiety of overt Communist mind control had subsided and the term *brainwashing* had slipped into everyday parlance, the mind-set, worldview, and emphasis on individuality that the concept initially inspired remained central components of the intellectual and cultural universe of postwar Americans. Perhaps more than any other popular conviction in the twentieth century, brainwashing destabilized postwar Americans' conceptions of individuality and influenced their anxieties about myriad threats to humanity and personal autonomy in the modern world. As the technique evolved from a sinister form of Communist mind control to a domestic tool of political and economic manipulation, it played a crucial role in shaping the nation's concerns about freedom, individualism, conformity, loyalty, and trust in authority. By looking at the complex and varied interactions between the Cold War and American society through the lens of brainwashing, *A Cold War State of Mind* aims to reestablish the concept's significance to postwar culture, politics, and popular thought. The mind-set and beliefs produced by brainwashing in the 1950s and 1960s have been among our central inheritances from the Cold War. Only by analyzing brainwashing from the perspective of ordinary Americans and exploring its evolution from the early 1950s until the end of the 1960s can one fully appreciate it.

I

"THERE IS NO 'BEHIND THE LINES' ANY LONGER"

1
The Origins of Brainwashing

On Friday, April 10, 1953, two months after being appointed director of the CIA, Allen Dulles stood before a gathering of the Alumni Conference for Princeton University in Hot Springs, Virginia. In less than two weeks the first exchange of prisoners of war (POWs) between the United States and North Korea, popularly known as Operation Little Switch, would take place.[1] The exchange would mark the beginning of the end of the Korean War, but as that war reached its final resolution in the fall of 1953 the Cold War continued unabated. As Dulles addressed the crowd it was clear that the future of the Cold War and the ever-escalating advances in weapons technology that helped fuel it weighed heavily on his mind. In a speech that touched on the country's fragile national security, the psychological aspects of modern warfare, and the ideological battle between the United States and the Soviet Union, Dulles began to articulate his concerns over sophisticated new Communist psychological weaponry that had the potential to alter the Cold War struggle forever. Looking out over the audience, Dulles said, "In the past few years we have become accustomed to hearing much about the battle for men's minds—the war of ideologies—and indeed our Government has been driven by the international tension we call the 'cold war' to take positive steps to recognize psychological warfare and to play an active role in it. I wonder, however, whether we clearly perceive the magnitude of the problem, whether we realize how sinister the battle for men's minds has become in Soviet hands. We might call it, in its new form, 'brain warfare.' "[2]

Fleshing out the contours of "brain warfare," Dulles claimed that the Communist enemy had invented new "brain perversion techniques" that had proven the human mind was "a malleable tool."[3] The result of the Communists' new technique was a "brain . . . [that] becomes a phonograph playing a disc put on its spindle by an outside genius over which it had no control."[4] Dulles concluded his speech with a dire prediction, speculating that "considerable numbers of our own boys there [in the Korean prison camps] might be so indoctrinated as to be induced, temporarily at least, to renounce country and family."[5] In the span of a few sentences Dulles had transformed the figurative concept of a "battle for men's minds" into a much more literal and horrifying conceit. The impetus for his worries was widespread rumors and classified military speculation that the Communists had successfully brainwashed a large number of American soldiers while they had been held captive in North Korea. A little over five months later, in the midst of Operation Big Switch, the behavior of twenty-three American soldiers appeared to confirm Dulles's predictions.[6]

On September 24, 1953, twenty-three American POWs arrived at the Neutral Nations Repatriation Commission in Panmunjom, Korea, in the back of Russian trucks. The men were dressed in smart blue Chinese uniforms, their jackets adorned with a small pin featuring Pablo Picasso's iconic white dove peace symbol. As they descended from the trucks and made their way into the complex, they loudly sang the Communist Internationale: "Arise, ye prisoners of starvation, arise ye starvelings of want." In a statement released to the press the soldiers said that "they love their country and some day will return—when the American people have achieved 'freedom.'"[7] As the American officers on the scene left the Neutral Nations Repatriation compound, a deep southern accent pierced the silence, directing its ire at a press correspondent: "Go home, you imperialist Yankee!"[8] A wave of American POWs then rushed the barbed-wire fence "and shook their fists" at the American officers.[9]

For all intents and purposes, the publicity surrounding the twenty-three American soldiers in Panmunjom signaled the arrival of brainwashing as a cultural phenomenon. As news of the soldiers who refused to come home made its way to the front pages of American newspapers, they became media sensations. Testifying to the importance of the soldiers' decision to remain with their Communist captors, John Chapple, the editor of the *Wisconsin Daily Press,* said, "The very history of civilization rests on the outcome of this case, for if we do not act courageously to rescue these boys we are admitting that the propaganda power of Communism is more effective than that of our way of life."[10] The behavior of the soldiers had temporarily pushed them into the center of the ideological struggle between the United States and international Communism and appeared to offer startling proof that American minds were under attack.

For the next three months the twenty-three soldiers remained at the United Nations compound, rejecting packages sent by their families and

Four of the GIs who refused repatriation to the United States and their mascot in Panmunjom on January 26, 1954. From left: Cpl. William Cowart, Sgt. Andrew Fortuna, Pfc. Lowell Skinner, and Sgt. Lewis W. Griggs. (AP Images / Gene Smith)

relatives and adamantly refusing to hold interviews with American officials. They were slightly less evasive with the media and continued to release statements lauding their captors and critiquing America. During the entire three-month period that they remained at the compound, interviews of their parents, siblings, girlfriends, wives, teachers, and neighbors were picked up by the national newswires, op-ed pieces analyzing their statements and behavior were splashed across the nation's editorial pages, and articles covering the twenty-three GIs became a daily feature in the mainstream media. The media indicated that the soldiers actually seemed to be enjoying the entire spectacle, enthusiastically singing Communist songs, joking with each other, and even "gulp[ing] down rice wine by the tin-cupful" on New Year's Eve.[11]

If the American government was quick to blame the episode on Communist torture and psychological manipulation, they were not above a little chicanery of their own. The American officers on the scene repeatedly told the POWs that if they simply agreed to return to the United States they would instantly be forgiven for their temporary shift in allegiance and never face a court-martial in American military courts—a promise that would not be kept. One POW received "tender letters" ostensibly written by his Japanese wife urging him to return to the United States, but they had actually been composed by members of the Associated Press in Tokyo.[12] Less deceitful, grassroots campaigns to entice the POWs to return to the United States sprang up around the country. There were earnest letter-writing campaigns, a plan sponsored by the American Legion to send all of the POWs' mothers to Panmunjom to convince them to return home, and an offer for a job in Major League Baseball from the president of the Cleveland Indians.[13] Several of the POWs' families recorded messages begging their sons to come home. Cpl. Arlie H. Pate's father attempted to convince his son to return to the family farm in southern Illinois through a combination of guilt ("Your mommy's in bad shape and can't stand it hardly at all, you being gone like that") and the lure of creature comforts and fried food ("We got the stock and everything here waiting for you and you can have fried chicken and everything, fried chicken, fried squirrel and fried rabbits and you can just have a big time").[14] However, despite the nation's best efforts, only two of the soldiers changed their minds, and when the deadline for repatriation arrived in January 1954, twenty-one American POWs opted to remain behind the Bamboo Curtain.

The group that stayed behind allegedly represented a typical cross section of young American men, an interpretation that appeared to be borne out by a quick glance at the soldiers. They consisted of eighteen Caucasians and three African Americans; there were ten Protestants, five Baptists, four Roman Catholics, an Episcopal and a Greek Orthodox Catholic; their ages ranged from twenty to thirty-three; and they hailed from twenty-one states and every corner of the country. In effect, noted one journalist, the "essential difference between the kid down the street and the twenty-one [POWs] is that he wasn't put into the front lines in Korea and didn't spend three years in prison camp."[15] In reality, these claims to normalcy were overblown and ignored a number of factors related to the POWs' backgrounds. But above all, during an era when Communism was a dirty word and any association with the Communist Party was deemed dangerously un-American behavior, the twenty-one POWs' disavowal of their home country and their decision to remain with their Communist captors was well outside the norms of the Cold War American ideological consensus.

According to the contemporary paradigm, communism, as both an ideology and a mode of government, was antithetical to fundamental American democratic values. Viewed within this context, the behavior of the soldiers in Panmunjom was hard for the American public to comprehend. How could members of the American military, the symbolic heart of American patriotism, be swayed by Communism? The fact that each POW was scheduled to collect roughly five thousand dollars in back pay, no small sum in 1953, only made their behavior more perplexing. As the sociologist Albert D. Biderman would later assert, for many "home-front Americans, only a mysterious and superhuman cause could explain how ordinary Americans, like themselves, could be made to serve such a diabolical creed as Communism."[16] That mysterious and superhuman cause became brainwashing, and as contemporary observers began crafting explanations for the soldiers' behavior they quickly latched onto the concept.

Through the prism of brainwashing, journalists were able to hypothesize that the behavior of the soldiers was the result not of any traitorous streak in America's fighting men but of advanced new techniques of psychological torture and mind control. Many writers saw the behavior of the twenty-one soldiers who refused repatriation to the United States as evidence of brainwashing's authenticity, claiming that Communism was so contradictory to the beliefs of America's fighting men that the only logical explanation for their behavior was mind control. An article in the *New York Times* in 1954 articulated this theory and the logic that supported it, claiming that "for men who were born and grew up in this country to say things like 'There is no freedom of speech in the United States' suggests that those making such statements have had their life memories wiped out and delusions put in their place."[17]

Eventually, brainwashing would become one of the most prominent explanations for the behavior of the twenty-one soldiers who refused to come home. More important, as the returning POWs faded into the background of American culture, the concept of brainwashing became an accepted, integral part of the intellectual and cultural Cold War milieu. Despite critical studies that attacked its validity, brainwashing became indelibly tied to concerns over national security, spies, and a Communist invasion and was one of the more prominent fears of the period. The potential for a technique that purportedly transformed patriotic young Americans into hard-core Commies was terrifying, and by placing a literal twist on the "battle for men's minds," brainwashing seemed to threaten the very basis of American democracy: free will and individual autonomy. As a result, the concept of brainwashing struck a deep nerve in the American public and became one of the most pervasive fears of the entire postwar era.

Initially, the explanation provided by brainwashing appeared to soothe fears over the seemingly inexplicable behavior of America's fighting men in Korea, but it quickly gave rise to new concerns over the presumed softness and mental weakness of the nation's fighting forces and the country at large, as well as the nation's ability to win the Cold War. Why did Americans so readily embrace brainwashing as a plausible explanation for ideological conversion, a symbol of Communist treachery, and a test of their own culture's strengths and weaknesses? The answer to that question lies in the events that led to the practice's large-scale exposure and how the concept was initially defined.

A Disturbing Pattern

Although the case of the twenty-one unrepatriated American soldiers marked the largest exposure of the concept of brainwashing up to that point, a number of incidents that occurred prior to Operation Big Switch played an important role in establishing the reality of Communist psychological warfare. Over the course of the Korean War there had been dozens of reports of American soldiers exhibiting bizarre behavior while they were held captive by the Korean People's Army and the Chinese People's Volunteers. This strange conduct manifested itself in signed pro-Communist statements, radio broadcasts extolling the virtues of Communism, confessions, interviews, and even letters to their families expressing their sympathies with the Communists. The recorded and written statements all included the same similarly worded pro-Communist messages. Initially, these reports were met with skepticism, but as the concept of brainwashing began to gain momentum in the early 1950s these incidents began to be perceived as evidence that the enemy was using the technique to extract false confessions from American soldiers and in some cases even successfully converting them into Communists.

Radio transmissions released by the Communist Party featuring captured American soldiers praising the Communist system and criticizing the United States appeared almost immediately. The first radio broadcast aired on "July 9, 1950, a mere four days after United Nations ground forces commenced military action against the North Koreans, [when] an American army officer of the Twenty-fourth Infantry Division 'made a nine-hundred word broadcast in the enemy's behalf over the Seoul radio.' "[18] As the fighting wore on pro-Communist broadcasts on the Communist Party's radio stations became relatively commonplace. Many captured American soldiers later admitted that they made the statements, either in response to threats or to receive better treatment in the prison camps. However, since most of these broadcasts reached only Communist nations, the American public never heard the kind of evidence that raised the specter of treason in the ranks.

The one exception to this general pattern occurred in 1952, when reports began to surface about the traitorous confessions of two air force officers, 1st Lt. John S. Quinn and 1st Lt. Kenneth L. Enoch. For months the North Koreans had been claiming that the United States was using bacteriological and germ warfare, specifically charging the air force with dropping containers filled with germ-infected ants on targets in North Korea and Manchuria. Secretary of State Dean Acheson publicly dismissed the claims as "nonsense," but the North Koreans never dropped the charges. Eventually, they publicized the presumed confessions of Quinn and Enoch, who had been captured in January and, in statements first aired over Peking radio in May 1952, purportedly confessed to committing germ warfare by dropping "germ bombs" on North Korean targets. A voice with a midwestern accent—later identified as Enoch, who was a native of Youngstown, Ohio—confessed to dropping "two germ bombs at Hwangju and four germ bombs at Tungwha, North Korea," on January 7 and 10.[19] Enoch concluded his statement by claiming he was determined "to become a new man . . . [and] struggle for peace in this war against capitalism to clear my conscience for my past errors."[20] In a nearly identical confession Quinn corroborated Enoch's statement regarding germ warfare, condemned the American government and their "Wall Street lies," and expressed remorse for his actions.

The fact that Lieutenants Enoch and Quinn confessed to germ warfare charges could not be denied—the U.S. government confirmed that it was indeed their voices on the Peking radio broadcast. Nevertheless, the confessions were widely perceived as Communist propaganda, and the authenticity of the germ warfare assertions was never taken seriously by the American press.[21] In a news conference on May 7, Secretary Acheson repudiated the statements, speculating that they had been signed by Enoch and Quinn under duress and were likely "dictated by Communist propagandists."[22] Examining the specific statements, Acheson said they contained "all the Communist clichés so alien to American youths" and were "another example of the incredible length to which they [the Communist Party] will go to propagate the 'big lie.' "[23]

Enoch and Quinn were not the only members of the American military to confess to war crimes. In the spring of 1953 a film distributed from Peking, China, showcased four American officers confessing to germ warfare. One of the officers stood, looked directly into the camera, and said, "I hope some day to marry like any normal man. When I have a child, how will I ever be able to face that child and tell it what I have been doing in this war when *I* know that *I* have been a criminal in the face of the world?"[24] The American media summarily dismissed these claims as well, pointing out that the men were using Communist stock phrases and that they seemed to be in a hypnotic state. As one news correspondent put it, the officer confessed "in a trance-like, evangelical fashion."[25]

The historian Ron Robin has documented "twenty-three airmen, including a marine pilot, Colonel Frank H. Schwable, [who] had made highly publicized public confessions of war crimes that included detailed statements of germ warfare bombing raids."[26] These pro-Communist statements and confessions were immediately derided as examples of Communist propaganda in the mainstream press, and journalists argued that they either had been completely fabricated or had been coaxed out of American soldiers through threats and torture. One common argument focused on the specific language and phrases in the confessions and concluded that the language was so alien to American thinking that it proved that the true source of the statements was the Communist Party. When Acheson commented on the confessions of Lieutenants Enoch and Quinn, he stated, "There are no two men in the whole United States Air Force who would of their own volition express themselves in such terms."[27]

Despite the government's and the military's public repudiation of the germ warfare confessions, in private there was rising speculation that American POWs were the victims of psychological torture. As a result, the American military quickly began to regard them with suspicion. For example, after Operation Little Switch "20 of the . . . returnees were diverted upon return to America to a special de- (or re-) brainwashing facility at Valley Forge near Philadelphia."[28] In an internal memo on the repatriated soldiers, a government official who visited the hospital cited the lack of coordination between the Department of Defense and the Far East Command and contradictory orders from army officials, which he blamed for the stories in the press about a "de-brainwashing" program. The memo also asserted that segregating the men in one hospital had been unnecessary, arguing they could just as easily have been sent to general hospitals near their home areas and claiming that the sloppy state of affairs had led to bad press and was making the soldiers anxious about their prospects "now that the press had insinuated that they had accepted communist indoctrination."[29] But the report also indicated that there was cause for concern, contending that several of the men were in fact "hard-core communists." The soldiers in the facility publicly denied ever having been brainwashed or being pro-Communist, and one of the army doctors there told members of the press, "I don't know where this idea started, but there's one thing for sure—we're not running a damned Laundromat here."[30] Despite the public denials, the incident raised concerns, and government officials clearly had reservations about returning POWs.

Those maintaining that the American soldiers were victims of brainwashing were further emboldened by reports coming out of the Neutral Nations Repatriation Commission in Panmunjom that a significant percentage of North Korean and Chinese soldiers captured by the United States refused repatriation to their home countries and "repeatedly have sworn to die rather than attend lectures or interviews given by the Communists."[31] There were reports that North Korean and Chinese soldiers, concerned that the United Nations would simply hand them back over to the Communists at the end of the war, were on the verge of rioting. And when Communist representatives arranged face-to-face meetings in "explaining" tents at South Camp in Panmunjom, where 14,500 Chinese and 8,000 North Korean POWs were being held, the first group of prisoners scheduled for interrogation "stripped to the waist, [and] armed [themselves] with clubs and stones."[32]

There were a number of intersecting political and personal factors motivating the North Korean and Chinese soldiers' decisions at Panmunjom. Commenting on their motivations, the historian Susan L. Carruthers pointed out that "almost two-thirds [of the Chinese prisoners] had served with Chiang Kai-shek's Nationalist forces during the civil war . . . and their loyalty to China's new regime was at best uncertain."[33] Many of the North Korean POWs also harbored little sympathy for Communism, in large part because their ranks included nearly forty thousand civilians who had been forced into the North Korean army against their will.[34] To further complicate matters, the Panmunjom compound was filled with officials and guards with Nationalist sympathies who began an active campaign of "physical terror including organized murders, beatings, [and] threats" to discourage North Korean and Chinese soldiers from repatriating to Communist nations.[35] All of these factors were largely ignored by the mainstream media in the United States, and several journalists asserted that the reason so many Communist soldiers adamantly refused to spend any time with their former compatriots was that they were aware that lectures and interviews were simply Communist euphemisms for brainwashing, and they would rather die than face the dreaded technique.

In August 1953 the media began publishing rumors based on reports from returning POWs that well over a hundred American POWs had "converted" to Communism and were not planning on returning to the United States. Commenting on this speculation, an editorial in the *Washington Post* stated, "The grim thought cannot be ruled out that a few Americans may remain behind as political zombies."[36] The behavior of North Korean and Chinese soldiers in Panmunjom, the Valley Forge episode, the germ warfare confessions, and the pro-Communist statements of American soldiers supported such an interpretation and offered compelling evidence that the most fiercely patriotic and anti-Communist of all American institutions, the military, might have Communists in its midst. Even more frightening was the background of these "political zombies"; they were products of the very American system which their actions and words denounced. During a time when American culture portrayed communism as irreconcilable with democratic forms of government based on personal freedom and individual liberty, an American soldier voluntarily changing his allegiance from the United States to Communism or even applauding Communist ideology was practically unthinkable. Brainwashing offered an explanation for these incidents that fit perfectly into the existing ideological paradigm, and by the time Operation Big Switch took place the perplexing developments in Korea were commonly perceived as examples of the dreaded Communist technique. This sequence of events played a crucial role in establishing brainwashing and provided the mainstream media with important examples of men who had fallen under the spell of Communist mind control. However, despite this evidence, defining brainwashing would prove to be a complicated process.

Defining a Concept

In the early to mid-1950s brainwashing was the topic of several books, dozens of newspaper articles, a handful of academic articles, and classified research sponsored by the government and the military. All of these sources agreed that the Communist Party was using increasingly heavy-handed techniques to influence individuals to fall in line with party doctrine. However, just how heavy-handed the techniques were and how the Communist Party implemented them became the focus of a heated debate. According to the literary scholar David Seed, after brainwashing was introduced two schools of thought quickly began to emerge: "the 'soft' view that brainwashing merely entails a newly systematic form of interrogation, and the 'hard' view that new technology has enabled new, more radical changes to be brought about in the human mind when the subject is isolated."[37] Despite the competing interpretations, the debate over the concept largely focused not on the validity of the technique itself but on how successful and severe it was.

The term first appeared in print on September 24, 1950, when the journalist Edward Hunter wrote an article for the *Miami News* titled " 'Brainwashing' Tactics Force Chinese into Ranks of Communist Party." Hunter claimed his Chinese informants had told him about a new technique being widely practiced by the Chinese Communist Party, which they called *hsi nao* ("wash brain.").[38] Hunter Americanized the phrase, and the term *brainwashing* was born. As a result, Hunter was the figure most responsible for introducing *brainwashing* to American life and would become one of the most vocal advocates of the hard interpretation of the concept. At the time the article was published, Hunter was an established foreign news correspondent, author, editor, and self-proclaimed expert on propaganda warfare and Communism. He also had extensive ties to the American intelligence community and had served as an undercover propaganda specialist for the OSS and the CIA. Over the next decade Hunter would create a steady output of material detailing the minutiae of brainwashing, and his professional career became intertwined with his work on the subject. Largely on account of his work on brainwashing Hunter became a minor, yet pivotal, figure in American Cold War culture.

Commenting on brainwashing's curious etymology, Hunter said, "The word came out of the sufferings of the Chinese people. Put under a terrifying combination of subtle and crude mental and physical pressures and tortures, they detected a pattern and called it *brainwashing*."[39] Hunter further speculated that "the term might well have been derived from the Buddhist expression 'heart-washing,' which goes back to the time of Mencius."[40] Hunter always maintained that *brainwashing* was a preexisting word and concept, one he did not make up or misinterpret but merely translated from Chinese into English. In truth, the Chinese word for brainwashing, *hsi nao,* never contained the sinister overtones of Hunter's adaptation of the term. The word was commonly used in a more metaphorical way than Hunter ever implied and actually referred "to the idea of washing away the vestiges of the old system (literally 'cleansing the mind') in the process of being re-educated to assume one's place in the new Communist society."[41] In other words, in its native language *hsi nao* was much more akin to the relatively innocuous concept of reeducation than to any literal technique that implied mind control or mental manipulation.[42]

To further complicate the early history of the term *brainwashing,* nine months prior to its appearance in print it was referenced in a classified CIA report. On the basis of these documents and Hunter's ties to the CIA, the historian Timothy Melley has speculated that "the *public* concept of brainwashing was from the beginning a creation of the CIA, which secretly invented and disseminated the idea as part of a propaganda campaign."[43] Given the duplicity of the CIA and the Cold War state, this remains a distinct possibility, and some members of the government clearly did employ brainwashing as a propaganda tool in an effort to portray the Communist enemy in a negative light. However, this interpretation of brainwashing's origins is hardly conclusive. The CIA's reference to brainwashing in early

1950 illustrates that the term was in circulation within certain circles in the government before it went public, but it is entirely possible that these early references were genuine attempts to describe actual techniques the U.S. government was observing on the ground in the Soviet Union and Red China. In 1950 the methods of psychological torture and manipulation that the Soviet Union and Red China were practicing to elicit confessions were not very well understood by the CIA, and it would take several years before the agency concluded that the Communists did not have mind control at their disposal. For his part, Hunter remained a vigilant proponent of the existence of brainwashing long after it retained any use as a propaganda tool. All of the available evidence indicates that Hunter, like several other cold warriors of the same mind in the government, genuinely believed that Communist brainwashing existed and posed a real threat to the United States.[44] The role he played in the CIA's original report on brainwashing is unclear, but he certainly took the idea and ran with it.

Hunter's first book on brainwashing, *Brain-washing in Red China: The Calculated Destruction of Men's Minds,* was published in 1951. Described on the dust jacket as the first disclosure of the "new and horrifying extremes in . . . psychological warfare being waged against the free world and against the very concept of freedom," the book was based primarily on Hunter's interviews with informants in China and Southeast Asia in 1950 and 1951, and it quickly became a seminal work in the burgeoning new field of brainwashing. In his introduction Hunter described an interview with a Chinese informant named Chi Sze-chen, a former student in Red China who had recently escaped to Hong Kong. In the interview Chi detailed his life in China, where he had been placed on a diet consisting of two small meals a day, routinely deprived of sleep, and enrolled in study sessions which sometimes lasted all his waking hours. This environment created what Hunter termed "a hypnotic state of fatigue," and the Chinese students were forced, "while in this trance, to repeat again and again, lengthily and in his own words the political dogma demanded of him."[45] This was "brain-washing," and according to Hunter it had become "the principal activity on the Chinese mainland."[46]

By the end of the book Hunter had shifted his focus from Chinese hearts and minds to their American counterparts. The strange psychology of Americans had led the nation down a perilous road of wishful thinking about the state of the Cold War. Overrun by ivory tower intellectuals and liberals, Americans had turned away from reality and were unprepared to face the perils at hand. "Blind conviction," Hunter warned, "can be persuasive around a conference table, but on a battlefield, if you make believe a rifle isn't there, you get shot."[47] Hunter's point was clear: Americans were unarmed on the psychological battlefield and overlooked new developments in Communist psychological warfare at their own peril.

The spectacle of the Korean POWs was the most notorious example of Communist brainwashing, but other cases appeared to substantiate Hunter's claims as well. In 1954 a female student at Peiping National University named Maria Yen wrote an account of life in Red China titled *The Umbrella Garden: A Picture of Student Life in Red China* that largely confirmed Hunter's claims about the rampant use of indoctrination and psychological manipulation in Chinese society. A year later two American students—a Fulbright scholar named Adele Rickett and a Harvard graduate studying at the Peiping Union Medical College named Malcolm Bersohn—emerged from China after being detained for three and a half years for allegedly committing espionage against the state and appeared so thoroughly indoctrinated that the press dubbed their case "a new high in 'brainwashing.'"[48] When they appeared in Hong Kong after being deported from China they told reporters they had been guilty of spying and expressed remorse for their crimes against the Chinese people. They also spoke in glowing terms of the Communist Party and their jailers, mixing party slogans into their comments to the press. When Bersohn began spouting Communist rhetoric at his first press conference back on American soil, members of his family literally pushed him into a waiting car and sped off before he could implicate himself any further. Meanwhile, before Rickett had even returned home, her family told reporters that they believed their daughter had been brainwashed and would need to spend time in a hospital to recover from her ordeal.[49] When the boat she was traveling on docked in San Francisco on April 3 her family hastily escorted her away from the press and denied all requests for a statement.

Bersohn's and Rickett's apparent devotion to Communism, especially in light of their lengthy prison sentences in Red China and their "parrot-like" responses to reporters, sparked new concerns that the Communists had cracked the code to brain warfare and added further credibility to Hunter's contention that the Communist Party had harnessed the power of brainwashing. Over the next several years the testimony and sporadic release of prisoners in Red China offered a seemingly endless stream of reports further validating the threat of brainwashing. In 1954 a Methodist official named F. Olin Stockwell released an autobiography detailing his "14 months in solitary confinement . . . [and] nine and one-half months of brainwashing" in China in the early 1950s.[50] A year later four American jet pilots who had been captured during the Korean War and were finally released from China in 1955 described their experience with brainwashing to reporters, claiming they had been kept in solitary confinement for months and forced to attend lectures and sign confessions.[51] In 1956 a member of a Baptist missionary group named Lee A. Lovegren was released after fifty months in a Chinese Communist prison and told reporters that while he had been in jail the "mental pressure was terrific." When reporters asked if the Communists had attempted to brainwash him, he responded, "And how! They even took my bible away."[52] In July of the same year a group of 335 Japanese prisoners were released after being imprisoned in China for years, and reporters immediately raised charges of brainwashing when the prisoners responded to Japanese reporters' questions with "stereotyped answers" and expressed Communist-inspired views of current events at a press conference.[53]

These cases received varying degrees of publicity in the mainstream media. Taken together, they offered compelling evidence that the Communists were indeed employing a variety of techniques—some physical, some psychological—in order to turn prisoners of the state into propaganda showpieces, lending credence to Hunter's claim that Communist brainwashing was not to be taken lightly. Although Hunter's *Brain-washing in Red China* has largely been forgotten by historians of the Cold War, it made a considerable impression on anti-Communists and foreign policy hawks and was met with generally favorable reviews in 1951. But Hunter could have hardly foreseen how little his brainwashing would resemble the popular understanding of the concept by the end of the Korean War only two years later. Initially, Hunter asserted that the technique was being used as a tool to extract confessions in Communist prisons in Red China, and he made a clear distinction between "brain-washing" and "brain-changing," comparing "brain-washing" to indoctrination and describing "brain-changing" as a much more sinister, complicated process that wiped away a person's memories and replaced them with new, Communist-sanctioned beliefs. Perhaps spurred on by the events unfolding in Korea, Hunter refined his interpretation of the technique over time, and he increasingly blurred the lines between brain-washing and brain-changing over the course of the decade, eventually dropping the term *brain-changing* and the hyphen between *brain* and *washing* altogether.

The methods Hunter's informants described were hardly innovative; physical and mental torture, indoctrination, propaganda, and even blackmail had been used by governments to exert control over their civilian populations long before the Cold War. By the middle of the decade, brainwashing would commonly be associated with overt mind control, a comparison Hunter was careful to disavow in his first book on the subject but eventually encouraged in subsequent writings. What made Hunter's brainwashing chilling in 1951 was its scale. Employed so broadly that it made earlier attempts at psychological warfare look minuscule in comparison, thousands of innocent Chinese civilians were being indoctrinated in Red China every day. Hunter's first book on the topic was a starting point, prefiguring much of what was to come. His brainwashing was ill-defined, linked to several preexisting methods of manipulation, and based almost entirely on anecdotal evidence.

A corollary to the early history of the notion of brainwashing was the nearly simultaneous introduction of other new words that attempted to describe the same technique. One was *menticide.* In February 1951 an article titled "The Crime of Menticide" by Joost Meerloo appeared in the *American Journal of Psychiatry.* Called the "more pretentious twin" of brainwashing by one Cold War historian, *menticide,* Meerloo admitted, was his invention.[54] The word was "derived from *mens,* the mind, and *cadeere,* to kill" and, according to Meerloo, described the "perverted refinement of the rack."[55] In 1951 Meerloo was already making much bolder claims about menticide than Hunter was about brainwashing. In a piece in the *New York Times,* Meerloo was quoted as asserting it was "a crime worse than genocide."[56] Meerloo clearly believed that the catastrophic potential of the technique was greater than Hunter had initially realized. In his first article on the subject Meerloo stated that the "concept of 'menticide' indicates an organized system of judicial perversion and psychological intervention, in which a powerful tyrant transfers his own thoughts and words into the minds and mouths of the victims he plans to destroy or to use for his own propaganda."[57]

In reality, menticide hardly appeared on the cultural radar during the 1950s, and the concept would never attain the same degree of cultural currency as brainwashing. For the duration of the 1950s *menticide* appeared in only 4 articles in the *New York Times,* while *brainwashing* appeared in exactly 251 during the same period.[58] Despite the fact that it went largely unnoticed in popular culture, menticide had a significant influence on Hunter's subsequent work. Hunter derisively referred to menticide as "a fine laboratory word,"[59] but it was apparent that he had absorbed the more dramatic and sinister overtones of *menticide* into his own expanding definition of *brainwashing.* In *Brainwashing: The Story of Men Who Defied It,* published in 1956, Hunter concluded that the two words were basically interchangeable and that both alluded to the same "quack science devised by the Reds to bring about the voluntary submission of people to an unthinking discipline and a robotlike enslavement."[60]

The term *menticide* largely disappeared after Meerloo's last publication on the concept, titled *The Rape of the Mind: The Psychology of Thought Control, Menticide, and Brainwashing,* appeared in 1956. However, Meerloo played an important role in raising brainwashing's profile. Not only did menticide have a large influence on Hunter's definition of brainwashing, but, equally important, it lent Hunter's concept some much-needed credibility. Meerloo held M.D. and Ph.D. degrees and was an instructor at Columbia. After his article on menticide appeared in the *American Journal of Psychiatry* both brainwashing and menticide began to be featured in a number of articles in academic journals. Meerloo would remain one of the most outspoken voices from the scientific community supporting the notion that brainwashing was synonymous with mind control, and his professional reputation gave brainwashing a degree of seriousness that it probably never would have attained in American culture if it had been solely associated with a news correspondent.

In the middle of the decade a group of army-sponsored scientists coined another word to describe the brainwashing process. In their studies they used the less sensational term *coercive persuasion* to describe what had happened to American POWs during the Korean War. At the head of this group was Edgar Schein, a psychologist who was employed by the Walter Reed Army Institute of Psychology in Washington, D.C. Schein had been involved in the repatriation process of American soldiers in 1953, and his study of the group, which was published in 1956, concluded that "the much-feared Communist program of 'brainwashing' was really more of an intensive indoctrination program in combination with very sophisticated techniques of undermining the social structure of the prisoner group, thereby eliciting collaboration which in most cases was *not* based on ideological change of any sort."[61] Like Meerloo's menticide, Schein's coercive persuasion never became very popular. In fact, by the time his second book on the topic appeared, Schein used the term *brainwashing* in his title, a tacit admission that his coinage did not have as much appeal to wide audiences. Despite its shortcomings, the term *coercive persuasion* illustrates the growing disparity between the popular and official interpretations of brainwashing.

Classified government and military documents from the Korean War era unmistakably reflect Hunter's and Meerloo's early work on Communist torture and psychological warfare, frequently even parroting their exact terminology and descriptions. On February 19, 1953, several months before the treatment and behavior of American POWs began to receive widespread media attention, Secretary of Defense C. E. Wilson wrote a memo to Under Secretary of State Walter E. Smith and the head of the CIA, Allen Dulles, that outlined his department's knowledge about the treatment of American POWs in North Korean prison camps and the Communists' use of "a 'new' form of war crime, and a new refinement in atrocity techniques; namely, 'mind murder' or mendicide [*sic*]." Noting that the treatment of American POWs was beginning to receive publicity, Wilson argued that "an appropriately coordinated release describing Communist attempts to indoctrinate our personnel, and explaining the techniques employed, may . . . allay natural public fears, and in fact provide the initial point for an effective counter propaganda campaign designed to create revulsion throughout the world concerning the Communist program."[62] Wilson forwarded to Smith and Dulles additional background material on Communist psychological warfare prepared by the Department of the Army, which included definitions of "brain-changing" and "mendicide" (which was repeatedly misspelled in the report) and defined "brain-washing" as the "calculated psychological attempt to destroy a man's previously-established moral code, religious and political beliefs, and personal associations, and to supplant those with rote adherence to Communist dogma."[63]

Significantly, the material prepared by the secretary of defense reveals that the Department of Defense, the Department of the Army, and potentially the State Department and the CIA were all influenced by Hunter's and Meerloo's work on brainwashing and Communist psychological warfare, indicating that their work factored into how government officials and policymakers interpreted events unfolding in Korea. In March, Hunter was interviewed by government officials associated with the Psychological Strategy Board.[64] Later that month the board suggested refining the government's policy on Communist psychological warfare, warning government officials "not to credit the enemy with a 'miracle-weapon,'" and advising "the word 'menticide' should not be used in reference to this problem. It is, on the one hand, too strong a word or too frightening a term for the American public, and on the other hand, in many quarters the meaning has to be explained. The Committee is searching for a better catch-word to describe the program."[65] This internal debate reveals that policymakers were struggling over how to address the Korean POW experience in public, but it also illustrates that they did believe some sort of new war crime had been committed behind enemy lines—in fact, before Operation Little Switch there was a general expectation in government and military circles that a significant percentage of American POWs had been indoctrinated or subjected to psychological torture.

The fact that government officials' first impulse was to use the specter of Communist brainwashing to stage a propaganda offensive against the Soviet Union and Communist China is equally telling and reveals their willingness to adapt the brainwashing narrative to suit their own purposes. By April, Wilson's vision of a counterpropaganda offensive had been rejected after other high-ranking policymakers decided it was more beneficial to gradually introduce the concept of brainwashing to the American public. This approach was due at least in part to "the fear that domestic reaction might be such that intolerable pressure would develop for the return of American troops from Korea."[66] After the prisoner exchanges with Korea, government officials appeared eager to utilize brainwashing in order to highlight Communist atrocities and push back on Communist accusations that the United States had used germ warfare in Korea. On October 26, 1953, Charles W. Mayo of Mayo Clinic fame appeared before the United Nations political committee and testified that the American pilots who had admitted to committing bacteriological warfare had been "shaken loose from their foundations of moral value—[they were] beaten down by the conditioning which the science of [the Russian scientist Ivan P.] Pavlov reserves for dogs and rats—all in a vicious attempt to make them accomplices to a frightful lie."[67] The comments are clear evidence that policymakers planned on using brainwashing in the months after Operation Big Switch. In private correspondence they expressed considerable worry about just how powerful this new Communist weapon was, scrambling to get expert feedback on the technique from prominent psychologists and psychiatrists. In public they attempted to get ahead of the media narrative on brainwashing by presenting a unified front on the technique, simultaneously telling the public it was no "miracle-weapon" but also employing it to further discredit the Communist enemy. As we will see, this linguistic tightrope ultimately proved untenable, especially as other sources began weighing in on the subject.

Perhaps the most important group to comment on brainwashing was the American POWs themselves, whose firsthand accounts began appearing with increasing regularity after 1953 and played an important role in the popular acceptance of the technique. A significant proportion of these "victims" of brainwashing had collaborated to varying degrees with the enemy and found their reputations on the line when they returned to the United States. In autobiographies and interviews they provided direct accounts of life in the Communist prison camps, the nature of Communist physical and mental torture, and the Communist system of indoctrination. On the basis of their reports, it was obvious that some form of organized indoctrination and psychological torture had taken place behind the Bamboo Curtain. However, when asked to describe the process, the majority of POWs described something that sounded more like an intense indoctrination program than anything approximating the sensational views of brainwashing espoused by Hunter and Meerloo.

Pvt. John E. Martin, for example, described being forced "to attend 'brainwashing' classes in a room supplied with books printed in Russia."[68] Sgt. Eddie Davis offered a more detailed description of the "brainwashing classes":

> They formed us into companies and every company had to show full attendance at "school" every day. In "class," anybody not paying strict attention was likely to find a Chinese gun butt in his face. The instructors were always saying they had a "leniency policy" toward us, but I never found them very lenient. The classes were held in the morning. They would start out with a lecture blasting what they called the American "warmongers"—Truman, Eisenhower, MacArthur, Acheson—almost any name they could pronounce. Then they'd have a lecture on "germ warfare."[69]

Many academics would later point to similar descriptions of "brainwashing classes" as proof that *brainwashing* was a misnomer for what had actually occurred in the prison camps. Citing these "classes," they would argue that the Communists had been indoctrinating American minds but not washing their brains. Returning prisoners of war also initially appeared confused by the very term *brainwashing* and were not exactly sure how to label their own experiences. As one returning POW put it, "I never even heard the term 'brainwash' before I got back home."[70] Despite this admission, returning POWs frequently cited the concept in interviews.

Summarizing these initial interviews, one authority on the Korean POWs said, "Some mentioned the overpowering effects of physical torture, others doggedly successful resistance to it; some stressed widespread American treachery, and others widespread American heroism."[71] Since many of the returning POWs were placed on the defensive regarding their wartime behavior before they had even stepped on American soil, the fact that they frequently brought up physical and psychological torture as well as their "doggedly successful resistance" is hardly surprising.[72] On the surface, descriptions of the torture prisoners were subjected to in Korea was simply a vivid, realistic depiction of what life in Communist prison camps had been like for a majority of the captured American soldiers. However, when soldiers alluded to their experiences as prisoners, they were not merely describing those experiences—they were simultaneously attempting to defend their reputations and offering crucial testimony that would color the public's perception of brainwashing.

Many returning soldiers latched onto brainwashing to explain away any behavior that could be viewed in an unfavorable light. For example, Col. John Knox Arnold Jr., who had confessed to conducting germ warfare, said he had been subject to "persuasion that civilized people simply do not know about."[73] In testimony at Colonel Schwable's court-martial hearing in 1954, his copilot, Maj. Roy H. Bley, blamed his confession on Communist psychological torture, lifting a passage straight from Hunter when he defined brainwashing as "nothing but a calculated destruction of people's minds."[74] Even the parents of the soldiers who had refused repatriation blamed brainwashing for their sons' behavior. Pfc. Richard F. Tenneson's mother's statement that it was "the only possible explanation I can think of" was typical.[75]

A common trend that began to emerge from interviews of returning POWs during this period was the caveats they frequently attached to accounts of their behavior in Korea. For example, after admitting he had signed a Communist petition that asked the United States to leave North Korea, Cpl. Donald Legay quickly added, "Don't be too cocky—after a couple of years of what the Communists call 'brain washing' you might have signed it too."[76] After this apparent rationalization of signing a Communist petition, Legay went on to say, "If you think brain washing threw me for a loss, look at the other 219 Americans in that camp on the Yalu. Twenty of them swallowed the Communist line. Fifty of them went off their rockers . . . about one of every three Americans there fell for the Red talk or went mad."[77] Although Legay may have been unique because he was so forthright about his collaboration with the enemy, his argument was fairly common. In essence, the argument was not only that brainwashing had an impact on many of the GIs in Korea, but also that most American civilians would have succumbed to it as well.

The returning GIs offered varying reports about the success rate of brainwashing. Some maintained that while they personally had been able to resist it, they had seen some of their fellow prisoners become diehard communists. Cpl. Harold Wilson, for example, told a story of an American in his camp who "had said he would 'kill his own mother and father if they interfered with him being a Communist.'"[78] Several declared that some soldiers may have appeared to agree with the Communists but that they were actually just doing so to get better food and treatment. A sergeant speculated about this possibility in an interview, stating, "Maybe there were guys who pretended to believe the Red Propaganda in the hope that the Commies might go easier on them, feed them a little easier. But these same prisoners, when the Reds weren't listening, would curse them for the liars they were."[79] Other returning POWs gave even vaguer reports on brainwashing, claiming they had no firsthand experience with it but had heard about other soldiers who had undergone it. Cpl. James Ball admitted as much when he said that "'a few' of the Allied prisoners of war may have succumbed to Communist propaganda but . . . he knew of no specific American cases."[80]

Firsthand reports of the physical and mental torture they endured and their determined battle against it were distinct attempts by the returning POWs to recast themselves from traitorous cowards to heroic, but ultimately helpless, victims. More important, amidst all of the confessions, denials, and rumors, the fact remained that a significant percentage of American GIs questioned about brainwashing reported that they had either witnessed or heard about new Communist techniques of mental manipulation. Until Operation Little Switch, reports of Communist brainwashing mainly consisted of hearsay and speculation, and there were only a handful of actual direct reports of the technique. The media coverage of the returning POWs quickly changed this, providing ample testimonial evidence in support of the existence of brainwashing.

There are three possible explanations for the frequent use of the term *brainwashing* by returning POWs. The first is that they simply adopted the term because by the time they returned to the United States it had become shorthand for what they had witnessed, namely, torture, starvation, and an organized indoctrination program. If this was their intent, it would indicate that the victims of the technique had a fundamental misunderstanding of what brainwashing implied to the American public. A second possibility is that returning POWs understood the popular definition of the word and believed that it accurately described their experiences. This was certainly true of a number of returning POWs, who seemed incapable of understanding why they or other members of their prison camp had behaved in the manner they had without falling back on the more sensational interpretations of brainwashing. Finally, there is the possibility that victims of the technique were being disingenuous when they employed the word in order to portray themselves in a more positive light and clear themselves of any unpatriotic behavior. Whatever the reason for their use of the term, by 1953 sensational interpretations of brainwashing were still largely uncontested in popular culture—the more balanced research sponsored by academia and the government would not begin to emerge until the middle of the decade.

The case of brainwashing illustrates a wider trend during this phase of the Cold War: namely, the Iron Curtain created such an absence of true expertise on Communism that being an expert on Communism did not require the traditional vestiges of cultural authority, which in turn created an atmosphere ripe for exploitation. At least in part this played a crucial role in the rise of the most infamous of Communist experts, Sen. Joseph McCarthy. The dearth of experts also elevated anyone who had firsthand experience with Communism into an expert on the subject. The historian Ellen Schrecker, who has focused on the politics of the Red Scare, emphasized the crucial role ex-Communists played in the American "anti-Communist network."[81] Informants like Benjamin Mandel, Louis Budenz, Elizabeth Bentley, and Whittaker Chambers were propelled into the limelight of this network solely because their experience as Communists lent them a high degree of cultural authority. When victims of Communist brainwashing came home, the media afforded them a similar degree of credibility on brainwashing.

The main proponents of a more nuanced view of the technique were chiefly academics, psychiatrists, and psychologists, many of whom were funded by the government. Their opinions on the topic were similar to Schein's, and, like Schein, their views on brainwashing remained predominantly confined to classified government and military reports, their own publications, several academic journals, and the academic and scientific community. On the opposite end of the spectrum were Hunter and Meerloo, who represented the popular view of the concept. In her groundbreaking study on the impact of the Cold War on domestic ideology, Elaine Tyler May made a compelling case that "postwar America was the era of the expert."[82] The competing popular and academic definitions of brainwashing and the battle for cultural authority they represented open a window onto the ascendancy of the expert during the 1950s. In the case of brainwashing, the experts were decidedly not the members of the academic and scientific community who espoused the more balanced, scientific interpretation of the concept.[83] Commenting on the ten-year anniversary of the introduction of the concept, one member of the academic camp resignedly proclaimed that "in the decade since the appearance of Hunter's book, the public meanings of the term have been determined largely by writings of journalists and autobiographies of victims, rather than by the research of scholars and scientists."[84]

Aside from a minor faction of right-leaning members of the military and the CIA who continued to view brainwashing as a radical new breakthrough in psychological warfare, by the middle of the decade majority opinion on brainwashing within the government began to reflect reports like Schein's and stress less alarmist interpretations of the technique. In 1956 two researchers at Cornell Medical Center, Lawrence E. Hinkle and Harold G. Wolff, produced what has been described as the definitive government report on brainwashing and Communist psychological torture.[85] The classified report, commissioned by Dulles and the CIA, acknowledged that some of the methods the Soviet Union and Red China had been using to elicit confessions and modify soldiers' behavior had been at least partially effective, but they held that the Communists' methods were not based on any exotic new breakthroughs in psychological warfare and emphasized that they had not been developed by scientists. Instead, they attributed them to well-established police tactics that predated the Russian Revolution, had been refined by the KGB, and were then borrowed by the Chinese state police and combined with their own particular variant of social pressures based largely on group dynamics and peer pressure. Declassified versions of their research appeared in the *Archives of Neurology and Psychiatry* and the *Bulletin of the New York Academy of Medicine* in 1956 and 1957. Taking specific aim at Hunter's and Meerloo's interpretations of Communist psychological torture in their published academic work, Hinkle and Wolff concluded, "There is no reason to dignify these methods by surrounding them with an aura of scientific mystery, or to denote them by terms such as 'menticide' or 'brain washing' which imply that they are scientifically organized techniques of predictable effectiveness."[86]

After holding public hearings on brainwashing in 1956, a congressional subcommittee chaired by Sen. John Little McClellan reported that the military had failed to prepare soldiers for the inhumane treatment they would face during the Korean War but stressed that the Communists had not developed any new groundbreaking technique of psychological manipulation. In a statement released by the Senate Investigations Subcommittee, McClellan attempted to officially put the most severe interpretations of brainwashing to rest, asserting, "It is my hope that this report will put to an end the widely held misconception about the meaning of 'brainwashing' and that our prisoners in Korea underwent this 'brainwashing' treatment. As a reading of this report will indicate, such was not the case."[87]

The government's understanding of brainwashing had clearly been fluid in the early 1950s and evolved over time. After the public had become aware of the extent of Communist psychological torture and indoctrination in North Korean prison camps, the government initially seemed intent on stoking fears of Communist brainwashing in order to delegitimize germ warfare charges and the Communist Party in general. The anxiety expressed by some members of the government about the technique in the early 1950s was indeed authentic, as evidenced by the sheer amount of money the U.S. government spent on studying it and attempting to reverse engineer it. By the middle of the decade these very studies helped reduce some of the anxiety about Communist brainwashing within the government, and many of the benefits of publicly embracing the more severe interpretation of brainwashing had subsided or been negated by the potential harm such an interpretation posed to American interests. The existence of Communist mind control could potentially lead to public hysteria that undermined support for the Cold War, make it difficult to recruit soldiers for future hot wars with the Communist enemy, and highlight the military's and the Eisenhower administration's incompetence in combating Communist psychological warfare. As Seed has pointed out, the government thus "had a self-evident vested interest in demystifying brainwashing," and the success of Communist psychological manipulation during the Korean War was eventually blamed on a lack of military preparation, individual frailties, and home and community issues rather than on an insurmountable new Communist weapon.[88] Despite these official attempts to discredit the authenticity of Communist brainwashing, by mid-decade the government had lost control of the brainwashing narrative, and more severe interpretations of the concept eventually dominated popular culture and Cold War discourse.

There were several reasons for this outcome. By the middle of the 1950s the very term *brainwashing* was loaded with cultural baggage that triggered a certain understanding of the concept with the American public. Whenever an article appeared in which a returning POW claimed he had been brainwashed in North Korea, the public would reach a number of conclusions based upon the popular understanding of the practice. As a result, the mere use of the word *brainwashing* by the alleged victims of the technique served as powerful testimony in many people's minds to the concept's validity. From a purely practical standpoint, Hunter's description of brainwashing reached the American public at a much earlier date than the academic description did. While brainwashing was slowly becoming a topic of conversation in relatively obscure scientific journals between 1952 and 1954, a more sensational view of it was being championed by Meerloo and Hunter and in turn was being picked up by other journalists and contemporary observers, mentioned by victims of the technique, and appearing in newspapers and nationally circulated magazines such as *Time* and the *Saturday Evening Post*. It was not until the mid-1950s that books and articles advocating a more balanced scientific understanding of brainwashing began to appear in significant numbers, but by this point the sensational view had already broadly infiltrated American culture.[89]

In addition to getting a head start, the sensational view of brainwashing held several other advantages over the academic view. From a linguistic perspective, the term *brainwashing* itself placed the academic view in a disadvantageous position. The academic view of brainwashing implied something akin to indoctrination, and this was simply not accurately reflected by the word *brainwashing*. The word implied a severe new technique—a literal washing of the brain—not something that was merely analogous to indoctrination. This, in part, explains the attempts that proponents of the governmental and academic view made to shift the focus of the discussion on Communist prison camps and torture methods away from brainwashing and their subsequent creation of such terms as *coercive persuasion*. Unfortunately for proponents of the academic view, *brainwashing* had become such a catchall term for Communist torture methods that it dominated the public discourse on the topic. This produced a linguistic catch-22 for the proponents of the academic view: they were simultaneously attempting to repudiate the severe interpretation of the concept of brainwashing, but their use of the word *brainwashing* served as a constant reminder of that severe interpretation to the American public.

Finally, there was a notable difference in the amount of exposure each view received, and this ultimately played a large role in the cultural dominance of the more sensational interpretations of the concept. The discrepancy between the exposure each view received was due to the aforementioned sources they appeared in, and Americans were not privy to the classified government reports that largely dismissed brainwashing. The sensational interpretation was also inherently more shocking and thus more newsworthy than the academic interpretations and consequently made frequent appearances in newspaper and magazine articles, television shows, and films. As a result of all of these factors, the sensational interpretation of brainwashing reached a larger audience and remained influential well into the 1960s, while the more balanced view of academics largely faded out of mainstream culture.[90]

The competing definitions of brainwashing and the fact that even the so-called experts on the technique were often vague about how it actually worked lent the concept an air of fluidity and open-endedness. According to one literary scholar, "The very attraction of the term 'brainwashing' was its vagueness, so that different expanding meanings could be projected on to it."[91] This "vagueness" afforded the concept ample room to expand, and what had initially been conceived of as a unique tool of the Chinese communists grew immensely. By mid-decade, supposed experts like Hunter claimed that brainwashing was used by every branch of the Communist Party. The differences between Hunter's first two books on brainwashing clearly illustrate the concept's malleable boundaries. In his first book Hunter confined the concept to the Chinese Communist Party and its prisons. By his second book he had extended the practice to the entire Communist Party and claimed they used it to manipulate entire civilian populations.

In the middle of the decade an army psychiatrist criticized how the concept had been popularly defined:

> I am afraid that the general conception has been that Communist techniques of manipulating human beings are so persuasive, so completely irresistible, that no prisoner can keep his integrity in the face of them—and, by analogy, that no people, including ours, can stand against such an enemy. This is what distresses me so much about the popular and improper use of a word like brainwashing. In our society, when we face a phenomenon that we do not completely understand, we are apt to give it a name that indicates there is something magical, something beyond the reach of man's powers of comprehension, about it. "My goodness," we say in effect by giving a process which has many aspects this particular name, "look at this! You can remove a man's brain and wash out what's in it, and wash into it whatever you want, the way you manage tape on a tape recorder!"[92]

Despite similar criticism from the academic and scientific community, brainwashing became popularly conflated with such techniques as propaganda and indoctrination and linked to threats against Americans' personal autonomy, freedom, and individuality. So just how, exactly, was the concept popularly defined in the early to mid-1950s? The American public was bombarded with different explanations and theories about who practiced it, whom it was practiced upon, and how it worked. At this point it was commonly described as a weapon that had been developed and implemented by the Communist Party and was thus commonly perceived as uniquely Communist in character. Although it was originally believed to be solely practiced by the Chinese Communist Party, writers eventually began to link it to the Soviet Union as well. Several contemporary observers and journalists cited Pavlov and his experiments on conditioning, conducted around the turn of the century, as evidence that the Soviet Union had been developing brainwashing for decades. By the time allegedly brainwashed American POWs were returning to the United States in 1953, the technique reportedly could be practiced on just about anyone. Explanations concerning how brainwashing worked remained vague but usually included the same list of methods, including physical or mental torture, hallucinogenic drugs, and hypnosis.

While the glut of competing definitions, explanations, and information about brainwashing did not make the concept any less confusing, the coverage of the concept never relented in the middle years of the decade, continuously hammering it into the nation's collective consciousness. In 1956 Hunter offered a lay explanation for the technique, defining it as "a system of befogging the brain so a person can be seduced into acceptance of what otherwise would be abhorrent to him."[93] This definition illustrates the murky outlines of the procedure, as Hunter does not explicitly describe how the brain is "befogged." In all of its various incarnations, the concept infused the "battle for men's minds" with new poignancy and was popularly portrayed and conceived of as a definite system of Communist mind control and manipulation.

Further elaborating on the concept, Hunter wrote, "The intent is to change a mind radically so that its owner becomes a living puppet—a human robot—without the atrocity being visible from the outside. The aim is to create a mechanism in flesh and blood, with new beliefs and new thought processes inserted into a captive body. What that amounts to is the search for a slave race that, unlike the slaves of olden times, can be trusted never to revolt, always to be amenable to orders, like an insect to its instincts."[94] Hunter's word choice—"puppet," "robot," "mechanism in flesh in blood," "captive body," "slaves," and "insect"—is telling. His language not only conjures up images that would come to shape the popular understanding and portrayal of brainwashing for the remainder of the decade, but also alludes to the themes of invasion, powerlessness, and the loss of self-control and personal autonomy that loaded the concept with such harrowing potential.

The Context of a Concept: Historical and Cultural Precedents

In light of all the competing definitions of the concept and the modern perception of brainwashing as a reminder of the "paranoid style" of the McCarthy era, it is important to emphasize that for the majority of the American public during the 1950s brainwashing was no laughing matter.[95] In fact, alongside the threat of nuclear war and a Communist takeover, it was one of the most prominent fears of the entire decade.[96] In promotional material for Edward Hunter's appearances on the lecture circuit in the 1950s, it was earnestly described as "a greater menace to peace than the Soviet H-Bomb."[97] Given how brainwashing was popularly defined, this claim was plausible to many Americans, and to classify the concept as a brief paranoid episode in American history would require one to ignore the historical and cultural context of the period; which made the more sensational interpretations of brainwashing appear as completely logical and rational steps in the evolution of preexisting techniques of manipulation.

One of the most significant influences on the early perception of brainwashing was the false confessions of several Communist leaders during the infamous Soviet purge trials of the 1930s and the show-trial confessions of non-Communists like Cardinal Josef Mindszenty and Robert Vogeler in the late 1940s and early 1950s.[98] During the purge trials of the late 1930s, dozens of high-ranking members of the Communist Party were accused of and publicly confessed to crimes against the state, participating in various assassination plots, and conspiring with Nazi Germany. The confessions quickly raised suspicions, especially as the allegations against the defendants became progressively more outlandish. A decade later the case against Cardinal Mindszenty made international headlines, in part because he was a man of the cloth and in part because of his jarringly sluggish demeanor during his trial for crimes against the Hungarian Communist government. Although Mindszenty admitted to a number of different charges, there was immediate suspicion about the validity of his confession because it was well known that he confessed to crimes he had never committed. For example, his confession that he was guilty of sponsoring anti-Semitic propaganda prior to the Second World War was directly contradicted by his behavior throughout the war, when he had used his position to champion Jewish rights. At his trial in 1949, Mindszenty repudiated his earlier confessions, further substantiating conjecture that his original confession had been the result of Communist manipulation. The case raised so many red flags for American observers that it prompted the CIA's head of Scientific Intelligence to travel to Western Europe to uncover what the Soviets had done to Mindszenty before his initial trial.[99]

Vogeler's confession and his eventual return to the United States also received a good deal of press coverage in the United States. Vogeler was an American businessman in Budapest who had been imprisoned in 1949 on charges of spying and sabotage, sentenced to fifteen years in prison, and eventually ransomed back to the United States in 1951. In his autobiography, *I Was Stalin's Prisoner,* Vogeler described the inner turmoil he suffered during his imprisonment and the mental and physical torture which eventually led to his confessions. Over the course of seventy days Vogeler lost nearly fifty pounds, was deprived of sleep to the point of hallucination, and was constantly interviewed by a team of interrogators. By the time Vogeler confessed, he was a shell of his former self, as his description of his trial illustrates: "At the time of my trial . . . I was in no condition to do anything but recite my lines. I had been imbued with such a feeling of desolation that my one desire was to say my piece and have done with it. My voice quavered as I spoke into the microphone that was placed before me. It sounded to me like the voice of another person, and in a sense, of course, it was. It was the voice of my Svengali, No. 2. [the name of Vogeler's main interrogator]."[100] Vogeler's imprisonment was eerily reminiscent of Arthur Koestler's fictionalized account of the imprisonment of an old revolutionary named Rubashov in *Darkness at Noon* (1951), and nearly all of the other documented cases of these types of false confessions followed their pattern.[101] The Communist hierarchy identified a potential threat or individuals who held some value as propaganda showpieces, arrested them and threw them in jail, and alternately starved them, deprived them of sleep, and interviewed them until they willingly acquiesced to their captors or became so incoherent that they no longer knew exactly what they were doing or saying. Frequently, this type of torture led only to signed confessions, but in several notorious cases the ordeal of physical and mental torture seemed to actually convince victims of their own guilt. As Vogeler's torturer boasted, "Make no mistake about it. Even if Jesus Christ were sitting in your chair, He'd tell me everything I wanted Him to say."[102]

By the time of the Korean War, a Communist confession trope had been well established, and "there were so many instances in which Communist propaganda involving 'confession' extortion and coercive indoctrination overtaxed the credibility of even the most credulous persons that all Communist use of 'confessions' in propaganda was easily discredited."[103] This would help explain the popular reaction to the air force men who confessed to germ warfare, whose confessions were met with disbelief from the time their story appeared in the media. These confessions formed a precedent of Communist techniques of manipulation that left a lasting imprint on the American cultural consciousness and helped pave the way for the widespread acceptance of the concept of brainwashing.

The long history of propaganda also helped set the conceptual foundation for brainwashing. Propaganda had been recognized as a central component of international relations long before the 1950s. In the nineteenth century, debates about propaganda were frequently linked to anxieties about foreign influence in the United States. One of the most prominent ongoing discussions about propaganda and foreign influence in the United States was directed toward Catholicism. According to anti-Catholic groups, the Vatican controlled American Catholic citizens and made them beholden to the pope, a situation that could potentially undermine the nation's entire democratic system. Variations of these concerns arose in anti-labor and anti-immigrant rhetoric throughout the late nineteenth and early twentieth centuries and illustrate that anxieties about foreign influences on the American mind have deep roots in American history.

During the First World War modern industrialized countries had thrown their might behind propaganda efforts, and the actions of Germany, Britain, and eventually the United States all supported the notion that national governments were intent on overtly manipulating the opinions and outlook of the public. This notion was strengthened during the interwar years and the Second World War, when the ascendancy of the Nazi Party in Germany was frequently attributed to its leaders' skills as master propagandists. In the aftermath of the Second World War, when the extent of Nazi brutality became clearer, this assumption took on even more popularity. As the international community searched for explanations for the behavior of normal citizens who had become willing and in some cases even enthusiastic Nazi collaborators, the Nuremberg trials appeared to hold out an answer: the Nazis had used a sophisticated, government-sanctioned system of propaganda that they disseminated frequently and widely via radio programs, public rallies, posters, and the popular press to gradually turn Germans into Nazis. Years later Meerloo would make an explicit link between the methods of the Nazi Party and the new technique of Communist brainwashing, asserting that the Nuremberg trials revealed the "systematic and coercive methods used by the Nazis" and claiming that their use of psychological torture could be traced back all the way to the early 1930s and the trial of Marinus Van der Lubbe, who was executed in 1934 for allegedly setting the German Reichstag building on fire. According to Meerloo, Van der Lubbe's appearance at his own trial bore all the hallmarks of psychological abuse, and "medical knowledge and psychiatric techniques had been misused in transforming the victim [Van der Lubbe] into a passive automaton."[104]

By the early 1940s the Americans' own early attempts at propaganda had evolved into concrete government programs such as the Office of War Information and Voice of America, which were primarily concerned with "explaining" American "government policy to the news media and the public, both domestic and foreign."[105] Voice of America was especially prominent, employing radio to broadcast news programs and American culture abroad. American attempts at psychological warfare were institutionalized under the supervision of William "Wild Bill" D. Donovan, head of the OSS, and, according to the historian Walter Hixon, during this period American efforts "encompassed a variety of activities, including propaganda in support of military operations; intelligence gathering; disinformation; sabotage; and myriad additional covert operations."[106] During the early Cold War it was evident that propaganda and psychological warfare were key aspects of both U.S. and Soviet Union military strategy. Hixon's analysis of this period highlights a crucial aspect of propaganda by the time of the early Cold War, namely, its increasingly subtle nature, as the exportation of jazz to Soviet bloc countries to advertise American culture illustrates.

One practical consequence of these developments on the home front was that cold warriors interpreted relatively innocuous activities and social programs as Communist-inspired propaganda and front organizations. In a letter to a high-ranking official in the Department of Commerce, Eisenhower's chief adviser on psychological warfare, C. D. Jackson, demonstrated just how pervasive such subterfuge was when he expressed concerns about an offer from the Soviet Union to buy $20 million worth of butter from the United States in 1954. After reviewing the request, he concluded that it was "very evidently Russian psychological warfare," noting, "I honestly do not think that for $20-million it is worth while falling into this trap."[107] Although it was certainly plausible that the Soviet Union may have had an ulterior motive for its request, Jackson's interpretation of the offer is indicative of how officials saw propaganda in even the most seemingly benign situations.

Policymakers believed propaganda was literally everywhere. An FBI report in 1957, for example, stated that Communists were utilizing propaganda "as a means of conditioning and influencing noncommunist Americans" and warned, "No part of the population and no sphere of activity in the United States has been overlooked or neglected by communists as targets of their propaganda."[108] Government officials increasingly began basing their policy decisions on this perception of Communist propaganda, and attempts to make the nation propaganda-proof would play a crucial role in domestic American politics from the civil rights movement to the Hiroshima Maidens program.[109]

At the dawn of the Cold War, U.S. propaganda and psychological warfare—whether via their obvious government-sponsored outlets, such as leaflets, posters, news programs, and radio broadcasts, or their subtler incarnations, including American music and films—dotted the cultural and political landscape and demonstrated openly that big government was in the opinion-making business. Both propaganda and psychological warfare served as immediate historical precedents to brainwashing and helped establish a framework for the eventual understanding and acceptance of the concept. Within this framework, brainwashing appeared as the next step in the evolution of propaganda and psychological warfare. By overpowering and controlling people's minds, brainwashing offered a much more authoritarian method of convincing the public to fall in line with a certain political party or ideology. Obviously more severe than propaganda, brainwashing was still at its base concerned with influencing individuals' beliefs, and this allowed it to be interpreted in the same vein as propaganda, psychological warfare, and other earlier forms of manipulation.

The popular understanding of brainwashing was also colored by America's cultural heritage, which by the middle of the twentieth century was littered with examples of techniques similar to mind control. These techniques had appeared in everything from folktales to science fiction, so mind control was by no means a foreign concept by the Cold War era.

The battle for men's minds, one poster at a time. Anti-American propaganda, U.S. Army Photo, from William Lindsay White, *The Captives of Korea: An Unofficial White Paper on the Treatment of War Prisoners* (New York: Scribner's, 1957).

In view of this cultural legacy, the techniques of mesmerism and hypnosis stand out. Mesmerism, based on the ideas of Franz Mesmer, first became well known during the 1830s as it spread throughout Europe. It reached its peak of popularity in the middle of the nineteenth century and eventually "came to refer to a wide range of different techniques, each claiming to give one person the power to affect another's mind or body."[110] Usually led by a male mesmerist, a mesmeric séance often focused on a female subject who had been placed in a trance. In front of a spellbound audience, the subject would proceed to "speak his [the mesmerist's] thoughts, taste the food in his mouth, move her limbs in a physical echo of his."[111] In 1843 the Scottish neurosurgeon James Braid published *Neurypnology: or the Rationale of Nervous Sleep*, which built on the earlier ideas of Mesmer and introduced the concept of hypnosis. According to Braid, having a subject focus on a small image at eye level would produce a hypnotic state, and, when a patient entered this state, a skilled therapist could reach and control his or her unconscious mind.

Mesmerism may not have been a household word in American society in the 1950s, but it was cited in descriptions of brainwashing and used to explain the mind-numbing power of the Communist Party. For example, the journalist Elizabeth Janeway cited mesmerism when she described the testimony of two ex-Communists who explained how Communism had slowly manipulated their perception of reality. Her sources, the atomic spy Klaus Fuchs and the ex-Communist poet Stephen Spender, both claimed that the lines between the "schizophrenic" world of Communism and reality had become blurred in their minds when they became members of the party.[112] Janeway attributed this "turning away from reality" to the party's "power of mesmerism."[113]

Hypnosis was even more influential on American's ideas about brainwashing. At the beginning of the twentieth century hypnosis was a prominent tool in therapy, but after Sigmund Freud abandoned the technique in favor of other methods, hypnosis slowly became "relegated to the entertainment stage, as magicians, vaudevillians, and illusionists used hypnotism for 'mesmeric' purposes."[114] The technique underwent a revival during the Second World War, as it began to gain publicity as a treatment for traumatized soldiers. During the early postwar period hypnosis became an accepted tool of therapists and psychologists, and it was not long before the press began to make outlandish claims about the practice, arguing that it helped cure everything from common phobias to "nail-biting, bedwetting, facial twitching, and masturbation."[115] By the early Cold War the hypnotized subject had been the topic of academic and popular fascination for decades, and experiments and public displays of hypnosis often tried to test the bounds of hypnotic suggestion and determine if a hypnotized subject could be willed to commit a crime or murder.[116] Speculation about the viability of hypnosis as a weapon of war was even becoming part of mainstream popular discourse, as evidenced by an article in a popular men's magazine by the Colgate University psychologist George Estabrooks which asserted that "a small corps of carefully trained hypnotists attached to an armed force could wreak more far-reaching havoc than an atom bomb."[117] The fact that the term *hypnosis* was repeatedly cited in articles explaining brainwashing alludes to the pivotal role hypnosis played in the early understanding of the concept. The attention hypnosis garnered in the late 1940s and early 1950s not only illustrates a midcentury fascination with the human mind and the possibility that it could be governed by outside sources, but also evinces that Americans were culturally predisposed to granting a degree of authenticity to brainwashing that it would not necessarily be met with today.

Fictional representations of mind control also had a long history, stretching back to Gothic fiction and serving as cultural precedents to brainwashing. As Seed has pointed out, mind control had become a familiar plot device by the late nineteenth century, when "hypnosis had become a staple of novels like *Dracula* where swirling lights are induced by the vampire . . . [and] *Trilby* where Svengali 'plays' his pupil like an instrument."[118] By the Second World War a number of fictional accounts of processes analogous to brainwashing were evident in popular literature. The most influential twentieth-century works of fiction on the popular perception of brainwashing were undoubtedly Aldous Huxley's *Brave New World* and George Orwell's *Nineteen Eighty-Four*, published in 1932 and 1949, respectively. These iconic novels painted a grim picture of what the world would look like if a totalitarian form of government ever came to power. *Brave New World* was set in twenty-sixth-century London and featured a World State which had come to power by implementing a hedonistic and mindless culture that revolved around the drug soma. In Huxley's dystopian vision, children were born in hatcheries, individuality and creative thought were fiercely discouraged, and humans were conditioned to behave in accordance with the World State government.[119]

Orwell's *Nineteen Eighty-Four* was equally bleak. The book is set in the ruins of late-twentieth-century London, and the protagonist of the novel, Winston Smith, was a discontented member of the Outer Party. Orwell's world-state Oceania was controlled by the Thought Police and Big Brother, who eventually arrested Smith and "cured" him of his discontentedness. Despite the fact that the totalitarian governments in Huxley's and Orwell's novels implemented their control in fundamentally different ways, both writers offered similarly dire predictions of the future state of individuality and freedom of thought under totalitarian rule. The concepts of Pavlovian conditioning, reeducation, and mind control were featured in the novels, and in addition to offering a literary portrait of a totalitarian government whose power rose as the amount of free will granted to the populace at large fell, both books were frequently cited in contemporary descriptions of brainwashing.[120]

The historical precedents of false confessions, propaganda, and psychological warfare and the cultural precedents of mesmerism, hypnosis, and the dystopian visions of Huxley and Orwell still do not completely explain why brainwashing became so easily accepted in the early 1950s. Just as important as these precedents was the larger historical context of the time period itself, which was extremely conducive to the widespread acceptance of brainwashing. In 1958 the science fiction writer Arthur C. Clarke aptly summed up the technological ethos of the period when he said that "at the present rate of progress, it is impossible to imagine any technical feat that cannot be achieved, *if* it can be achieved at all, within the next five hundred years."[121] On the heels of the explosion of the atomic bomb, the 1950s was a period when nearly any scientific breakthrough seemed within reach, and brainwashing was no exception.

In addition to a general sense of progress and the notion that anything was possible, midcentury American culture was marked by a fascination with mental health and the human mind. In 1957 an article in *Life* magazine claimed that the 1950s was "the age of psychology and psychoanalysis as much as it [was] the age of chemistry or the atom bomb."[122] Although this fascination with the mind was palpable, postwar Americans' relationship with the burgeoning field of behavioral science was marked as much by distrust as by enchantment. The dangers posed by the misuse of psychiatry and psychology were frequent topics in the mainstream media, and the media took special note of cases in which the tools of behavioral scientists had fallen into the wrong hands. For example, an article titled "Hypnotism Is Dynamite" published in the *Los Angeles Times* in 1952 noted the dangers posed by the rampant use of hypnosis by amateurs, sometimes to deadly effect. Citing one amateur hypnotist who practiced out of his cellar and placed ads in the local paper, the article revealed that he had learned his craft from a book advertised in a mystery magazine ten years earlier and had gone on to treat "hundreds of people—for insomnia, stuttering, smoking and drinking, and even inferiority complex."[123] As a psychiatrist had asserted earlier in the article, this was indeed cause for consternation, since "the lay hypnotist can do irreparable harm by producing hypnotic effects which he doesn't understand and doesn't know how to use."[124] The notion of brainwashing substantially heightened these anxieties, indicating that foreign states were exploiting modern psychiatry and behavioral sciences and turning them into weapons of war. One of Hunter's sources, a psychiatrist from New York named Leon Freedom, captured these concerns when he asserted, "The methods devised by the Free World to combat illness are used by the communists to create it. . . . That is why brainwashing can only be properly understood and dealt with as man-made illness."[125] Simultaneously playing on Americans' fascination with the human psyche and their anxieties about its potential as a site of external abuse, the brainwashing narrative fit perfectly within the broader climate of popular postwar American medical and scientific discourses.

The general atmosphere of the Cold War also contributed to the widespread acceptance of brainwashing. In 1949 the Soviet Union dropped its first atomic bomb, shocking the American intelligence community, who had predicted that the Soviets were at least five years away from harnessing nuclear power. As a result, within the environment of Cold War secrecy, the nuclear arms race, and technological one-upmanship, practically anything within the realm of plausibility, from death rays to advanced missiles, was imagined to be on the shop floor of Communist scientists. In this light, brainwashing was viewed as frightening evidence that the Communists were pulling ahead in the "race" for the mind. Fred Schwarz, who toured the lecture circuit in 1953 and spoke extensively on Communism, articulated this point of view when he claimed that "they [the Communists] are as far ahead of us in the control of the human mind as we are ahead of the Hottentots of Africa in the production of automobiles."[126]

The midcentury popular understanding of Communism also produced a favorable climate for the ready acceptance of brainwashing. Remarking upon this climate, David Seed said, "Undoubtedly one reason why the term 'brainwashing' caught on so quickly was that it harmonized easily with already existing metaphorical discourse."[127] Two cultural artifacts that exemplify the broad outlines of this discourse are the figure of the Communist dupe and Hannah Arendt's influential book *The Origins of Totalitarianism.* In the late forties and fifties any American who displayed pro-Communist beliefs was commonly referred to as a dupe by the mainstream media. The figure of the dupe offers a snapshot of the American mindset on Communism during this period and suggested that the success of Communism was widely attributed to some form of trickery or mental subterfuge. Arendt's *The Origins of Totalitarianism,* published in 1951, elucidates another central aspect of midcentury American thought on Communism. Remarking on the goals of totalitarianism, Arendt wrote that it "strives not toward despotic rule over men, but toward a system in which men are superfluous. Total power can be achieved and safeguarded only in a world of conditioned reflexes, of marionettes without the slightest trace of spontaneity."[128] Arendt was not the first, nor would she be the last, to insinuate that the main goal of totalitarianism was total control. This conviction became a central component in the popular understanding of the alleged international Communist conspiracy for global domination and made brainwashing appear to make perfect sense. If the Commies' intention was not to simply rule over other men but to have total power over them, as Arendt and other cold warriors frequently asserted, what could be a more definitive symbol for their aims than mind control? Beyond all these factors is the simple fact that a great deal of evidence indicated that the Soviet Union and Red China were using propaganda, indoctrination, and psychological torture on an unprecedented scale during the early Cold War. As the psychiatrist Robert Jay Lifton would later note, "Despite the vicissitudes of brainwashing, the process which gave rise to the name is very much a reality: the official Chinese Communist program of *szu-hsiang kai-tsao* (variously translated as 'ideological remolding,' 'ideological reform,' or as we shall refer to it here, 'thought reform') has in fact emerged as one of the most powerful efforts at human manipulation ever taken."[129] Some scholars have taken to describing brainwashing as a "cultural fantasy," and although this interpretation has merit, it does not fully acknowledge just how deeply rooted in reality brainwashing was.[130] Brainwashing was not simply a cultural fantasy, it was a flawed interpretation of political realities. That it was flawed did not make it any less real to home-front Americans living through the Cold War.

With all of these factors in the background, the publicity surrounding the American POWs in 1953 raised concerns, and while the commotion caused by the POWs in North Korea may have been the proverbial match that lit the fires of a widespread acceptance of brainwashing, the concept's historical and cultural precedents as well as the general historical context of the period had already gathered and laid the cultural and ideological kindling that allowed that fire to blaze so brightly for the remainder of the decade.

The Appeal of Brainwashing

When brainwashing first appeared on the American intellectual and cultural landscape in the 1950s it was intrinsically linked to the American soldiers who had been imprisoned by the Communist Party during the Korean War. However, even as the media attention surrounding the soldiers began to fade by the middle of the decade, brainwashing retained an integral place in American culture. All of the evidence and incidents that touched on brainwashing, the historical and cultural precedents of the concept, and the general cultural and intellectual atmosphere of the early Cold War era created a specific framework for understanding the concept. That framework heavily favored conceptualizing the technique as a sinister and overt form of mind control, one that allowed outside forces to manipulate individuals to behave and think in specific, often unwanted ways.

The rapid ascension of brainwashing in American culture can be largely attributed to the fact that it seemed to simultaneously support what Americans thought they knew about Communism and offer new insight into what they didn't. A central example of this was the appeal of brainwashing as an explanation for the international success of Communism. Within American culture, Communism was commonly portrayed as a mode of government that was diametrically opposed to capitalist democracy. As a result, many Americans found it difficult to understand how Communist ideology attracted so many converts around the world. For Americans to admit that the reason for this success was that Communist ideology best served the interests and concerns of certain groups would have meant that capitalist democracy did not—a conclusion most Americans in the early 1950s could not accept. Instead of examining why Communism truly appealed to certain groups, Americans had long chalked up its success to authoritarian methods and intellectual trickery. Brainwashing worked in the same way, offering what Timothy Melley has called "a crude theory of ideology" and shifting the focus from a fair and balanced analysis of the appeal of Communism to a reflexive concentration on mind control and overt manipulation.[131]

From the American perspective brainwashing also served as symbolic and metaphoric shorthand for the differences between democracy and Communism. Brainwashing represented mental slavery, the dominance of the party or group over the individual, and the denial of inherent human freedoms—all prevailing aspects of the popular portrayal and conceptualization of Communism during the 1950s. According to the contemporary paradigm, the United States, on the other hand, was marked by freedom and individuality. Brainwashing tapped into this dominant comparative framework, and as a result it became a popular conceptual tool during the period.

All of these factors played an important role in endowing brainwashing with immense explanatory power and help explain why the concept became both ubiquitous and dominant. During the early 1950s widespread reports that the Communist enemy had drained American soldiers of their personalities and turned them into pawns of the Communist state infused the Cold War with a new psychological dimension and encouraged Americans to believe that their own mental autonomy might be at risk. This new landscape was emphasized by policymakers. In 1955 the secretary of defense's Advisory Committee on Prisoners of War highlighted the fact that new developments in Communist psychological warfare represented a challenge for all Americans: "America must view the Communist treatment of captives as but another weapon in the world-wide war for the minds of men. . . . The battlefield of modern warfare is all inclusive. Today there are no distant front lines, remote no man's lands, far-off rear areas. The home front is but an extension of the fighting front."[132]

This new psychological battlefield would have far-reaching ramifications on modern American life, and from its introduction brainwashing would offer Americans a new way of thinking about the Cold War and the threats posed by the postwar world. It is clear that the concept was created and defined within the larger American cultural and intellectual milieu of the early 1950s. However, it did not merely reflect the main themes of American postwar culture—it played a key role in shaping them. Touching on a disparate range of topics and issues, brainwashing would reverberate within America's cultural consciousness for decades to come.

2
The Many Faces of the Communist Enemy

Two weeks before the presidential election of 1952, Gen. Dwight D. Eisenhower appeared before nearly one hundred thousand enthusiastic Bostonians on Boston Common to highlight his case for the presidency. Addressing the largest crowd of his presidential campaign, Eisenhower began his speech by differentiating himself from the Democratic nominee, Adlai Stevenson. Telling the crowd he could not "dress up . . . [his] ideas in witty and pretty talk," Eisenhower clearly and simply articulated his qualifications for the presidency, claiming that the main reason the United States needed new leadership was because it faced an enemy that represented "a definite and self-proclaimed threat to the individual lives, the individual freedom, of each one of us on this ancient common ground." The threat Eisenhower was referring to was "godless communism," which he described as a "menace to the free world's unity . . . [that] creeps through every unguarded gateway . . . [and] strikes at the jugular vein of freedom."[1] Presenting himself as a man of the people and the only candidate who had the spiritual strength to protect American's "individual freedom" from the Communist threat, Eisenhower was met with thunderous applause. His message that day, oft-repeated during his campaign for the presidency, struck a nerve with the entire nation, and he was elected president on November 4 in a landslide victory.[2]

The Boston speech offers a revealing glimpse of the cultural and political landscape of the period because Eisenhower's invocation of a vague and elusive Communist Party was typical. During the late 1940s and early 1950s, communism was only vaguely defined by reporters, Cold War experts, and even prominent politicians like Eisenhower. Alternately described as a menace, a specter, and a vast international conspiracy, the

Communist Party was almost universally deemed by the mainstream media a dire threat to all the free peoples of the world and consistently portrayed as an un-American totalitarian movement bent on world domination. However, the reasoning behind such assertions was frequently clouded by vague allegations and even vaguer rhetoric.

This portrayal derived in part from a number of high-profile political trials in the late forties and early fifties that allegedly revealed a Communist network of spies living in American society and working in the upper echelons of the federal government. The Cold War historian Ellen Schrecker has argued that these trials helped transform "the vague and largely ideological threat of Communism into something much more concrete: real people taking real actions that seemed to be part of a Moscow-led conspiracy."[3] The trials undoubtedly helped establish an explicit Communist threat, namely, atomic espionage committed by some American citizens and a Soviet Union emboldened by atomic secrets and nuclear weapons, and, as Schrecker points out, they further "demonized" the popular image of the Communist enemy.[4] However, by highlighting "real people" like the alleged traitors Julius and Ethel Rosenberg, an American-born married couple living in New York City, the trials also blurred the lines between foreign, Communist others and apparently normal American citizens. The Communist enemy appeared both diffuse and omnipresent in the nation's cultural consciousness: Communism was a political party with totalitarian aspirations; it was a subversive and un-American idea; it could be practiced by your next-door neighbor.

While he was still on the campaign trail in 1952, Eisenhower unambiguously communicated the new battle lines drawn by the Cold War, telling a crowd in San Francisco, "Our aim in 'cold war' is not conquest of territory or subjugation by force. Our aim is more subtle, more pervasive, more complete. We are trying to get the world by peaceful means to believe the truth. The truth is that Americans want a world at peace, a world in which all people shall have opportunity for maximum individual development. The means we shall employ to spread this truth are often called 'psychological.' Don't be afraid of that term just because its [*sic*] a five dollar, five syllable word. 'Psychological warfare' is the struggle for the minds and wills of men."[5] If Eisenhower's caricature of the Communist enemy was unclear, his description of the nature of the Cold War was much more specific. This was a war being waged on a psychological battlefield to protect Americans' "individual development." And in this war the true prize was the "minds and wills of men." As brainwashing began to receive increased publicity in 1953 it began to figure prominently in this worldview and the popular portrayal and understanding of the Communist enemy. The rise of brainwashing as an explanatory device and a means of gaining insight into Communism evolved from two central factors. The first was the ambiguity surrounding the contemporary portrayal and understanding of Communism in American society, which left the popular image of the Communist enemy in a state of flux and allowed it to continue to evolve. The second factor was that brainwashing provided the mainstream media, politicians, and Cold War experts with a unifying concept that allowed them to connect all of the various narrative strands related to Communism together.

Because the Communist enemy, as ambiguous as it was, had already been exhaustively sketched by the mainstream media, and the Cold War had long been perceived as a battle for the "minds and wills of men," brainwashing did not redefine Communism or the nature of the Cold War as much as it extended and deepened preexisting ideas. Consequently the concept would play a central role in shaping American anti-Communist culture and give the vague Communist menace of Eisenhower's speech a more definitive shape.

The Evolution of the Communist Threat

With the exception of the Second World War, when the United States and the Soviet Union formed a short-lived alliance against a common Nazi enemy, a prominent strain of anti-Communist sentiment ran through American culture for most of the early twentieth century. The historian Cecilia O'Leary has argued that anti-Communism first became prominent as a response to increased union activity as early as the 1880s, when "industrialists joined publishers in branding labor activism as communist, anarchist, and un-American."[6] When the Communist Party came to power in Russia after the Bolshevik Revolution of 1917, the nation's suspicion of Communism developed into the first Red Scare, which lasted until 1920 and was at least partially responsible for riots that broke out in twenty-five towns and cities across the United States during the so-called Red Summer of 1919.

The mainstream media's portrayal of Communism during the Cold War era was clearly indebted to pre–Cold War imagery and ideas, and the manner in which politicians, journalists, and Cold War pundits described Communism after the Second World War would have sounded familiar to earlier audiences. Central to pre–Cold War perceptions of Communism were three main ideas: Communism was godless, it valued the collective over the individual, and it represented an un-American ideology. Americans would largely filter new developments in the Cold War through these long-established modes of thought. However, despite overt similarities, something had fundamentally changed in the way Americans perceived Communism during the middle of the century. The nation had long viewed it as a threat, but prior to the Cold War the media and politicians focused primarily on the American Communist Party (CPUSA) and its disruptive effect on labor and the economy. During the early Cold War, the nation's focus began to shift to the Soviet Union and international Communism, which led many Americans to reexamine the nature of the Communist enemy.

The new realities of the post–Second World War geopolitical landscape and the Soviet Union's ascendancy as a nuclear superpower in 1949 prompted this reexamination. Yet the mainstream media and prominent members of Congress did not simply portray Communism as the threat of nuclear war. Of at least equal import in American Cold War culture was the notion that the Soviet Union would use the threat of nuclear war as a means to an end: world domination and the total control of civilian populations. During the early years of the Cold War, the American public was repeatedly informed that the Soviet Union governed its citizens with an iron fist. The Truman administration and the print media both focused on gulags (Glavnoye Upravlenye Lagerei, or Department of Penal Labor Camps), which contemporary journalists estimated contained anywhere between two million and twenty million slave laborers. Anticommunists often failed to distinguish between the camps and life outside them, and over time the "slave world came to define everything east of the Iron Curtain."[7] This belief reached the highest levels of the American government, as evidenced by the policy paper NSC-68, which stated that the Soviet Union was "held together by the iron curtain around it and the iron bars within it."[8] As the historian Susan Carruthers has pointed out, despite the fact that the image of the gulag had faded from the public eye by the midfifties, the Soviet Union remained linked to the unlawful captivity and imprisonment of innocent civilians in the popular imagination and continued to be depicted as one vast prison camp in the media.

The existence of the gulag brought attention to the Communist Party's ability to exert physical control, but a number of other sources during the same period indicated that the dangers posed by the Soviet Union went far beyond enforced servitude and physical annihilation. In 1951 Hannah Arendt explicitly described Communism as a threat to Americans' minds and bodies. Classifying both Nazism and Communism as totalitarian movements, Arendt declared that they came to power through propaganda, the imposition of mass conformity, and a general climate of fear. Once they assumed leadership, however, their goal was "not the transformation of the outside world or the revolutionizing transmutation of society, but the transformation of human nature itself."[9] In order to accomplish this transformation, Arendt claimed that totalitarian movements killed the moral, individual, and juridical essence of every citizen, until nothing remained "but ghastly marionettes with human faces, which all behave like the dog in Pavlov's experiments, which all react with perfect reliability even when going to their own death, and which do nothing but react."[10] Arendt's analysis, word choice, and description of the Communist threat evoked many of the main themes of Edward Hunter's first book on Communist brainwashing, which was also published in 1951.[11] One of the central arguments of both works was that the Communist Party aimed to control American minds and bodies, not simply eradicate them.

Over the course of the 1950s the notion that the Communist Party was aggressively waging an international psychological war against humanity became one of the most dominant narratives of American Cold War culture and became closely linked to the nation's perceptions of the Communist enemy. Reporters and politicians frequently cited brainwashing and indoctrination as evidence that the Communist enemy engaged in a new and brutally total warfare. Commentators like Hunter went a step further and used the practice to draw conclusions about Communist society, maintaining that the Communist Party's willingness to use techniques like brainwashing on their foes and even on their own citizens demonstrated a brazen lack of respect for human rights and illustrated their ruthless, inhumane nature.

When the treatment of American POWs in North Korean prison camps began receiving national exposure in 1953, it was immediately cited as evidence of the Communist Party's desire to control minds as well as its abhorrent disregard for basic human rights. In an op-ed piece that appeared on September 13, 1953, the military editor of the *New York Times,* Hanson W. Baldwin, argued that the Communist treatment of American POWs "reaffirm[s] once again the ruthless nature of the enemy and emphasize[s] his unlimited aims."[12] In a particularly revealing passage, Baldwin linked the North Korean prison camps to the Communist Party's central objectives: "The Communists are trying to recreate man after their own image. Domination of his mind and spirit is an essential, and usually a preliminary, to physical subjugation. Conformist man—robot man—man cowed by fear or blindness—this is the objective of a world-wide conspiracy implacable in its ruthlessness."[13] Baldwin's analysis illustrates how quickly reporters began to contend that the treatment of American POWs in North Korea was a critical indication of what the Communist Party intended to do on an international scale, and how the media began to refer to Communist citizens in language that unmistakably referenced brainwashing. Baldwin's examination also stands out because his reference to "conformist man" and "robot man" was an early example of what would become a hallmark of the popular portrayal and description of the Communist enemy by the middle of the 1950s: the inhuman, foreign Communist other. When reporters like Baldwin used words like *conformist* and the more loaded term *robot* to describe the Communist enemy, they were explicitly pointing out that Communist citizens were losing their individuality and perhaps even their humanity.

In addition to *conformist* and *robot*, politicians and writers frequently referred to Communist citizens as *slaves, pawns, automatons, puppets, drones,* and *zombies.* This rhetoric left ample room for interpretation of how this dehumanizing process was actually accomplished. In the early 1950s a sizable number of prominent social commentators insinuated that the minds of Communist citizens were literally being controlled by the Communist hierarchy. At the forefront of this group was Hunter, who averred that the Communist hierarchy was using heavy-handed, inhumane methods to turn innocent citizens into a new breed of human beings who behaved and thought in perfect accordance with the party. For example, in *Brainwashing: The Story of the Men Who Defied It,* Hunter wrote that the party intended to use a Pavlov-inspired "conditioned-reflex" system to make citizens behave and think in perfect accordance with the party and the ideology promulgated by its leaders, a process he called "the insectivization of human beings."[14] Hunter called the end product of this process the "new Soviet man," a citizen who had "the conception of the individual *I* . . . replaced by the *we* of collectivity."[15]

Although many authorities in the political and media establishment may have been slightly more reluctant than Hunter to draw such a clear connection between brainwashing and the character of Communist citizens, their description of the Communist threat drew heavily from the concept of brainwashing and similar methods of manipulation and control. Even reporters who disagreed with Hunter regarding the severity of Communist brainwashing did not disagree with his basic premise that the Communist hierarchy intended to control and manipulate its citizens' behavior. For example, in an anonymous op-ed piece that appeared in the *New York Times* in 1955 the writer argued that the notion that Communist citizens were being turned into robots was largely overblown, writing, "Even after ten years of Communist rule the 100,000,000 people of this area [Eastern Europe] have not yet been turned into the servile automatons who are the ideal citizens of a totalitarian state."[16] In the very same article, however, the writer said that "over the long run, Moscow hopes to have its way by indoctrinating the young, who have no memories of other ways of life."[17]

The article testifies to the diverse claims being made in regard to the Communist hierarchy's purported success in controlling "men's minds." Some commentators indicated that the Communist party was using only indoctrination and propaganda, not the more severe methods outlined by Hunter. Nonetheless, and despite differences of opinion about the relative success and exact nature of Communist mind control, a consensus was developing in the mainstream media and the public at large that the Communist hierarchy was employing manipulative measures to control its civilians' thoughts and actions and to systematically root out dissent and resistance. As a letter to the editor of the *Chicago Daily Tribune* explained, "The materialistic system of communism appreciates human beings only as work tools."[18] The notion that Communist citizens were systematically dehumanized and afforded little personal autonomy or individual liberty was not exactly novel, and in fact had been a long-running theme in American anti-Communist culture. What separated the new consensus from older ideas about the Communist Party was largely based on the assumption that they had evolved as a military threat and were now in possession of and actively using modern scientific methods of overt psychological manipulation to accomplish their objective of total authoritarian control.

By the middle of the decade the mainstream media and Cold War experts alike had absorbed the main themes of brainwashing, and the concept had become incorporated into the popular portrayal and understanding of the Communist enemy. J. Edgar Hoover's *Masters of Deceit: The Story of Communism and How to Fight It,* a best-seller in 1958, illustrates the extent of brainwashing's impact. Hoover's description of the Communist Party was filled with allusions to brainwashing, indoctrination, and enforced mass conformity. In one especially revealing passage Hoover wrote that the Communist Party believed that "man can be completely redesigned from a child of God into a soulless social cog." According to Hoover, the Communists specifically designed and produced this "soulless social cog" through "discipline, education, the Party press, recreation, literature, organizational structure, [and] the arts." The end result of this process was "the 'communist man,' the terror of the twentieth century."[19]

Hoover's description illustrates how pervasive the notion of a total Communist threat had become by the end of the 1950s. Simply put, the Communist threat was not conceptualized or portrayed as simply a danger to American power abroad, or the struggle over foreign markets or foreign nations like Korea. Instead, experts like Hoover frequently depicted it as a modern struggle between American freedom and Communist "twentieth-century slavery." In this war, American citizens' very humanity was at stake. Hoover's description of the Communist threat built on preexisting ideas about the soul as a central battleground of the Cold War struggle. Communism had long been derided by American critics such as the radio personality Father Charles Coughlin for its atheism and secular stance on religion and, as a result, was commonly described as being godless and un-American. The media also reported that the Communist Party was not only in the process of eradicating organized religion but also attempting to take its place, forcibly transitioning its subjects' traditional feelings of loyalty to and reverence for the Russian Orthodox Church to the party, turning Communist literature into a new Bible, and worshiping Joseph Stalin as "a deity."[20] By emphasizing how the Communist Party intended to turn children of God into "soulless social cogs," Hoover put a new twist on these old worries.

This concern for American souls was clearly reflected in popular culture. For example, in the prologue of *The Ten Commandments*, the highest-grossing film of 1956, the producer Cecil B. DeMille claimed that the film was about "whether men are to be ruled by God's law—or whether they are to be ruled by the whims of a dictator. . . . Are men the property of the state? Or are they free souls under God?"[21] Because Communist brainwashing and manipulation seemed to potentially threaten Americans' souls as much as their minds, a number of national religious leaders cast the struggle between the Soviet Union and the United States as a holy war, a line of thought that found a particularly receptive audience among American evangelical Christians and helped propel the careers of preachers like Billy James Hargis, Carl McIntire, and Billy Graham.

Hoover's description of how the Communists designed and produced the "communist man" illustrates how even innocuous activities, such as "discipline, education, the Party press, recreation, literature, organizational structure, [and] the arts," had become filled with potentially traitorous and dangerous implications in Cold War America. Hoover was arguing that even seemingly harmless behavior should be regarded with suspicion because of the Communist Party's ability to impact and modulate individual behavior through increasingly subtle methods. Hoover's warning illustrates how the logic of brainwashing had influenced the larger national discourse on Communism by the middle and late 1950s and how the portrayal and perception of the Communist peril had evolved. From the inception of the Cold War the Communist enemy had been characterized as a vague and menacing threat to American lives. Brainwashing played a central role in popularizing the belief that not only Americans' lives but also their minds and souls were at stake.

Slaves, Aliens, and the Foreign Communist Enemy

In the aftermath of the Second World War, American policymakers faced a formidable dilemma: how to sell the Cold War and the notion of an irrational, aggressive Soviet Union to Congress and the American public in light of nearly five years of popular culture that had portrayed the Soviet Union as a nation of rational allies.[22] By 1946 politicians had already constructed a new narrative to demonize the Communist enemy: the leaders of the Soviet Union were insane. In his famous long telegram to Secretary of State James Byrnes in 1946, George Kennan claimed that the Communist Party's leadership suffered "a psychosis which permeates and determines [the] behavior of [the] entire Soviet ruling caste."[23] The historian Frank Costigliola has argued that "the discourse of psychological pathology privileged Kennan and his listeners—they had the authoritative gaze of physicians—while it positioned the Soviet Union as a mental patient without a legitimate subjectivity."[24] The claim that the leaders of the Soviet Union were insane would play a vital part in the national discourse on Communism for the next twenty years, and it helped turn one of America's closest allies during the Second World War into an illogical, irrational, and aggressive threat.

Although the Communist enemy was routinely deemed a formidable adversary during this period, it was portrayed as a bellicose and belligerent one: an insane, power-hungry monster that was met in the United States with equal parts contempt, condescending derision, and war-weary concern. This vision was reflected in the general attitude of politicians and intellectuals like Kennan, who argued that the Communist enemy was simply a madman writ large and should be treated as such. Kennan's focus on Communist pathology in part explains his desire to contain the Soviet Union, and his containment thesis eventually became a principal component of the Truman Doctrine and U.S. foreign policy during the early years of the Cold War. In his influential article "The Sources of Soviet Conduct," written in 1947 under the pseudonym X, Kennan argued that the Soviet Union must be met with "unalterable counterforce" whenever it showed "signs of encroaching upon the interests of a peaceful and stable world." Kennan's argument for containment derived in part from midcentury attitudes toward the insane, albeit on a much larger scale. Those deemed by the public to encroach upon peaceful and sane society were simply contained in psychiatric wards. In the case of the Soviet Union, which Kennan held was being run by a psychotic ruling caste, it was the duty of the rational United States to contain Communist insanity so that it could not spread or infect the civilized world. As Mike Hammer, the most notorious detective in popular fiction during the period, explained to one of his Communist foes, "You were a Commie, Oscar, because you were batty. It was the only philosophy that would appeal to your crazy mind."[25]

The madman school of thought as professed by Kennan and illustrated by the logic of the containment thesis became increasingly hard to support in the early 1950s. Once the Soviet Union acquired atomic power in 1949, the mainstream media and government leaders continued to conceptualize and portray the Soviet Union as an insane, irrational enemy, but that picture was complicated by mounting evidence that the USSR was an emerging scientific and military superpower. As a result, politicians, intellectuals, and the media began to change the discourse on the Communist enemy; the image of the Soviet madman of the early Cold War fell out of favor and was slowly replaced by the new image of the Soviet mad scientist. This perception of the Soviet Union was exponentially more terrifying than the earlier belief that the Communist enemy was simply mad because now its madness was coupled with a vast, sophisticated scientific proficiency that was at least on par with that of the United States.

In the U.S. government's view the Soviet mad scientist was not a testament to Communist brilliance so much as another reminder of the authoritarian nature of life in the USSR. American profiles of the Soviet education system frequently emphasized that Soviet children were not allowed to choose their own career path and were force-fed political indoctrination at all stages of their education. In 1957 a report from the U.S. Office of Education highlighted the differences between the American and Soviet education systems, noting that in the United States "the individual is of surpassing worth and the goal of education is the development of each person as an individual with freedom and with opportunity to choose his life's work in his best interests."[26] Meanwhile, according to the report, in the Soviet Union "the goal of education is to meet the needs of the state," and students' occupations and courses of study were almost entirely dependent on the whims of the party.[27] Given that students were educated six days a week in a curriculum that focused on science, mathematics, and political indoctrination, the report indicated that the Soviet system was based on the complete inverse of the values embodied by American public education. Soviet scientific progress was thus not the result of individual initiative but the end product of an undemocratic exercise in Communist social engineering.

The media often criticized Soviet education, but an article written by a military correspondent for the *New York Times* in 1958 illustrates how, by the midfifties, such criticism masked a legitimate fear and even grudging respect. In the article, titled "The New Soviet Man—In Diplomacy,"

Drew Middleton claimed that the new generation of Soviet diplomats was more sophisticated, well-spoken, and devious than their ill-mannered and unworldly predecessors. Analyzing a number of the new Soviet diplomats' traits, Middleton praised their table manners, their preference for a martini or Scotch and soda instead of vodka, their ability to take part in intellectual conversations, and their stylish clothing. In apparent astonishment Middleton even made note of the fact that at the recent diplomatic conventions in Geneva he "failed to see a Russian who was obviously drunk or even a bit off center."[28] Despite Middleton's praise for the "ingratiating urbanity" of this new breed of Soviet diplomats, he indicated that they still had much in common with their boorish, uncouth forebears. Underneath the polished veneer Middleton saw the same streak of inner ruthlessness and "single-minded devotion to the interests of the Soviet Union above the interests of any group of countries or of mankind as a whole."[29]

Perhaps the most revealing aspect of Middleton's article was how he reconciled the sophistication and worldly demeanor of the new Soviet diplomats he encountered with their devotion to Communism. According to the contemporary paradigm, Communism was illogical and irrational, and its followers were either blind to reality or insane. How, then, could these intelligent, articulate, sophisticated men be such devoted Communists? Faced with this apparent contradiction, Middleton fell back on the logic of brainwashing, asserting that the new Soviet diplomats would never realize the follies of Communism, even after increased exposure to the outside world, because their "view of the world . . . has been implanted in their minds by years of propaganda."[30]

Middleton's explanation illustrates the key role of the concept of brainwashing in explaining the contradictions in the mainstream media's portrayal of the Soviet enemy. Commenting on the anti-Communist imagery of the Cold War era, Schrecker has argued that the mainstream media and prominent American politicians simultaneously evoked the image of the superhuman and the subhuman when they described the Communist enemy. On the one hand, the Soviet enemy was the master of the atom, an intellectual and scientific juggernaut, and a snazzy dresser to boot. On the other, he was cold and inhuman, blind to reality, the unthinking, indoctrinated follower of an insane worldview. The concept of brainwashing, which inherently implies the existence of a lopsided power dynamic between those using the technique and those who are victimized by it, allowed these contradictory images of the Soviet enemy to coexist. Within this context, the unwilling "new Soviet man" was patently the victim of brainwashing and propaganda, while the Communist hierarchy was the evil enemy using modern psychology to exert ruthless control.

Brainwashing also allowed for a considerable amount of ambiguity in the anti-Communist imagery of the era. In light of nearly a decade of Soviet scientific progress, culminating with the launch of *Sputnik 1* in 1957, the old myth that Communism was simply a reflection of the illogical and irrational Soviet mind seemed to be contradicted by ample evidence to the contrary. However, by using brainwashing and propaganda to explain how normal Soviet citizens were being turned into unthinking party members, the mainstream media were able to dispel the apparent contradictions between the reality of Soviet scientific progress and a popular and intellectual culture that insisted that the Soviet enemy was delusional. And, equally important, brainwashing reiterated one of the main underlying assumptions of American Cold War culture: Communism was so blatantly absurd, one literally had to be brainwashed or a member of the power-hungry, insane ruling elite to advocate it.

Many sources pointed out that the most notable result of this dynamic in the Communist world was that its citizens lacked all outward signs of self-expression and freedom of thought. In an article documenting his trip to Czechoslovakia in 1959 Bill Ball asserted, "An American sticks out like a sore thumb in a communist country. Not only because of his clothes or speech, but because he talks, laughs, and acts *spontaneously.*"[31] An advertising executive for a Chicago-area savings and loan association, Ball was especially exasperated by his inability to find anyone willing to have an actual, frank conversation with him about life behind the Iron Curtain. He wrote that it was not "unusual . . . for party members in the lower echelons to talk almost entirely in party slogans." In fact, Communist party slogans had become so ingrained in everyday conversation that Ball had difficulty determining whether they truly reflected public opinion or had simply become part of the popular idiom. The effect of nonstop propaganda on the civilian population was less of a mystery. "Is it any wonder, then," Ball asked, "that at the frequent Marxism–Leninism lectures, meetings, seminars that one must attend, we find whole audiences stone-faced in rapt attention? As the speakers or discussion leaders grind the same old ax, no one yawns, no heads nod, no eyes shift to gaze at the pretty blonde with the red hat."[32] The citizens of Czechoslovakia, Ball indicated, were starting to lose their humanity.

After accompanying the press corps on Vice President Richard Nixon's tour of Russia and Poland in 1959, the *Los Angeles Times* Washington bureau chief, Robert T. Hartmann, confirmed Ball's diagnosis of life in a Communist state. The main culprit in Hartmann's view was the rise in "Pavlovian thinking," which impacted "virtually every process of Soviet life from the toddler's day nursery to the brainwashing chambers of the

MVD [Ministry of Internal Affairs]."[33] Hartmann reported that citizens in the USSR and Eastern bloc countries were being conditioned so extensively that they barely controlled their own actions. Throughout the trip Nixon had repeatedly told Soviet officials that granting their citizens a greater degree of autonomy would pay dividends for Communist society, but Hartmann was not optimistic that any changes would ever occur under Khrushchev's leadership. He concluded, "For Khrushchev to permit really free intercommunication of ideas and information . . . would really wreck the system which has been so carefully erected to permit the Kremlin to control even the subconscious thoughts of its 208 million subjects. This much, however, may be hoped. If a divine spark does exist within the human soul—as communism denies and we affirm—it will someday burst into flame."[34]

The notion that Soviet citizens had become psychologically distinct from Americans from living under absolutist, authoritarian rule was not confined to popular culture or simply designed for public consumption by figures like Hoover. It was also readily apparent in the classified documents of U.S. policymakers. A memo circulating through the upper levels of government in July 1959, titled "A Strategy for Peace," documents how elite policymakers' perceptions of the "new Soviet man" mirrored the portrayal of Communism in the mainstream media and popular culture. Written by an unnamed "man, outside of government, who is knowledgeable in the business of collecting and disseminating information in the world," the memo made a distinct impression on President Eisenhower, who forwarded it to the secretary of state, Christian A. Herter. He also requested additional commentary from Karl G. Harr Jr. of the Operations Coordinating Board (OCB) and the National Security Council, George Allen of the U.S. Information Agency, and Allen Dulles of the CIA on the memo's recommendations for developing psychological warfare and public opinion initiatives in order "to defeat the international communist conspiracy."[35]

In addition to outlining various methods of "public-opinion formation" and emphasizing the importance of "organizing a publicity apparatus" in order to shape international public opinion and secure America's objectives abroad, the memo argued that the unique psychology of Soviet citizens required close attention:

> The psychology of the peoples behind the Iron Curtain is different from that in free countries. The history of Russia is one of absolutism and indicates to us that there is among the peasants generally a slavish acceptance of autocratic rule. These people are accustomed to discipline such as the Czars imposed. Many, therefore, acquiesce in the discipline of the men in the Kremlin because they are accustomed to it. It is a habit of life.

> We must take into account this psychology and find means of penetrating it. . . . Too many of us like to see policies formed on the basis of what would appeal to Americans, and too little on what would appeal to the Slavic races.[36]

As the memo illustrates, even government officials were not immune to the notion that Soviet citizens were a people apart, racially and historically predisposed to accept the discipline and lack of freedom imposed by the Kremlin.

The popular portrayal of America's other main foreign Communist enemies during the 1950s, the People's Republic of China and the Democratic People's Republic of Korea, was based on equally dire assumptions about the state of their respective humanity and largely filtered through the racial politics of the era. Unlike citizens of the Soviet Union, Asians had been racially vilified in American popular culture since at least the 1880s, when tensions over Chinese immigrants on the West Coast gave way to xenophobia and immigration reform. The anxieties of that era gave birth to a Yellow Peril tradition in American culture. By the middle of the 1880s the musical comedy *The Mikado* by Gilbert and Sullivan was already playing on popular stereotypes of Japanese men as subhuman puppets as the authors had a choir of Japanese noblemen sing, "If you think we are worked by strings, / Like a Japanese marionette, / You don't understand these things: / It is simply court etiquette."[37]

This racist cultural tradition was exacerbated by the rise of Japan as a world power and by the Second World War, which produced an outpouring of negative stereotypes and images that portrayed the Japanese as sinister, aggressive, and devious. The historian John Dower has written that "the Western Allies . . . consistently emphasized the 'subhuman' nature of the Japanese, routinely turning to images of apes and vermin to convey this."[38] Prowar propaganda posters, editorial and popular cartoons, and popular culture from films such as *Menace of the Rising Sun* (1942) to the Warner Bros. short *Bugs Bunny Nips the Nips* (1944) widely trafficked in this imagery.[39] The long history in the United States of conceptualizing and portraying Asian nations as racial others served as an important precedent and provides crucial insight into how Red China and North Korea came to be popularly understood and depicted during the Cold War. As David Seed has indicated, the racist images of Asians that had been so prevalent in pre–Cold War American culture were still evident in the widespread portrayals of Red China and North Korea in the 1950s and early 1960s. For example, as Seed points out, Yen Lo, the Asian Communist scientist in *The Manchurian Candidate* (1962), bore a striking resemblance to Fu Manchu, the most iconic character to emerge out of the Yellow Peril tradition.

The parallel was not an unintended coincidence, as Frank Sinatra's character in the film described Yen Lo as a "Chinese cat . . . smiling like Fu Manchu." The scene led Seed to conclude that some "Cold War themes merely continue those of an older Yellow Peril tradition."[40]

Although the earlier perceptions and images of a racialized Asian other did not simply disappear in the 1950s, they were largely co-opted by a new, less overtly racist discourse that relied heavily on the concept of brainwashing and informed the way the foreign Communist enemy would be portrayed and thought about for much of the Cold War. Central to this new discourse was the idea that Red China and North Korea were mentally and physically controlled by the Soviet Union. During the presidential campaign of 1952, Adlai Stevenson said, "[The] root of the Korean problem does not lie in Korea—it lies in Moscow."[41] The same argument was made by numerous politicians and writers throughout the fifties. An op-ed piece in the *New York Times* declared that common sense dictated such an interpretation: "The idea that the Soviet Union would tolerate a strong and fully independent state, even if that state were Communist, on its longest land frontier is beyond belief."[42]

The consequence of such logic was that during the early Cold War era Red China and North Korea were both broadly portrayed as subservient to the Soviet Union. At best, they were represented as a junior partner. At worst, they were the subhuman puppets of the superhuman and insane Communist hierarchy in Moscow. Both narratives vastly oversimplified the complicated alliance between the Soviet Union and Asian Communist nations, which was commonly rendered as a master–slave relationship in the media.[43] Kurt Vonnegut Jr.'s short story "All the King's Horses," published in *Collier's* in February 1951, is one of the earliest and most memorable examples of this logic in American popular culture. In the story a group of American soldiers led by Col. Bryan Kelly, who is accompanied by his wife and twin sons, crash-land in the Asiatic mainland and are immediately captured by an Asian Communist guerrilla chief named Pi Ying. The captured Americans are taken to an abandoned palace, where Ying offers to let the entire group go free if Kelly can best him in a game of chess. But Ying does not have an ordinary game of chess in mind. Rather, the game is played on a life-size chessboard, and Ying uses giant, hand-carved black chessmen, while Kelly, his family, and the men under his command serve as the white pieces. Whenever Kelly loses one of his pieces to Ying, the "piece" is swiftly escorted out of the room by Ying's guards and shot.

When Kelly tries to explain the situation to his men, he says that Ying is intent on getting some entertainment out of his newfound captives, which prompts one of his men to ask, "Is he nuts?" Vonnegut used the game to underscore Ying's personality, which served as a veritable caricature of the Asian Communist enemy and alluded to the specter of Communist cruelty and insanity. However, Ying is not the only Communist enemy in the story. A military observer from the Soviet Union named Major Barzov is also present, and he watches the entire game unfold with Ying on a balcony overlooking the giant chessboard. Barzov literally lurks in the shadows behind Ying, claiming he is powerless to intervene for Kelly and his men yet constantly whispering in Ying's ear, who seems eager for his approval. When a young American corporal attempts to break up the game and attack a guard, Barzov laughs and yells, "He'll learn to be a pawn yet. It's an Oriental skill Americans could do well to learn for the days ahead."[44] In the story's final scene Ying is murdered by his mistress, who sympathizes with the American prisoners and is being kept as a slave, and Barzov is unveiled as the true mastermind behind Ying's war games.

Vonnegut's story is an example of the emerging narrative in American culture and the mainstream media that depicted the Soviet Union as the root cause of aggressive Asian Communism. The leaders of Asian Communist countries were certainly represented as being evil and ruthless as well as a complicit and integral part of the worldwide Communist conspiracy. However, the mainstream media and American popular culture ultimately depicted them as pawns of the Soviet hierarchy in Moscow, and the notion that a master–servant power dynamic was at the heart of the relationship between the Soviet Union and Communist Asia directly shaped American foreign policy from the Korean War until Vietnam. This misguided perception served to obscure the true nature of international Communism. Instead of perceiving Communism as an international political party that encompassed a number of diverse and often competing interests, countries, and people, the media and prominent American leaders continued to describe and to read international Communism as a monolithic menace headed by the Soviet hierarchy in Moscow. As a result, the American intelligence community failed to recognize the depth of the Sino-Soviet split for the entirety of the 1950s, and they misinterpreted the inherently nationalistic goals of many Asian Communist nations, regarding them as further proof of Asian Communist aggression.[45]

Since Red China and North Korea were supposedly nothing more than subservient, puppet regimes of the Kremlin, all of their tactics and advanced weapons, including brainwashing, were accredited to the Soviet Union. Hunter claimed that brainwashing had been developed in the 1920s and 1930s by Pavlov and other Russian scientists and that the Soviet hierarchy kept the technique a well-guarded secret until they passed it on to Red China in the late 1940s. According to Hunter, as soon as Red

China's leaders acquired the technique they began to use it against their entire civilian population. An October 1953 editorial in the *New York Times* made similar allegations, claiming that "of the countless crimes of the Red regime of Mao none has been as terrible as the crime against the minds and hearts of the good Chinese."[46] Basing their report on accounts of the lucky few who had escaped, the editors stated that the Communist Party of China indoctrinated their young, turned them into unthinking party members, and forced them to spy on their family members.

By the midfifties this view passed for common knowledge. An editorial by William Henry Chamberlin in the *Wall Street Journal* in 1956 articulated the new consensus. Aptly titled "The Silent People: Communists Brainwash the Once-Individualistic Chinese into Gloomy Conformity, Fear and Mental Atrophy," Chamberlin claimed that reports by veteran Far East correspondents based in Europe indicated that "brainwashing, in a somewhat milder form, has been the fate of the whole Chinese population under Communist rule."[47] After touring Communist China, the left-leaning British journalist Kingsley Martin offered a slightly more tempered interpretation of life in Red China in the *Nation* in 1955, arguing that Mao's regime emphasized idealism as well as uniformity. But even Martin conceded that "as far as possible, liberalism and individualism are being purged." Contemplating the future of Red China, he wondered, "Will the next generation even know that there are other intellectual worlds to conquer? Will they become tolerant as they become safe from external and internal attack? Or will uniformity grow until Big Brother's lightest word is law?"[48] The majority of Western newsmen believed the last option was the most likely outcome.

In the months leading up to the Hundred Flowers Campaign, which supposedly loosened the rigid controls on public discourse in Red China, many major American newspapers continued to maintain that Mao's regime severely curtailed the identity and individuality of its citizens. An article by the longtime government adviser and China scholar A. Doak Barnett in September 1956 titled "Mao's Aim: To Capture 600 Million Minds" unabashedly asserted that Red China's indoctrination and propaganda campaigns were larger and more successful than anything ever attempted in the Soviet Union. Barnett contended that in less than a decade, Mao's regime, despite its public pronouncements to the contrary, had started "to 'remold' the thinking of almost a quarter of the human race."[49] The methods they used were extremely similar to the techniques employed against American civilians and POWs who had fallen into the hands of the Communist Party, and, as Barnett noted, "The 'brainwashing' which Americans imprisoned in China have undergone is not a process reserved for foreigners. It is merely part of the Communists' over-all program of 'thought reform.' "[50] In China, this had produced an entire nation of "regimented yes-men, parroting the Communist party line and speaking in one repetitious, monotonous voice."[51] Media coverage of China remained deeply cynical even when there was evidence that positive developments were taking place behind the Bamboo Curtain. In an appraisal of the Hundred Flowers Campaign, for example, the *Saturday Evening Post* insinuated that Mao's critics would face the same repercussions as free thinkers in China a decade earlier, who were invited by the Chinese Communist party to offer their thoughts on Communism only to be isolated and punished for being brave enough to speak out. As the *Post* reminded its readers, "The only flowers that bloomed for them were the few that might have decorated their graves."[52]

Widespread reports of thought control in Red China were reinforced in 1957, when the deputy director of Communist Party propaganda in China announced at a news conference attended by members of the Western news establishment that party members would be "brainwashed" through "persuasion and argument" in order to resolve arguments within the party.[53] A cartoon titled "Brainwashing" that appeared in the *Portland Oregonian* in 1959 perfectly captured the popular perception of Red China by the end of the decade. In the center of the cartoon was a larger-than-life military officer overlooking a large bucket filled with "100% Pure Communism." To the officer's left were China's millions, waiting in a line that stretched into the horizon to be dunked by the officer into the bucket and have their brains washed. The drawing was not a very flattering picture of Chinese society, but it indicated that China's masses might also be victims, as opposed to America's natural-born enemies, in the international Communist conspiracy to take over the world.

The American mainstream media depicted Red China and other Asian Communist countries as modern slave societies ruled with an iron fist by the local Peking hierarchy, who in turn were subservient to their Soviet masterminds in Moscow. Despite this chain of command, the media portrayed the Moscow and Peking leadership very similarly. They were both painted as inhuman, insane regimes, forced to rely on authoritarian methods of control to keep their civilian populations in line. According to the media, the civilian populations of the Soviet Union and Red China had much in common as well and were the victims of propaganda, indoctrination, and brainwashing. Other Communist nations were interpreted within a similar framework, and the dominating theme of news coverage and popular culture was that Communism did not appeal to people's intellect but deposed it. For example, in 1959 the *Chicago Tribune*'s Latin

American correspondent Jules Dubois told an audience at the fiftieth anniversary of the journalism fraternity Sigma Delta Chi that Fidel Castro had taken control of the mass media in Cuba and established one of the most sophisticated brainwashing operations in the world. Although Dubois noted that the Cuban people were actually fiercely anticommunist, "the brainwashing to which they are subjected is mesmerizing many of them."[54]

The notion that Communist governments systematically manipulated and controlled their civilian populations became one of the underpinning justifications for American foreign policy throughout the fifties and early sixties, especially after the decline in Communist aggression after the death of Stalin and the subsequent rise of Khrushchev's comparatively more diplomatic regime in 1953. The media and politicians used the bugbear of Communist cruelty and manipulation to frame the Cold War as a struggle between American freedom and Communist slavery, and this construction allowed them to argue that the United States had to fight in North Korea, direct an invasion of Cuba, and send troops to North Vietnam, not only to protect the United States from Communist aggression but also to save the peace-loving citizens of those countries from the psychological effects of Communist tyranny. The perception of the foreign, Communist other tied all the divergent strands of this cultural narrative together. On the one hand, the American public was continually confronted with the image of the superhuman and insane Communist hierarchy, which was vast in intellect and ruthless in nature. On the other hand, the mainstream media continually portrayed the citizens of these countries as innocent victims who had been turned into subhuman pawns through brainwashing and indoctrination.

After returning from a trip to Moscow in 1959, the publisher of an aircraft magazine named George Haddaway was moved to inquire, "Can people stay human under Communism?"[55] If they were influenced by the popular culture of the era, many Americans would have had their fair share of doubts. Nowhere was the theme of the superhuman and subhuman Communist enemy more prevalent than in the science fiction and horror films of the 1950s. The plots of nearly a dozen films, including *Invaders from Mars* (1953), *It Came from Outer Space* (1954), *Invasion of the Body Snatchers* (1956), *The Brain from Planet Arous* (1957), *I Married a Monster from Outer Space* (1958), and *The Brain Eaters* (1958) featured alien invaders who had the ability to mimic normal American citizens, control their minds, and turn them into cold, inhuman slaves. As the journalist and cultural critic Peter Biskind has pointed out, this genre represented more than simple sci-fi fantasy, and the film's depictions of "possession by pods—mind stealing, brain eating, and body snatching—[was] an overt metaphor for Communist brainwashing, which had just turned GIs into Reds in Korea."[56] For our purposes, the size of these films' respective audiences and the marginal impact they had on mainstream American culture are not of central importance. They stand out because of how they articulated widespread fears about national security and highlighted the themes of infiltration, powerlessness, and mind control that had become so central to American Cold War culture.

These films routinely treated audiences to harrowing visions of American powerlessness in the face of superior alien invaders. Although they varied markedly in appearance, the aliens in these films served as metaphorical representations of the superhuman Communist hierarchy. In her exploration of Cold War cinema, the film critic Nora Sayre offered an insightful appraisal of the alien invaders in these films, writing that they were "always endowed with an intelligence that's far superior to ours; characteristic of the Fifties, intellect was suspect—in these movies, it was often evil. Martian technology outdistanced our latest inventions, as we feared that the Russians' might."[57] But the link between intellect and evil in these films has another crucial dimension that Sayre and other cultural historians have largely ignored. In *Invaders from Mars* the main evil-monger was a Martian head encased in a glass sphere replete with eerie tentacles emitting from its sides. In *Invasion of the Body Snatchers* the aliens were soulless yet foreboding pods. In *The Brain from Planet Arous* the monster was literally a giant floating brain. The common link between the disembodied heads, cold-blooded pods, and levitating brains was not simply their overpowering intelligence or their ability to control the behavior of others, but the fact that they were literally heartless. Having no heart or soul to ground them, the aliens had intellects that were empty of compassion and empathy. In this light, the films were not simply giving voice to some deep-seated strain of anti-intellectualism in American culture. In fact, they frequently championed the folksy wisdom and resourcefulness of the American townspeople who found themselves threatened by alien invaders. The films were not offering a blanket critique of intelligence but warning of the dangers of intelligence devoid of human morality.

If the films' alien invaders represented the unchecked and insane intelligence of the superhuman Communist hierarchy, the cold and inhuman townspeople who were turned into unwilling but complicit slaves represented the subhuman, brainwashed disciples of Communism the world over. After coming into contact with extraterrestrials the characters in these movies would become oddly emotionless, distant, and almost unrecognizable to their friends and spouses. They would start working for

Heartless 1950s sci-fi villains with powers to mesmerize, replicate, and brainwash. Stills from (*above*) *Invaders from Mars* (1953), (*below*) *Invasion of the Body Snatchers* (1956), and (*opposite*) *The Brain from Planet Arous* (1957).

the alien enemies, recruiting more pod people or sabotaging the towns' defense systems. And slowly but predictably more and more townspeople would come under the spell of the invaders until the central protagonists were vastly outnumbered and left to battle the outsiders and their mental slaves all alone or forced to bring in the American military for help. In this respect the films were as much about the threat of internal subversion by manipulated American citizens as they were about invasion from external, alien forces, and they illustrate how expansive the image of the Communist enemy was in American popular culture. The United States was manifestly under attack from the external, foreign Communist other, but that threat was balanced by the equally frightening prospect of internal subversion and the CPUSA. In the climactic scene of *Invasion of the Body Snatchers* the main protagonist addresses this dual threat when he rushes into oncoming traffic after narrowly escaping the clutches of the "pod people." As passing motorists speed by, he shouts frantically, "They're not human! Listen to me! . . . There isn't a human being left in Santa Mira!" Breaking the fourth wall, he then turns to the camera and offers a warning that must have resonated with the film's Cold War audience: "They're here already! You're next!"

The Danger of Ideas and Internal Subversion

As much as the mainstream media portrayed Communism as a tangible physical threat, many Americans were equally apprehensive about communist ideas, to which journalists, politicians, and local community groups regularly ascribed dangerous powers. Although the logic behind such assertions was always ambiguous, the media frequently portrayed Communist ideology as an entity with diabolical abilities to deceive, manipulate, and convert normal American citizens into spies and die-hard apparatchiks. Ideas were practically construed as physical entities in American popular culture, and Communist ideas did more than just enter one's mind: they could magically manipulate one's behavior and blind one to reality. When rehabilitated American Communists spoke about how they had mindlessly converted to the party, they frequently referred to a Communist spell that eventually was broken by some form of spiritual or mental awakening. Even though brainwashing itself was popularly embodied with magical qualities, the concept served an important cultural desire for a more nuanced framework for understanding the spell of Communist ideas and the nature of their influence. Ultimately, Communist ideas were portrayed as yet another enemy that could prey upon weak-minded Americans, effectively wash their brains, and potentially undermine the safety of the nation. And yet again, the mind was envisaged as a central battleground in the war between Communism and the United States.

Behind closed doors U.S. policymakers expressed anxiety about both the potential for Communist ideas to invade and subvert the nation and an ever-widening idea gap. In a direct attempt to counteract Communist propaganda, policymakers had spent years coming up with imaginative new ways of scoring points in the international war for men's minds, ranging from plans in 1953 to exploit Stalin's death for psychological effect to a proposal in 1957 by the OCB to launch "a highly visible large inflatable satellite designed to achieve significant psychological gains by being visible as it traverses the populated areas, including the Soviet Union and Red China."[58] Policymakers engaged in mind games that were unsavory and often bordered on the absurd. Motivating them was the belief that, in a war for hearts and minds, ideas could be as powerful as bombs. The "Strategy for Peace" memo circulated by the White House in 1959 made this point clear: "It can be argued logically that the United States has no right to incite or foment revolution in a foreign land, but there is no rule which says that the United States cannot transport an idea across a boundary. Nor is there any rule which says that American citizens cannot do the same across boundaries, or that private organizations cannot be set up to transmit ideas and express themselves in language far more forceful than the government is privilege to use."[59] If the United States could not directly "incite or foment a revolution in a foreign land," it would do the next best thing: export an idea abroad, let it take root in the minds of Communist citizens, and then watch it blossom into a full-blown revolution that accomplished America's objectives without getting the State Department's hands dirty.

Although this plan displayed an overtly cynical, propagandistic impulse equal to anything displayed by the Communists, the public viewed Communist ideas differently from democratic and capitalist ones. When the United States attempted to export its ideas, it was simply trying to communicate the truth to foreign audiences. When Communists exported their ideas, they were engaging in psychological warfare and propaganda. The notion that Communist ideas and rhetoric had the power to trick innocent civilians into becoming confused and falling for the "big lie" can be traced back to the 1940s, when the CPUSA came under increasing public scrutiny as government officials and news outlets sought explanations for its rise. In the late forties and fifties, the media frequently warned against the dangers of American feeble-mindedness and attributed the rise of the CPUSA to deceit and chicanery. Over time, the perception that Communist ideas were not simply deceiving naïve, wide-eyed Americans but also completely clouding their judgment and dictating their behavior began to take on an increasingly hysterical tone.

In an interview in 1953 an ex-Communist and former member of the CPUSA said that what truly amazed him "was to find that communism could not only control a party member's theory and behavior, but also *his awareness of actuality*."[60] Other ex-Communists echoed this sentiment and compared the Communist Party to a new religion that blinded its followers to rationality. The ex-Communist writer Howard Fast, for example, called Communism a "naked God" and described his time in the party as "a long, and terrible nightmare." Extrapolating on how the Communist Party muddied the lines between good and evil, Fast asserted that the great majority of CPUSA members were earnest, good people who saw in Communism an opportunity to change the world for the better. However, Fast stressed that by emphasizing its ends over the inhumane means the party forced its members to accept a skewed worldview, and, as a result "the road became more important than the destination [and] in time, the road became sacred and real, whereas the destination blurred into increasing unreality."[61]

The nation's highest authorities on Communism used similar arguments to explain the rise of the CPUSA. Hoover chalked up the party's ability to acquire converts to their "double-talk," "Aesopian language," and propaganda, which was used to "fool noncommunists [and encourage] them to believe that communism stands for something desirable."[62] Hoover also touched upon the quasi-religious nature of the party, writing that "in many instances we know, joining the Communist Party comes from a loss of faith, so to speak, in our Judaic-Christian heritage and earnest, though perverted, seeking for a new faith."[63] Hoover's assessment is indicative of the mainstream media's depiction of the CPUSA, and its very existence was attributed repeatedly to a combination of Communist deception, American weak-mindedness, and the decline of traditional American values.

Communist ideas were to be guarded against because they could dupe innocent Americans into committing potentially subversive behavior. In one of the most fascinating passages in his 1956 book on brainwashing, Hunter directly warned the American public to be wary of Communist stock phrases and words. Hunter claimed that the Soviet-made short film *The Nervous System* illustrated the Communist Party's ability to use words and ideas to trigger certain types of prescribed behavior.[64] For Hunter the highlight of the short film was several scenes depicting Pavlov's conditioned reflex experiments with dogs. After Communist scientists were shown classically conditioning a dog and eventually inducing it to salivate whenever they flashed a light, the film showed a boy sitting on a chair with a rubber tube inserted into his mouth to collect his saliva. The following scenes showed the boy being fed small cakes whenever a light flashed, and by the end of the film the boy had been conditioned to salivate whenever the lights flashed. According to Hunter the film illustrated that with a little patience and the right science human beings could be as easily conditioned as a dog. Hunter conjectured that "instead of a light, the Kremlin could use words as signals—any words would do—*imperialism, learning, running dog of the imperialists, people, friend of the people, big brother.*"[65] In this scenario words could condition American minds and act as unconscious triggers, a plot device that would become common in anti-Communist popular culture and spy films in the late 1950s and early 1960s. More important, Hunter's assertion showcases the tendency of many Americans to associate Communist ideas and words with danger and subversion.

It was widely assumed that the CPUSA was transmitting Communist ideas, slogans, and double-talk into American life through a variety of mediums in order to affect Americans' behavior. The most obvious manifestation of Communist ideas was produced by the CPUSA in its publications, ranging from pamphlets to newspapers such as the *Daily Worker*. A report by the FBI in 1957 claimed that the CPUSA, proportionate to its size, had "distributed more literature than any other organization in the United States" and intended to use it "to indoctrinate its members and sympathizers and to reach and propagandize the noncommunist masses."[66] The desire to protect innocent American minds from Communist influence was one of the driving forces behind the cultural blacklist that affected these types of publications as well as film, radio, and television throughout the late forties and fifties. The blacklist, designed to ensure that Communist ideas were not disseminated, was directly responsible for the refusal by libraries and newsstands to carry Communist literature as well as for the demise of countless careers in Hollywood, the censorship of allegedly subversive films such as *Salt of the Earth* (1954), and what Schrecker has termed the "dumbing down" of American popular culture. As several historians have pointed out, the blacklist was abused by politicians and powerful business interests, who became trigger happy with the subversive label and used it to squash dissent, racial integration, and aspects of postwar culture that they deemed unfavorable to capitalism.[67] Despite its obvious potential for abuse, the blacklist cast a shadow over American culture for nearly two decades.

By attributing the blacklist to powerful political and economic interests, historians have tended to overlook the widespread public support for censorship. One of the more fascinating examples of local censorship of Communist ideas came in an unusual case in 1952, when a public high school in Sapulpa, Oklahoma, burned several books in its library collection. A local women's civic group had been appointed the task of examining every textbook and reference book used in the local school libraries. The group deemed several books objectionable, including a history book they found to be "too approving of socialism" and several books that dealt with sex. The women's group did give all of the other history textbooks a clean bill of health, stating that they "found nothing un-American or communistic or fascist in them," although presumably those would have been burned too if they had contained any hints of Communist propaganda.[68] In Oklahoma, censorship was simply another means of protecting young minds from falling under Communist control.

The Sapulpa incident may have been unique in its extremity, but censorship on a local and national level was not. In 1954 the U.S. Post Office refused to deliver seventy-five copies of Vladimir Lenin's *State and Revolution* to Brown University on account of its supposedly subversive ideas. In the early 1950s one of the most popular high school civic textbooks in the country, Frank A. Magruder's *American Government*, was banned in Houston, Little Rock, and the entire state of Georgia and was attacked in several other communities after a review in the *Educational Reviewer* avowed in 1949 that it was overly sympathetic to Communism. The State Board of Education in Arkansas even removed a civics textbook from classrooms for acknowledging the existence of Communist theory. As the historian Jonathan Zimmerman has pointed out, the attack on textbooks was especially prominent in the South and was championed by influential members of the far right, but it also represented a great deal of grassroots activism and support for the censorship of textbooks that exhibited "statism, New Dealism, and socialism."[69]

In an editorial written in 1952 the *New York Times* journalist Benjamin Fine described the consequences of the rabid assault on textbooks, writing that "libraries have been persuaded to remove textbooks or not to order materials that might create a controversy in the community."[70] Perhaps the most striking aspect of the entire debate was that the educators who stood in opposition to censorship claimed that the groups who wanted to ban books were actually the ones trying to control the minds of America's youth. The former chairman of the American Library Association's Committee on Intellectual Freedom, David K. Berninghausen, called the members of the voluntary groups that advocated censorship "volunteer educational dictators" and harshly criticized them, saying that "copying the Nazis or the Communists in thought control techniques in communications and education is not the way to meet our problem."[71]

In a speech at Dartmouth College in 1953 President Eisenhower entered the fray of the debate on censorship when he implored, "Do not join the book burners. . . . Don't be afraid to go in your library and read every book. . . . How will we defeat communism unless we know what it is?"[72] Somewhat paradoxically, however, Eisenhower later clarified that his remarks did not extend to outright Communist propaganda, which he believed should be destroyed.[73] Straddling the lines of the debate on censorship, Eisenhower cautioned against the impulse to burn books but simultaneously acknowledged that Communist propaganda was dangerous enough to warrant its outright destruction. The upshot of this debate is hard to assess. As Fine's editorial makes clear, across the country some books were taken off library shelves and others were simply boycotted. Anything that could possibly be labeled subversive or, worse yet, Communist became culturally off-limits. And, despite the protest of members of the intellectual elite such as Berninghausen, behind the clamor for censorship in communities across the country was a palpable sense that Communist ideas really were dangerous and subversive and really could lead young Americans to commit unspeakably un-American acts.

During the same time period, there were mounting calls for an end to this type of mentality, and several government officials and members of the media indicated that a McCarthyist ethos that banned free and open discussion of Communist ideas was at least partly responsible for the susceptibly of some American POWs to Communist psychological warfare during the Korean War. The father of Lowell Skinner, one of the American POWs who had refused repatriation to the United States, commented on this issue and admitted to a reporter, "I don't know what Communism is, frankly." However, he believed that such ignorance, far from keeping his family safe, had made his son vulnerable, and he was convinced that if Lowell had been provided with an adequate education on Communism "he would have learned all about it and this wouldn't have happened to him."[74] In the concluding analysis of her book on the twenty-one American POWs who refused repatriation, Virginia Pasley reinforced this point, writing, "We must not let fear of Communism keep us from being fully informed about it—good points as well as bad—so that future generations are not taken in when they find out that Communists don't beat their grandmothers."[75]

One of the central ironies of the brainwashing discourse of the 1950s was how different parties promoted interpretations of the technique that worked at cross purposes. In the hands of censors, the logic of the brainwashing narrative justified the purging of Communist ideas and the delegitimizing of the CPUSA.[76] Meanwhile, in the hands of writers like Pasley the same narrative was used to argue that public consumption of Communist ideology could actually provide immunity against Communist psychological warfare. Although obviously at odds with one another, the two interpretations rested on the assumption that the Communist enemy was waging a war on Americans' hearts and minds. Ultimately what was at stake in this war was what Eisenhower had called Americans' right to individual freedom. In this context it was clear that although Communists might not actually beat up your grandma, it was entirely possible they might try to wash her brain.

As several Cold War historians have pointed out, communism was frequently conceptualized as a contagious virus that could contaminate and infect an entire nation. The domino effect in American foreign policy theory represents how this perception took hold of the worldview of America's policymaking elite. In popular culture, nowhere was the threat of contamination in greater relief than in another classic science fiction film of the era, *The Blob* (1958). In this film a meteorite from outer space lands in a small town and when it breaks open, the blob emerges to consume and contaminate everything in its path. As one townsperson after another is contaminated by the blob, it becomes larger and larger, slowly spreading across the town and absorbing innocent American citizens into its gooey mass. As Sayre has argued, science fiction films like *The Blob* "yielded metaphors for the larger malignancies of the Cold War, when a neighbor or one's former teacher might suddenly be labeled as a subversive, when a nuclear attack (or accident) might expunge all questions of who was right or who was wrong, or safe or sorry or secure."[77]

In the world of *The Blob,* contamination was irreversible at the point of contact, and infection meant death. In the real world, during a period when many Americans were calling for a return to traditional values in order to strengthen American society, the specter of contagion, contamination, and internal subversion served to undermine loyalty and trust in communities across the country. After being warned about a pervasive Communist enemy that came in many forms and threatened American citizens on multiple fronts for the better part of a decade, Americans had learned to be on the lookout for external threats as well as internal signs of subversion. Behind the many faces of the Communist enemy was the concept of brainwashing, compelling Americans to reframe the Cold War, in Hunter's words, as the "conflict between the influences that dehumanize and collectivize people and those that develop individuality and free will."[78] By the middle of the 1950s it had become impossible to divorce Americans' perceptions of the Communist enemy from brainwashing because they had become so intertwined in the popular imagination. And just as it had prompted them to reevaluate the Communist enemy, brainwashing led Americans to conduct a critical inquiry of themselves in the wake of the Korean War.

3

Korean War POWs and a Reevaluation of the National Character

After the Korean Armistice Agreement was signed on July 26, 1953, there was a palpable sense of relief that American boys were coming home. The majority of the returning POWs received warm homecomings. As a group, they benefited from largely positive and sympathetic press coverage in the fall and winter of 1953, and the highest-ranking American POW, Gen. William F. Dean, was graced with a ticker-tape parade in New York City. Over time, however, these initial good feelings were overshadowed by critics who questioned the mental fortitude and patriotism of the men who had served in Korea.[1] As the first large contingent of Americans alleged to have undergone Communist brainwashing, the returning American POWs were studied extensively.[2] According to one of their principal defenders, by the end of the decade the American public had concluded that "there had been wholesale collaboration by the American prisoners with their Communist captors and that this unprecedented misbehavior revealed alarming new weaknesses in . . . [the] national character."[3] As a result, the concept triggered a reevaluation of America's fighting men and helped underwrite a searing critique of the state of American patriotism, mental toughness, and resolve at the height of the Cold War.

Widespread reports that American POWs had failed to stand up to brainwashing led many contemporary observers to conclude that American men had been mentally unprepared and outmatched in Korea. A photographer for the Associated Press who had spent thirty-three months in a North Korean prison camp gave firsthand testimony in support of this interpretation, calling the American POWs "babes in the woods" and claiming that "they were not mentally equipped or fortified in any way on how to take care of themselves against this intense indoctrination that was poured on day after day and hour after hour."[4] By the middle of the decade this line of thought had blossomed into a full-blown national debate about the soldiers who had been imprisoned in North Korea. The concept of brainwashing became indelibly tied to reports of their supposedly un-American behavior and led many Americans to believe that the country's defenses against this new Communist weapon left much to be desired.

The journalist Eugene Kinkead, one of the most outspoken critics of the POWs throughout the decade, would claim in a book published in 1959 that "when our contact with the enemy was on the field of battle, we fared better than when we met him on a personal basis, face to face, mind to mind, culture to culture, in his prison camps. In a high percentage of these personal meetings, we not only did not hold our own, but we failed signally."[5] A number of experts attributed these failures not only to the potency of Communist methods of manipulation but also to the weaknesses of the POWs. These analysts protested that the Communists had successfully exploited a number of inherent flaws in the prisoners that were indicative of shortcomings in the American character. Their criticism turned brainwashing from an indictment of Communist cruelty into a commentary on American life.

Maj. Clarence L. Anderson, a doctor in the army who had been a POW in the first North Korean Communist prison camp, said that what stood out the most in regard to the behavior of the POWs was "their almost universal inability to adjust to a primitive situation—a regrettable lack of the old Yankee ingenuity, you might say."[6] In Anderson's opinion, the POWs' inability to adjust to captivity was directly linked to "a new softness" in American men.[7] Kinkead expanded on Anderson's comments by connecting the behavior of POWs in the Korean War to American society. He wrote, "It was not just our young soldiers who faced the [Communist] antagonist, but more importantly the entire cultural pattern which produced these young children."[8]

For many Americans brainwashing highlighted a precipitous decline in traditional American values and the nation's inability to conjure up the psychological tenacity the Cold War demanded. In a letter to the adjutant general in Washington, a dean of cadets in Chicago named Maj. Bert E. Grove claimed that the current publicity surrounding the returning POWs was making it difficult to "inculcate [his cadets] with true Americanism here at Morgan Park Military academy." Grove said he could not "go along with this 'brain washing' hokum, for a real American never, no matter what, renounces his country." To Grove the main issue at stake had never been brainwashing, which he said was a dubious excuse for inexcusable behavior, but the fact that it revealed American men did not have the mental wherewithal to withstand anything the Communists could throw at them. As Grove put it, "A man can steal and lie and, if he is sorry and knows he will never do it again and has paid his debt to society, can be forgiven; but when he prefers communism to Americanism, and encourages others to do likewise, he has defiled Bunker Hill, Gettysburg, [and] Pearl Harbor."[9]

The Korean War had simultaneously been a test of individual American men's ability to fight the Communist enemy on a new psychological battlefield and a test of American society in producing men capable of defending themselves on that field of battle.[10] Results on both fronts had been underwhelming. The concept of brainwashing brought these concerns to the fore, and the reaction to American POWs opens a window onto the nation's insecurities at midcentury. An editorial in *Collier's* in 1955, attempting to pinpoint who was to blame for the POWs who had succumbed to Communist propaganda and indoctrination, asked its readers, "Did these failures reflect inadequate training, or were they symptoms of a broader national weakness?"[11] Throughout the nation educators and politicians addressed this question, and they frequently blamed the behavior of POWs in North Korea on the mental softness of the American people and used the episode as a clarion call to double down on traditional values. Eventually, the assumptions surrounding brainwashing and the behavior of the POWs would lead to a national crisis in confidence and a number of harsh appraisals of American society. How Americans thought about and addressed these concerns would fundamentally alter the cultural landscape of the nation.

A Tenuous Homecoming

By the winter of 1954 the ticker-tape parades had given way to a much more solemn homecoming, as the behavior of American POWs became the topic of intense, prolonged debate. For the POWs who had refused repatriation to the United States, public opinion was unforgiving from the start. An article in the *New York Herald Tribune*'s *This Week* magazine by one of the mothers of a POW who had refused repatriation illustrates just how extreme reactions to the soldiers ran. Commenting on her son John, Irene Dunn grimly conceded, "I guess I'll never see my boy again. If they have really converted him to Communism it would be better if they buried him."[12] Public opinion about the POWs who were returning home was decidedly less fanatical but still marked by suspicion.

The government's sensitivity about the returning prisoners was on display as soon as they began returning home in April and May 1953. In a letter to Gen. Wilton B. Persons regarding a proposal to have a national day of dedication for the returning POWs, C. D. Jackson, a special assistant to the president and one of Eisenhower's chief advisers on psychological warfare, highlighted the government's uneasiness over the entire situation. Although "under normal circumstances I would be all for something like this," Jackson wrote, "it would be premature and inadvisable to have a great national hoopla for these prisoners, as some pretty bad customers would inadvertently be dined and wined by Mayors and citizens' groups and then a lot more trouble would arise."[13] As the letter reveals, from the start policymakers viewed the returning POWs as potential war criminals and collaborators rather than as heroes worthy of national veneration.

By 1954 President Eisenhower was one of the most prominent voices still advocating a sympathetic approach to the returning POWs. Discussing the case of Cpl. Edward Dickenson, who had initially refused repatriation but then changed his mind, Eisenhower urged Americans "to read the lesson of the prodigal son" and stated that "those sitting in the comparative safety of Washington could not be sure how they would have acted under the same circumstances."[14] The supporters of the returning POWs would repeatedly emphasize this point, insisting that the incidents of un-American behavior were primarily the result of Communist psychological warfare. In the view of these advocates, the POWs were victims and should not be blamed for their actions.

An editorial in the *Washington Post* was typical. Maintaining that POWs who had been "taken" by brainwashing were "victims of propaganda," the editorial argued that they "need[ed] sympathy rather than condemnation."[15] Col. John Driscoll made a similar argument in an article about the germ warfare confessions of 1st Lt. John S. Quinn and 1st Lt. Kenneth L. Enoch. According to Driscoll, Quinn and Enoch were the victims of "the Communist-devised methods of interrogation," and "these fiendish techniques forced the two U.S. Air Force lieutenants to lend their names to the Soviet propaganda."[16] Other publications alleged that the POWs' critics were sanctimonious hypocrites. An editorial in the *Saturday Evening Post,* for example, hypothesized, "The twenty-three supposed converts to communism have been denounced as weaklings and cowards by writers and others who have probably never experienced or been threatened with physical torture since they were initiated into the mysteries of their college fraternity."[17] Hunter also weighed in on the topic, asserting that the men who collaborated with the enemy were "sick, and they should be treated as if they were sick. And I don't think they should be condemned any more than you should be condemned if you picked up a polio germ and I didn't."[18]

Not everyone believed that brainwashing was solely responsible for the behavior of the American POWs who had collaborated with the enemy. Months before the Korean armistice, a spokesperson for the Defense Department downplayed the severity of brainwashing, claiming "the much-discussed communist 'brainwashing' technique has been overestimated—at least in the extent it was used on American POW's. All of the prisoners . . . were exposed to the Red propaganda indoctrination, but there is no evidence as yet that any of the Americans were subjected to severe psychological torture."[19] In an editorial that appeared in the *Marion Star* in Ohio several months later, the influential Hearst journalist George Sokolsky wrote, "So far, little evidence has been abduced [*sic*] to justify the charge of brainwashing by drugs of our sons." Sokolsky speculated that the Communists had been able to manipulate American soldiers with promises of "a better bed, by access to women, by extra food," and that the soldiers gave in because they were "weak-willed creatures."[20] Although the Defense Department and Sokolsky tried to downplay the impact of brainwashing on the behavior of the POWs, the variety of reports regarding the severity of the technique left ample room for interpretation. Because nearly every report about the returning POWs included at least a brief allusion to brainwashing, the veterans of the Korean War would become popularly linked to the technique for the remainder of the decade. Further, although the opinions of writers like Sokolsky illustrate that differences of opinion on brainwashing did exist, it is significant that even the skeptics believed that the Communists had been able to exploit and manipulate American men.

Two letters to the *Oakland Tribune* in September 1953 illustrate the range of emotions the reports of brainwashing and manipulation of American male soldiers initially produced. The first letter, written anonymously by a woman from Richmond, California, focused on the purported germ warfare confessions made by members of the air force. The letter writer felt compelled to "question the loyalty of those men and their ability to serve" and believed that "the various air arms are commissioning the wrong caliber of men." After declaring that the men should have been able to withstand Communist torture, she concluded her letter by saying, "To be a prisoner of war for even three years does not make a man a hero . . . five minutes of loyal action can! As the happy wife of a Reserve Naval officer, who saw duty in both World War II and the Korean crisis, I can honestly say that I would rather be the widow of an unsung hero than the wife of a coward."[21] Although the intensity of the letter writer's position may have been unique, the letter articulates some of the worries many Americans harbored about the steadfastness of a new generation of American fighting men. On the other end of the spectrum was a letter written two weeks later by someone from Alameda, California, in response to the allegations made by the woman from Richmond. The writer argued that the Richmond woman should have read Hunter's books on brainwashing in order to appreciate the severity of Communist psychological torture. Calling the Communists "mental destroyers," the letter concluded with a rhetorical question: "If a man is driven temporarily out of his mind, is he still to blame for what he does or says?"[22]

The exchange of letters in the pages of the *Oakland Tribune* was indicative of the mixed emotions the return of American POWs initially generated. An editorial that appeared in the *New York Times* two years later reflected the general mood of the public with its title, "For the Brainwashed: Pity or Punishment?"[23] Citing several military reports on the returning POWs as well as a handful of high-ranking members of the armed forces, the article made it clear that members of the military had not reached a consensus on the victims of brainwashing either. Despite differences of opinion, it is obvious that POWs were regarded as either objects of derision or objects of pity. Neither viewpoint held the returning POWs up as shining examples of American patriotism. On their return home many POWs attempted to combat the negative public perception of their behavior and defend their honor by emphasizing their resistance to the Communist enemy. As Susan L. Carruthers has pointed out, they were assisted by the mainstream media, and they "faced ceaseless entreaties to elucidate communist brutality, the more gruesome their stories—or emaciated their bodies—the better."[24] In comments to the press, POWs time and again emphasized their physical and mental resistance to their Communist captors in an attempt to reassert their bravery and loyalty under duress.

Some men simply recounted their physical resistance against the Communists. Leonard Brewton described an incident in which a Chinese guard jumped him because he refused to listen to Communist propaganda. Brewton retaliated with his fists because, as he put it, "Hell, I was not taking that from anybody."[25] Other soldiers described more subtle forms of resistance. Sgt. Edward Hewlett recalled a Communist propaganda lecture that was broken up by the insubordination of a quick-witted GI. The Communist lecturers had been passing around pictures which they said showed North Koreans picking up insects with chopsticks in fields that the U.S. Army had deliberately infected with germs. When the North Korean guards showed the American soldiers their evidence, a jar with a supposedly infected bug, one GI calmly grabbed the jar, opened it, and ate the bug. Although he was punished, he never became ill from eating the

A group of POWs excited to be returning home after a long ordeal in captivity. Before long, they and their cohorts would become some of the most heavily scrutinized and vilified American soldiers in U.S. history. U.S. Army Photo, from William Lindsay White, *The Captives of Korea: An Unofficial White Paper on the Treatment of War Prisoners* (New York: Scribner's, 1957).

"poisonous" bug, and he helped stem the onslaught of propaganda in that particular prison camp.[26]

Another soldier described the subtle form of insubordination and resistance that developed in Camp No. 5 at Pyoktong: singing what Cpl. Carlton G. Marmorman described as the number one hit song in the camp. The song featured a refrain that lamented life in the Communist prison camps: "Now come here, friends, let me tell you a story. / I'll tell you of Lin [a Chinese guard] in all his glory./I'll tell you of lectures and roll calls, too./But beware, my friends, they'll make a commie out of you/And I just don't like this kind of living."[27] Although less confrontational than the physical resistance of Brewton and less contentious than the bug eating described by Hewlett, the song nonetheless demonstrated the independence and resistance of the men in Camp No. 5. The common denominator in these various narratives of resistance was their emphasis on the physical and mental autonomy of the returning POWs.[28]

Over time these heroics would be left by the wayside, and the legacy of the veterans of the Korean War would become largely associated with the men who had capitulated and collaborated with the enemy. The media's portrayal of American soldiers during the Korean War played a large role in how they were perceived. From the onset of the war, soldiers fighting in Korea were portrayed in more realistic terms than their Second World War brethren. Taking stock of the "warrior image" of the Korean War, the historian Andrew Huebner has noted how the cheerful, winking American soldier of the Second World War was replaced by imagery that predominantly featured American soldiers showcasing fatigue, sorrow, stoicism, and suffering. Huebner has argued that for the American public "it was hard not to commiserate with the soldiers in the pictures, men with bloodshot eyes, men crying over the loss of a friend, men slumped dejectedly against each other, men pitifully wounded, men fated to die moments later."[29] This was undoubtedly true of a sizable percentage of Americans, who expressed heartfelt sympathy for American soldiers during the Korean War, especially during the early stages of the war and right after its conclusion. But this imagery also indicated that American soldiers in Korea were different from their Second World War predecessors. This transformation was largely a media and government creation and had more to do with the media's new frankness in covering the war than with the realities of Korea. In fact, five of the POWs who refused repatriation had actually served in the Second World War. Nonetheless, as the public image of American soldiers during the Korean War became increasingly linked to the behavior of the American POWs who had collaborated with the enemy, the initial sympathetic view of the prisoners' war record as espoused by the likes of Eisenhower, Driscoll, and Hunter gave way to much more critical attitudes about this "new breed" of soldiers.

In addition to media coverage there were several other reasons for this shift in attitudes. One noteworthy factor was the disappointing conclusion of the Korean War, which prompted American leaders to warn about the dangers of complacency and led to an atmosphere marked by self-examination and insecurity. Public reaction to the truce that ended the war in 1953 illustrated how the public had internalized these warnings. In comparison to the chaotic scene of nearly half a million celebrating men, women, and children in Times Square in New York City on V-J Day, marking the end of the Second World War, when the truce that ended the Korean War was announced Times Square was described by the *New York Times* as "a comparable ghost town." Noting that the crowd of about nine thousand people briefly applauded and then went about their business after the truce was announced, the *Times* observed that the largest celebration in Times Square that evening had been "a well-staged scene by television newsreel men who were in desperate search of action for their cameras and coaxed a small crowd to 'react.'"[30] The euphoria of the post–Second World War era was conspicuously absent. In addition, the irrefutable fact that some American men had collaborated with the enemy, confessed to war crimes that they had not committed, and even refused repatriation to the United States was extremely damaging within the confines of domestic American culture. Most important, over the course of the 1950s the POWs who had collaborated with the enemy were increasingly blamed for succumbing to Communist brainwashing and psychological torture. In the eyes of many critics, if the POWs had had a firmer allegiance to their country and exhibited the traditional characteristics embodied by generations of American men, they would never have capitulated in the first place.

In American popular culture the individual POWs who had been allegedly brainwashed came to symbolize an entire nation of men who lacked the internal strength and resolve to fight the Cold War battle for the mind and were mentally weak enough to be manipulated and controlled by the Communist enemy. A number of overlapping factors were responsible for creating this impression. One of the earliest and most authoritative indicators was the army's actions and comments regarding the American POWs in the aftermath of the Korean War. Their words and deeds not only gave the American public cause for concern by substantiating the assertions that a considerable number of POWs had succumbed to Communist brainwashing and collaborated with the enemy, but also seemed to legitimize fears that something was fundamentally wrong with American men in general.

From Prison Camps to Courtrooms

After the final prisoner exchange between the United States and North Korea ended in December 1953, the army took control of the American POWs. Instead of immediately sending these men home, the army conducted interviews and psychiatric and intelligence tests on each of them for nearly two months. Over one thousand soldiers were interviewed by a psychiatric task force headed by the army psychiatrist Maj. Henry Segal. After Operation Little Switch, Segal's comments about the men were among the first public statements made by anyone affiliated with the military who had actually interacted with the returning POWs. His comments were not reassuring.

In an article in the *New York Times* titled "Red Methods on G.I.'s Effective," Segal admitted that a large percentage of American men had succumbed to Communist indoctrination. As Segal explained it, "If someone told you to eat a certain breakfast food over and over again every day for months on end you would probably try it, even though you were sure you wouldn't like it. The Communists used the same methods."[31] Segal's claims were reinforced by comments from several returning POWs, who told reporters that "some of their fellow prisoners who fell for the Communist line were being sent through in the prisoner exchange to try to spread the Red doctrines in the United States."[32] These accusations charged American men with more than simple collaboration with the Communist enemy, and they quickly turned the issue of American men's ability to withstand Communist brainwashing into a matter of national security.

Equally damaging were reports that a number of prisoners had been so brainwashed that they were returning to the United States as diehard Communist spies. One article reported that a number of "the returning prisoners include[d] agents deliberately 'planted' by the Communists to inoculate U.S. citizens with Red propaganda."[33] The writer's sources included several returning POWs, such as Cpl. Thomas R. Murray, who avowed that even though some of the men "may not act like it . . . they are [Communists]."[34] Another article quoted Cpl. Leslie E. Scales, who said "he knew of 30 pro-Reds who had been sent back from his 306-man company."[35] Scales told reporters he had overheard the group planning a meeting in San Francisco, where they intended to organize a Communist cell.

These types of reports were grossly exaggerated and often based on nothing more than hearsay. A small number of American POWs had indeed collaborated with the enemy, but if the military had conducted a fair, scientific analysis of the returning POWs they would have certainly downplayed the initial reports of collaboration, brainwashing, and Communist spies. The army and its psychiatric task force, however, were predisposed to finding examples of collaboration and un-American behavior. The Communists had sent over a number of pro-Communist "progressives" during Operation Little Switch, which, as noted earlier, took place about four months prior to the close of the war and Operation Big Switch.[36] The army's experience during Operation Little Switch colored their expectations for the remaining POWs. One of the men connected to the army repatriation effort, Maj. Gen. Arthur G. Trudeau, admitted that "the psychiatrists on each transport had been warned in advance . . . that it looked as if many of the prisoners had been indoctrinated."[37]

The military was also likely inspired by the popular portrayal of brainwashing. The extent of this influence is evident in a report that was eventually submitted to the U.S. surgeon general by Major Segal. In the report Segal and his team took special note of the apparent apathy of the men after the prisoner of war exchange.[38] Segal termed this behavior the "Zombie Reaction." One of the psychiatrists on his staff elaborated upon this point, saying that "most of the returnees . . . showed a lack of feeling . . . as though they cared little one way or the other what was transpiring."[39] Although Segal's dramatic terminology was not made known to the public, the word *zombie* echoes in the popular descriptions of the victims of brainwashing in the mainstream media during the same period and demonstrates how pervasive the negative casting of the returning POWs had become.

After a short interval in Inchon with Segal's staff, the majority of the soldiers were placed aboard ships in late August and early September. The army and Counter Intelligence Corps had "assigned to each shipload of returnees . . . a psychiatric task force consisting of five psychiatrists, one clinical psychologist, and four enlisted technicians, the last either social workers or psychology experts."[40] The psychiatric task force conducted Rorschach and sentence-competence tests as well as "a seventy-seven page battery of questions for each returnee and . . . a biographical statement as well."[41] Their job was to analyze each returning POW, determine the conditions he had lived under during his imprisonment, and assess how he had been affected by his time in a prison camp. The attention the soldiers received was unprecedented, and the army's decision to focus on the mental state of the POWs before their return home, illustrated by the sheer number of psychiatrists and psychologists stationed at Inchon, bolstered the assumption that it was the men's minds, not their bodies, that had been under attack during their time in Communist prison camps.[42]

After the soldiers landed in San Francisco the military and the government escalated the controversy by initiating a handful of high-profile inquiries and court-martials. Since collaboration with the enemy was so commonplace, the men who had been singled out for court-martial had not simply collaborated with the enemy but were being put on trial also for what the military deemed gross misconduct. The accusations ranged from collaborating with the enemy to informing on fellow prisoners to partaking in assorted propaganda activities on behalf of the Communists and even to murdering fellow POWs. Sgt. James C. Gallagher, for example, was accused of murdering three POWs in the permanent prison camps in North Korea. Gallagher was court-martialed, found guilty by a military court, and sentenced to life in prison in 1955.

The great majority of the evidence presented against the former POWs came from the testimony of their fellow prisoners. Speaking anonymously to the press, one senior officer said that the court-martials were based on "literally hundreds of accusations by former prisoners," and he called the accused "a particular handful of rats."[43] In total, fourteen cases went to trial, and they offered the public compelling proof that some American soldiers in the Korean POW camps had not lived up to military standards. The trials kept the issue of the American soldiers' behavior in captivity before the public eye throughout the middle years of the decade. Among the most prominent of these trials were the cases of Cpl. Edward Dickenson, Cpl. Claude J. Batchelor, and Col. Frank H. Schwable. Each case contained its share of high drama, from Dickenson's mother passing out outside the hearing room to Schwable's emotional testimony on the stand in his own defense. Significantly, they also employed variations of the same defense: the men had been victims of Communist mental torture and should not be held accountable for their actions.

Dickenson was one of the infamous twenty-three American soldiers who had refused repatriation to the United States before having a change of heart. At his trial the court heard the testimony of General Dean. On his return home Dean was awarded a Medal of Honor and was widely regarded as one of the few true heroes of the Korean War. Speaking on behalf of Dickenson, Dean claimed that the psychological torture he had faced was so intense that he had actually "once tried to commit suicide in a prison camp because he feared he might break under Communist torture and disclose military secrets to the enemy."[44] The military court also heard the testimony of various doctors, including Morris Kleinerman, who said that Dickenson was not at fault for his actions because the Communists could manipulate people who had his personality type. As Kleinerman put it, Dickenson was " 'basically emotionally unstable' and might be an easy prey for Communist bullies."[45] Another expert witness, Philip Bloemsma, offered a different psychological defense for Dickenson's alleged crimes. Citing a mental condition he called "fence complex," Bloemsma said that nearly every POW " 'loses his sense of right and wrong' after he is held captive behind a fence for any length of time" because "the fence is stamped in his mind."[46] The military court did not find the defense's argument or their expert witnesses convincing: Dickenson was found guilty and sentenced to ten years of hard labor.

Corporal Batchelor's lawyers crafted a much more explicit connection between his behavior and Communist brainwashing. Like Dickenson, Batchelor was one of the twenty-three soldiers who had initially refused repatriation, and he was accused of collaborating with the enemy and informing on other POWs. His highly publicized decision to return to the United States before the repatriation deadline in January 1954 had already led to several less-than-sympathetic reactions in the court of public opinion. For example, *Time* magazine claimed that he had "gobbled up the Communist line almost from the day in 1951 when he was taken prisoner in Korea," and, after flipping "like a trained seal from democracy to Communism, prepared to flop right back again" when it served his best interests.[47] Batchelor's lawyers initially decided to base their defense on the notion that he had been brainwashed while he was in captivity, claiming that "Red brainwashing techniques had made Corporal Batchelor believe he really was acting in the best interests of the United States by collaborating with the Communists."[48] However, the court ruled that this defense was inadmissible, which forced Batchelor's defense team to shift to a plea of temporary insanity.

The army used its own expert witnesses, including Major Segal, to refute the defense's claims. They concluded that Batchelor had been "in perfect contact with reality when he returned from Communist captivity."[49] But Batchelor's lawyers would not let the insanity claim die. According to them, the insane world of Communism had distorted Batchelor's ability to reason and led him to temporarily lose control of his thoughts and actions. This contention was vaguely similar to their initial brainwashing defense. Unfortunately for Batchelor this argument did not find a particularly receptive audience in the military court, and, like Dickenson, Batchelor was found guilty and received a life sentence. Around the time of Batchelor's sentencing, one of his lawyers told the press, "I'm not worried about Corporal Batchelor's future, nor is he. I'm only worried about the Army's lack of understanding of the evil insanity of Communism."[50]

Colonel Schwable's court inquiry featured many of the same elements as Batchelor's, including a brainwashing defense and the testimony of psychiatrists and other medical experts. Schwable was a decorated senior officer and a Marine Corps pilot who had become infamous for his role in the germ warfare confessions and was accused of bearing false witness against the United States. He openly admitted to making the false confessions but maintained he had been the victim of severe psychological torture that had broken his mind and therefore could not be held responsible for his actions. Several POWs who had been imprisoned in the same camp as Schwable in North Korea were called to the witness stand, and their testimony painted the picture of a broken, tortured man. One POW testified that Schwable had lost so much weight while he was in captivity that he was barely recognizable, saying, "His face was so drawn and thin he looked like a little mouse." Several other witnesses testified that they had seen Schwable being kept in a tiny, windowless cell, where he was continually tortured and barely fed. Disturbingly, several of the POWs witnessed Schwable in the throes of what appeared to have been a mental breakdown. When several of them were transported to another prison camp, Schwable muttered to himself continuously and stared blankly at the floor of the truck they were in until he suddenly sprang to his feet and shouted, "I'm surrounded by oil." When they finally arrived at their destination, the prisoners witnessed Schwable nervously shadow boxing. Describing the scene, a marine, Cpl. Melvin J. Gaynor, said Schwable did not appear "to be in his right mind."[51]

Schwable's defense team used this evidence to portray him as an innocent victim. In order to make their case the defense called the father of menticide, Joost Meerloo, to the stand. Meerloo told the court that a victim of Communist methods of mental coercion "could be induced to identify himself completely with his interrogator. In the end . . . the victim will do anything he is told and, in a state of auto-hypnosis, believe he is acting correctly."[52] Meerloo declared that the only way Schwable could have avoided his fate after the Communists had begun the brainwashing process was by committing suicide. The highlight of the court inquiry came in a dramatic exchange between Meerloo and Schwable's lawyers. The lawyers asked Meerloo "if anyone alive, if subjected to this condition, over a long period of time, will inevitably capitulate?" Meerloo answered in the affirmative, which prompted Schwable's lawyers to push the point further: "And that includes anyone in this room?"[53] Once again Meerloo answered in the affirmative, thus setting up Schwable's prime defense: no one alive could stand up to Communist brainwashing.

In the final days of the inquiry Schwable took the stand and attempted to explain why he had confessed to committing germ warfare, stating "the words were mine, but the thoughts were theirs."[54] Schwable said that after spending months in solitary confinement and enduring Communist brainwashing he had been reduced "to feeling like an animal in the zoo."[55] He described the psychological torture he underwent, explaining that "when a person has gone through such an experience . . . he is so tormented by fears and doubts that he feels as if 'the devil is whispering' in his ear."[56]

In closing remarks Schwable's lawyer said, "No one can judge Colonel Schwable who does not recognize that brain-washing can put false words in the mouths of the bravest of men," and he suggested that instead of

Col. Frank H. Schwable attempting to explain his germ warfare "confession" during an interview in Inchon following his repatriation on January 23, 1954. (AP Images)

demonizing Schwable the Marine Corps should award him the Navy Cross or the Medal of Honor for his role in saving another pilot prior to his capture. The military court decided not to court-martial or discipline Schwable, but they publicly denounced him.[57] The secretary of the navy, Robert Anderson, claimed that Schwable's usefulness to the navy had been "seriously impaired." The commandment of the corps, Gen. Lemuel C. Shepherd Jr., echoed these sentiments when he claimed that Schwable had been an "instrument, however unwilling, of causing damage to this country," and as a result he should only be given "duties of a type making minimum demands upon the elements of unblemished personal example and leadership."[58]

At first the court-martials were unpopular with the public, with Dickenson and Batchelor evoking the most sympathy.[59] The discrepancies between the sentences handed out by the different branches of the military were the most visible source of controversy. In May 1954 the air force decided to throw out all eighty-three court-martial cases it was preparing, explaining that "the mental and physical torture of prisoners of war by the Communists was something unprecedented in our history" and that the members of the air force who had collaborated with the enemy were not going to be punished for their actions.[60] This led to outcries about the harsher sentences doled out by the army and the Marine Corps and the desire for a more uniform policy toward the returning POWs. When President Eisenhower was asked to comment on the Schwable case, he "asserted that allowance[s] must be made for the rigors to which prisoners had been subjected," adding that the returning POWs "must not be condemned too severely."[61] At the same time, Eisenhower preached common sense and said none of the men who had "cracked" under Communist pressure should ever be restored to positions of command. The public's perception of the soldiers generally reflected Eisenhower's sentiment, and many Americans, although viewing the POWs with some degree of sympathy, were beginning to envision them as possible weak links in the battle against the Communist enemy. As a result, the court-martial cases were a first step in the direction of a harsher evaluation of the American POWs.

During the same period, the military created a widely publicized new code of conduct for American soldiers. The fact that the government and military found it necessary to articulate the most elementary rules governing the behavior of American soldiers—for example, an article in the new code of conduct stipulated that all members of the armed forces were to "never forget that . . . [they were] an American fighting man, responsible for . . . [their] actions, and dedicated to the principles which made . . . [their] country free"—further eroded the public image of the American soldiers who had served in Korea. Speaking anonymously to the press on the topic of brainwashing, a general who had fought in the Korean War said that the future of the United States "depends on young men who have iron in their souls and guts in their bellies."[62] The implication was clear: many of the men who had fought in the Korean War had not been tough enough to withstand Communist methods of manipulation, and if the country did not start producing "real men" who could, the United States was in store for a bleak future.

The POWs had been on trial not only for their actions in North Korean prison camps, but also for the way they embodied the nation's concerns about the state of the Cold War and the purported decline in American strength and resolve. To put things in perspective, at least 7,000 American soldiers were captured during the war, and "of the approximately 4,400 who survived, 192 were found 'chargeable with serious offenses against comrades of the United States.'"[63] Only eighty-two of these cases were ever approved for court-martial by the army's Board on Prisoner of War Collaboration, and those cases were further whittled down to fourteen court-martial cases and brought to trial in court tribunals around the country between 1954 and 1955.[64] As these numbers illustrate, the army decided that the overwhelming majority of POWs in Korea were not likely to be found guilty in an American or military court. In fact, the Advisory Committee to the Secretary of Defense on Prisoners of War set up by the Department of Defense concluded in 1955 that on the whole "the record [of the POW's] seem[ed] fine indeed."[65] By the time the Marine Corps decided to decorate five prisoners who had refused to "bear false witness against their country" in 1954, an act which a reporter for the *New York Times* called an "implied rebuke to those United States prisoners who signed germ warfare confessions and in other ways did the bidding of their captors," the damage had already been done.[66] In 1955, while it was preparing for another round of trials, the army publicly denied that any of the men being charged had ever been brainwashed, and although they admitted that the Communists had used mental pressures in the prison camps they claimed there was no evidence to support the widespread use of brainwashing in North Korea.[67] Nonetheless, the popular image of veterans of the Korean War had become irreversibly associated with the concept of brainwashing and the image of the brainwashed American man; subservient, powerless, and completely at the will of the Communist enemy.

Kinkead, Mayer, and the Perpetuation of a Negative Interpretation

The most prominent defender of American POWs in the late 1950s and early 1960s, the sociologist Albert D. Biderman, deemed Kinkead and the army psychiatrist Maj. William Erwin Mayer to be the two experts most responsible for perpetuating a negative stereotype of the American soldiers and turning them into a symbol of the country's shortcomings. Both men were closely affiliated with the army, which lent their viewpoints considerable authority and guaranteed the widespread dissemination of their ideas in the middle and late fifties. Taken together, their work reveals how sources close to the military attempted to minimize the role of brainwashing in the POW narrative and place the focus on American social and educational institutions instead.

Kinkead first wrote on the topic in a *New Yorker* article of October 26, 1957, titled "The Study of Something New in History," which he then expanded into a book, *In Every War But One* (1959). Basing his writings on the army's five-year study of the POWs, Kinkead called the Korean War "a war with an enemy who had fought not only on the battlefield but also in prison camps, by manipulating the minds of the prisoners" and claimed that "our government and the Army had come to see that our servicemen not only had to be trained how to fight physically—they had to know how to fight back mentally and morally as well."[68] Kinkead focused on these moral and mental failings but continually attributed them to larger societal issues rather than to psychological warfare, specifically taking issue with those who blamed the record of American soldiers on brainwashing. Indeed, he trumpeted the official army position, asserting that "the prisoners, as far as Army psychiatrists have been able to discover, were not subjected to anything that could properly be called brainwashing."[69] His sources in the army made a distinction between what had occurred in the prison camps—namely, interrogation, indoctrination, and a mixture of "mental pressure and physical hardship"—and brainwashing, which led Kinkead to conclude that the story of American POWs was "a good deal more complex than brainwashing and simple brutality."[70]

Major Mayer also wrote and spoke extensively about American POWs in the middle and late 1950s. According to Biderman, his articles and speeches were "disseminated to thousands by the playing of a tape-recorded speech to active and reserve units of the Armed Forces, government training institutes, schools and colleges, civic associations, and by radio stations in various cities."[71] One of Mayer's main contributions to the popular image of the POWs was his contention that "at least one-third [of the prisoners] 'co-operated'" with their captors.[72] By mid-decade, cooperation and collaboration with the enemy had become popularly associated with the POWs in Korea and included a range of behavior "from writing propaganda for the enemy or informing, to such innocuous activities as broadcasting Christmas greetings home and allowing the enemy to appear in a 'good' light."[73] Unlike Kinkead, Mayer explicitly stated that POWs had been given the brainwashing treatment, but he felt the term was "generally and widely misused" and was not, as the public appeared to believe, "an inhuman system of unnamed tortures and magic designed to 'destroy the mind' and will." Defining brainwashing as an educational program augmented by a "psychiatric management and treatment regimen" to produce anxiety, Mayer's conclusions about the effectiveness of Communist psychological warfare and manipulation ultimately echoed those of Kinkead.[74] American soldiers had proven easy targets because of deficiencies in the national character and the education system, not because they had been rendered helpless by brainwashing.

Kinkead and Mayer used several aspects of the American POWs' war record to paint a dismal picture of the modern American soldier. One of their recurring points was that the lack of escapes, and even escape attempts, from the prison camps reflected a dearth of intestinal fortitude and cunning on the part of the American men in captivity. Kinkead wrote, "In every war but one a respectable number of prisoners managed, through ingenuity, daring, and plain good luck, to escape. That one war was the Korean War."[75] Mayer expanded on Kinkead's observation by stating that "there was not a single successful escape from Communist camps despite extraordinarily light restraints."[76] As evidence, Mayer cited "a camp of 600 Americans that was run successfully by six Communist guards with only a single strand of barred [*sic*] wire between the docile prisoners and freedom."[77]

Reports that the punishment for escape attempts in the prison camps sometimes consisted of little more than a slap on the wrist made the lack of escape attempts even more troubling. In his memoir *I Was a Captive in Korea*, Philip Deane, a war correspondent for *The Observer* who had been captured by the North Koreans in 1950 and released in the spring of 1953, gave an account of two American GIs who had attempted to escape and were caught three days later. The soldiers told Deane "they had not been in any way brutalized" and admitted that their only punishment "was deprivation of tobacco for a week."[78] After the war the military explicitly stated that American soldiers were duty bound to at least attempt to escape: the third article of the armed forces new code of conduct read, "If I am captured I will continue to resist by all means available. I will make every effort to escape and aid others to escape."

Kinkead believed that the same lack of courage and mental toughness that led many American POWs to become complacent in the prison camps and fail to escape in any meaningful numbers was also responsible for the high mortality rates in Korea.[79] Basing his claims on the testimony of Major Anderson, Kinkead reported that a considerable number of American prisoners became afflicted with a mysterious illness called give-up-itis. The term *give-up-itis*, allegedly coined by the POWs themselves, described soldiers who "seemed to will themselves to die."[80] Most of the men who came down with the so-called disease were young, and, after refusing to eat or take care of themselves, they would slowly succumb to starvation unless other soldiers intervened on their behalf and force-fed them. Kinkead charged that the disease was due "to poor discipline and defects of character of the average POW," which implied that many of the deaths of GIs in Korea were the result of the softness of the average American soldier rather than of any physical illness or Communist maltreatment.[81]

Kinkead and Mayer employed these examples to support one of their main contentions: the American men who had served in Korea were somehow incapable of the courage and quick thinking of earlier generations of American men. As Biderman pointed out, the central "historical allusion in the title *In Every War But One* gives emphasis to Kinkead's thesis that Americans aren't what they used to be."[82] Although they were perhaps the most renowned purveyors of this degradative school of thought, Kinkead and Mayer were not unique. In fact, as Biderman observed, they "merely reflected a simplified picture of the Korean events that had been developed and fixed before . . . [they] began . . . [their] work."[83]

As early as 1953 contemporary observers, journalists, and even military and government officials were declaring that the veterans of the Korean War compared unfavorably to previous generations of American soldiers. For example, in a *New York Times Magazine* editorial of August 9 of that year, the war correspondent George Barrett called the Korean veteran "a different breed from his older brother who came back from World War II." Describing Korean veterans as "disquieting machine-like products of their special times," Barrett went on to assert that "there seems to be an almost robot-like disinterest about him that is in disturbing contrast to the assertive individualism of the World War II soldier."[84] Barrett's word choice and generalizations illustrate how fuzzy the line between the effects of brainwashing and the inherent qualities of a new generation of American men had become in popular culture and how quickly the image of the brainwashed American man became associated with social and generational decay. In an op-ed piece of September 1953 in the Ohio daily newspaper the *Marion Star* titled "These Days," Sokolsky argued that veterans of the Korean War did not measure up to earlier generations of American soldiers. Criticizing the soldiers who had refused repatriation, Sokolsky admitted that it was "perhaps true that in World War I and World War II some Americans were missing." However, Sokolsky attributed these missing men to a very manly reason: "They shacked up with native women and got lost."[85] The title of the article conveyed Sokolsky's central message: "these days" American men were simply not as brave, courageous, or dedicated to the United States as they used to be.

As the articles by Barrett and Sokolsky show, the notion of social and generational decay neither originated in nor was restricted to the work of Kinkead and Mayer. Although Kinkead and Mayer would attempt to minimize the role of brainwashing in the record of American POWs, their work did little to stop the popular association between brainwashing and the

Korean War, as evidenced by numerous artifacts in popular culture. The central role of Kinkead and Mayer, then, was to reiterate the argument that American POWs had demonstrated shortcomings that reflected larger problems in American society, broadcast that argument to large audiences, and further entrench it within the collective cultural consciousness.

By the middle of the decade several government officials working behind the scenes attempted to push back on the cultural and political emphasis on the inadequacy of American POWs, thereby divulging the general lack of consensus in government and military circles on the POW episode. Members of the OCB and officials in the State and Defense Departments provided the journalist William L. White with access to classified material on the POWs, documents that colored his interpretation of their behavior and led him to write a generally sympathetic account emphasizing Communist brutality instead of American cowardice. Titled *The Captives of Korea: An Unofficial White Paper on the Treatment of War Prisoners,* the book initially did not find the audience that the OCB had anticipated, which prompted the board to coordinate a clandestine publicity campaign on the book's behalf after it was published in 1957. The special assistant to the president Robert Cutler approached the editors at *Reader's Digest* and *Life* to see if the book could be condensed or serialized, and members of the OCB also made inquiries at USIA about abridging the book for an international audience or potentially turning it into a film. In a letter to Jackson, Cutler wrote, "This is a book which every American ought to read. The incredible bravery of some of our boys simply squeezes the heart."[86] Despite these efforts, *Reader's Digest* and *Life* passed on the book, it was never turned into a film, and it never found a wide audience.

Throughout this period the government was sending mixed messages on the POWs, and White and Kinkead reached starkly divergent conclusions because their work represented different supposedly official narratives about what had transpired in Korea. White's research had been influenced by the State Department, the Department of Defense, and members of the OCB, who were intent on downplaying the effectiveness of Communist brainwashing and highlighting the inhumanity of the Communist enemy. Kinkead, on the other hand, was articulating the point of view of the army and other conservative voices in the military, who were sensitive about accusations that the military had not prepared American soldiers for the psychological components of the Korean War and were attempting to put the public focus on the new code of conduct and the behavior of the POWs themselves. Other government officials would become the primary sources for numerous television programs, films, articles in major magazines like *Look* and the *New Yorker,* newspaper coverage, plays, and academic literature. At times these sources contradicted each other or emphasized very different aspects of the war. Ultimately, though, it was Kinkead and others like him who produced the enduring popular narrative of the war. The primary reason this negative perception of the war became entrenched in the popular imagination is that it harmonized with what many government and military figures were saying about the POWs in the media and was repeatedly broadcast through popular outlets. More subtle and nuanced accounts of Korea and the POW experience there, such as White's, were relatively rare, only occasionally reached mass audiences, and never successfully overcame the image of twenty-one POWs renouncing home and country and countless others succumbing to Communist indoctrination and propaganda.

The most wide-ranging critique of the negative point of view typified by Kinkead and Mayer was Biderman's *March to Calumny: The Story of American POWs in the Korean War* (1962). Biderman held that "(a) the prevalence of misconduct, susceptibility to Communist indoctrination, and poor adaptability to stress among the American POW's have been exaggerated greatly, (b) the conclusion regarding Korean events being 'unprecedented' represents a failure to make comparisons with truly comparable events, and (c) those captured in Korea were, in any event, a highly unrepresentative group of Americans."[87] One of Biderman's main critiques of the Kinkead and Mayer school of thought was that it largely overlooked the reality of the American POW experience in Korea. Assertions that the war record of Korean War veterans represented vast social and generational decay since the Second World War ignored the records of men like Colonel Schwable, who had in fact fought in the Second World War and was forty-five years old at the close of the Korean War. In addition, when the lack of escape attempts and high mortality rates are examined in light of the conditions of the Communist prison camps, it becomes clear that the war record of American POWs during the Korean War was not nearly as damning as Kinkead, Mayer, and other critics made it out to be.[88]

Simply put, the circumstances surrounding their imprisonment discouraged American POWs from embarking on certain courses of action. The majority of them were captured between June 1950 and March 1951. This period was marked by high casualty rates and exceptionally inhumane treatment of the captured soldiers. After a brief stay at temporary internment camps, the POWs were led on "death marches" to the permanent prison camps located near the North Korean and Manchurian border along the Yalu River. The most infamous North Korean officer during this era, known simply as the Tiger, led one of these marches, and under his command any man who could no longer walk or who dropped out of the ranks because of fatigue was shot and left to die.[89] The fact that many of the men were not appropriately dressed for a march through northern Korea in the middle of winter meant that many suffered or died from exposure. It is impossible to calculate the exact number of men who died during this period, but Biderman estimated that "well over half of the men captured during this period did not survive."[90]

By the spring of 1951 the majority of the surviving American POWs were housed in a series of permanent camps along a fifty-mile stretch of the Yalu between Chang-song and Changhung-Dong, with the center at Pyoktong.[91] Poor diets, dirty drinking water, and inadequate shelter and clothing during the winter months led to outbreaks of scurvy, pneumonia, and dysentery, and casualty rates remained high. The conditions in the prison camps slowly began to improve in 1952 as the North Koreans and Chinese began to prepare for truce negotiations, but prior to that point the majority of the POWs simply lacked the physical strength an escape attempt would have required.

Despite the improvement in their diets and health after 1952, only a relatively small number of American POWs ever managed to escape from their new homes along the Yalu River. However, Mayer's account of a contingent of six hundred American soldiers imprisoned by only six Communist guards and Deane's report of the light punishment meted out for escape attempts were extremely misleading. A simple matter of geography made escapes not only impractical but nearly suicidal. UN forces had pushed deep into North Korean territory in the fall of 1950, almost reaching China and the Yalu River. But Chinese intervention quickly prompted a full UN retreat, and by December of that year battle lines hardened around the 38th parallel, where it would remain for the duration of the war. Because of the war's shifting geographical landscape, American POWs located in Communist prison camps along the Yalu River found themselves extremely deep in enemy territory by 1951, meaning a successful escape would have entailed a trek though practically the entire length of North Korea. In addition, as Biderman pointed out, during the period when American POWs began to regain their health, persistent rumors of truce negotiations between the Communists and the United Nations spread around the camps, further discouraging escape attempts. Their ill health in the early years of their imprisonment, the location of the prison camps, and the fact that they were armed with the knowledge that the war could possibly end at any moment gave the American soldiers imprisoned during the Korean War a number of rational reasons not to risk an escape attempt.

Even so there were a handful of successful escapes and a notable number of escape attempts. Ward M. Millar, an air force pilot who was shot down in Communist territory and suffered two broken ankles on impact, wrote a stirring memoir of his escape in 1955. Millar faced nearly insurmountable obstacles to escape. But through a little good luck, determination, and the aid of a North Korean defector, he was able to signal an American aircraft until it landed and rescued him. Gen. Otto P. Weyland, the commander of the Far East Air Forces during the Korean War, wrote the foreword for Millar's memoir, part of which reads,

> Our fighting men have met the test of combat wherever and whenever called upon, but the insidious attempts of the Communists to alienate men from the country of their birth by torture, threats, and brainwashing was something new. Faced with these conditions, Air Force personnel downed behind Communist lines, even when badly wounded, managed to survive by sheer wits and an almost unbelievable courage. The courage of those who did escape is an inspiration to the youth of future America, and such exploits well deserve their place of honor in our nation's history. I have never doubted the physical, mental, and moral fiber of our air crews. These qualities have been proven wherever the Air Force has been called upon to fight, and they will prove again if required.[92]

Despite General Weyland's praise, Millar's escape received little publicity in the mainstream media, and many reporters and social critics continued to denounce the "physical, mental, and moral fiber" of American soldiers.

The proliferation of give-up-itis as an explanation for the high mortality rates in Korea further shows how the reality of the POW experience became obscured by inflammatory rhetoric that promoted a distorted perspective of the war record of POWs. American soldiers had as little control over outbreaks of disease and the temperament of their captors as they had over the location of the prison camps. Still, the very soldiers who paid the ultimate price in Korea were blamed for their own deaths, and the public was presented with an explanation for their perceived poor war record that focused on their lack of mental fortitude.

A political cartoon by Herblock in 1954 highlighted the hypocrisy of Americans who criticized the behavior of American POWs. Featuring two well-dressed, older men sitting comfortably in armchairs in a posh living room, the cartoon pokes fun at the false bravado and ignorance of home-front Americans who were divorced from the realities of the POW experience but still found it possible to condemn the men who had experienced Korea firsthand. One of the men is smoking a cigar and holding a newspaper with the headline, "Officers testify on brainwashing in prison camps" prominently splashed across the front page. The other man, a glass of liquor in his hand, points to the newspaper and declares, "I'd have said to those Reds, 'Now see here!' "[93] By 1962, when Biderman's critique was published, a predominantly negative outlook on the POWs had become firmly embedded in American popular culture. In large part this perspective was determined by military officials, members of the media, and citizens who naively proclaimed, "I'd have said to those Reds . . ." Swayed by a number of factors, the public discourse on the POWs became dominated by accusations of social decay and a vaguely defined new softness in American men. The portrayal of POWs in American films during this period sheds light on how popular culture reflected this pessimistic attitude and magnified preoccupations about the state of American society.

On the Silver Screen

Advertised in promotional posters as "the Star-Spangled, laugh-loaded salute to our P. W. Heroes," the film *Stalag 17* premiered in New York City on July 1, 1953, nearly a month before the Korean armistice was reached. Based on an earlier Broadway play about a group of American POWs in a Nazi prison camp during the Second World War, the film quickly became a commercial and critical success and was lauded as "one of . . . [the] year's most smashing films."[94] The movie hearkened back to an earlier epoch when American men were brave, quick thinking, and capable of standing up to indoctrination and torture, and at least part of *Stalag 17*'s success can be attributed to the way it framed broader concerns about the behavior of American POWs in North Korea.

Stalag 17's plot focused on the prisoners' suspicion that a member of their camp had been thwarting their escape attempts by serving as a Nazi spy. Suspicion within the camp immediately fell upon Sgt. J. J. Sefton, who had become notorious in the camp for bargaining with the Nazis for luxury items. This plot point was finally resolved when Sefton, who had never actually collaborated with the enemy beyond his financial dealings, revealed the identity of the true spy, a Nazi who had infiltrated the American prison camp and posed as an American. In the film's concluding scenes the prisoners tricked the Nazis into killing their own spy while Sefton and an American lieutenant escaped from the camp.

In the film the POWs made escape attempts, exhibited nimble thinking and self-control, and ultimately outsmarted their Nazi captors. Comparing the supposed weakness and traitorous behavior of American veterans of the Korean War with the supposed strength and heroism of their Second World War predecessors would become a recurring motif in American popular culture for the remainder of the decade, and although *Stalag 17* never made a direct comparison between veterans of the two wars, it served as a timely reminder that the behavior of contemporary American POWs paled in comparison to that of previous generations of American soldiers. The fact that Sefton, who was self-serving and somewhat detached from the other members of his camp, did not collaborate with the enemy underscored one of the film's main messages: true American men, no matter how questionable their character, were simply incapable of collaborating with the enemy. Even Sefton thought it was beneath him and indirectly criticized the American soldiers who had collaborated with the enemy in Korea when he said it was "sort of rough, one American squealing on other Americans."

Throughout the film the soldiers steadfastly resisted all forms of Nazi torture. For example, in one tense scene the head of the Nazi prison camp, Colonel von Scherbach, attempts to force Lt. James Dunbar to confess to blowing up a Nazi ammunition train. Although Dunbar had in fact blown up the train, he never capitulates. Scherbach uses sleep deprivation torture, which was commonly associated with the techniques the Communists used to brainwash American soldiers in North Korea, but throughout the interrogation session Dunbar maintains his innocence and continues to sleepily utter, "I didn't do it. I didn't do it." In this battle of wills and test of mental fortitude Dunbar is the clear victor, indicating not only that American men could stand up to psychological torture but also that they had indeed done so in the recent past.

The reaction of the POWs to Nazi attempts at political and ideological indoctrination in *Stalag 17* gave further proof of their unwavering allegiance to the United States and their mental toughness. When the gravel-voiced American camp messenger, Marko the Mailman, announces, "The Kommandant is sending every barracks a little Christmas present. A copy of *Mein Kampf* [Adolf Hitler's autobiography]," he is met with an immediate chorus of boos. The messenger shows his own disdain for the Nazi propaganda by remarking, "In the words of Oberst Von Scherbach, now that the German victory is in sight, all American prisoners are to be indoctrinated with the teachings of the Fuhrer. Unquote. In my own words, [belches], unquote." When the Nazi barracks supervisor enters the barracks after copies of *Mein Kampf* have been handed out, he finds the entire company intently listening to one of the American prisoners, Harry Shapiro, loudly reading from the autobiography. In astonishment the Nazi sergeant calls for order, and Shapiro, who is holding the book in front of his face, lowers it to reveal a fake Hitler moustache. With an absurd German accent, Shapiro yells, "Quiet! We are indoctrinating." Then, turning to the company, he yells, "Is you all indoctrinated?" The crowd of American prisoners gleefully responds in German, "Jawohl!" Addressing the company again, Shapiro asks, "Is you all good little Adolfs?" The men

American popular culture frequently glorified earlier generations of American men, who had, supposedly, had the "guts" to stand up to physical and mental torture. Still from *Stalag 17* (1953).

respond again, "Jawohl! Jawohl!" Finally, Shapiro says, "Then we will all salute Feldwebel Schulz. About face! *Sieg heil!*" At that instant the entire company turns to Schulz to give the Nazi salute and reveals that they too have adorned their faces with fake Hitler-style moustaches. As this scene indicates, in the fictional world of *Stalag 17* the enemy's indoctrination was not simply unsuccessful, it was laughable.

Long before the writings of Kinkead and the pontifications of Mayer, *Stalag 17* subtly relocated techniques associated with brainwashing into an earlier time period and indicated that during the Second World War American men had been capable of maintaining their courage and strength under fire. In *Stalag 17* the characters exhibit true Americanism by not succumbing to indoctrination or the enemy's attempts at manipulation and by remaining loyal to the United States in the face of indoctrination, torture, and harsh conditions. At the time, the film's portrayal of POWs was praised for its nuance and realism. The *New York Times* film critic Bosley Crowther said the film "stripped the pretty wrappings off . . . [our] brave heroes," and he concluded that *Stalag 17* was "a sharply perceptive indication of the ironies contained in modern men."[95] Since the film was filled with such inherently human and flawed characters, it should not be read as cinematic hero worship of an earlier generation of American men, but as a subtle indicator of the cultural and social norms governing the behavior of American soldiers.

The fact that every single POW film set in the Second World War and produced and released between 1953 and 1965 revolved around or featured escape attempts was another reflection of the popular impression that American men were no longer living up to the legacy of previous generations of American soldiers.[96] In 1963 *The Great Escape* made the connections between escaping from a prison camp and fulfilling one's loyalty and patriotic duty particularly explicit. Based on an autobiographical book of the same name, the film recounts Paul Brickhill's personal recollection of his experiences as a POW during the Second World War and an escape attempt he had witnessed firsthand. Set in a Nazi prison camp, the movie focuses on the main American protagonist, Captain Hilts, played by Steve McQueen. After a group of Allied prisoners organizes a tunnel-digging operation, Hilts becomes involved and, along with seventy-six other prisoners, escapes into the German countryside with forged papers and civilian clothes. Nearly every man who escapes is eventually captured. In the midst of being transported back to the camp, one large group of the Allied escapees is taken to an empty field and executed by a Nazi wielding a mounted machine gun. Just prior to their deaths, the British squadron leader Roger Bartlett, the primary figure behind the escape attempt, says to the Allied men in his company that even though the escape had been unsuccessful it had kept him alive in the camp.

In the final scene Captain Hilts, one of the few men to survive after being recaptured, is taken back to the isolation unit in the prison camp, called the cooler, where he had spent a great deal of time throughout the film for various thwarted escape attempts. After he is handed the ball and baseball glove he had customarily used to entertain himself with while in solitary confinement, Hilts slyly smiles, leaving the audience with two possible impressions. Either Hilts is smiling about the unsuccessful escape attempt, which had given the men a common goal and a "reason to live," or he is already plotting his next escape. Either interpretation clearly alludes to the central theme of the film: what allowed the men to sustain their pride, patriotism, and dignity was their choice to think and act for themselves, as opposed to becoming the passive, subservient prisoners of their captors. The film implies that the latter fate would have been worse than death.

Of the many films about POWs set in the Second World War and released during the post–Korean War period, only one featured men collaborating with the enemy. That film, *The Bridge on the River Kwai,* was released in 1957 and focuses on Colonel Nicholson, played by Alec

Guinness. Nicholson convinces the British soldiers under his command to willingly collaborate with the Japanese running the camp by helping them build a bridge over the River Kwai in order to complete a railway connecting Bangkok with Rangoon. The British soldiers had initially wanted to sabotage the bridge, but Nicholson reasons that the bridge would give them a purpose while in the camp, instill discipline in the men, and illustrate the Allies' technical and mental superiority over their captors. The film deftly illustrates how life in a prison camp could obscure reality and the outside world, as Nicholson slowly begins to envision the bridge as a life accomplishment and, through self-deception and misplaced pride, willfully ignores the fact that building the bridge significantly aids the enemy's cause.

Interestingly, the only film of the era to depict Second World War POWs collaborating with the enemy is one featuring primarily British characters. In fact, the lone American prisoner in the camp, Commander Shears, escapes and helps lead a reconnaissance mission back to the camp to blow up the bridge, offering cultural testimony yet again of the heroism of American POWs in World War II. Despite the British POWs' initial collaboration with the enemy in *The Bridge over the River Kwai*, by film's end they have reverted to their heroic mold. In the tense final scene Nicholson uncovers the reconnaissance mission to detonate the bridge, and, with the first train quickly approaching, he alerts the Japanese colonel and several Japanese guards to the plot. After Shears is shot in a last-ditch attempt to reach the detonator, Nicholson is shot in the crossfire, but he finally comes to his senses, stumbles to the detonator, and falls over it just as the train is crossing the bridge. The film, which won seven Oscars, including the award for best picture, indicated that even if it was possible that Allied POWs could temporarily lose sight of their loyalties, they ultimately were able to think and act on their own and fulfill their duty, even if it meant certain death.

As the historian Charles S. Young has argued, the majority of POW films produced during this era were "built in a heroic region of the cultural landscape," and, with few exceptions, they focused on "the enemy without, not weaknesses within."[97] The exception to this rule was the POW films set in the Korean War. Their portrayal of American soldiers stood in stark contrast to the heroics, self-control, inner strength, and personal autonomy possessed by Hollywood's Second World War POWs. Between 1953 and 1962 only a handful of films featured Korean POWs, and the picture they present is far from flattering: the men in the films collaborate with the enemy, suffer emotional and mental breakdowns, and lose the ability to think for themselves or control their actions.[98] In her analysis of these films, Carruthers remarks, "In their depiction of 'brainwashing' and their treatment of 'collaboration', the films powerfully testify to the moral confusion surrounding the POWs, and the shifting meanings which attached to these most scrutinized men in 1950s America."[99] The films also represent many of the most iconic cultural images of Korean War soldiers and demonstrate how a predominately negative perception of the military men who fought in the Korean War was perpetuated by American popular culture.

One film that stands out in this genre is *The Rack,* which made its debut on November 2, 1956, while the court-martial trials were still fresh in the minds of Americans.[100] The main character in the film is Capt. Edward Hall Jr., played by a young Paul Newman, an officer who had been imprisoned for two years in a North Korean prison camp. As the film opens, Hall has returned to the United States and is recovering in a military hospital. His sister-in-law immediately notices he is a changed man, as Hall appears conflicted and emotionally unstable. The source of Hall's mental anguish, which is slowly revealed through dialogue, was his behavior in North Korea—he had allegedly mistreated his fellow POWs, made propaganda lectures on the enemy's behalf, and informed on Americans who had attempted to escape.

Hall's actions are made all the more shocking by his background. Born into a military family—his father had been a colonel—Hall and his brother were raised to be soldiers. In the ultimate act of self-sacrifice Hall's brother had died in combat in North Korea. Like his brother, Hall had been nurtured at the core of Americanism and had been a distinguished soldier and the recipient of a Silver Star during the Second World War. In many ways, Hall represented the best the country's military had to offer—the product of a military family, a career soldier, and a Second World War hero. The fact that such a decorated soldier breaks under Communist psychological torture is one of the film's central points and indicates that, in the words of Hall's lawyer, "few of us would have been immune under the same circumstances."

Like many Americans, Hall's father takes the news of his son's collaboration with the enemy as a personal affront. In one especially emotional scene, he yells at his son, "Why didn't you die like your brother did? It would have been much better that way." Hall Sr. goes on to accuse his son of treason and breaking faith with "your country and me," to which Hall angrily responds, "With you? What about me? . . . I sold my soul for a blanket that smelled of fish and urine and three lousy hours of uninterrupted sleep!" The remainder of the film strikes an uneasy balance between condemnation and sympathy, focusing on Hall's court-martial case. The defense attorney, Lt. Col. Frank Wasnick, argues that although Hall had collaborated with the enemy, his crimes had not been "committed willingly, willfully, or knowingly." Featuring a defense strikingly similar to the real-life defense of Colonel Schwable, Wasnick attempts to portray Hall as the victim of a "new moral perversion where the mind can be placed upon the rack and made to suffer agony for which there is no measure." After several of his fellow POWs testified against him, Hall took the stand and attempted to explain how the Communists had changed him. Forced to endure six months of solitary confinement, a starvation diet, and brutally cold conditions, Hall finally broke after he was given a letter from his father telling him that his brother had been killed. Once he capitulated, Hall signed everything the Communists put in front of him, including propaganda leaflets and a statement informing on a group of American POWs who had attempted to escape from the camp. According to Wasnick, the Communists' goal was not "to eradicate the mind" but just "to make it suffer." Still, it was clear that Hall had changed as a result of his experience and had returned to the prison camp a broken man.

A key portion of Wasnick's defense is to describe the stages of the Communist technique of manipulation to demonstrate how Hall had methodically been broken down. First, the Communists broke down health and morale in the camp and separated the officers from the enlisted men. Then they spread rumors and created an atmosphere of terror. In the final stage, they infantilized the American men by turning them "into small boys who depend[ed] on . . . [them] for childish rewards and punishments." Finally, they focused on the most psychologically and emotionally fragile of the group and, in the words of Wasnick, they found that man's "personal, hidden key," which "everyone of us has." In the case of Hall, the hidden key was the news of his brother's death, which triggered a flood of emotions from his childhood, including the loneliness of his formative years, his mother's illness and death, and his father's subsequent emotional detachment.

By exploiting the emotional and psychological fault lines in Hall's psyche, the Communists had been able to "break" him, manipulate him, and finally control him. In his closing remarks, Wasnick attempts to shift the blame for Hall's actions to the whole of American society. Looking directly at the members of the military court, Wasnick asks, "Gentlemen, if there is guilt, where does it lie? In that small number who defected under pressure as Captain Hall did? Or do we not share it? At least those of us who created part of a generation which may collapse because we have left it uninspired, uninformed, and, as in the case of Captain Hall, unprepared to go the limit because he had not been given the warmth to support him along the way." Wasnick's query unmistakably reflected the widespread notion that the behavior of American soldiers in North Korea was linked to American society and representative of deep-seated shortcomings in the American people. However, in the film the court is not swayed by Wasnick's defense and sides with the prosecution, who argued that even though "in some instances society may seem to be responsible for an individual criminal and his crime, this does not release society from the further responsibility of bringing the criminal to justice."

The reason *The Rack* remains such a compelling example of the social commentary surrounding brainwashing and Korean POWs in the midfifties is that it contradicted many of the claims that would later be popularized by Kinkead and Mayer. The fact that Hall was a decorated veteran of the Second World War contradicted the popular claim that veterans of the Korean War were somehow less courageous or capable than their earlier counterparts. One of the main witnesses for the defense testifies at length about a group of men who were deemed troublemakers by the Communists because they would not comply with their demands and recounts his own failed escape attempt, which contradicted claims that American GIs had never attempted to escape from the prison camps in North Korea. As a result, the filmmakers seemed to point out that some of the popular critiques of the men who had fought in the Korean War were overblown or simply incorrect.

However, although the film was certainly one of the most nuanced and sympathetic examinations of the men who had succumbed to Communist psychological torture in American popular culture, it still condemned Hall for his actions and portrayed veterans of the Korean War as emotionally and mentally unequipped to withstand the "new duress" of Communist psychological torture. Throughout the film, the mental toughness of American men is repeatedly questioned or deemed insufficient to meet the task at hand. Hall testifies to the prevalence of give-up-itis among enlisted men, and he describes young soldiers who "just folded up" and died because they stopped eating and taking care of themselves. And Hall had been completely at the mercy of his captors after his ordeal in solitary confinement and he suffers an emotional breakdown on the stand as he relates his experiences in captivity and his lonely childhood.

Compared to the films focusing on Second World War POWs that were produced during the same period, *The Rack* is noticeably more critical of America's fighting men. Commenting on the film's central message, Young has argued, "The film called on society to steel its young soldiers for anything or face the shattered spirits who come home."[101] More specifically, it implied that the nature of the Cold War and the battle for men's minds necessitated the development of tenacity and courage in American men. As Hall's emotional and mental breakdown in *The Rack* illustrated, the physical toughness of the veterans of the Second World War was no match for the psychological warfare waged by the Communists, and if the country wanted to beat the Communist enemy it would need to start producing men who were psychologically equipped to face the obstacles of a new age.

POWs and American Society

In the introduction to his book on the negative public perception of the men who had been POWs in North Korea, Biderman wrote, "We can learn less about pathologies of our society from the behavior of the Americans captured in Korea than we can by attempting to understand the reasons for the complaints that have been made against them."[102] The public uproar over the behavior of American men in North Korea has always provided more insight into the nation's insecurities during a particularly sensitive period of the Cold War than it has on any national shortcomings or supposed flaws in the national character. Prompted by the disappointing conclusion of the Korean War, critics and the public alike latched onto the most outlandish examples of disloyalty and collaboration in North Korea and used them as the basis for a searing critique of the state of the nation's strength and resolve against the Communist enemy. In many cases what commentators stressed in their critiques of POWs revealed their own anxieties at midcentury. As Carruthers has written, the captivity of POWs "came to function as something akin to a Rorschach test for social commentators in the fifties [and] the shapes Americans discerned there mapped an intricate set of cold war anxieties."[103]

From the start brainwashing had played a central role in shaping these anxieties, firmly gripping the public's imagination and indicating that POWs had been powerless, impotent, and weak while in captivity. Beyond instituting the new code of conduct, the military was at a loss for how to respond, as evidenced by a short-lived brainwashing program at Stead Air Force Base in Nevada that was abruptly suspended in 1955 after the media reported that it trained air force cadets in "brainwashing interrogation" methods by actually subjecting them to psychological and physical torture.[104] Rear Adm. D. V. Gallery of the U.S. Navy suggested a more basic solution: a "tell-anything policy" in the military, which he inferred would seriously diminish the propaganda value of confessions and "leave no further motive for brainwashing except sadism."[105] But the consensus among a number of prominent politicians and military officials was that a more expansive reimagining of U.S. policy was in order. They indicated that the only sensible solution to the dilemma posed by the behavior of American POWs was to essentially turn Communist brainwashing on its head and indoctrinate a new generation of Americans with traditional values and "true Americanism." As Hunter put it, education could defuse the threat of Communism and provide Americans with a "mental vaccination" against the contagious powers of Communist ideology.[106] Reflecting on his experience in Communist prison camps, General Dean observed that the American POW experience offered several lessons that "Americans should take to heart." Notably, one of Dean's lessons was that "the meaning of true Americanism and Democracy should be taught by practice as well as words."[107] As early as 1952 Lewis K. Gough, the national commander of the American Legion, declared, "We cannot afford to be lukewarm Americans any longer." Gough's solution was to "not only get Communism out of schools . . . [but] get Americanism into schools."[108] Two years later Mildred Younger, a candidate for the state senate in Los Angeles, took Gough's ideas a step further, arguing that teacher loyalty checks were necessary to ensure that the youth of the nation were getting the proper training to prepare them for the perils of the Cold War. In an appearance at the Metropolitan Business and Professional Women's Club, Younger stated, "The function of our public schools is to teach the fundamentals of true Americanism."[109]

In 1959 one of the largest congressional efforts at addressing this issue became the basis for a bill to create a Freedom Commission and a Freedom Academy. The proposed commission would feature a seven-person full-time staff that reported to the Joint Congressional Freedom Committee and supervised Freedom Academies around the country, which would be open to students from the "free world" and would promote "the development of the science of the counteraction to the world Communist conspiracy and . . . the training and development of leaders in a total war." Essentially, the driving concept behind the bill was to create an institution that taught students how to effectively combat Communist psychological warfare. On the second day of hearings on the bill, the Senate Internal Security Sub-Committee called Hunter to the stand. Hunter praised the bill and testified that it "would be a positive aggressive step by the United States which would at one and the same time dissipate the defensive psychology prevailing in the United States and the West vis-à-vis Communism and arm the Free World with a powerful weapon against world Communism."[110]

Although several high-ranking senators agreed with Hunter's comments, the bill became stuck in legislative purgatory for the better part of the next decade and ultimately never got off the ground. The impulse behind the bill, however, continued to hold meaning. In essence, the legislation was based on the perception that Communist psychological warfare and brainwashing had stripped American soldiers of all the traits associated with true Americanism at midcentury: the courage, bravery, and mental fortitude that had served earlier generations so well. For many policymakers the most logical solution to this dilemma was to create freedom academies and indoctrinate students in Americanism. Almost immediately after the war, critics like Kinkead and Mayer began to argue that the success of Communist brainwashing and psychological manipulation was not truly the result of the Communists' new technique but the result of widespread shortcomings in American society. In the view of these critics, the Communist enemy had found ways to exploit a new softness in the American people, and if American soldiers had truly been psychologically and mentally prepared to face the Cold War enemy they would never have succumbed to the Communists' methods of manipulation in the first place. This interpretation was dependent on the incomplete, vague understanding of brainwashing and on what practically amounted to a willful ignorance of the reality of the North Korean prison camps and dozens of examples of American men behaving bravely in the face of adversity during the Korean War.

Despite the holes in the logic of this school of thought, it had practical consequences with regard to American life. Citing the purported lack of escapes, the deadly give-up-itis disease, and the general weakness of American men in North Korean prison camps, many contemporary observers began to claim that the behavior of American men during the Korean War was the result of rampant social decay. Frequently, these allegations went hand in hand with assertions that the veterans of the Second World War had somehow been better equipped to handle the demands of modern warfare than the veterans of the Korean War, a view that was reflected in the POW films of the period. Critics proclaimed that if the nation was going to defend itself against Communist brainwashing and psychological warfare, individual Americans would need to be as self-reliant and mentally tenacious as their forefathers. As a result, Americans around the country began to believe that the best way to combat Communism was to emphasize traditional values and make free will and individuality the cornerstones of modern American democracy.

4

Motherhood and Male Autonomy during the Cold War

In the fall of 1953 Portia Howe became a minor cause célèbre and a short-lived media sensation when it was revealed that her son, Pvt. Richard R. Tenneson, was one of the twenty-three American POWs in Korea who planned to remain with his Communist captors and refuse repatriation to the United States. Part of the publicity was owing to Tenneson's age: he was only seventeen when he enlisted in the army in 1950 and was one of the youngest Americans to decide not to come home. But what really captured the public imagination was Howe's response to the news. Instead of sitting idly by, she sprang into action. Telling reporters that all she needed was ten minutes alone with her son to "make a dent in that kind of thinking," she immediately recorded a message for him at a radio station in Mankato, Minnesota, and then arranged with the Defense Department to have the message sent to the Repatriation Commission in Korea. In the message she told her son, "Make up your own mind . . . as you've been brought up to do."[1] Over the next several weeks Howe began laying the groundwork for a face-to-face meeting with her son despite considerable roadblocks. By December she had obtained a passport to travel to Korea and had raised enough money for the flight through donations from her local church and by cashing in nearly seventeen hundred dollars' worth of her son's war bonds. On December 9, after telling members of the press she was "fighting for [her] son's soul" and intended to bring him "back to his senses and back home," she boarded a plane for Tokyo.[2]

Upon her arrival in Japan, Howe was immediately escorted by military officers to a private conference with the commander in chief of the Far East Command, Gen. John. E. Hull, who rejected her plan to see her son in Korea on the basis of the Department of Defense's policy on POWs. Caught up in bureaucratic red tape, Howe remained in Tokyo for another week and a half, appealing to the public and Congress through foreign correspondents in Japan. Ultimately, however, it was her son who persuaded Howe to abandon the mission. After she wired him a telegram with details of her visit, he wrote her a letter stating that she could visit him if she wished but that she would never accomplish her goal of persuading him to return home. In the letter Tenneson criticized U.S. authorities and defiantly told his mother he was staying with his Communist captors, writing, "I know that you want to take me home with you but I have made up my mind and I am not going." He closed the letter by snidely recommending she "go over to GHQ and take a loyalty oath" before returning home. Standing before assembled members of the press with tears in her eyes and a Bible in one hand, Howe broke down, almost sobbing as she asked, "Where did I fail?—I don't know where I failed." Regaining her composure, she mocked her son's naiveté: "He was only 17—what does he know of life in the United States? He was in combat seven weeks. What does he know of war? The whole argument falls apart." She asked the reporters present to make the entire letter available to the public. "I think people should know how vicious a thing communism is," she said. "If it can destroy a home, it can disintegrate a nation."[3]

Tenneson's story was tailor-made for the press, and Howe's every move received intense media scrutiny for weeks. In the years after, every time Tenneson wrote a letter home to his mother the press would revisit the entire story. In September 1955 Howe received the first indication that Tenneson was tiring of life in Red China. Two months later the Chinese government abruptly agreed to release him. On December 16, after being away from his hometown for nearly five years, Tenneson returned to Alden, Minnesota, where he was greeted with a warm family homecoming and a roast turkey dinner. The press made special note of the dessert at the dinner, a cake in the shape of an open Bible that was inscribed with two quotations from scripture. The first read, "Commit thy way unto the Lord; trust Him and He shall bring it to pass"; the second, "I can do all things thru Christ which strengthened me." The Associated Press ran a photo of the scene, showing Howe and her son smiling as they looked down at the cake. After all her effort, it appeared Howe had indeed saved her son's soul. The army dropped all charges against Tenneson, averring that the case was outside their jurisdiction, and after NBC televised a one-hour drama based on the story in 1956, aptly titled "Mother of a Turncoat," Howe and her son quickly faded from the public eye.

If the story appeared to have a happy ending on its surface, several aspects of the episode would have given critics reason to pause by the middle of the decade. First, there were the statements Tenneson made on his return home about the generosity of his captors and the authenticity of the germ warfare charges against the United States, which prompted one reporter to label him "a well-indoctrinated victim of the Communist propaganda machine."[4] Further, there was the continued evidence of Tenneson's naiveté and immaturity, attested to by the Associated Press's reference to him as a "22 year old farm boy," which many critics would see as indicative of a larger national problem: the stunted development of a new generation of American men who were hardly men at all. Next, there were the persistent rumors of Tenneson's unhappy childhood, which some pointed to as the primary reason for his behavior in North Korea. While he was in Hong Kong, Tenneson fueled this speculation when he told reporters that he may have succumbed to Communism because of lingering resentment over beatings he had suffered at the hands of his stepfather. Notably, press coverage of Tenneson frequently contained allusions to the fact that the Howe family was not the traditional nuclear American family of the 1950s and pointed out that Tenneson was Howe's son from a previous marriage, referring to his siblings as his half brother and half sister. And, finally, there was the simple fact that he had a stepfather in an era when divorce was relatively uncommon and a cause for social ostracism. When Howe was pressed to discuss the whereabouts of Tenneson's father, whom she had divorced when her son was four, she frankly stated, "We don't know whether Richard's father is still alive."[5]

Howe's supporters ignored many of these details and portrayed her as a devout Christian and loving mother. For example, John Chapple, the editor of the *Ashland Press* in Wisconsin, publicly applauded her efforts to visit her son in Korea and claimed that "mother love, mothers' prayers and tears, and the fervent prayers of Christians everywhere, and above it all the supreme power of Jesus Christ are awakening these boys in spite of the difficulties of personal contact."[6] Although Howe represented a sympathetic figure, many critics nevertheless indicated she was at least partially responsible for her son's behavior and insinuated that perhaps the root cause of Tenneson's actions stemmed not from Communist brutality but from his childhood in Minnesota. Howe hinted as much herself when she conceded, "Richard resented discipline. Perhaps I over-did it. Perhaps that is where I made my mistake."[7] Commentators would come to agree with Howe's statement that if Communism could destroy a home it could "disintegrate a nation," and by the middle of the 1950s they were armed with a variety of responses to her inquiry, "Where did I fail?"

The story of Howe and her son illustrates a broader dimension of the history of brainwashing and postwar American society. Just as Tenneson was, returning POWs would be portrayed as naive, immature weaklings who had succumbed to the "Communist propaganda machine," and, as the search for the source of their supposed lack of manly fortitude in the face of Communist psychological warfare moved beyond the confines of the barbed wire enclosing North Korean prison camps, their mothers would be thrust into the limelight. Prominent social critics and the mainstream media would link the behavior of POWs to a number of economic and cultural developments in post–Second World War American society, including the relative comfort of the postwar welfare state; a decline in traditional American values; the shortcomings of the American public education system; and, according to Lt. Col. William Erwin Mayer, even the "ready availability of installment credit."[8] But it was the family and the nation's mothers in particular that were pinpointed as the source of a troubling new softness in American men and blamed for what many deemed a precipitous and potentially disastrous decline in the state of male autonomy and independence in the United States. A number of historians have identified Americans' anxieties over gender roles during the Cold War, but they have largely overlooked how closely the development of these apprehensions paralleled the rise of brainwashing. Throughout the 1950s the specter of Communist brainwashing played a central role in underwriting a critical reexamination of American motherhood and inspiring a new focus on the vulnerability of men's minds. These fears would eventually bind American boys' physical fitness and mental toughness to national security and led to new training methods in the army, new public policies related to physical education, new models of masculinity that prioritized normative sexuality and mental toughness, a general climate of mother bashing, and an emphasis on parenting strategies intended to toughen up American boys. The history of brainwashing is also a history of gender and domesticity at midcentury.

Class, Race, and American POWs

Initially there was widespread speculation that the behavior of American POWs who capitulated in Communist prison camps could be credited to class and racial factors. The Communists had attempted to stoke discord within the camps by emphasizing segregation and class inequality in the United States in their propaganda and in the mandatory classes the POWs were subjected to, and several sources anxiously speculated that blue-collar whites and African Americans would be highly susceptible to this approach because of their experiences or lack of education back in the States. Rep. William Wampler from Virginia, for example, opined that American POWs were "mere country boys victimized by a shrewd propaganda . . . technique."[9] Media discussion of several of the POWs who were caught up in the repatriation scandal, including Tenneson, Arlie Pate, and Edward Dickenson, often referenced their humble origins and rural upbringings, insinuating that blue-collar boys made easy targets. A letter by Alonzo M. Mercer printed in the *Chicago Defender* made similar points about the three African American soldiers who had refused repatriation to the United States, bluntly hinting that America's race problem was the underlying factor in their defection. Addressing his own experiences with segregation in the South, Mercer cited an episode in which he was refused room and board along the Texas border but welcomed back into Mexico, writing he was thus forced to leave "the democracy of the US to find food and shelter in a foreign country." Admitting he was "at a loss to explain why 20 white boys want to stay," Mercer said, "The reason for the Negro boys wanting to remain is not too hard to explain."[10]

When the media began taking a closer look at the GIs who remained in Korea, it became apparent that many displayed class and racial characteristics that distinguished them from the majority of Americans. Almost all of them had come from the ranks of the working class, and eight had grown up in extreme poverty.[11] Generally, the soldiers were the sons of farmers and laborers, not of suburban, middle-class parents. The majority of them had never completed high school, and a significant percentage had come from broken homes. Commenting on their backgrounds, the journalist Chalmers M. Roberts argued that "a group portrait" of the soldiers who refused repatriation "sheds some new light on their strange decision." In an article titled "The GIs Who Went Red? A Portrait of Poverty, Ignorance, Strife," Roberts wrote that their backgrounds as members of "the lower, often the lowest, economic strata of American society" and a general lack of "intellectual capacity—or parental urging" played a large role in what had transpired in North Korea.[12]

Virginia Pasley's book *21 Stayed: The Story of the American GI's Who Chose Communist China* (1955) presented the clearest distillation of this argument. Each chapter in her book focused on a POW who had refused repatriation and was based on a biographical account of his life and interviews with his family and members of the town and community he grew up in. In lieu of a title, each chapter was preceded by a page containing biographical information about the POW, including his race, religious affiliation, and IQ level. One of the more revealing aspects of the book was its appendix, which compiled the biographical information of each POW and broke it down into several sections, including "Home background—Material Circumstances," "Schooling," and "I.Q." The fact that the book ends with a statistical overview of the POWs points to how instrumental these statistics were to Pasley's analysis. At least in part on the basis of this statistical impression Pasley concluded, "No one reading the unhappy life stories of the twenty-one—stories of broken homes, poverty, brutal treatment, serious emotional problems and scanty education—could fail to see how vulnerable they were, how pitifully ill-equipped to withstand the psychological warfare the Reds waged against them."[13] Although Pasley qualified her remarks by writing that "no one, however stalwart, however secure, however ideal his background . . . could withstand the full force of the cruelly corroding methods the Communists use," her book indicated that specific types of men were especially vulnerable.[14] The numbers she provided show that the majority of POWs who refused repatriation had low to average IQ's and came from poor, working-class backgrounds.

Despite the unmistakable pattern in this statistical portraiture, several issues complicated the narrative. With regard to race, early reports suggested that African Americans had actually held up admirably well to Communist propaganda and psychological warfare. After being segregated from the rest of their company—an irony, incidentally, that did not go unnoticed—African American POWs were subjected to a near-constant barrage of propaganda highlighting the racism rampant in American society. An article in the *Christian Science Monitor* suggested that African American men in the prison camps had specific qualities that made them impervious to Communist manipulation, including their "unquenchable talent for the comic, their sense of the ridiculous, their in-group ability to spot pretense whether Caucasian or Oriental, and their resentment at being 'used' anew."[15] Such an interpretation transformed African Americans' stereotypical racial characteristics from a liability into an asset.

Attribution of the behavior of American POWs to their status as members of the working class was contradicted by the simple fact that economically privileged soldiers had also capitulated under Communist pressure, including officers in the air force and marines. At Col. Frank H. Schwable's trial, Maj. Gen. William Dean appeared as a witness for the defense and when questioned about his own ability to give only his name, rank, and serial number in response to Communist brainwashing he frankly acknowledged that even though he had been treated leniently compared to other American POWs, he "did not have the strength or intelligence" to abide by army regulations and withhold other information from his captors.[16] Dean was not only, as noted earlier, the highest-ranking American POW during the Korean War but also a graduate of the

University of California at Berkeley. His testimony indicated that someone's behavior in a prison camp could not be projected on the basis of their class or education status. Other reports corroborated Dean's testimony and offered further evidence that education and IQ levels were poor indicators of men's response to Communist psychological warfare. A returning POW who had been acquainted with seven of the men who ultimately refused repatriation directly contradicted reports that all the men were ignorant and uneducated, telling a reporter for the *Washington Post* that several had been voracious readers and that the Communists' methods affected both "heavy readers who were swayed by Communist literature, and the uneducated who, after several hours of pep talks, were easily persuaded that life under the Reds was the best for them."[17]

The initial focus on the class and racial background of American POWs promoted two narratives. The first held that African Americans and members of the working class were not up to the task of meeting the Communist enemy on the psychological field of combat. Based above all on racist and classist notions of the intrinsic deficiencies of these groups, it was a view predicated on widespread skepticism about the abilities of African American and working-class soldiers. The second perspective on class and racial factors shifted this narrative by putting the onus back on American society, arguing that if African Americans and working-class soldiers had proven easy prey for Communist propaganda, it was primarily because their experiences in the United States had left them with little reason to feel sufficiently patriotic enough to jeopardize their mental or physical well-being for the nation. In fact, Communist propaganda in the POW camps dwelled on the racial and class injustices that were a particularly vulnerable aspect of postwar American society, and the mainstream media's reservations about how the "Negros" and "farm-boys" would respond to such material betray deeper misgivings with racial and class inequality in 1950s America. Ironically, although the overwhelming majority of POWs who refused repatriation were members of the lower and lower middle classes, their alleged softness and inability to stand up to Communist psychological warfare would consistently be linked to the excesses of postwar mass consumption.[18]

Doubts about working-class and African American soldiers would continue to rear their head occasionally in public discourse and in the media's discussion of American POWs, but there was simply too much evidence to the contrary to allow the POWs' behavior to be attributed solely to class and racial factors. In search of a common denominator among all of the soldiers, and since race and class had largely proven to be a nonstarter, their sex and age became the focus of scrutiny. All of the POWs were male, and they were predominantly young: 93 percent were between twenty and thirty-four years old on their return to the United States. It was widely reported that the youngest soldiers in North Korea had fared the worst.[19] This led the media to express worries over a crisis of American manhood in the 1950s and early 1960s and to report that the masculine vigor and toughness of the nation were in a state of decline.

"A New Softness"

An article titled "The Ordeal of Colonel Fleming" published in the *Chicago Daily Tribune* on November 14, 1954, reveals how mounting disquiet over American POWs began to evoke a broader critique of the state of American manhood. In the article, the *Tribune*'s war correspondent, John H. Thompson, commenting on the military court-martial of Lt. Col. Harry Fleming in Fort Sheridan, Illinois, wrote that "his unprecedented trial raises questions about [the] conduct of U.S. service men which all America must answer." At the time of the trial Fleming was forty-six years old, and he had a long and decorated career in the army. Given his background and the fact that he was the first officer tried for collaborating with the enemy, the case received considerable publicity in 1954.[20] Fleming had been charged with leading Marxist study groups, making pro-Communist propaganda recordings, and informing on his fellow POWs. After the court heard the testimony of several POWs who had been under his command and of a former army psychiatrist who testified that Fleming had been "subjected to communist brain washing," Fleming took the stand and wept openly as he described the scenes he had witnessed as a prisoner. In the long run Fleming's emotional testimony may have hurt him more than it helped, as the military tribunal found him guilty and sentenced him to a dishonorable discharge in November 1954.

According to Thompson, "Much more than the fate of Harry Fleming rode on the decision and on the testimony in the Fort Sheridan courtroom."[21] Thompson wrote that the proceedings against Fleming proved the United States was in dire need of stronger leadership and of men with "more built-in backbones," but he was not optimistic that the nation had men who were mentally strong enough to endure Communist psychological torture. In short, Thompson believed Fleming was not an anomaly but representative of the American people in general and American men in particular. Voicing his concerns, Thompson asked his readers, "Does the Korean POW experience highlight a basic softness in America?"[22]

Picking up on these themes, prominent critics like Kinkead ascribed the disconcerting record of American POWs to a variety of factors, writing,

"The roots of the explanation go deep into diverse aspects of our culture—home training of children, education, physical fitness, religious adherence, and the privilege of existing under the highest standard of living in the world."[23] Mayer supported Kinkead's assessment, claiming that the frailty of American POWs raised "serious questions about American character, and about the education of Americans."[24] The former POW and army doctor Maj. Clarence L. Anderson narrowed it down even further, saying that the general ineptitude of young American POWs was "the result of some new failure in the childhood and adolescent training of our young men—a new softness."[25]

The reference to "a new softness" is especially notable, as hard and soft imagery became a prominent theme in discussions of American POWs.[26] For example, at an awards ceremony in 1954, Secretary of the Navy Robert B. Anderson praised five Marine Corps POWs who did not collaborate with the enemy "for choosing the course of 'stern duty' over that of 'flaccid collaboration.'"[27] Preoccupations over the state of American manhood and the nation's child-rearing practices had been present in Cold War culture before the Korean War, and the association between Communism and softness was not a midcentury development.[28] The etymology of *pinko* is a case in point of the long-standing affiliation in American culture between liberal politics, Communism, and soft femininity. *Pinko* was a derivative of the older term *parlor pink* and was first widely used in the mainstream media in the 1920s to deride "liberals [and] those who were close to, and thus tainted by, *red* Communists."[29] The innuendo of the term was obvious: Americans who harbored liberal or pro-Communist sympathies were effete and unmanly.[30]

During the early Cold War acute gender distress extended well beyond mere political attacks—it permeated American political and private life. In the late 1940s and early 1950s conservatives began to carry out a systematic assault on Democrats for the perceived loss of China, Franklin Roosevelt's appeasement at Yalta, Alger Hiss's sabotage against the nation, and Dean Acheson's handling of the Korean War.[31] The Department of State under the Truman administration came in for special derision, and conservatives labeled the department a haven for Communists, homosexuals, and, as Chief Justice William Clark asserted, "cookie pushers."[32] The historian Robert Dean has persuasively argued that this brand of politics led to a so-called lavender scare against homosexuals in the United States as conservatives "conflated fears of domestic political subversion and foreign aggression with anxieties about the maintenance of domestic social and sexual order."[33] The nationwide purge of homosexuals from American government had disastrous political and personal ramifications and may have encouraged many politicians to assert a more aggressive and thus more "masculine" stance on a variety of issues for the remainder of the fifties.[34] Since the nation was already expressing considerable angst over the state of American manhood, allegations about the softness of American POWs after the Korean War fit neatly into the era's dominant consternation about masculinity.

Public apprehensions over manhood led Arthur Schlesinger Jr. to conclude that there was a "crisis of American masculinity" in 1958, confirming the existence of some underlying tensions beneath the public veneer of a country in the midst of a baby and consumer boom and a Cold War consensus that celebrated the family and the marketplace as extensions of American health, vitality, and progress.[35] As historians have pointed out, this climate did not institutionalize a single model of acceptable American manhood but instead opened the doors for a variety of models of male behavior, the traditional breadwinning patriarch championed by conservatives standing alongside the male playboy embodied by Hugh Hefner.[36] However, Americans were not simply reacting to broad transformations in American life. Directly influenced by the events of the Korean War, the phantom of Communist brainwashing added a new dimension to the nation's unease over American manhood and linked all of the various responses to the gender crisis by establishing a newfound emphasis on male autonomy, independence, and mental toughness.

The Rape of the Mind

When American POWs returned to the United States in 1953, worry about their mental autonomy coexisted alongside more traditional concerns about normative masculine behavior. Not surprisingly, tensions over male sexuality surfaced in the mainstream media's initial coverage of the American POWs. For example, an article in *Newsweek* published in 1954 and titled "Korea: The Sorriest Bunch" judged half of the twenty-one American POWs who had refused repatriation to be "bound together more by homosexualism than Communism."[37] An article in the *Washington Post* made similar charges, stating that "some, perhaps four, of the 22 are homosexuals who have taken to letting their hair grow long and using language so foul as to repel the regular soldiers of the Indian Army who are their guards." The article paraphrased an earlier Associated Press account that had reported that "two of the 22 were seen by American correspondents to be dressed in women's clothes."[38] Rumors of their sexual "perversity" had become so far-reaching that it spurred the twenty-one POWs to respond to the accusations, and at a press conference in Panmunjom in January 1954, Pfc. Samuel D. Hawkins told members of the press, "We are all normal. There are no homosexuals and no perverts."[39] The charges were unfounded, but they illustrate how the media filtered the behavior of POWs through preexisting stereotypes that associated pro-Communism with soft masculinity and homosexuality.

The media's attempt to connect American POWs behavior in Korea to sexual perversion was colored by the larger historical context of the era and reflects the dubious allegations about Communism and sexuality that were circulating in American political discourse during the period. Just two years before the Korean War, in his landmark work *Sexual Behavior in the Human Male,* Alfred Kinsey had shocked the nation by publishing his studies, which had found that a high percentage of American men had engaged in homosexual activities at least once in their life. Kinsey's data ignited a great deal of trepidation about perversion and homosexuality and were consistently cited by politicians and the media as evidence of a troubling new "homosexual menace" in American society.[40] For those who knew where to look, this menace was becoming more and more visible, as a homosexual subculture was beginning to emerge in cities across the nation.[41] After February 28, 1950, when Undersecretary of State John Peurifoy admitted under questioning that ninety-one employees had been dismissed from the State Department since 1947 because they were homosexuals, issues of sexual perversion and homosexuality became even further politicized.

In June the Senate launched a full-blown investigation of homosexuals in government, based in part on the claims of the Republican floor leader Kenneth Wherry that the chief of the District of Columbia vice squad, Lt. Roy E. Blick, had acquired "the names of between 300 and 400 Department of State employees [who were] suspected or allegedly homosexuals."[42] The investigation concluded that there was a significant homosexual presence in American government. According to the historian John D'Emilio, the Senate report justified excluding homosexuals from government service for two overlapping reasons. First, the report asserted that homosexuality was not normal behavior, and individuals who practiced it lacked "emotional stability" and "moral fiber." Second, the report concluded that homosexuals were security risks, and their behavior made them susceptible to blackmail. As D'Emilio observed, Americans believed that "homosexuality [was] . . . an epidemic infecting the nation, [and] actively spread by communists to sap the strength of the next generation."[43] The ramifications of the Senate investigation were immediate: governmental oversight of the personal lives of employees was increased, security measures that made homosexuality and sexual perversion roadblocks to federal employment were enhanced, and a national campaign against homosexuals, carried out by conservatives in Washington and local civic and religious groups across the country, was launched.

These measures placed male sexuality at the center of national politics and cast additional suspicion on the returning POWs. In December 1952, less than a year before the end of the Korean War, the publicity surrounding Christine Jorgensen served to draw the masculinity of American GIs into even greater question. On December 1 the *New York Post* made Jorgensen perhaps the most infamous GI in the entire country when it reported that he had undergone a sex change operation in Denmark. Under the headline "Ex-GI Becomes Blonde Beauty: Operations Transform Bronx Youth," the story detailed Jorgensen's transformation from a GI to "a striking woman." With the appearance of numerous articles, interviews, and a five-part autobiographical account of her life in *American Weekly,* Jorgensen became one of the most widely reported upon American servicemen in 1953. When two other former servicemen underwent similar procedures it became clear that hers was not an isolated case.[44]

Not all returning POWs were accused of sexual perversion, but indoctrination and brainwashing were both popularly portrayed as emasculating processes. This was especially apparent in Joost Meerloo's work on the subject, as indicated by the title of his book on the subject, *The Rape of the Mind: The Psychology of Thought Control, Menticide, and Brainwashing.* Meerloo's word choice suggests he thought there was an overwhelmingly sexual component to brainwashing. In his view the Communist enemy had dominated American male POWs, who were psychologically raped against their wills. Because their minds had been "penetrated" by the Communist enemy and they were manipulated into "mental submission," American POWs had essentially been feminized in North Korea.

For many Americans it only made sense that a return to normative heterosexual behavior might counteract Communist indoctrination and return Communist POWs to full-blooded American manhood. This notion was on display when the second group of POWs released during Operation Little Switch returned to the United States in April 1953. On disembarking at Hickam Air Force Base in Honolulu, the POWs were greeted by dancing hula girls who outfitted the men with leis made from flowers. The reception served as a reminder of normative American sexual guidelines, with scantily clad women serving as the objects of the men's lustful gaze. The

Associated Press seemed to approve of the proceedings, reporting that "the men craned their necks from the windows of the ambulances to watch the hula girls whirling before them."[45]

But heterosexual behavior was not deemed a cure-all, especially in light of assertions that the Communists had influenced some men to refuse repatriation to the United States by promising them "they could have plenty of women."[46] During the same period, popular magazines such as *Look* and *Life* connected the perversity of the Communist system to Soviet women, who were commonly depicted as sexless, brutish, and unfeminine. As the historian K. A. Cuordileone has pointed out, "The idea that Communism reversed somehow the natural order of gender relations and even empowered women at the expense of men . . . [was] a more complex reflex of deep anxieties rooted in American life, not Soviet reality."[47] In postwar America, then, only a specific type of heterosexual relationship had become acceptable, namely, one in which women either played a subservient role to men or risked emasculating them.

A short story titled "The Brainwashed Pilot" by Sidney Herschel Small that appeared in the *Saturday Evening Post* on March 19, 1955, served as powerful testimony to the notion that only monogamous heterosexual relationships contained in marriage could restore POWs' manhood. The story followed Anne Holmes, a nurse working in a Hong Kong infirmary whose husband's airplane had been shot down over Korea. Anne has traveled to Hong Kong because it is the closest she can get to Red China, where, she believes, her husband, Johnny, is a prisoner of the Communists. An elderly Chinese patient confirms her suspicions when he describes a white man living in his village who is suffering from amnesia and does not remember who he is or where he comes from. When Anne arranges a meeting with the mysterious villager and discovers that he is indeed Johnny, she rushes into his arms and passionately kisses him, but as she pulls away from his embrace she notices something is wrong. Johnny does not recognize her. In tears, Anne pleads with him, "I'm Anne, Johnny. Don't you remember? I'm Anne. Oh, darling, I'm your wife."

Convinced that Johnny has suffered a head injury, Anne cautiously tries to restore his memory without shocking his psyche. At the infirmary, the neurologist concludes that Johnny "had been subjected to brainwashing by the Reds." He clearly is no longer himself: he cannot speak a word of English and is convinced he is a Chinese peasant whose name is Yan Hai. But something of the old Johnny remains nevertheless, and Anne is quick to pick up on the way he casts "appraising eyes on her," which she interprets as "Yan Hai's instinctive attraction for John Holmes' wife."[48] After that first passionate kiss, Yan Hai begins to court his onetime wife, and in the process he seems to be on the verge of remembering his past life. In the final scene of the story, when Anne is attacked and sexually assaulted by a number of Communist soldiers, Johnny jumps to her rescue, fights them off, and finally recognizes his wife.

The historian Elaine Tyler May has argued that the media, the military, and private industry made marriage and parenthood the only safe avenues for patriotic American male and female sexuality by affiliating supposedly deviant sexuality and the threat of internal subversion. According to May, both heterosexual men who could not control their sex drives and homosexual men were seen as security risks "because they could be easily seduced, blackmailed, or tempted to join subversive organizations."[49] May posits that these concerns helped support the intellectual and moral underpinnings of the baby boom and the domestic politics of containment. In "The Brainwashed Pilot" it is evident that the containment of Johnny's sexual impulses in marriage plays a role in his eventual mental breakthrough. But Small's short story indicates that containing male sexuality in monogamous relationships is only one part of a larger equation. Drawing a parallel between the psychological violation of Johnny's psyche and the attempted rape of his wife, Johnny overcomes Communist brainwashing in the end by protecting his wife's chastity. Johnny's salvation is propelled by his initial attraction to Anne, but ultimately what breaks the final vestiges of Communist control is protecting the sanctity of his marriage by thwarting an attempted rape of his wife. The sexual innuendo in the final dialogue of the story is nearly comical, as Johnny, finally recognizing his wife, mutters, "Anne, Anne. Yes." Anne replies in a whisper, "Yes. Oh, yes, Johnny." If the pillow talk in the concluding scene signals that the fictional couple is seconds away from reconsummating their marriage, it also hints at how American men who had been emasculated by Communist brainwashing could become men again: by returning to normal heterosexual relations with their spouses and reestablishing their authority over Communist men.

Child Rearing in the Age of Brain Warfare

As the nation searched for solutions to the dilemmas brainwashing posed to American manhood, many critics began questioning why men had become so soft in the first place. Increasingly, the critics homed in on mom, who was blamed for everything from the stunted growth of American boys to a nationwide epidemic of homosexuality. Blaming mom for national shortcomings was nothing new in the 1950s, as several historians have pointed out.[50] In 1942 Philip Wylie's widely read nonfiction essays collected in *Generation of Vipers* introduced the concept of "momism."[51] Expressing a marked despair over a national decline in masculine power and prestige, the book warned that women were turning the country into a matriarchy by upending the traditional gender hierarchy, emasculating their husbands, and infantilizing their sons.[52] As Wylie later claimed, his vitriolic diatribe against American women earned him the moniker of "the all-out, all-time, high-scoring world champion misogynist." During the Korean War his thesis reemerged with a vengeance.[53] Military insiders, child-care experts, and even returning POWs blamed the nation's mothers for the misconduct of American soldiers in Communist prison camps, arguing that they were guilty of overprotecting and spoiling their sons, which stunted boys' physical and mental growth and made it impossible for them to develop the necessary masculine toughness to stand up to the diabolical, mind-bending Communist enemy.[54]

In the aftermath of the Korean War, the momentum to blame mothers for the POWs' weakness in regard to brainwashing continued to grow. In a letter of October 12, 1955, to the *Christian Science Monitor* Gaylen V. Pyle of Fayetteville, Arkansas, articulated the connections between overbearing motherhood and a new generation of weak American men: "In looking for those weaknesses in our society which have been reflected in the character of our young soldiers when faced with the coercion, intimidation, and indoctrination of Communist captors, the finger of blame is being pointed first one place and then another. Let 'Momism' not be excluded. There can be no doubt that this blighting influence weakens our young men, making them less effective in combat."[55] Other military insiders expressed similar logic. Major Mayer said, "A boy who has been brought up largely by his mother alone, a boy who has become what in psychiatry we refer to as a dependent character, something like the result of 'momism' as described by Philip Wylie . . . [could] not withstand the stresses of captivity."[56] In 1956 Mayer embarked on a national speaking tour to explain the new military code of conduct and army reforms, which he said would make American soldiers tough again. Speaking to groups of officers and enlisted men around the country, Mayer emphasized the importance of nurturing the independent character of American men so that they developed a sense of personal responsibility and the requisite toughness to bear Communist psychological torture.

Sgt. Lloyd W. Pate of Columbia, South Carolina, who had been a POW in the prison camps alongside the Yalu River in North Korea and eventually wrote a memoir based on his experiences there, also attributed the misconduct and weakness of his fellow POWs to their spoiled childhoods and passive characters. Speaking to a reporter from the *Saturday Evening Post*,

Pate said the reason so many POWs had collaborated with the enemy was that they were "'spoiled and pampered kids . . . no guts here'—Pate pointed to his belly—'or here'—he pointed to his head. 'Too much mamma,' he finished laconically."[57] Elaborating further, Pate drew a direct line between an overfeminized army and overbearing mothers, claiming the army "just isn't tough enough to fight this new kind of war, on account of women are always softening it up. They don't want their men to be tough. Do they want them dead?" Asked if he would ever consider reenlisting, Pate said, "I'll re-up when they make this man's army a man's army again."[58]

The military was not the only sector of American society to link the behavior of American POWs to momism, as, by the end of the 1950s and early 1960s, child-care experts began to weigh in on the subject as well. One of the nation's preeminent authorities on how to care for infants and children during the postwar era, Benjamin Spock, became convinced that the behavior of American POWs was the product of the nation's child-rearing practices. Since the publication of his best-selling seminal work, *The Common Sense Book of Baby and Child Care,* in 1946, a book that became a virtual parenting bible throughout the country, Spock had publicly advocated a flexible, affectionate approach to child rearing.[59] In 1962 Spock wrote, "Nothing has shaken thoughtful citizens as much as the behavior of the American soldiers taken prisoner during the Korean War." In light of that behavior, Spock said he was "shocked, not so much at what the Communists did, but at how easily these Americans went to pieces." The entire episode prompted him to question whether America's youth had become dangerously "underdisciplined" and "overcoddled."[60]

In her landmark work of 1963, *The Feminine Mystique,* Betty Friedan also accepted that momism was a central reason for American misconduct during the Korean War. Friedan stated that the generation of Americans fighting in Korea had proven itself "helpless, apathetic, incapable of handling freedom," and she claimed that American men were beginning to develop personalities "'strangely reminiscent' of the familiar 'feminine' personality as defined by the [feminine] mystique."[61] Elaborating on the source of the personality deficiencies displayed by American POWs in North Korea, Friedan wrote, "There was certainly something terribly wrong with these young men. . . . I would call it ego-failure—a collapse of identity. . . . Adolescent growth can and should lead to a completely human adulthood, defined as the development of a stable sense of self. The Korean prisoners, in this sense, were models of a new kind of American, evidently nurtured in ways inimical to clarity and growth at the hands of individuals themselves insufficiently characterized to develop the kind of character and mind that conceives itself too clearly to consent to its own betrayal."[62]

In Friedan's analysis the blame was placed not solely on American mothers, but also on American society because it had forced modern women to funnel their hopes and aspirations for professional and personal fulfillment into motherhood. However, even in Friedan's nuanced examination, the nation's mothers were called to task for stunting the emotional, physical, and mental maturity of their children.

Some dissenting voices argued that mothers were not entirely responsible for the behavior of the nation's youth. In the opinions section of the *Portland Oregonian,* E. Newton of Vacaville, California, wrote that the "ills of our youth" were also the fault of inattentive fathers and that "it is a rare, rare father who will lay down his newspaper for the sake of his child. Men are quick to accuse mothers of 'momism,' . . . [but] aren't fathers guilty, too, of that overpowering disease called 'newspaperitis'?"[63] Other Americans were defensive about the increasingly vocal charges against mothers. An indignant mother writing to Mary Haworth's daily mail column in the *Washington Post,* for example, protested the popular association between the word *mom* and overparenting, writing, "It really gets under my skin to read your frequent references to the author—what's his name? [Wylie]—who hit upon the word 'mom' to designate the overly possessive female parent, who wants to run her children's lives in detail."[64] These protests notwithstanding, others argued that a critical reexamination of American mothers was necessary. A letter from C.B. to the *Washington Post* chastised the possessive, immature mothers who instinctively recoiled from criticism instead of addressing their shortcomings as parents. In C.B.'s opinion, the "injured protest" of some mothers toward Wylie and other critics "indicates a lurking conviction of personal guilt."[65]

For nearly a decade after the Korean War the nation's concerns about motherhood remained front-page news, as a number of critics, journalists, and politicians argued that American mothers played a central role in a nationwide breakdown in the moral and physical fiber of the youth of the country. One of the high watermarks of this debate was initiated by a report published in the midst of the POW scandal in December 1953. Based on research by Hans Kraus and Ruth P. Hirschland of the Institute of Physical Medicine and Rehabilitation at New York University, the report compared the physical fitness of American and European children on the basis of a battery of physical and agility exercises, including leg lifts, sit-ups, and toe touches. The study found that 56.6 percent of the 4,458 American children tested failed to meet minimum health requirements. Worse yet, the children were vastly outperformed by their European counterparts: only 8.3 percent of the European children in the sample failed even one of the tests. In their concluding remarks, Kraus and Hirschland blamed the poor physical fitness of American children on the "highly mechanized society" in which they lived, with its prevalence of "cars, school buses, elevators . . . [and] other labor-saving devices."[66]

By 1955 interviews of Kraus had appeared in *U.S. News & World Report, Sports Illustrated,* and *Newsweek,* and the two researchers' findings had been widely publicized. Other reports appeared to corroborate their findings. In 1952 the media revealed that the army had rejected 42 percent of draftees on "physical, moral or mental grounds."[67] This represented a 6 percent increase over the rejection rate during the Second World War, even though the military's physical standards had not been substantively altered and the army was primarily drawing from a younger demographic. In 1956 the National Sports Council announced that American boys and girls ranked last in physical fitness in the world.[68] And in 1960 it was reported that British girls had posted higher scores than American boys on the same fitness tests.[69] It was widely stressed that this was not just a youth issue: it was a national issue with implications for foreign policy and the strength of the adult population. A YMCA brochure noted this fact, quoting Thomas Cureton of the University of Illinois, who said, "Most men of today are middle aged physically at the age of 25 years." The picture was not much rosier for adult women. The fitness expert Bonnie Prudden declared, "Girls round into beautiful curves at 16 and become flabby with no muscles to support this beauty by 25 years."[70]

In 1954, in a letter to his television consultant, the actor and producer Robert Montgomery, President Eisenhower conveyed his interest in making political hay out of youth fitness, divulging that he had had a conversation with an unnamed adviser who "suggested a talk some day on physical fitness in America . . . [and] urged that Teddy Roosevelt rode this subject hard and always to good effect."[71] A former running back on West Point's football team who had developed a penchant for golf in his thirties, Eisenhower had advocated sports and fitness throughout his adult life. This background predisposed Eisenhower to take sports and fitness issues seriously. The Kraus and Hirschland report conveniently combined Eisenhower's interest in athletics with a ready-made political issue he could use to boost his image before the presidential election of 1956. On July 11, 1955, the White House invited Kraus to speak at a luncheon attended by Eisenhower and Nixon as well as by some of the most well-known professional athletes and sports figures in the country, including the baseball star Willie Mays, the Celtics' basketball legend Bob Cousy, the commissioner of Major League Baseball, and the president of the Olympic Committee.

In his brief talk at the luncheon Kraus didn't pull any punches, declaring, "Underneath a veneer of Olympic heroes, 'All-Americans,' and professional sports stars, this country has a soft core."[72] Eisenhower was immediately taken aback by Kraus's report, telling associates he was shocked by its findings and disturbed that young people might "lack the spirit" to take care of their bodies. Vice President Nixon had a similar reaction, and in public comments asserted, "While we are not a nation of softies, we could become one, if proper attention is not given to the opportunities for normal physical, health-giving exercises."[73]

Kraus's attendance at the White House luncheon set the stage for the President's Conference on the Fitness of American Youth, held on June 18 and 19, 1956, at the U.S. Naval Academy in Annapolis, Maryland. Even though the conference emphasized that physical fitness was a national issue and that the physical well-being of young girls was a problem, the mainstream media's focus was predominantly on the fitness of young men and boys.[74] The fact that the conference was held at one of the nation's male-only service academies was no coincidence, and politicians and social critics began to pair the fitness of American boys with broader issues of national security, especially after it was reported that the army had rejected nearly one-third of its draftees between 1950 and 1956.[75]

In 1956 the *U.S. News & World Report* disclosed that "around 23 per cent of the American men who could be tapped for military service in a national emergency are physically or mentally unfit for fighting."[76] On the basis of this and other accounts, several politicians and military experts indicated that the mental frailty displayed by American POWs during the Korean War was emblematic of the state of physical and mental fitness of the nation's youth. Eisenhower appeared to agree with this sentiment, saying that the regrettable state of physical fitness in the country was responsible for the high percentage of rejections by draftee boards, and he expressed his apprehensiveness about what the future held if Americans didn't start stressing what he called the total fitness of young Americans' bodies and minds.[77]

Given that Kraus and Hirschland had imputed the poor physical shape of America's youth to general societal trends in the United States, the problem could not be laid entirely at the feet of parents. For example, two pictorial sections in the *U.S. News & World Report* in 1957 illustrate how the media linked concerns over physical fitness with the excesses of postwar American consumer society. The first, titled "How Father Built His Muscles," featured pictures of a child filling a wood-box with logs, children walking to school, and a boy helping his father plow a field by hand. The next series of pictures, titled "Why Sonny May Be Soft," showed children

The reported crisis in children's physical and mental fitness was attributed to a combination of bad parenting, new gadgets, and consumer excess. For many critics, television represented a potent mix of all three. "Is American Youth Physically Fit; Today's Children are Bigger, Softer, but Harden Up Fast," *U.S. News & World Report*, August 2, 1957, 71.

partaking in a number of physically undemanding activities like sitting in front of a television set, doing chores with "gadgets" (a vacuum cleaner) that made household tasks easier, lying on the couch while conversing on a telephone, and getting into cars and school buses.[78]

Although the pictures illustrate the existence of worries over American consumer society, many journalists and social critics claimed that parents and mothers in particular were the root cause of the national epidemic in unfit youth because they spoiled their children and allowed them to participate in postwar consumer culture. Prior to the formation of a new council on youth fitness headed by members of the cabinet, President Eisenhower accentuated this point by publicly declaring, "The essential responsibility for the fitness of our young people is a home and local community problem."[79] The media made similar proclamations. An article in the *New York Times* by Dorothy Barclay reported Kraus's and Hirschland's findings, concluding that the "overprivileged, overprotected, overindulged child of the oversolicitous parent may well grow up with problems as difficult to himself as those of the youngster who has had too few of the good things of life."[80] The illustration accompanying the article featured a mother holding her young son back as he eagerly looked at a jungle gym crawling with children. An article by the *Chicago Tribune*'s child guidance writer, Marcia Winn, titled "Why Is Johnny Always Tired?" echoed this point of view, asserting, "Today's children sit. It isn't their fault. Their parents have sought only 'the best' for them, and the best has been misinterpreted as getting them off their feet—into a stroller, a car, a school bus, a movie, or onto a cushion in front of the television set. The result is that American children have the most used buttocks and the least used back and leg muscles of any children in the world."[81] Although journalists admitted that parents of both sexes were guilty of spoiling their children, most reporters echoed Barclay's assertion that the majority of the time it was female parents who stunted the physical and psychological growth of American children, and only "in some cases" were fathers guilty of the same behavior.

Kraus's and Hirschland's original report had warned that in the absence of sufficient physical exercise, American children would have "inadequate outlet[s] for nervous tension." Other commentators picked up on this and began to associate physical fitness and overprotection with psychological neuroses and mental health. In her article Barclay wrote, "The problem has psychological as well as physical aspects, of course."[82] She quoted Milton M. Berger, a staff psychiatrist at Lenox Hill Hospital on Manhattan's Upper East Side, who estimated that "early overprotection in various forms might be a factor in the difficulties of some 25 per cent of . . . [his adult] patients."[83] In a message to participants in the first President's Conference on the Fitness of American Youth, Eisenhower underscored the relationship between physical fitness and mental fortitude, stating, "There is a need for arousing in the American people a new awareness of the importance of physical and recreational activity that our young people may achieve a proper balance of physical, mental, emotional, and spiritual strength."[84]

The softness of American POWs in Communist prison camps continuously informed the national discourse on the fitness of America's youth and imparted a sense of urgency to the debate. Throughout the late fifties and sixties, child-care experts, politicians, and journalists connected the poor shape of the nation's youth to the Cold War, the necessity for mental toughness, and the struggle against the Communist enemy. The *Los Angeles Times* ran a series of articles titled "U.S.—A Nation of Softies?" by Mary Ann Callan in April 1959. In the articles Callan referred to the Kraus and Hirschland report and asked, "What are we being physically fit for?" In the first article Callan suggested, "Let's look at the evidence first, then examine the other factors and the time-tested rebuttal: 'I'd stack up American kids with anybody, any time—including the Russians.' We have been stacked up—at least momentarily—with other countries and have been found wanting."[85] For evidence, Callan described "the breakdown of some U.S. servicemen in Korea . . . reports that some present Army recruits have a hard time, even with a light knapsack, of lasting through a 12-mile march . . . and the ever-present peacetime plea of mothers to 'go easy on my son.'"[86]

What stood out in Callan's article, which was representative of how fitness, overprotective mothering, and national security had become popularly intertwined, was her contention that a hard physical exterior was worthless without mental fortitude and tenacity. To demonstrate this point, she quoted Robert Kiphuth, the chairman of the physical education program and head swimming coach at Yale University, who was quoted as saying, "The shell's there, but what are we doing to put guts in it?"[87] Joining the alleged breakdown of American POWs to a lack of mental toughness and momism, Callan's article exemplifies how the Cold War and Communist psychological warfare informed preoccupations about American boys' physical and mental health. The answer to her central premise—"What are we being physically fit for?"—was clear: to ensure that future generations of American soldiers were physically and mentally strong enough to defend the nation and stand up to the insidious tactics of the Communist enemy.

In 1960 the executive director of the President's Council on Youth Fitness, Shane MacCarthy, pointed out the connections between physical well-being and character to an audience of college students and their parents at Trinity College, saying that "adults must provide the environment in which youth can grow into sturdy, self-reliant individuals."[88] MacCarthy was one of the key figures in the fitness campaign, and during his reign as the executive director of the council he toured the country extensively, warning communities about the dangers posed by unfit youth. His speech at Trinity pinpoints how youth fitness began to be related to self-reliance and individuality, which demonstrates that the fitness campaign was not simply a quest to remodel American boys' bodies but also an attempt to reshape their character and harden their minds. The burden of this mission increasingly fell on the shoulders of American parents, especially mothers, who now had a patriotic duty not simply to bear children but also to train a new generation of individualistic cold warriors who were physically and mentally tough enough to win the Cold War.

Raymond Shaw and Mrs. Iselin

The most articulate cultural representation of the frenzied agitation surrounding brainwashing, American manhood, and momism appeared in *The Manchurian Candidate*, a film that played in theaters in October 1962.[89] The film was adapted from Richard Condon's best-selling novel of the same name, which was published in 1959 and largely panned by critics. Yet even the book's most vocal critics acknowledged that Condon's tale of a brainwashed American POW programmed to assassinate the president of the United States was sure to captivate audiences. A book review in *Time* averred that Condon's novel deserved a place on a list of "the Ten Best Bad Novels," with "a superstructure of plot that would capsize Hawaii." Despite this critique, the reviewer predicted that the book would be read and enjoyed because Condon's "malicious humor" offered its audience a satirical take on almost every aspect of American disorder, "including incest, dope addiction, war, politics, brainwashing and multiple murder."[90]

When the director of the film, John Frankenheimer, adapted the novel for the screen, he dropped some of the more outlandish aspects of the book but stayed true to its main plot. The movie followed a conspiracy centered on Sgt. Raymond Shaw, played by Laurence Harvey. Shaw's platoon had been captured during the Korean War, smuggled into Manchuria, and brainwashed by a group of Communist scientists. The purpose of the entire operation was to turn Shaw into the perfect assassin, a sleeper agent who would be publicly regarded as a patriotic war hero but who would have no memory of his treasonous actions. The extent of the Communists' control over the men is revealed in a scene that shifted between shots of the alternate reality the American GIs had been conditioned to see in Manchuria and the actual events taking place. Conditioned to believe they are in the United States at a talk, "Fun With Hydrangeas," sponsored by the local Lady's Garden Club at the Spring Lake Hotel in New Jersey, Shaw's platoon is actually sitting in front of a group of assorted Communist politicians, military officials, and scientists. The head brainwasher demonstrates the extent of Shaw's conditioning by ordering him to strangle one of the men in his company in cold blood and then shoot another. Raymond complies with both commands, murdering the men with a cold efficiency as the rest of his platoon casually looks on.

The film's central plot twist is that the Communist operative working the American side of the conspiracy is Shaw's mother, the domineering Mrs. Eleanor Shaw Iselin, whom Raymond despises. Played by Angela Lansbury, who was nominated for Best Actress in a Supporting Role for her portrayal, Mrs. Iselin uses her son as a pawn in a scheme to win the presidency for her second husband, Sen. John Iselin. She can order Raymond to do virtually anything she wants simply by asking him to shuffle a deck of playing cards. Appropriately, the queen of diamonds—symbolic of female power—is Raymond's subconscious trigger mechanism. Although the film alludes to the powerlessness of the modern American man, it makes clear that all hope is not lost. In the end, with the help of Maj. Bennett Marco, who had been a member of Shaw's platoon and is played by Frank Sinatra, Shaw is able to block the subconscious trigger, unlock the shackles of control, and, propped up in the rafters of an auditorium and aiming the rifle meant to execute the assassination plot, shoot Johnny Iselin, his mother, and finally himself.

As Susan Carruthers pointed out in her article "*The Manchurian Candidate* and the Cold War Brainwashing Scare," the real target of the film is not the external Communist enemy but overbearing American mothers in the United States who were corrupting and controlling American men.[91] In the view of some contemporary psychologists, momism was the result of misplaced sexual desire. This interpretation, born during the Second World War and adverting to a midcentury fascination with dysfunctional sexuality and Freudian psychology, argued that American women could become sexually frustrated while their husbands were away at war and that "female sexuality . . . would become warped and misdirected toward sons in a dangerous Oedipal cycle."[92] The incestuous overtones of momism are reflected in a disturbing scene in *The Manchurian Candidate* when Mrs. Iselin passionately kisses her son while he is in a brainwashed trance. Harvey's and Lansbury's embrace was tame compared to Condon's original version of the scene because Frankenheimer had decided to omit a number of the more controversial aspects of the original novel, including the fact that Mrs. Iselin had seduced her father while she was still a teenager. In the novel the scene that eventually culminates in the passionate kiss was much more disturbing:

> Mrs. Iselin: "How much you look like Poppa! When you smile, Raymond dearest, for that instant I am a little girl again and the miracle of love begins all over again. How right that seems to me. Smile for me again, sweetheart. Yes. Yes. Now kiss me. Really, really kiss me." Her long fingers dug into his shoulders and pulled him to her on the chaise, and as her left hand opened the Chinese robe she remembered Poppa and the sound of rain high in the attic when she had been a little girl, and she found again the ecstatic place she had lost so long, long before.[93]

Alluding to momism at its most perverse, the rape of Shaw represented the pinnacle of Mrs. Iselin's mental and physical control of her son.

Commenting on this scene, the historians Matthew Frye Jacobson and Gaspar González have argued that "the character of Eleanor Iselin . . . is a patchwork creation whose elements are the very ideological elements of sexualized nationalism—neither Elaine Tyler May nor Cynthia Enloe could improve the character to better illustrate the argument about gender, sexuality, the family, and the politics of citizenship during the Cold War."[94] But the scandalous relationship between mother and son in *The Manchurian Candidate* moves well beyond "sexualized nationalism" and reflects broader tensions about male autonomy in Cold War America. In Condon's fictional universe, the correspondence between female power and male subservience is closely related and frankly on display in the relationships between Mrs. Iselin and the two men in her life. Johnny Iselin is so overcome by the unbalanced power dynamic between himself and his wife that he is both literally and figuratively impotent in her presence. As Condon put it, Iselin had "found himself as impotent as a male butterfly atop a female pterodactyl when he tried to have commerce with Raymond's mother."[95] Meanwhile, Shaw becomes an unwitting tool of his mother, carrying out her demands to their perverse ends. Furthermore, his rape at the hands of his mother alludes to the popular and the academic understanding of brainwashing.[96] While Iselin has lost his ability to perform, Shaw is mentally and physically subjugated by his mother. In this sense both men have lost their claim to American manhood because they have been deprived of their inherent masculine autonomy and become dependent on a woman.

The character of Mrs. Iselin is notable not only because she is one of the most manipulative female characters in the history of American cinema, but also because she contradicts so many of the platitudes about supposedly permissive mothers. Permissiveness is definitely not an issue with her. Rather, her character represents a warning against mothers who were too strict and too controlling: permissive motherhood, that is, was not the only type of motherly behavior that was under attack. At least in the movies, the domineering, unfeminine, and overbearing mother was just as likely as the passive mother to produce a weak son who was subservient to the Communists abroad and a submissive caricature of masculinity at home.[97] Extremes in either direction produced men ill-equipped to deal with the stresses of the postwar era, a signal that mothers needed to find some happy medium between the parenting styles of Spock and Mrs. Iselin or risk producing an effeminate turncoat.

The fact that *The Manchurian Candidate* debuted nearly a decade after the close of the Korean War and primarily focused on a platoon of American soldiers who had been brainwashed by Communists demonstrates the lasting association between Korean POWs, brainwashing, and declining male power. By counterbalancing Hollywood's image of the self-governing, manly Second World War POWs from the same period with that of the mentally enslaved, emasculated Korean POW, the film served as further cultural testimony of a national decline in male power and autonomy. Finally, and perhaps most important, by associating brainwashing with a Communist plot to take over the country, the film mirrored the popular yoking the media had forged of individual American men's minds and matters of national security and further supported the notion that men's mental and psychological independence from both Communist brainwashers and overcontrolling women was of crucial importance in the Cold War era.

The Doolittle Reforms

After the Korean War the military began to take direct action and implement new rules meant to instill better discipline and toughen up the nation's soldiers. In addition to the new code of conduct governing the wartime behavior of American soldiers in prison camps, the army instituted a range of substantive new polices that marked a major reversal of the reforms of the Doolittle Board that had revised the army's disciplinary code and recruitment policies after the Second World War. One colonel, speaking anonymously, proclaimed that the "Doolittle Board turned up the permissive road, giving us a loose, undisciplined system in the Army."[98] According to the colonel, the entire Korean POW debacle was a result of this lack of discipline. Lamenting the differences between the well-disciplined soldier and the soldiers who collaborated with the enemy in North Korea, he was quoted as saying, "[A] well-disciplined kind of soldier probably won't get captured. But if he does—and there is no disgrace in it if his ammunition runs out, if he is wounded, or if he is overpowered—he will still be a proud, efficient American soldier in the prison camp. The enemy won't indoctrinate *him,* by God."[99]

To ensure that the enemy would never indoctrinate another American soldier, the army implemented new measures that focused on rugged physical conditioning during basic training, reinstated the practice of saluting superior officers when GIs were off post, and granted noncommissioned officers more authority and prestige. An *Associated Press* editorial in 1954 analyzed the changes and concluded that "after years of seeking to lure men into enlistment with promises of good pay, security and 'learn a trade,' it has decided that such promises do not produce men physically and mentally conditioned to fight."[100] Military insiders who commented on the changes admitted that they were a direct response to the behavior of American POWs in North Korea and stressed that one of the cardinal lessons the army had learned as a result of the Korean War was that soft soldiers would die quickly in combat and would not fare well in captivity.

In 1954 a panel of seven of the highest-ranking officers in the army's organization and training division reevaluated army regulations and recommended increased physical training and harsher discipline.[101] In comments to the press, one of the members of the panel criticized the softness of the army and questioned the virility of veterans of the Korean War: "We're going to have to tell the people who come into the Army they aren't coming in for a feather bed. We aren't going to call them 'boy' and lead them around by the hand. They've got to learn to be men."[102] Another panelist compared Chinese and North Korean Communist troops with American soldiers, finding the former to be tough and knowledgeable about how to endure harsh conditions on meager rations, while the latter "had to have three squares [meals] a day—and two of them had to be hot or junior would write his Congressman or his mother."[103]

Malvina Lindsay of the *Washington Post* wrote an editorial in response to the new policies in which she argued that although the reforms were necessary they raised an important question: "Can physical toughness be superimposed in a few months on the softness of muscle that so many American youths are developing . . . [and] what is to be done about mental toughness?"[104] As we've seen, heightened sensitivities over physical fitness were prevalent in the middle of the decade, echoing traditional scares about American masculinity. However, even the fixation on children's physical fitness revealed that a strong body was no longer enough—it needed to be accompanied by a strong mind, or what Eisenhower, as noted, had called total fitness. Lindsay preached the necessity of educating recruits about Communist psychological warfare and preparing American men to endure propaganda and brainwashing so that in the future they would not break down or capitulate to Communist demands. As her editorial demonstrates, the Korean POW experience and the specter of Communist psychological warfare were vital in reshaping the nation's expectations of American men and helped displace traditional anxieties over manhood from their locus in men's physicality. The mind had become the new site of vulnerable American masculinity.

The nations' mothers, too, the targets of so much criticism in the aftermath of the war, were given new instructions about how to raise their children. Many women internalized this criticism, as shown by the AMVETS Auxiliary's "Code of an American Mother," created in 1956 and meant as a counterpart to the new code of conduct for American soldiers. The code defined a mother's responsibility as a parent: "I am an American mother.

It is my privilege to guide the destiny of my children." Moreover, it identified America's mothers as cold warriors, declaring in their name, "I realize that I must instill in my child a deep understanding of American politics and American history to serve as a bulwark against enemy political indoctrination."[105] In the auxiliary's new code, mom was conceptualized as the first line of defense in the fight against Communism, responsible for guiding children—as opposed to coddling them—and preparing them for psychological warfare with the Communist enemy. As a female subordinate organization of AMVETS, the auxiliary was composed of women who were manifestly aligned with the military and conservative forces in American life, but its new code constituted the ideas and fears of mothers all over the country. Moms had come under fire across the nation, and the public discourse surrounding the Korean War proves that many emerged from this debate intent on remodeling their parenting in order to produce boys who would never repeat the disgrace of Korea.

The epidemic of physical unfitness would receive periodic coverage in the mainstream media well into the sixties, ultimately making physical education a new battleground on which to inculcate masculine toughness and shaping policy well into the administration of John Kennedy.[106] The practical consequences were far reaching. The President's Council on Youth Fitness, now named the President's Council on Fitness, Sports and Nutrition, is entering its fifty-sixth year. The council promoted public awareness as well as considerable trepidation over fitness levels in the country, was directly affiliated with twenty-five governors' councils on youth fitness, and was responsible for both a reexamination of physical education programs and the creation of a national youth fitness testing program, now known as the President's Challenge. But the legacy of the social upheaval surrounding the Korean POW experience, motherhood, and the broad deficiencies in physical fitness goes much deeper than a handful of programs.

Brainwashing raised a central question for American men, the fathers and mothers who raised them, and the institutions dependent on them in the postwar era: What exactly constituted tough American manhood in a world of brain warfare? Although ideal masculinity had always had some intellectual components to it in American culture, physicality had traditionally received the lion's share of attention. Even character issues were related to physicality, such as the turn-of-the-century debate surrounding politicians' backbones. The tensions fostered by brainwashing helped reshape Americans' ideas about masculinity by affirming that a strong will and psychological tenacity were at least as critical as a strong body, since a strong, muscular man could still be psychologically raped and effeminized

The President's Council on Youth Fitness, created in 1956, would promote public awareness about America's fitness levels and ballooning waistlines for the next five decades. Ad for the President's Council on Physical Fitness during the Kennedy administration. (Courtesy of the President's Council on Fitness, Sports and Nutrition and the Ad Council Archives, Historical File, RS 13/2/207)

by the enemy if he was not mentally up to the task of fighting on the psychological battlefield. This climate of unease was responsible for a new sensitivity to men's psyches as well as to a new mental machismo. By the end of the 1950s, after hearing that members of the American Legion were voicing their discomfort about Khrushchev's scheduled trip to the United States, Sen. Lyndon B. Johnson confidently stated that Americans could "take in stride the best brainwashing he can offer."[107] Like other American men at the end of 1950s, Johnson was attempting to project confidence in the midst of a new age. Downplaying the threat of Khrushchev and his would-be brainwashers, Johnson attempted to demystify the threat of brainwashing by reassuring Americans they could stand up to the Communist psychological threat. Not everyone was so confident, as evidenced by the wide-ranging panic brainwashing provoked.

Looking back on the anxieties over motherhood, male autonomy, and physical and mental toughness in the wake of the Korean War, one can discern that Americans' concerns derived from structural changes that had radically transformed the nation after the Second World War. The United States was in the midst of an unprecedented baby boom, which naturally made motherhood and child care topics of intense debate. During the same period, many Americans were adjusting to life in the television and suburban age, and social critics simultaneously praised the benefits of postwar innovations and warned of the consequences of a sedentary lifestyle.[108] The hovering threat of Communist brainwashing and the ability of American soldiers to withstand it transformed these worries from a matter of lifestyle to a matter of life and death.

The intense focus on motherhood was rife with contradictions. The nation's mothers were publicly celebrated in public life and TV sitcoms but simultaneously derided for being overly affectionate and controlling of their sons. And, amazingly, women came under fierce criticism for what had occurred in North Korean prison camps. Notably, the convergence on male sexuality and child rearing was a way of reframing the critique of Korea. Instead of putting the blame on men and martial values, which had come up short, critics consistently argued that the principal cause of the nation's poor showing in North Korea was excessive femininity. Many critics indicated that if American mothers continued to infantilize their sons, the nation would fall to the Communist enemy. The nation reacted by formulating new ideals for boys and men that called for hard bodies and strong minds and began to idealize more stern styles of parenthood. As part 2 will show, however, by the middle of the 1950s social critics and the mainstream media would begin to point out that a number of domestic American political, economic, and cultural institutions were employing methods akin to those of Communist brainwashing and that women were just as likely to be psychologically manipulated as men. Brainwashing, initially a testament to the inhumanity of the Communist enemy and the new psychological dimensions of the Cold War, was being employed in America's own backyard.

II

"A DISQUIETING INVASION OF OUR MENTAL DOMAIN"

★ 5 ★
Hidden Persuaders on the Home Front

A B-movie released in the fall of 1958 illustrates just how far brainwashing had come by the end of the decade. Directed by Jacques Tournier and starring Dana Andrews as Alan Eaton, a former POW in North Korea, *The Fearmakers* opens with a scene that evokes many of the Korean War POW films that had come before it. As the title sequence rolls and ominous music plays in the background, a haggard-looking Eaton is repeatedly struck across the face by his Communist captors, shoved into a prison cell, and finally released at a United Nations compound with other prisoners. In the next scene, a clean-shaven Eaton, who has exchanged his filth-encrusted prison garb for a clean dress shirt and slacks, is sitting on an examining table as a doctor inspects his eyes with a penlight. After the doctor gives him a clean bill of health, Eaton appears noticeably distracted and stares blankly into the distance. Sitting down on the examining table next to him, the doctor removes his glasses, peers intently into Eaton's eyes, and warns him of the difficulties that lie ahead: "Remember, captain, you've had almost two years of Chinese prison camps. I don't need to tell you that brainwashing isn't just a word. Some of these symptoms will take time. Fatigue, the dizzy spells, lapses of memory. . . . [Don't] push yourself too hard, physically or mentally." As the doctor leaves the room, Eaton stares at his reflection in the mirror, and it is clear he will be on his own as he attempts to reassimilate into American society.

Despite the film's opening scenes, which imply that the movie deals with American POWs' experiences in recovering from Communist brainwashing, the real subject of the film is not Communist psychological warfare but its American-style equivalents. The film quickly transitions from Eaton's treatment in the prison camp to his life back home, where he had worked as an executive at a public relations firm in Washington, D.C. On attempting to return to the career that had been disrupted by the Korean

War, Eaton discovers that the firm he had built from the ground up with his partner, Claude Baker, has been taken over by Jim McGinnis, a brash, middle-aged executive who replaced Baker after he died under mysterious circumstances. Hearing the news of his longtime partner's death, Eaton nearly faints as McGinnis gruffly explains that Baker had sold Eaton's share of the company to him shortly before he had died and Eaton no longer has any control over the company he founded. Even more shocking, the firm has been radically transformed under McGinnis's leadership, and is no longer solely occupied with collecting and analyzing public opinion polls. As one character puts it, Eaton's public relations firm is now in "the profession of mass persuasion."

As Eaton struggles to adapt to his new life he becomes increasingly suspicious of McGinnis, and, after receiving a little encouragement from a former client in the Senate, he decides to work for McGinnis in order to observe his operation firsthand. To his dismay, he discovers that McGinnis is actually responsible for Baker's death and is spearheading a plot to "package politicians" and "peddle propaganda" in order to manipulate public opinion for his clients, who include an antinuclear group headed by Dr. Gregory Jessup and a Capitol Hill lobbyist named Fred Fletcher. When he finally has enough proof to expose McGinnis, Eaton angrily confronts his new boss: "You know, it's a funny thing, they have pure food and drug laws to keep people from buying poison to put in their stomachs, and you're peddling poison to put in their minds."

In the film's climactic scene Eaton chases McGinnis through the National Mall and up the steps of the Lincoln Memorial, where the two men struggle as the camera zooms in on the statue of Abraham Lincoln and then pans around them to reveal the Washington Monument in the background. After knocking McGinnis down, Eaton yells, "This is for Claude Baker and a lot of guys in Korea" and then delivers a final blow to McGinnis, who falls awkwardly down the steps of the memorial and is quickly surrounded by approaching police. Standing tall, Eaton has finally recovered from Communist brainwashing, which has plagued him with recurring fainting spells throughout the film, and has been able to summon the courage and strength to strike a literal blow for democracy. As McGinnis is dragged off in handcuffs, Eaton stands next to his secretary and, nodding toward the statue of Lincoln, says, "You know he was right. You can't fool all the people, all the time. But nowadays, you don't have to fool all the people. Just enough to swing it for the Fletchers and the Jessups." Eaton reveals that he plans to testify before a senator's committee in order to bring McGinnis's clients to justice, neatly tying up all of the film's loose ends. He then turns to his secretary and kisses her passionately, and they descend the steps of the Lincoln Memorial together.

Since the movie industry was still reeling from the aftereffects of operating under the blacklist for nearly a half decade, overt criticism of the capitalist system in Hollywood was still rare, and in many respects *The Fearmakers* was intended to be a reassuring film: a veteran of the Korean War returns to the United States, overcomes the lingering effects of Communist psychological torture, beats up the bad guy, and even secures a love interest by the film's final scene. Despite these positive outcomes, however, *The Fearmakers* offers a deeply disturbing vision of American democracy, and it is clear that Eaton has escaped Communist brainwashing only to discover similar practices being employed in the United States. Although there are vague allusions to a Communist plot behind McGinnis's operation, America's own political institutions and mass media are at the heart of the conspiracy. In a review of the film, a movie critic for the *Los Angeles Times* pointed out that the movie uncovered "the well skeletoned closets of the shadowy world of Washington lobbies and invisible pressure groups."[1] *The Fearmakers* indicated that American institutions could use billboards, radio, television, and other media to potentially pervert the entire political system and turn the United States into a fictional democracy in which elections were won by the parties with the deepest pockets and the most sophisticated advertisements.

In its implicit association of Communist psychological warfare and political machinations in the United States, *The Fearmakers* offers a riveting example of an emerging narrative in American popular culture and illustrates how popular culture stressed the similarities between brainwashing and a number of supposedly manipulative trends in domestic American society. Timothy Melley has pointed out that while brainwashing was a recurring theme in the literary fiction of the 1960s, the discourse had shifted, "converted from a conservative hysteria about foreign enemies to a liberal attack on corporate power, political conformity, and social conditioning."[2] As the plot of *The Fearmakers* demonstrates, literary fiction was part of a larger cultural reimagining of brainwashing, and by the time the film reached movie theaters in late 1958 a growing number of social critics and intellectuals were claiming that the Communist enemy was not alone in his attempts to control and manipulate American minds. These sources hinted that potential brainwashers might, in fact, be much closer to home. Such concerns went far beyond Hollywood, and anxieties generated by the work of these commentators played an important role in several congressional inquiries, a national debate on juvenile delinquency, and a critical reassessment of advertising and the mass media at midcentury. Perhaps more important, their work fueled a critique of the capitalist system at the end of the Red Scare, one which seriously undermined the Cold War consensus and cast doubt on long-held assumptions that American-style capitalist democracy was a safe haven for freedom and individuality.

Wertham, Comic Books, and Juvenile Delinquency

In the pivotal brainwashing scene of Condon's *The Manchurian Candidate* (1959), the architect of the Communist brainwashing program, Dr. Yen Lo, claims that Raymond Shaw can be manipulated to commit "antisocial actions" against his will.[3] Before inducing Shaw to provide a demonstration for the audience of eager Communist onlookers, Lo cites some legitimate academic scholarship to establish his point, including research on hypnosis, criminal behavior, and self-injury. Interestingly, he also cites a book by a renowned German American psychologist that explored the impact of American comic books on children. His inclusion of a study addressing the manipulative nature of American mass culture shows how, in American popular and literary culture, brainwashing was undergoing something of a transformation. After the concept had first come to national attention in the aftermath of the public uproar surrounding American POWs during the Korean War, it was quickly imported into the domestic political and cultural landscape, and an American public that had repeatedly been warned about the threat of sophisticated new methods of mind control began to identify techniques analogous to brainwashing on the home front.

Many of these suspicions were still directed at the Communist enemy and linked to angst about various supposed Communist plots against the American people. The right-wing opposition to the fluoridation of public drinking water in the early 1950s exemplifies many of the hallmarks of such conspiracy theories.[4] Protests contesting fluoridation had sprung up around the country, and by mid-decade debate over the issue had led to local referendums in over three hundred communities and a handful of court cases debating its constitutionality at the state and national levels. Many protestors took issue with fluoridation on scientific and religious grounds, believing the idea that the campaign was based on unsound science and bypassed individuals' freedom of choice. A vocal minority, however, held that fluoridation was part of a larger Communist conspiracy and a direct attack on American autonomy. A housewife from San Francisco named Golda Franzen, for example, said that fluoridation would turn Americans into "moronic, atheistic slaves" and ultimately "weaken the minds of the people and make them prey to the Communists."[5] Ultraright groups like the Ku Klux Klan and the John Birch Society echoed variations of Franzen's sentiments, and paranoia over fluoridation remained prominent in some circles for decades. The links these groups made between fluoridation and Communist psychological warfare highlights how the threat posed by brainwashing had moved out of Manchuria and into America.

Because brainwashing had made Americans extremely self-conscious about their subconscious, for the rest of the decade the entire nation collectively had its mind on the brain, and the themes of brainwashing, mind control, and psychological manipulation would continuously inform public discourse. Prior to the outbreak of the Korean War a number of scholars and cultural critics had been charging for years that American society and culture were psychologically manipulative—in fact, this had been a recurring critique throughout the twentieth century. In the midst of a heated public debate over the psychological effects of the mainstream media, popular culture, and advertising, these critics started to discuss American culture in terms that directly evoked Communist psychological warfare, arguing that it was almost equally oppressive. The notion that Communists were alone in their pursuit of the American psyche was quickly dispelled, as both grassroots protest groups and several congressional hearings began to examine the supposedly overt psychological manipulation being employed on the home front by American cultural mediums and the mainstream media.

One of the most prominent social critics to link psychological manipulation with American popular culture and the establishment media was the man cited by Yen Lo in *The Manchurian Candidate,* Fredric Wertham. A Jewish German American expert on child psychology who had immigrated to the United States in the 1920s and served as a senior psychiatrist in the Department of Hospitals in New York City for nearly two decades, Wertham was a relatively well known public figure by the 1940s, but in the 1950s he became a household name. Starting in 1951, when he evaluated Ethel Rosenberg at the request of her lawyer while she was awaiting trial for espionage, he began to appear with greater frequency on the national stage. In the same year, the Delaware chapter of the National Association for the Advancement of Colored People enlisted Wertham's expertise in its attempt to overturn segregation in the state's public school system. At the association's request Wertham embarked on a series of studies to determine the psychological impact of school segregation on schoolchildren. His findings would eventually be cited in *Brown v. Board of Education,* the landmark Supreme Court decision in 1954 that arguably helped pave the way for the desegregation of the nation's public school system.[6] His work on these matters thrust him into the national spotlight, but it was his research on comic books that truly captured the public imagination, in large part because it linked three issues that had a strong grasp on postwar American society: popular culture, juvenile delinquency, and the subconscious American mind.

Wertham's specific target was crime comic books, and he worked tirelessly to establish a connection between children's comics and juvenile delinquency. One of his first articles about comic books aimed at a popular audience, published in 1948 in the *Saturday Review of Literature,* opened with a troubling anecdote:

> An anxious mother consulted me some time ago. Her four-year-old daughter is the only little girl in their apartment house. Whenever they get a chance the boys in the building, ranging in age from three to nine years, beat her with toy guns, tie her up with rope. They manacle her with handcuffs bought with coupons from comic books. They take her to a vacant lot and use her as a target for bow and arrow. Once they pulled off her panties, to torture her (as they put it). What is the common denominator in all this? Is it the "natural aggression" of little boys? Is it the manifestation of the sex instinct? Is it the release of natural tendencies or the initiation of unnatural ones? The common denominator is comic books.

The anecdote became a blueprint for Wertham's subsequent allegations, which were filled with similar stories of children and adolescents reenacting scenes culled from comic books. According to Wertham, comic books directly acted on children's behavior and were responsible for an epidemic in juvenile delinquency. As he explained to a reporter the same year, "We are dealing with the mental health of a generation—the care of which we have left too long in the hands of unscrupulous persons whose only interest is greed and financial gain."[7]

For the next several years Wertham addressed audiences around the country about the unsavory effects of comic books. In 1948, at a symposium titled "The Psychopathology of Comic Books," he announced, "You cannot understand present-day juvenile delinquency if you do not take into account the pathogenic and pathoplastic influence of the comic books."[8] A few months later Wertham told an audience of prison officials that an ordinance against comic books was necessary in order to protect children's minds from "pollution" that suggested "criminal or sexually abnormal ideas and [created] an atmosphere of deceit, trickery and cruelty." Some comics, Wertham suggested to the officials, might even encourage racism.[9] By 1951 he had taken his criticism all the way to the New York State legislature, where he testified in a public hearing before the Joint Legislative Committee to Study Comics and condemned comics as "the cause of a psychological mutilation of children."[10]

The critique of comic books predated Wertham by nearly a decade and can be traced back to the early 1940s, when a handful of religious groups began questioning their morality and a number of literary critics, educators, and librarians disparaged their quality.[11] In 1940, for example, Sterling North, the *Chicago Daily News* literary editor, pronounced that comic books were "badly written and badly printed—a strain on young eyes and young nervous systems—the effect of these pulp-paper nightmares is that of a violent stimulant."[12] Like North, many of the early critics denounced comics' artistic value and raised concerns about their potential impact on young readers, but, as the historian David Hajdu has noted, Wertham was the first to give the crusade against comics a public face.[13] With his penchant for theatrics, heavy German accent, and horn-rimmed glasses, Wertham was a veritable stereotype of the 1950s academic, and if a comic book illustrator at the time had been tasked with producing a drawing of a psychologist, she or he might have come up with an image approximating Wertham's likeness. Wertham also made for a memorable and authoritative public figure, and although the comic book industry attempted to paint him as a humorless social conservative who favored censorship over free speech, his track record proved he had been a staunch progressive reformer of social causes for decades.

Throughout the early 1950s, partially spurred on by Wertham's work, the debate over comic books would become a national issue, and although Wertham was the most ambitious and authoritative figure in the professional ranks of the anticomics crusade, the movement was also the product of a great deal of grassroots activism. Starting with a handful of Catholic schools in 1945, public burnings of comic books began to occur with alarming regularity in the years after the Second World War. In December 1947 a public burning was organized by students at St. Gall's School on the southwest side of Chicago, where over three thousand comic books were gathered and burned. Roughly six months later, in the fall of 1948, a group of students in Spencer, West Virginia, encouraged by a teacher who had the backing of the local parent–teacher association, started a local campaign against comics and, after collecting over two thousand of them, lit them ablaze in a giant bonfire behind the school with all of the students and staff looking on. In the next two months there were similar burnings at two Catholic parochial schools in New York. And early the next year a Girl Scout troop in Missouri organized a campaign against comic books that culminated in a public burning at a local Catholic high school.[14]

The grassroots activism against comics was eventually matched by legislation, starting in Detroit, which banned thirty-six comics from newsstands in 1948. Fifty municipalities and nineteen states quickly followed suit until the Supreme Court ruled that many of these legislative acts were unconstitutional. Despite the Supreme Court's ruling, the door was left wide open for future regulation of the comic book industry.[15] By the middle of 1948 comic book publishers were attempting to combat this negative publicity by promoting their own attempts at self-regulation, which led to the creation of the Association of Comic Magazine Publishers and a new regulatory code. Although much of the anticomics legislation in the late 1940s was ultimately unsuccessful and the comic book industry's efforts were met with a great deal of skepticism, together they helped temporarily subdue the furor.[16] That American comic books were banned in Britain in the 1950s implies that the groups working to censor them in the United States were not simply emblematic of some conservative puritanical streak in the American public. Even a cursory analysis of the actual comic books of the period makes it clear why they were beginning to raise some alarms. By almost any contemporary standard, a sizable percentage of the comics depicted scenes that were gory or sexually suggestive, and many of the stories were violent. But the reaction to the comics was at least as disturbing as their content.

Although the crusade against comics had much deeper roots and extended far beyond Wertham, his emphasis on the relationship between comic books and the psychology of American children distinguished him from other critics. Wertham held that comic books were not simply a bad influence in that their negative consequences extended beyond mere mimicry. Using examples from his experience as a psychiatrist to support his argument, Wertham averred that the impact of comic books on the nation's youth was visible in a number of disturbing new trends in the behavior of American children. These previously overlooked tendencies pointed to widespread psychological maladjustment in the nation's youth, including the increasingly violent images children saw in Rorschach tests, a precipitous rise in eye gouging and eye injuries in children, frequent reports of violent and sadistic torture play taking place in playgrounds and school yards nationwide, and the rise of juvenile delinquency and petty vandalism across the country.

In 1954 Wertham's magnum opus on the topic, *Seduction of the Innocent,* was published to broad acclaim and helped reignite the national debate on comic books. The book reiterated many of the arguments Wertham had been making for years, contending that comics had an adverse effect "on the minds and behavior of children who come in contact with them" and classifying *Superman, Batman, Wonder Woman,* and a number of other popular comic books as crime comics.[17] "Children's minds are at least as sensitive and vulnerable as a man's stomach," Wertham argued, and children's constant exposure to violence, racism, sexist imagery, and crime represented a form of "comic-book indoctrination" that had a profound psychological effect on budding American minds.[18]

One of the most serious allegations in the book was Wertham's assertion that the proliferation of crime comic books was a central factor in the rise of drug use among minors. Pointing to the cases of nearly "1,500 teen-age dope addicts" in New York City by the late 1940s, Wertham maintained that before the spread of comic books there were nearly no documented cases of drug use among children, and he wrote that in his experience "all child drug addicts, and all children drawn into the narcotics traffic as messengers . . . were inveterate comic-book readers."[19] Wertham thought this was not a coincidence and that comic books were promoting drug use in children by "softening them up for the temptation of taking drugs and letting themselves be drawn into participation in the illegal drug traffic."[20]

In addition to contributing to a new epidemic in drug use by young people, comic books, Wertham contended, encouraged racial hatred. Analyzing the plots of several popular comic book series, he pointed out that they routinely separated humanity into two distinct groups: "On the one hand is the tall, blond, regular-featured man sometimes disguised as a superman . . . and the pretty young blond girl with the super-breast. On the other hand are the inferior people, natives, primitives, savages, 'ape men,' Negroes, Jews, Indians, Italians, Slavs, Chinese and Japanese, immigrants of every description, people with irregular features, swarthy skins, physical deformities, Oriental features."[21] Almost universally, the blond men and women were superheroes while nonwhites and Eastern Europeans were depicted as "criminals, gangsters, rapers, suitable victims for slaughter by either the lawless or the law."[22] Based on his interviews with children and a handful of violent, racially charged incidents, Wertham believed this imagery was beginning to sway children's perception of racial groups and leading many young comic book readers to conflate the qualities of comic's bad guys with the inherent characteristics of nonwhite races. The frequency of "rape-like" scenarios featuring white women being attacked and physically threatened by nonwhite men, often to be rescued by a white superhero, was especially troublesome because it upheld old stereotypes of the lascivious nature of nonwhites. Wertham noted that while white female characters' sexuality was something to be honored and safeguarded in the comics, nonwhite females were portrayed as willing, even eager, victims of sexual exploitation, and it was deemed acceptable to draw them, but not white females, with "bared breasts" and in various sexually suggestive poses. This pattern was yet another sign of the racism on display in comic books, and, Wertham warranted, the racial stereotypes they promoted were beginning to turn some young children into hardened racists before they even reached middle school.

Given the national obsession with sexuality during the early postwar years, not surprisingly Wertham devoted an entire chapter to comic books' impact on children's sexual development. The chapter begins with an anecdote of a young comic book reader who, on being asked what he wanted to be when he grew up, blurted out, "I want to be a sex maniac!"[23] To Wertham, the child's comment testified to the hypersexuality of comic books, which he claimed were almost universally homoerotic, sexually stimulating, and replete with imagery that featured the muscular physique of male characters and commonly depicted female characters in tight-fitting, revealing clothing. If a child knew where to look, there were even subliminal pornographic images hidden in plain sight. Wertham documented one example of a subtly salacious "picture within a picture" in a male character's shoulder and right arm, which when magnified and turned to the side appeared to bear a striking resemblance to a woman's bare legs and genitalia. These accusations indicated that comics were essentially no better than pornography, and Wertham questioned the morality and long-term consequences of exposing young children to such sexually explicit material.

Because comics frequently intertwined sex and cruelty or violence, Wertham believed they were inducing an entire generation to become sexual sadists. As he put it, "The short circuit which connects violence with sex is a primitive pattern slumbering in all people. It can easily be released in children if it is drilled into them early enough and long enough."[24] In boys, the consequence of this onslaught on the senses was a connection between sexual arousal and violence, which often had a devastating effect on their behavior and interactions with women. In girls, it led to "fear of sex, fear of men and actual frigidity."[25] In addition to inculcating in the nation's youth unhealthy attitudes toward members of the opposite sex, Wertham argued, comics instilled or reinforced homoerotic tendencies in children. Wertham pinpointed the "psychologically homosexual" relationship between Batman and Robin, describing their home life as "a wish dream of two homosexuals living together"[26] and their "Lesbian counterpart" in the Wonder Woman and Black Cat comics, whose stories were "anti-masculine" and featured female superheroes that symbolized "the cruel, 'phallic' woman."[27] In sum, Wertham alleged, comics contributed to the unhealthy sexual development of children and in some cases even subconsciously affected their sexual practices later in life.

According to Fredric Wertham, if children knew where to look they could find pornography in comic books. This image of "subliminal sexual imagery" from Jungle Comics #98, published by Fiction House in February 1948, was highlighted by Wertham in his seminal work, *Seduction of the Innocent* (1954).

Several years before the publication of Wertham's book, parents around the country had articulated their apprehensions about the impact of comic books on their children's minds. For example, a mother wrote to Wertham in 1948 that when her two boys were "in the presence of comic books they behave as if drugged, and will not lift their eyes or speak when spoken to." After attributing her sons' behavioral problems to comics, she stated somewhat hysterically, "We consider the situation to be as serious as an invasion of the enemy in war time, with as far reaching consequences as the atom bomb. If we cannot stop the wicked men who are poisoning our children's minds, what chance is there for mankind to survive longer than one generation, or half of one?"[28] The arguments about the negative impacts of comic books published in *Seduction of the Innocent* not only substantiated these fears about the medium, but also postulated that comics reached further into young children's psyches than parents had ever imagined.

Wertham framed the battle over comic books as a war between the nation's democratic ideals and the comic industry, with young American minds hanging in the balance. On the basis of years of research and ample anecdotal evidence, he concluded that comic books represented the "mass conditioning of children" and argued that they had the potential to shape children's "super-ego" and subconsciously indoctrinate them into a life of crime, drug abuse, and homosexuality.[29] *Seduction of the Innocent* went on to become a minor best-seller, but, more important, it thrust comic books back into the national spotlight. Its publication in April 1954 was particularly timely in light of the fact that the book was published in the midst of a national debate about the behavior of American POWs, who had been released from Communist prison camps only a few months earlier. By affirming that comic books "conditioned" and "indoctrinated" those who read them and by relating American children's behavior, desires, ideas, and sexuality to external forces that aimed to psychologically seduce them and appeal to their most base instincts in order to turn a profit, Wertham offered compelling evidence that American mass culture was waging its very own brand of psychological warfare and intruding on young Americans' minds as forcibly as Communist brainwashing.

"The Wild Orgies of Cavemen"

In the fall of 1953 Sen. Robert C. Hendrickson of New Jersey announced plans for a congressional subcommittee on juvenile delinquency to carry out investigations in twenty cities with "juvenile gang problems" around the country. In comments to the press, Hendrickson said that the main objective of the subcommittee was to "find out what is causing this increasingly serious problem and what can effectively be done to prevent it. It is not simply an urban or a poor people's problem and we intend to gather information concerning our rural situations as well."[30]

In February 1954 Hendrickson referenced the "significant public concern over the possible harmful effects of comic books on the young mind" when he announced that the committee would explore the possible links between juvenile delinquency and comic books.[31] As one of the nation's preeminent experts on comic books, Wertham caught the committee's attention, and in the same month that *Seduction of the Innocent* was published he was called to New York City to testify before the Senate Subcommittee on Juvenile Delinquency.[32]

When Wertham appeared before the subcommittee on April 21 he was armed with a handful of obscene comic books and prepared to make his case. He began by launching into an extensive discussion of his credentials as an authority on child psychology and stated that there were connections between his early research on brain disorders and his more recent work on the psychological effects of comic books on children. After his opening statement, Wertham essentially reiterated the main arguments in his book, testifying that "normal children" were harmed by comics the most because they presented them with ideas and images they otherwise would never encounter. The subcommittee was responsive to Wertham's argument, and Sen. Estes Kefauver, a Democrat from Tennessee, responded to his testimony by commenting on the similarities between comic books and Nazi propaganda. Wertham emphatically agreed, announcing, "I think Hitler was a beginner compared to the comic-book industry. They get the children much younger. They teach them race hatred at the age of four, before they can read."[33]

Of all the testimony given at the day's proceedings, nothing caused more of a stir in the press than the oft-quoted exchange between Senator Kefauver and the president of EC Comics, William Gaines. Gaines's company was behind some of the most infamous comic books of the period, including the horror-themed *Tales from the Crypt* and *Weird Science* and the wildly popular *Mad* magazine. In 1954 the company sold nearly two million comics a month. In testimony to the committee, Gaines said he opposed censorship and heartily disagreed with Wertham's contention that comic books contributed to juvenile delinquency. Gaines emphasized that he did not believe any normal, healthy child had ever been ruined by a comic book and that everything EC Comics published was within the limits of good taste. This prompted Senator Kefauver to hold up a recent EC comic book titled *Shock SuspenStories* that prominently depicted an axe-wielding maniac holding the severed head of a woman on its cover, and he asked Gaines, "Do you think that is in good taste?" Gaines responded, "Yes, sir; I do, for the cover of a horror comic. A cover in bad taste, for example, might be defined as holding the head a little higher so that the neck could be seen dripping blood from it and moving the body over a little further so that the neck of the body could be seen to be bloody."[34]

Kefauver claimed that the cover and Gaines's defense of it were shocking. As the literary scholar Bart Beaty has written, "The negative reaction to this particular exchange harmed the comic book defenders as much or more than anything that Wertham testified to, especially as it seemed to prove that comics publishers were out of touch with the concerns of the day."[35] Certainly, the exchange between Kefauver and Gaines highlights one of the overarching themes in the national debate about the effects of mass culture on the American people in the 1950s, namely, the distinction between good and bad taste. The issue of aesthetic value would crop up repeatedly, and the debate over such questions signaled the beginning of a major culture war in American society, as diverse groups battled for cultural supremacy and contested the limits of mass culture and public decency. On the one hand, businessmen like Gaines advocated consumer rights and fought for freedom of expression. On the other, men such as Wertham proclaimed the necessity of establishing community standards in order to protect America's youth.[36]

When Wertham testified in front of members of Congress, he had declared, "As long as crime and horror comic books are published, no American home is safe."[37] The subcommittee agreed with him, and although the final report of the hearings did not directly blame the comic industry for juvenile delinquency, it recommended that comic book companies begin censoring their products by toning down scenes of overt violence and sexuality. In the face of mounting public pressure, the Comics Code Authority was formed in 1954 to enforce industrywide standards and to counteract the negative publicity surrounding comics. Gaines's EC Comics was one of the first victims of the new code. Because the words *horror, crime, weird,* and *terror* were no longer allowed in comic book titles, several of EC Comics' long-standing and most popular publications were forced to change their titles or were simply discontinued. In addition, the Comics Code Authority's restrictions on the depiction of vampires, werewolves, and zombies forced EC Comics to stop producing several of its popular horror-themed comic books. By 1955 EC Comics was nearly bankrupt, and the only EC title to survive was *Mad* magazine.

After the congressional hearings on comic books adjourned in April, the issue of comic book regulation captured national attention. Commenting on the public's reaction, a journalist for the *Los Angeles Times* proclaimed, "High feeling against filthy comic books is reaching the boiling point. The menace of criminal comics is a point of discussion whenever two parents of young children meet."[38] The comic industry's efforts at sanitizing their product ultimately did not suppress the public's outcry for action, and grassroots activism against comics started becoming prominent yet again, as a rule culminating in public comic book burnings. Eventually, regulations were passed by state legislatures around the country, and it would take the comic book industry nearly a decade to recover from the negative publicity. Although the Senate Subcommittee on Juvenile Delinquency never completely adopted Wertham's position, his testimony subtly shaped the tone of the entire congressional debate and shifted the subcommittee's focus from the supposed obscenity of comic books to their impact on children's minds.

T. E. Murphy, a columnist for the *Hartford Courant* and a central figure in the campaign for comic book regulation in Connecticut, captured the sentiments of many parents in a *Reader's Digest* article published in June 1954. In order to understand the comic book phenomenon more fully, Murphy began reading the books in question, only to discover "the most

A scoutmaster drops several comic books into a bonfire in October 1954, as the boy scouts who participated in a house-to-house collection of horror, crime, and sex comics look on in the background. (AP Images)

depraved pictorial material I have ever seen." In the article, Murphy sensationally related his findings:

> I have waded through hundreds of comics in recent weeks. I feel as though I have been trudging through a sewer. Here is a terrible twilight zone between sanity and madness, an area peopled by monsters, grave robbers, human-flesh eaters. Here everything that the human mind has come to venerate and respect through the years of civilization is spat upon and trampled. Here ordinary murder is mild—mix it with sex, mayhem, adultery, patricide, matricide, necrophilia, vampirism. Only in the tamest volumes is a character permitted to die by knife or gun. This is the literary offal we have been permitting a few conscienceless publishers to pour into the minds of our children—for profit![39]

For critics like Murphy and Wertham, the issue posed by comic books was not strictly a matter of taste, but of the long-term consequences of "pour[ing]" bad taste "into the minds of our children."

Several historians have concluded that the comic book scare was primarily fueled by anxiety over new cultural mediums and an emerging commercial youth culture. For example, James Gilbert has described the debate over mass culture in the 1950s as "a struggle in which the participants were arguing over power—over who had the right and responsibility to shape American culture."[40] And Hajdu has written that the central issue in the public debate over comics "was not really juvenile crime or mental health or literacy or the effect of comic-book printing on the eyes, but the idea of *taste*."[41] As the press coverage of Gaines's responses to Kefauver's pointed questions demonstrates, these issues were without doubt factors in the public's obsession with comics. But ultimately Wertham's testimony before members of Congress reminded observers of what was truly at stake in the battle over comic book regulation. The issue raised by supposedly indecent comics was not simply about who was exercising cultural authority or the supposedly debased quality of mass culture, but also about the danger mass culture posed to the psychological development of American children. The sanctity of young children's minds was the overriding concern of the entire debate and the issue that motivated so many Americans to push for legislation and take part in public demonstrations in the first place.

Throughout the fifties Congress explored this issue again and again, specifically analyzing the ties between new cultural mediums, juvenile delinquency, and young American minds. In 1951 Rep. E. C. Gathings of Arkansas pushed for a congressional inquiry into television because he believed the new mass medium was "corrupting the minds and morals of the American people."[42] On the floor of the House of Representatives in June 1952, Gathings decried the prevalence of violent crime shows and the "low necklines" of female entertainers and blamed perceived obscene television entertainment for a rise in juvenile delinquency and the "recent panty raids at colleges."[43] Between 1952 and 1955 there were three separate congressional inquiries that explored the effects of television violence on young children. In 1954 the Senate Subcommittee on Juvenile Delinquency began to review films and televised gangster and western programs to determine, as Senator Hendrickson put it, "what effect these programs have on the juvenile mind."[44] And in 1955 psychiatrists testified in front of another congressional inquiry on film violence that "impressions gained by viewing pictures would . . . serve as 'trigger mechanisms' to set off latent tendencies of abnormal behavior."[45]

By the end of the 1950s and the early 1960s psychiatrists and the media were discussing television in terms that implied it had a much more powerful effect than Gathings had originally imagined.[46] For example, the clinical psychologist Murray Korngold of Los Angeles publicly likened television to propaganda, stating that "any kind of sustained propaganda will influence the people who are being propagandized. If you expose a child often enough to the explicit statement that killing is commonplace, then surely he's going to believe that killing is commonplace."[47] A number of prominent psychologists made similar arguments, contending that television desensitized children to violence and murder and as a result could potentially mark their behavior.[48] Many ordinary Americans shared this sentiment. In 1957 a woman serving on the Citizens' Committee on Literature in Newport, Rhode Island, compared American mass culture directly to brainwashing. After watching two films specifically marketed to teenage audiences, *Rock All Night* (1957) and *Dragstrip Girl* (1957), she reported her experience to the committee: "Isn't it a form of brainwashing? Brainwashing the minds of the people and especially the youth of the nation in filth and sadistic violence. What enemy technique could better lower patriotism and national morale than the constant presentation of crime and horror both as news and recreation?"[49] The implication of her comments was clear: American popular culture was potentially as destructive as Communist psychological warfare.

Misgivings about popular culture was not limited to comic books, television, and film. Nearly as soon as it emerged as a viable form of commercial youth culture, rock 'n' roll also provoked a wave of negative publicity. As early as 1952 Aldous Huxley had written about the potential music had to shape individual behavior:

> No man, however highly civilized, can listen for very long to African drumming, or Indian chanting, or Welsh hymn singing, and retain intact his critical and self-conscious personality. It would be interesting to take a group of the most eminent philosophers from the best universities, shut them up in a hot room with Moroccan dervishes or Haitian Voodooists, and measure, with a stop-watch, the strength of their psychological resistance to the effects of rhythmic sound. . . . Meanwhile, all we can safely predict is that, if exposed long enough to the tom-toms and the singing, every one of our philosophers would end by capering and howling with the savages."[50]

Experts and parents around the country agreed that rock 'n' roll had a similar effect on teenagers, and in 1955 the Senate Subcommittee on Juvenile Delinquency once again explored the relationship between juvenile crime and mass culture, this time by homing in on the effects of rock 'n' roll.

When the rock 'n' roll craze swept the nation in the early 1950s many social commentators questioned its long-term impact on the youth of America and nervously explored its effects on teenage behavior. In a worried letter to the *New York Times*, the clinical psychologist Stanley Rudin argued that rock 'n' roll was simply one part of a larger corporate assault on young American consumers, who had become the main "target of as greedy and conscienceless a bunch of disk jockeys, song writers, motion picture producers, TV writers and other assorted hucksters as ever peddled opium."[51] Other critics agreed that rock 'n' roll was potentially as addictive, morally corrosive, and mentally destructive as comic books and television and perhaps even opiates.

An event hosted by Alan Freed, one of the most prominent rock 'n' roll disc jockeys in the country, at the Paramount Theatre in Times Square on February 22 and 23, 1957, underscored many of the reasons parents and psychologists fretted over rock music. The theater was hosting a two-day screening of the film *Don't Knock the Rock,* starring Freed, who was on hand to publicize the film with a number of live music acts. On the opening day teenagers began lining up outside the theater at 4 a.m., and when the doors opened at eight o'clock that morning the disorderly crowd rushed forward, breaking the glass window of the box office in the process. For the remainder of the day teenagers poured into the theater by the thousands, and outside the Paramount the crowd at its peak was estimated at 10,500. Traffic on the surrounding streets came to a standstill, and for nearly two and a half hours Forty-third Street was blocked off to motorists. As the day wore on, the crowd still waiting to get in grew more and more restless, until the city sent 175 policemen to the theater to keep the peace. The *New York Times* reported that by late morning teenagers were throwing the contents of their lunch boxes, shouting at mounted police officers, and pushing each other and the officers in a frenzied attempt to get into the theater. Once they made their way inside, they danced in the aisles and enthusiastically stamped their feet to the music, prompting inspectors from the fire department to temporarily shut down the second balcony.[52]

The next day the theater had 279 officers on hand to keep the teenage audience in line, and police patrolled the aisles, chased dancers back to their seats, and ordered teenagers who were standing on their chairs to sit down. According to media coverage of the event, despite the enhanced police presence the scene remained chaotic, especially inside the theater. Members of the audience continuously attempted to rush into the aisles to dance, and a line of police officers standing shoulder to shoulder had to block the stage to prevent teen revelers from rushing Freed and the musicians.[53] Only one arrest was made—a twenty-year-old woman struck a female police officer and was arrested for simple assault—but the main reading of the event, at least judging by the mainstream media, was that rock 'n' roll turned teenagers into crazed, gyrating delinquents.

The *New York Times* described the audience as "devotees of the rock 'n' roll cult," while a headline in the *Chicago Daily Tribune* blared, "Rock 'n'

"Rock 'n' roll addicts" dancing in the aisles of Paramount Theatre in New York City during a screening of Alan Freed's film *Don't Knock the Rock* in February 1957. (Bettman/Corbis/AP Images)

Roll Addicts Take Over Times Sq."[54] Many experts at the time agreed that there was indeed something cultish and addicting about rock 'n' roll. By sheer coincidence a meeting of the American Psychopathological Association took place at the Park Sheraton Hotel in midtown Manhattan, just down the block from the theater, the same day as the Paramount concert. Given the hotel's proximity to the theater, it is likely that many attendees of the association's meeting had come in direct contact with the teenage crowd, and the event became a hot topic of debate throughout the day's proceedings. Several of the psychologists present asserted that their profession had already established that "10 to 20 per cent of all children did 'some act like rocking or rolling,' " and although they likened the rock 'n' roll "craze" to "rhythmic behavior patterns" as old as the Middle Ages, the consensus that day was that rock 'n' roll was potentially dangerous and called for further study.

Joost Meerloo, who had formerly played a central role in the scholarly debate over brainwashing, was a primary figure in the debate over rock 'n' roll and made public comments about the incident at the Paramount. He compared the teenage crowd's behavior to St. Vitus Dance and Tarantism and argued that rock 'n' roll's ability to get teenagers to dance themselves "into a prehistoric rhythmic trance" could have potential political implications if politicians used music to manipulate large public crowds. He concluded that "rock 'n' roll is a sign of depersonalization of the individual, of ecstatic veneration of mental decline and passivity. If we cannot stem the tide with its waves of rhythmic narcosis and of future waves of vicarious craze, we are preparing our own downfall in the midst of pandemic funeral dances."[55] According to experts like Meerloo, rock 'n' roll represented a real threat to the nation's mental health and could potentially be used to exert control over a naïve public, which only further fueled public speculation that rock 'n' roll was turning naïve American teenagers into crazed delinquents.

A great deal of the public debate on rock 'n' roll dwelled on its inherent quality, or lack thereof, as critics reacted to the popularity of the new cultural medium with equal parts condescension and perplexity. For example, a quip reprinted in the "Pepper . . . and Salt" section of the *Wall Street Journal* in 1957 snidely observed, "The advantage of buying rock and roll records is that when they wear out you can't tell the difference."[56] Even the Soviets got in on the act when the former foreign minister Dmitri T. Shepilov told an audience of Soviet composers that rock 'n' roll was a symptom of America's lack of sophistication and derisively sniffed, "All this nervous and insane boogie woogie and rock 'n' roll are the wild orgies of cavemen."[57] The article reporting Shepilov's comments slyly noted that Elvis Presley records were the latest rage among the youth of Leningrad, where they were reportedly being sold on the black market, so it appeared that the youth of the Soviet Union was just as addicted to the rock 'n' roll craze as their American counterparts.

Experts and the public alike agreed that the merits of rock 'n' roll as a new cultural medium were not as potentially catastrophic as the music's tendency to turn teenage audiences into frenzied addicts who lost all vestiges of self-control and inhibition. The larger historical context was that at that time the United States was actively using American popular music as propaganda in Soviet bloc countries, an activity that did not go unnoticed in America.[58] A satirical article in the *Wall Street Journal* published in the wake of the Soviet Union's launch of *Sputnik 1* played on this theme when it claimed that Western pop music could turn the "Red propaganda victory" into another example of "Soviet crimes against humanity" by simply changing the public narrative of the event. After listing a variety of ways in which humans' exploration of space would change lyrical norms in popular music, the article closed by saying, "Once these songs begin orbiting around the world's loud-speakers and jukeboxes, the tide of world opinion will turn against Russia."[59] If American popular music was being used to shape public opinion abroad, did it not stand to reason that it could shape public opinion in domestic American society?

Anxieties about mass culture predated the rise of television and rock 'n' roll, and there was similar consternation about the hypnotic powers of film dating back to nearly the dawn of the cinema age.[60] By the late 1940s these long-standing uncertainties had merged with the anti-Communist fervor of the era, and this ethos hung over the examination of Hollywood by the House Un-American Activities Committee and that body's perception that Communists were not only controlling popular culture but also using it to deploy propaganda to an unknowing public. If worry over the effects of mass culture on the youth of the nation was part of a larger cyclical or "episodic notion," as at least one historian has asserted, by the 1950s it had become noticeably more severe and underscored new doubts about the vulnerability of American's minds.[61]

Between 1952 and 1960 the public debate over the supposed cause-and-effect relation of juvenile delinquency and the new commercialized youth culture of the 1950s occurred virtually in lockstep with an equally contentious discussion of the extent of Communist brainwashing on American servicemen in the Korean War. Brainwashing offered a new way of thinking about and discussing mass culture, and although mass culture had certainly been coupled with propaganda and psychological manipulation before the Korean War the rise of brainwashing as a cultural phenomenon led the public and experts to adopt an even more radical interpretation of the psychological potential of mass culture and its ability to influence, manipulate, and control the youth of the nation. Many Americans judged that there was good reason to be wary of certain forms of popular culture, and the work of several well-known scholars gave politicians like Senators Kefauver and Gathings an intellectual impetus to favor censorship. More significant, since academics and politicians equated the mass media with propaganda and indoctrination, the American public was told that just as the Communist enemy could potentially infiltrate the country and brainwash unwilling Americans, so comic books, television, movies, and rock 'n' roll could prey on young minds and turn a nation of innocent adolescents into violent delinquents. For the first time during the Cold War, the citizenry was expressly informed that their minds were being attacked by an enemy that was not Communist. In the mid- and late 1950s, this perception would be amplified by the work of Vance Packard and James Vicary.

"I Think I Want a Hot Dog"

An article titled "Most Hidden Hidden Persuasion" published in the *New York Times* on January 12, 1958, described a coming revolution in American advertising, the "hidden commercial, or phantom plug," which the article claimed was "painless, odorless, non-fattening and very sneaky."[62] The commercials were projected on television and movie screens so quickly that viewers were not even conscious of receiving a sales pitch, and although the technique had reportedly been used only to push specific consumer products so far, the article reported that it could potentially be used to promote almost anything: "Vote for Lionel Smudge. Drink More Strega. Take Off Your Hat. Abjure Fleshy Lusts."[63] The story was accompanied by a series of illustrations that painted a vivid portrait of these new commercials in action. The first showcased an entire family in their living room, their faces all transfixed by a larger-than-life television set. There was a western on the screen featuring two cowboys with guns drawn and pointed at each other, but the real focus of the illustration was nine tiny little angels—or demons, depending on your perspective—floating through the ether and whispering into each family member's ear. Cigarettes and shaving products were being pitched to the father, the virtues of a particular brand of household cleaning products were being extolled to the mother, a line of cosmetics was being described to the teenage daughter, and the infant son, standing alertly in his crib and staring at the television, was being sold a prescription against, of all things, subliminal ads. Even the family dog was not immune to the subliminal Madison Avenue sprites, as one held up its ear and whispered into it a sales pitch for dog food. Another illustration showed a pair of waif-like hands eerily stretching out of a television screen, with a male viewer seemingly under their spell. On the last page of the article appeared an image of a man and woman walking side by side, the subconscious sprites now looming larger than both adults and apparently continuing to impress their victims even after they were no longer in front of a television screen.

The article and the illustrations were a direct response to the work of the social critic Vance Packard, the author of *The Hidden Persuaders* (1957), which quickly climbed to the top of the *New York Times* best-seller list and was described by one reviewer as "easily the most frightening book of the year."[64] Packard's central argument was that politicians, corporate executives, and big business were employing "large-scale efforts . . . often with impressive success, to channel our unthinking habits, our purchasing decisions, and our thought processes by the use of insights gleaned from psychiatry and the social sciences."[65] Writing that Americans were being "treated like Pavlov's conditioned dog," Packard argued that hidden persuaders had probed deep into the collective American subconscious, exploring "why we are afraid of banks; why we love those big fat cars; why we really buy homes; why men smoke cigars; why the kind of car we draw reveals the brand of gasoline we will buy; why housewives typically fall into a hypnoidal trance when they get into a supermarket; why men are drawn into auto showrooms by convertibles but end up buying sedans; why junior loves cereal that pops, snaps, and crackles."[66] Putting this research to work, advertisers and the psychologists and social scientists they had on staff were finding new ways to prey on Americans' hidden insecurities and desires in order to "manipulate our habits and choices." Nothing was sacred to these researchers, and they left no stone unturned, as Packard documented by citing their use of "psychiatric probing" of little girls and their exploration of the effect of women's menstrual cycles on family food purchases. These types of practices led Packard to deduce that the United States was quickly moving "from the genial world of James Thurber into the chilling world of George Orwell and his Big Brother."[67]

Packard built on the work of several postwar intellectuals who criticized the manipulative aspects of consumer culture and the advertising industry, but he offered new insight into how American corporations used the tools of modern psychology to shape public opinion in their favor.[68] To demonstrate the corporate use of psychology, he focused on examples that illustrated the tools corporations and businesses had at their disposal. One relatively banal example that encompassed many of his points was the commercial resurrection of the common prune. According to Packard, depth probers and motivation researchers using word-association tests had discovered that the prune had become commonly associated with a number of negative words and images: *old maid, dried up, laxative.* Applying the results of their studies, they recommended advertisements that pictured the prune in bright, lively colors and being eaten by young, happy children. Sales immediately went up, and "in its public image the prune became a true-life Cinderella!"[69] As this example illustrates, Packard was not arguing that the use of new advances in market research and psychology were entirely diabolical or sinister. In some cases, as in the case of the prune, the results were hardly foreboding. Still, Packard found many of the recent developments in marketing, advertising, and political campaigns to be disquieting.

In 1956 the president of the Public Relations Society of America told a meeting of the society's members that "the stuff with which we work is the fabric of men's minds."[70] Packard said that the comment was proof that merchandisers, publicists, fundraisers, personnel experts, and politicians were pushing the United States away from its traditional ideals of personal autonomy and freedom. Packard concluded that "our expanding economy can manage to thrive without the necessity of psychoanalyzing children or mind-molding men or playing upon the anxieties we strive to keep to ourselves. America is too great a nation—and Americans too fine a people—to have to tolerate such corrosive practices."[71]

Some in the mainstream media questioned this prognosis. For example, Henry Greene of the *Chicago Daily Tribune* believed that Packard had unveiled some alarming advertising practices but that in a free market all advertisers would use the methods Packard described and thus cancel each other out. According to Green, only in "a totalitarian economy" would motivational analysts and depth probers truly pose a problem.[72] By and large, however, the mainstream media and the American public reacted to Packard's study with equal measures of shock and concern. In a letter to the editor of the *Hartford Courant,* B. Gough of Hartford reported that after reading a review of Packard's book he questioned the role of psychology in American society, emphatically stating that Americans "should never be used by every 'trick' in the 'book' to be the subject of various stimuli."[73] In a book review in the *Washington Post,* the Washington lawyer and writer Jerome Spingarn called Packard's book "a hair-raising progress report on the march of time toward 1984."[74] Writing in the *New York Times,* the social critic and writer A. C. Spectorsky asserted that Big Brother no longer had to worry about watching Americans to ensure they conformed to the system because "with the probes and prescriptions of applied psychology and psychiatry, Big Brother (or Big Business, or Big Government) is manipulating your daily life so the surveillance is unnecessary; puppet-like, you do as you're told and, puppet-like, you yourself don't know you're being manipulated."[75]

One practical result of Packard's study was an outpouring of articles alerting the public to specific instances of manipulative advertising practices. Everett G. Martin of the *Wall Street Journal* warned readers of the dangers of background music in television ads, which might "be mounting a subtle psychological attack against your sales resistance."[76] In the *New York Times,* June Owen referred to Packard's description of manipulative practices in the supermarket and offered her readers a simple list of instructions aimed to beat the supermarket "motivation men." Her directions included going to the grocery store with a list and making sure that the man of the house was never entrusted with the responsibility of grocery shopping because men were more susceptible to the subconscious impulse purchases the stores slyly promoted and would probably end up buying a "five-pound wheel of cheese . . . because he happens to have a taste for sharp cheddar."[77] Reflecting on his work a year after the publication of his book, Packard reached a more sober conclusion: "If marketers persist in devising strategies to invade the privacy of our minds, we should begin training our younger people to protect their privacy. . . . The monumental problem we seem to face is that of working out a spiritually tolerable relationship between our fabulous, dynamic economy and our free people."[78]

In September 1957 a market researcher named James Vicary caused a similar stir when he announced that his firm, the Subliminal Projection Company, had discovered a groundbreaking new method for projecting subliminal messages to consumers. At a press conference in New York Vicary went public with his new projectors, which he had already tested in the field for several months at a movie theater in New Jersey. According to Vicary, repeated flashing of the words *Coca-Cola* and *Eat Popcorn* at speeds of up to 1/3000th of a second during each showing caused sales of the two items to rise, respectively, by 18.1 and 57.5 percent.[79] In an editorial commenting on Vicary and subliminal advertising, Donald Craig of the *Los Angeles Times* dramatically fused "hidden commercials" to Communist psychological warfare and asserted that "for diabolical skill in thought control through the use of words, the Russians are as far ahead of us as they were in shooting Sputnik I into space. . . . Now, however, America has come up with a new propaganda 'weapon' with the most sinister thought-control potentials of anything ever devised."[80] Craig dramatically warned of dire consequences if the technology fell into the wrong hands, from unscrupulous American politicians to the Communist party itself.

The public reaction to Vicary's findings was immediate, overwhelmingly negative, and similar in tone to Craig's anxious objection to the new advertising method. Writing in the *Washington Post,* the journalist Phyllis Battelle declared, "I have just had my subconscious mind tampered with—by a group of gentlemen who, I solemnly believe, have no business meddling in my id." Describing subliminal messages as perhaps "the most appalling assault upon the human brain and nervous system yet concocted by civilized man," Battelle asked her viewers to imagine the following scene: "A housewife is sitting placidly beside her husband, watching a Western-Mars movie on their 62-inch screen, when suddenly she darts to the bathroom and begins shampooing her hair. The reason for this sudden suds-conscious urge, of course, is that every five seconds during the movie, the name of a dandruff-remover shampoo has been flashed into the dark depths of her mind. Without logic—possibly without even dandruff—she has obeyed this Svengali impulse."[81] The highly regarded television critic John Crosby described a similar scene: "I can just see someone who has hated popcorn all his life stumbling down the aisle blindly driven to the popcorn dispenser, muttering 'eat popcorn, eat popcorn, eat popcorn.' "[82] And Larry Wolters, a television critic for the *Chicago Daily Tribune*, averred that subliminal advertising had come right out of the pages of George Orwell's *1984*, and opened his article on Vicary's enterprise by simply stating, "There's a new scheme afoot to capture men's minds and stimulate them into action."[83]

Vicary had attempted to avert this type of negative press by describing subliminal advertising as a boon to consumers, saying it would offer "two substantial gains to the viewing public: Fewer interruptions for sponsor messages and added entertainment time."[84] However, not many journalists were buying what Vicary was selling, and a great deal of what was said and written about subliminal advertising in the fall and winter of 1957 centered on the technique's potential to sway public opinion and suggested that there was much more at stake than the wayward purchase of a little popcorn or a bottle of pop. Jack Gould, the chief television reporter and critic for the *New York Times*, described subliminal television as "the idea of secretly tickling a viewer's subconscious so that he will be hypnotically impelled to cozy up to Big Brother or, even better, buy the king-sized package" and addressed the emerging criticism of the new, "invisible" advertisements in an article that December. He argued that what primarily had motivated critics of subliminal advertising was "the specter of remote control of national thought. If campaigning on a platform of the subconscious ever gets started, these individuals fear, it will be no time before the electorate goes goose-stepping to the polls."[85] One of Vicary's most vocal critics in Congress, the Utah congressman William Dawson, did not mince words—he believed that it was "made to order for the establishment and maintenance of a totalitarian government if put to political purposes."[86] A group of religious leaders meeting in New York also quickly condemned the new sales method, wary of its ability to convince an unsuspecting public to increase their consumption of alcohol and sleeping pills.[87]

Public intellectuals like Betty Friedan framed manipulative business and advertising practices in a similar light, indicating that if advertising firms could subconsciously influence American's decisions the potential for corporations to alter human behavior might not be limited to the marketplace. For example, in 1963 Friedan wrote that American housewives had been victimized by the advertising industry's "sexual sell" once businesses and corporations discovered that subconsciously promoting "the perpetuation of housewifery" was economically advantageous to their bottom line.[88] To explore corporations' motivation for utilizing the "sexual sell," Friedan spoke with a man who had "got in on the ground floor of the hidden-persuasion business in 1945." According to her informant, if

American housewives were "properly manipulated . . . [they] can be given the sense of identity, purpose, creativity, the self-realization, even the sexual joy they lack—by the buying of things."[89]

Addressing the sexual sell and the role of the advertising industry in limiting women's options outside the home, Friedan offered a damning critique of its pervasive influence on postwar American society:

> The manipulators and their clients in American business can hardly be accused of creating the feminine mystique. But they are the most powerful of its perpetuators; it is their millions which blanket the land with persuasive images, flattering the American housewife, diverting her guilt and disguising her growing sense of emptiness. They have done this so successfully, employing the techniques and concepts of modern social science, and transposing them into those deceptively simple, clever, outrageous ads and commercials, that an observer of the American scene today accepts as fact that the great majority of American women have no ambition other than to be housewives. If they are not solely responsible for sending women home, they are surely responsible for keeping them there. Their unremitting harangue is hard to escape in this day of mass communications; they have seared the feminine mystique deep into every woman's mind, and into the minds of her husband, her children, her neighbors.[90]

What stands out here is that Friedan was joining hidden persuasion and the manipulative nature of the advertising industry not only to people's purchasing decisions but also to their actual behavior and worldview. By subconsciously and repeatedly indicating that being a housewife was the only acceptable venue for the aspirations and dreams of American women, hidden persuaders had hoodwinked an entire generation of women into feeling guilty about wanting a career and not being drawn to the home and the world of the housewife. On Friedan's analysis, it would appear that hidden persuaders had almost omnipotent powers to control the decisions of Americans, from their purchase of a new dishwasher to their decision to get married—a prospect that would not have sat well with many Americans in the early 1960s.[91]

Although there was a great deal of trepidation about subliminal advertising and hidden persuasion, there was also much curiosity. The economic potential of these methods proved alluring enough for a flurry of imitators to spring up around the country. A television station in Bangor, Maine, and the Canadian Broadcasting Corporation tested the technique on viewers, who reported mixed results, and the promotion manager of a radio station in Seattle reportedly used subliminal messages in a practical joke, sending barely audible messages to the station's audience to drink a cup of coffee for three consecutive days before revealing the joke to listeners.

Movie houses and radio stations around the country carried out similar experiments, and some were economically motivated, such as that conducted by a radio station in Chicago that began to sell "sub-audible" advertising time for a thousand dollars a week. Several companies that had apparently been working on similar schemes also came forward, including Precon Process and Equipment Corporation, which was in the process of applying for a patent for special projectors that flashed subliminal ads and had been in talks with 20th Century Fox about utilizing such messages to enhance the entertainment value of their films. One of their techniques was to overlay the screen with invisible "psychologically pleasing geometric figures," which they claimed subconsciously enhanced the audience's enjoyment of the film. They also claimed their system could be used by film directors to manipulate an audience's reaction, citing as an example a gunfight in a Western that contained hidden images of a six-shooter that slowly got larger and larger, building up to a tense, subliminal cinematic climax.[92]

Like Vicary, Precon was forced to defend its new advertising technology, and in comments at a meeting of the Los Angeles Advertising Club in January 1958 one of the men behind Precon's projectors, Robert Corrigan, dismissed direct comparisons between subliminal advertising and brainwashing, stating that the process their company had discovered was "completely contrary to the 'brainwashing' concept[,] which implies a passive role by an observer."[93] The majority of professional psychiatrists who made public comments at the time agreed with Corrigan in theory, not because they believed subliminal advertising was any different from brainwashing but because they were skeptical that that kind of advertising would work. Nonetheless, the technique had received enough negative publicity that Congress decided to look into it, and in January 1958 Vicary's Subliminal Projection Company was ordered to demonstrate their projectors before the Federal Communications Commission (FCC) in Washington. On January 13 Vicary demonstrated his method at a television studio in Washington to an audience of congressmen and members of the FCC, who were subjected to subliminal ads to "eat more popcorn" or "fight polio" for one-twentieth of a second every five seconds during a four-minute screening of *The Gray Ghost*. Vicary again attempted to downplay the severity of the technique, describing it as a "mild form of advertising" and a "very weak persuader." His assessment was supported by the subliminal ads' utter failure to produce their intended results on the group of assembled politicians that day, highlighted by Sen. Charles E. Potter's reaction to the four-minute screening, who turned to another politician and confusedly remarked, "I think I want a hot dog."[94]

Rep. Peter Frelinghuysen Jr. (left), New Jersey, Rep. William A. Dawson, Utah, and Sen. Charles Potter, Michigan, attending a screening of subliminal advertising techniques in 1958. The original title of the photo was "Legislators study new Brainwash gimmick." (Bettmann / Corbis / AP Images)

In the wake of the demonstration, the FCC publicly declared that any use of subliminal ads in the future would need to meet with federal regulations, and all the major television networks vowed not to use them in their broadcasts, which essentially ended the public debate on the topic. One of the only independent television stations in the country that had publicly proclaimed they were going to be adopting subliminal messages, KTLA in Los Angeles, announced that it would no longer be moving forward with Precon's specially made projectors at their station. Publicly, the station officials stated they were indefinitely suspending their use of the projectors until the FCC made a clearer statement on the use of subliminal advertising, but privately it was speculated that it was a sizable, overwhelmingly negative mail response to the station that prompted their decision.[95]

The publicity surrounding the marriage of advertising and psychology in the late 1950s encouraged Americans to approach consumer culture with a newfound skepticism and to reevaluate the supposed transparency of the capitalist system. In a review of Packard's *The Hidden Persuaders* published in the *Nation* in 1957, Michael D. Reagan, a political science professor at Williams College, drew an explicit parallel between Communist brainwashing and capitalist "persuasion," documenting the affinities between Packard's analysis of domestic consumer practices and William Sargant's analysis of brainwashing in *Battle for the Mind* (1957). The column struck a cautionary tone about the dangers of living in a new "Age of Manipulation," surmising, "Given the increasing pressures upon our minds and emotions described in the books reviewed here, the injunction, 'Know Thyself,' becomes essential to our survival as individuals."[96]

Public discourse during the era indicates that the resemblance between Communist and capitalist psychological intrusion was not lost on the American people. In a letter printed in the *Los Angeles Times* in 1959, a citizen inquired, "As far as the human mind is concerned, is there any difference between brainwashing and advertising on television and radio?"[97] A letter to the editor in the *Washington Post* echoed this sentiment, asserting that jingles in televised ads "bore themselves into your brain until you find yourself humming them as you reach, with blinded eye and shaking hand, for the product on the shelves when you finally capitulate." In this letter-writer's view, the earworms pitching products on television were an aural invasion of the American consumer's mind. The letter concluded, "This is as good an example of brainwashing as anything Moscow ever dreamed up."[98] These letters indicate how Americans were equating Communist psychological warfare to domestic practices with greater regularity.

Another letter to the editor, printed two weeks after the launching of Sputnik, captured the unease many Americans were beginning to harbor about the growing manipulative state of American capitalism. Tirzah Stuart King of Pigeon Cove, Massachusetts, wrote, "Those who have scanned the sky for a glimpse of Soviet mechanical progress [Sputnik] . . . will find revealed in a book by Vance Packard, 'Hidden Persuaders,' a disquieting invasion of our mental domain as important as the little moon now invading our sky." In one eloquent passage, King wrote, "People will be mentally manipulated through the mechanism of the subconscious mind, so that when they are looking at motion pictures or television they may be bombarded with suggestions that urge them to act as the unseen suggester wishes them to act. Could there be a more fertile field of susceptibility to 'brain washing' and indoctrination by unprincipled elements seeking world domination? Let us be alert to our Christian heritage of individuality and cherish it, as well as our American right to think for oneself."[99] Describing advertisements, motion pictures, and television as an internal "invasion" that should give cause for as much fearfulness as the external invasion of the Communist enemy, King's letter illuminates how, in a profound sense, the end of the 1950s witnessed the beginning of a critical breakdown in the Cold War consensus.

According to the logic of the Cold War, overt psychological manipulation was employed by the Communist enemy because it was the only way they could win followers. The United States was different in that it promoted freedom of choice and individuality, and the consumer and voter had the capacity to determine the popularity of goods and candidates based on their merits and of their own free will. However, in the midst of the Second Red Scare, a period historians have traditionally described as marked by an anti-Communist fervor bordering on hysteria, institutions that were central to consumer identity and the capitalist system came under scrutiny for their apparent ability to intrude upon the American psyche. Thus the debate over mass culture and advertising in the 1950s ultimately served to blur the lines between Communist brainwashing and its capitalist cousins and seriously undermined the existing paradigm that framed the Cold War as a battle between American freedom and Soviet mental and physical oppression.

It is difficult to say with any certainty how many Americans experienced these anxieties, or how the Americans who expressed them might have divided along lines of class, race, and religion. But the association between Communist brainwashing and domestic popular and consumer culture was pervasive and extended far beyond academia. Writers like Wertham and Packard may have popularized some of these ideas, but their books had a broader impact than their readership might suggest because they raised topical concerns that garnered a great deal of media and even congressional attention. Certainly, the middle class was the target audience of many of these publications, and there was a discernible class element to some of their anxieties over rock 'n' roll and comic books and the supposed indoctrination of middle-class kids with working-class culture and values. But the anxieties over mass culture were not felt exclusively by middle-class or college-educated Americans, as the widespread protests against postwar mass culture among rural grassroots segments throughout the country reveal. In the 1950s a suburban mother might have chafed at the impact of television on her children while a Baptist minister told his congregation that rock 'n' roll was a bad influence on American teenagers and a rural parent–teacher group organized a public comic book burning. Alarm over the domestic misuse of psychology and the ability of culture to corrupt and influence American's behavior cut through many layers of American society.

Although perhaps not many Americans saw big business and consumer practices in quite as oppressive a light as Tirzah Stuart King, the journey of the concept of brainwashing from a weapon of the Communist enemy to a tool of American politicians and big businesses is a revealing one. By the end of the 1950s the American public had been repeatedly warned that they had more to fear than Communist mind control, and they began lashing out against all manner of internal manipulators. Those more prone to action, their faces illuminated by the soft glow of burning comic books, angrily called for congressional hearings on rock 'n' roll and mass culture and federal oversight of the advertising industry. Less reactionary Americans argued it was time for the nation to collectively take a hard look in the mirror and reexamine its values and the materialism of modern American life. As a self-proclaimed "garden-variety housewife" writing to the *New York Times* stated, "Perhaps it is high time we stopped tearing out every pay day to get one more thing that we 'can not live without.' "[100] No matter their course of action, it was obvious to many Americans that the presumed freest country in the world was being subjected to a number of forces that were subconsciously altering their personalities and utilizing psychological methods to undermine their free will.

6

The Limits of Individuality in Postwar America

In his commencement address at Smith College in 1955, Adlai Stevenson warned the graduating class of the small women's liberal arts college in Northampton, Massachusetts, about the growing trends of specialization and conformity within American society that were threatening to dehumanize the "typical Western man, or typical Western husband." In Stevenson's view these new trends were part of a historic crisis between collectivism and individualism, and even though he derisively informed the audience that, whether they liked it or not, the majority of them would go on to fulfill "the humble role of the house-wife," he avowed that nonetheless they had a central role to play in this struggle. As Stevenson saw it, the young women graduating from Smith would soon be wives and mothers, and as such it was their duty "to restore valid, meaningful purpose to life in your home: to beware of instinctive group reaction to the forces which play upon you and yours, to watch for and arrest the constant gravitational pulls to which we are all exposed, your workaday husband especially, in our specialized, fragmented society." They would accomplish this vital task in their homes, Stevenson told them, "with a baby in your lap or in the kitchen with a can opener in your hands." If they were really clever, he noted, maybe they could even practice their "saving arts on that unsuspecting man while he's watching television!"

By encouraging their husband's and son's individuality, Stevenson claimed, the graduates could help distinguish the United States from the Communist world, which at that very moment was "busy brainwashing all over Asia," and thwart the efforts of American leaders, "who certainly have a brainwashing glint in their eye when they meet with an unfamiliar idea." However, defeating these looming threats was going to take a great deal of effort and mental fortitude since it was so easy "to accept the conditioning which so many social pressures will bring to bear upon you." Ultimately, if they put themselves to the task and utilized their education, Stevenson was confident the graduates could conquer the forces working to destroy American individuality and produce "homes and whole human beings in whom the rational values of freedom, tolerance, charity and free inquiry can take root."[1] To Stevenson there could be no higher calling for college-educated women.

The speech reflects the social and gender norms governing mainstream society in the midst of the baby boom, but, given the presence of such budding feminist luminaries as the poet Sylvia Plath in the graduating class that spring and Gloria Steinem in the class of 1956, it is hard to imagine that many Smith students were eager to heed Stevenson's advice. For his part, Stevenson appeared totally unaware of the inherent irony of exhorting college-educated women to combat conformity and groupthink by rushing back into the home, getting married, being supportive wives, and raising children. Although Stevenson had apparently not given much thought to the plight of modern women, he had long-standing issues with the state of American society. A year earlier, in an engagement as a commencement speaker at Vassar College, he had made similar remarks about the dangers plaguing the nation, professing that conformity was "a more certain threat to the validity of your education and to your immortal soul than the blandishments of the flesh and the devil."[2] Stevenson viewed the rising encroachments on individuality as a serious threat, one that American men and women alike needed to vigilantly resist.

Stevenson's critique of the perils of conformity and groupthink that afternoon in Massachusetts was hardly unique, and, as K. A. Cuordileone has written, "If one were to judge mid-twentieth century American culture by a selected assortment of popular books, novels, and films, it would appear singularly preoccupied with the self and its fragility."[3] Taken together, this material offered the most critically disparaging introspection of the United States in the early postwar period, and, although the earliest examples of this new critique of American selfhood predated the Cold War by several years, by 1950 it had emerged as a well-defined school of thought. By the end of the decade it was practically omnipresent, informing a wide range of popular and political debates about American corporate and domestic life. As concerns about American individuality gained traction with the public, it was transformed from an intellectual issue into a practical one. After being continuously reminded of the inherent sameness of modern American life for the better part of the 1950s, Americans began to consciously set out to pursue more individualistic lifestyles, which ultimately would help ignite the cultural rebellion of the 1960s and 1970s and produce a new set of social expectations governing American behavior.

Historians who have analyzed the midcentury fascination with individuality have alternately interpreted it as a sign of male discontent with the corporate status quo, anxiety over the implications of living in a postindustrial mass society, the increased reverence afforded to psychiatry and psychology, and widespread uneasiness with a bevy of postwar trends, including the rise of the mass media, domesticity, suburbia, bureaucratic institutions, and all the usual "self-crushing forces of modernity."[4] But to truly understand Americans' fixation on the state of American individuality, the critique of the domestic institutions that supposedly threatened it needs to be reexamined in light of the contemporary understanding of Communist psychological warfare. After the Korean War ended, an outpouring of academic works, novels, films, and television shows depicted the rigid conformity of the postwar age in terms that echoed the more severe interpretations of Communist psychological warfare and likened the methods and culture of American corporate and social institutions to propaganda, indoctrination, and even brainwashing. Thus Stevenson's reference to Communist brainwashing in an address about conformity in the United States was no mere coincidence and shows how the concept was used to highlight similar processes that many believed were endangering Americans' civil liberties at home. In the context of Stevenson's speech, apparatuses of the state in Red China employed brainwashing and various forms of psychological warfare to control public opinion and curtail freedom of thought, while at home Americans' individuality was being threatened by social, corporate, and economic institutions rather than governmental ones. Nonetheless, the outcome was essentially the same: dehumanization, the loss of personal identity, and a decline in individual autonomy.

Analyzing several of the phrases used to describe suburbia, the sociologist William H. Whyte reported that he had heard it jokingly referred to as "a Russia, only with money." It's a fascinating anecdote, and although Whyte noted its wry sarcasm, it reflects a deep level of suspicion about the new environs of postwar America. Like the suburbanite comparing the communal character of his neighborhood to the Soviet Union, colloquial attempts at linking the Soviet Union and the United States were often purposefully exaggerated in order to draw attention to the supposedly authoritarian aspects of modern American society. Yet these comparisons also indicate how Americans began to perceive the United States in a new light over the course of the 1950s, and just as they were being warned about the manipulative aspects of mass culture and the advertising and public relations industries, they were constantly being informed that corporate entities and the new suburban landscape were transforming their nation from a free democracy into a dehumanizing, conformist society. This vision of the United States was eerily similar to the popular perception of the Communist world and would leave an enduring legacy on American behavior and thought as the nation emerged from the 1950s.

Individuality under Attack

Long before the Cold War a number of intellectuals held that modern institutions posed a threat to individuality. One of the central concepts in psychology and critical theory informing their arguments was the notion of the mass man, which can be traced back to the 1930s and 1940s and the work of prominent psychoanalysts such as Erich Fromm and Wilhelm Reich. Fromm and Reich both explored the rise of fascism and attributed its success to the psychological burdens of freedom and, according to Reich, to sexual repression in early childhood and an authoritarian family structure that inhibited psychological development and made individuals susceptible to totalitarianism later in life.[5] Their work provided the foundation for public intellectuals such as Arthur Schlesinger Jr., who warned that the United States was in danger of producing its very own mass man in the 1950s.

The sociologist David Riesman's *The Lonely Crowd,* published in 1950, was one of the foundational works in a new, critical literature on the United States that was heavily informed by sociology and psychoanalysis. In this classic study of American social character, Riesman posited that the nation was in the midst of a radical transformation in social values and that a new type of American was beginning to dominate the country. As opposed to the "inner-directed" Americans of earlier epochs, who were largely independent and motivated by their personal goals, the twentieth century witnessed the emergence of "other-directed" individuals, who adapted themselves to the expectations of their peers and had largely lost their autonomy in the process. Although Riesman acknowledged that previous generations, whether they were what he termed "inner-" or "tradition-directed" individuals, were forced to adjust and conform to their own set of social expectations, he argued that modern Americans faced new obstacles to autonomy in both their professional and private lives. In large part this was because modern industrialized societies forced individuals to embark on careers they were not passionate about and because their leisure activities were influenced by the mass media, their peer groups, and "one's location on the American scene."[6] Ultimately, Riesman concluded that "the idea that men are created free and equal is both true and misleading: men are created different; they lose their social freedom and their individual autonomy in seeking to become like each other."[7] The book quickly became a best-seller, thrusting the terms "inner-directed" and "other-directed" into the public discourse in the process, and is indicative of an emerging critique of American society which warned that Americans were in danger of becoming products of mass society and fleeing from individuality.

The Lonely Crowd illustrates that in 1950 the debate over modern American individuality was influenced by academics and psychologists who were, by and large, not directly engaging with ideas related to psychological warfare. At the time, even critics whose work directly addressed the burgeoning Cold War typically argued that the success of Communism was largely the product of the psychological frailties of modern man rather than the result of external forces preying on his psyche.[8] During the Korean War, as the concepts of brainwashing, propaganda, and indoctrination began to seep into American intellectual culture, many thinkers began to reassess this narrative and argue that individuality in the United States was being directly targeted and attacked by forces that were much more powerful than previously imagined. Perhaps no study was more influential in this regard than William Whyte's *The Organization Man*, published in 1956.

Central to Whyte's argument was the notion that a pronounced shift had occurred in the United States over the course of the twentieth century, as Americans abandoned the traditional Protestant ethic of their forefathers in favor of a new social ethic based on "a belief in the group as the source of creativity; a belief in 'belongingness' as the ultimate need of the individual; and a belief in the application of science to achieve the belongingness."[9] In this respect, Whyte's analysis of contemporary American society was, at least on its surface, similar to Riesman's, and they both held that, whether because postwar society was "other-directed" or because it had started to prioritize the group over the individual, Americans were losing the personal autonomy possessed by earlier generations. What distinguished Whyte from Riesman was whom he blamed for this development: whereas Riesman identified new historical, cultural, and social forces, Whyte predominantly blamed the organization itself, which used psychological manipulation and indoctrination to turn members of the middle class into subservient "company-men." The main characters of Whyte's study, the members of the middle class who had taken "the vows of organization life," were clearly successful, but their success had come at a steep price because they did not simply work for the new, "self-perpetuating institutions," they belonged to them. And though Whyte largely classified this growing "collectivization" as an outgrowth of new trends in the corporate world, he was convinced that its social ethic had spread far and wide and reached into almost every profession in the country.[10]

One of the main reasons Whyte believed that Americans were willing to acquiesce to the organization was that they were becoming thoroughly indoctrinated in its values. Colleges around the country had altered their curriculums to better prepare students for the new corporate model, and once students graduated from college they were frequently enrolled in organizations' training programs, which focused on developing a certain type of "social character" that would seamlessly adapt to life in the corporation. As a result, a new generation of Americans was being educated and trained to place a higher value on group work than on individual initiative and taught how to manage other people's ideas rather than think for themselves. In those rare cases that a worker or scientist slipped through the cracks and retained some vestige of her former individuality, by the time she reached the Organization she was quickly put through a "good indoctrination program" which stamped out her independence and made her fully "company-oriented."[11]

Whyte particularly noted the incestuous relationship developing between colleges and the Organization, as American higher education had become so thoroughly infiltrated by the new corporate ethic that colleges were starting to actively seek out high school students who fit the corporate model. One dean of freshman students confided to Whyte that since corporations liked "a pretty gregarious, active type," his college had taken to recruiting students "who had an 80 or 85 average in school and plenty of extracurricular activity. We see little use for the 'brilliant' introvert who might spend the rest of life turning out essays on obscure portions of D. H. Lawrence's letters."[12] Since industry was well on its way to becoming one of the principal financial benefactors of the nation's institutions of higher learning, Whyte expected this trend to increase over time until eventually colleges would be dominated by anti-intellectualism, a process he believed was already under way. In large part Whyte believed this was because the new focus on "Business English," communication skills, management, and general education was eroding the traditional emphasis on the liberal arts and the sciences. Looking at the new landscape of higher education, Whyte judged there was little room for optimism unless a radical reappraisal of university teaching practices took place. He derisively noted, "Once the uneducated could have the humility of ignorance. Now they are given degrees and put in charge."[13]

Of all the Organization's methods Whyte documented and criticized, the one he went to the greatest lengths to undermine was the use of personality tests. In a chapter devoted to these "inquisitions into the psyche," he argued that the tests gave the organization such a thorough picture of a job candidate, from his politics to his "personal sexual behavior," that they practically amounted to a psychological X-ray.[14] In many companies personality tests were not only used to screen job applicants, but also given to existing personnel in order to provide the organization with a detailed record of all of its employees and to inform management's decisions on everything from promotions to layoffs. Whyte believed this was especially frightening because the tests were presented as a totally benign means of assessing candidates and employees rather than as a form of psychological invasion. To demonstrate that the tests rewarded mediocrity and conformity, Whyte carried out a case study by giving the principal versions of the personality test to uniquely talented individuals working in the Organization, namely, a cross section of a dozen of the nation's most successful corporate leaders, sixteen leading scientists, and thirty-eight of the most promising men in middle management. Roughly half of the applicants scored extremely poorly, and not a single corporate leader scored in the acceptable range. Two corporate leaders did so poorly on the test that Whyte predicted that if they had been applying for a job at a corporation they would have "failed to meet the minimum profile for foremen."[15] To Whyte, the case study demonstrated the test's inability to measure true leadership qualities and individual brilliance, so, in addition to representing a psychologically invasive practice, the tests did not even operate in the best interests of American industry because they precluded exceptional candidates from ever being hired.

In order to combat personality tests Whyte offered his readership a sample test and, in an act of open rebellion, encouraged them to cheat if they ever applied for a job that required one.[16] As he explained, "When an individual is commanded by an organization to reveal his innermost feelings, he has a duty to himself to give answers that serve his self-interest rather than that of The Organization."[17] Ultimately, Whyte believed that the tests divulged "the voice of The Organization" and showed where it was heading in the future. The tests, alongside the companies' use of psychological consulting firms, were an indication of the Organization's desire to get inside their employees' heads, map their psyches, and eventually mold their personnel to fit a particular psychological blueprint. With regard to personality tests and the Organization's use of psychology, Whyte postulated, "The Bill of Rights should not stop at organization's edge. In return for the salary that The Organization gives the individual, it can ask for superlative work from him, but it should not ask for his psyche as well."[18]

Whyte maintained that perhaps the most disturbing aspect of the new social ethic promoted by the Organization was that it was no longer confined to the corporate world, but, in addition to infiltrating academia and the sciences, had followed the Organization man home. His assessment of the "dormitory" of the Organization man, in which "everyone lives in an identical house," was part of a growing critique of the new suburban communities dotting the postwar landscape. Noting the interchangeable quality of the people living in suburbs, from as far afield as Levittown, Pennsylvania, to Park Merced, San Francisco, he indicated that suburbanites started to lose their identity almost as soon as they moved into that new ranch house on the cul-de-sac. A large part of the sameness was a conscious desire to keep up with the Joneses, and Whyte argued that suburbanites, through a sort of social "osmosis," began to mold themselves into the image of their neighbors, conforming to community standards on relatively superficial issues such as clothing and home décor as well as on such intensely personal issues as politics and religious denomination. Even though suburbanites were aware of what was going on and sensed they were losing themselves in the process of adapting to life in the suburbs, their training in college and within the Organization had led them to believe that "responding to the group is a moral duty—and so they continue, hesitant and unsure, imprisoned in brotherhood."[19]

Although *The Organization Man* did not call for a revolution against the capitalist system, it did call for a reevaluation of it, especially with regard to the practices that curtailed individual autonomy. Historians who have examined the book generally emphasize Whyte's attack on suburbs and the corporation, and many see it as Jackson Lears did, that is, as "the locus classicus of the 1950s critique of conformity."[20] To these historians *The Organization Man* is representative of a larger body of work produced by sociologists and other intellectuals throughout the postwar period that criticized corporate America. Among these studies are Riesman's *The Lonely Crowd* (1951), C. Wright Mills's *White Collar: The American Middle Classes* (1951), Packard's *The Status Seekers* (1959) and *The Waste Makers* (1960), and Daniel Bell's *The End of Ideology* (1960). In their various analyses of Whyte, historians have pointed to several themes, classifying *The Organization Man* as an angry, nostalgic call for a return to "competitive capitalism and rugged individualism," a confirmation of "male critics' declaration of a 'masculinity crisis,'" and a reflection of the widespread "paranoid suspicion of psychotherapy being used for manipulative purposes."[21] All of these interpretations are easily supported and have been well documented. But of at least equal significance is the fact that Whyte's indictment of contemporary American society paralleled contemporary platitudes about life in the Communist world, and the methods he claimed the Organization employed were remarkably similar to Communist psychological warfare.

In Whyte's view the Organization was an authoritarian, tyrannical force in American life whose main goal was nothing short of capturing the American worker's soul.[22] Using methods borrowed from psychologists, the Organization relied on indoctrination, psychological manipulation, and social engineering to ensure worker conformity, primarily because they "equate[d] the lone individual with psychic disorder."[23] The danger of suburbs and the Organization lay in the fact that, on their surface, they appeared benevolent, and, as a result, their invasion of the American psyche was going unchallenged and had led to a general deterioration of individual autonomy and free thought, leaving many Americans to powerlessly conclude that they were "more acted upon than acting—and their future, therefore, [was] determined as much by the system as by themselves."[24] In an especially revealing chapter that considered how the ethic of the Organization man had spread throughout American popular culture, Whyte analyzed the dominant themes of postwar popular film and literature and stated that their primary message was simply, "*Accept.*" Americans should learn, popular culture drummed into them, to accept the corporate social ethic, to accept their role in the group, to accept the system. Whyte compared this to the conclusion of Orwell's *1984,* when Winston Smith finally breaks down in tears because he realizes that "he had learned to love Big Brother." Whyte noted that although *1984* was a commentary on Communism, the outcomes of the new American social ethic and of Orwell's communist dystopia were "hauntingly similar."[25] The only reasonable course of action for Americans, said Whyte, was to rebel.

If this conception of American society was confined to Whyte, one might conclude that he offered a rare perspective on American society in the 1950s, but the substance of his critique was echoed by literally dozens of intellectuals and social critics, practically all of whom employed rhetoric that alluded to the specter of psychological warfare and further internalized the brainwashing thesis in a domestic context. The psychiatrist and social critic Robert Lindner wrote a collection of essays titled *Must You Conform?* (1955) that sounded a similar panicked alarm over the state of American identity.[26] Discussing what he termed "Mass Men" and "Mass Manhood," Lindner described a new breed of Americans as "mechanized, robotized caricature[s] of humanity" who had become "slave[s] in mind and body."[27] Lindner contended that the twin evils of conformity and adaption had weakened Americans' individual egos to the point that they had begun to subconsciously identify with the "mass." This loss of self was spreading like an "infection" across the country, and Lindner warned that if it was not treated, "the qualities that make up the humanity of man [will] disappear, and in the place of a man stands a goose-stepping automaton driven by animal lusts."[28]

In a section that identified how Americans were being subconsciously transformed into Mass Men, Lindner provided a disturbing timeline that documented the forces weighing on Americans' psyches from infancy to adulthood. Starting at birth, Americans were raised to adjust themselves on the basis of the larger demands of society, and the motto "You must adjust" became a subconscious and oft-repeated command that shaped their personalities and their fate. The motto first appeared on "the walls of every nursery," where "slowly and subtly, the infant is shaped to the prevailing pattern, his needs for love and care turned against him as weapons to enforce submission."[29] Children who would not conform were ostracized or cured by specialists until they were old enough to enter the schools, which had "become vast factories for the manufacture of robots" in which children were taught how to socialize in a group setting.[30] Such socialization would continuously be reinforced later in their lives by institutions of higher learning, religious organizations, and the American political system. The rare individual who escaped these forces with his or her individuality intact was forced to undergo therapy, medicated, and in extreme cases treated to shock therapy or even a lobotomy until, finally, "a walking zombie, the penultimate conformist, stands where a man once stood, 'cured' of his humanity."[31] For Lindner, the only silver lining to this Orwellian vision of American society was that everything in humans' nature forced them to rebel against this system, and, although he did not give many practical solutions to the problems he diagnosed, he was optimistic that through nonconformity and rebellion Americans could defeat the forces that were working to dehumanize and destroy them.[32]

In Riesman's detailed study of the values promoted by suburbs, aptly titled "The Suburban Sadness" and published in 1958, he pointed to similar forces that were working to socialize Americans "into 'organization men' and family men" and leading them to "homogenizing modes of thought and feeling."[33] Riesman argued that many facets of suburban life represented an "individual, only barely self-conscious, protest against the values inherited from industrialism and the low-birth-rate middle-class metropolis."[34] This protest had subconsciously influenced men to seek their identity outside of commerce and industry in what had traditionally been considered women's domain: the home, leisure activities, and civic life. At the same time, women were leaving the home to take temporary jobs, and an increasing "homogenization of roles" was taking place. Despite these opportunities, women had become captives of the suburbs, "tied down . . . by their young children, the lack of a car, and the lack of servants." Their children, who unlike their parents were not afforded the benefits of growing up outside suburbia, were similarly enslaved by the suburb and the suburban public school system, which left them "dependent on whatever art and science and general liveliness their particular school happens to have."[35] Even the layout of the typical ranch-style suburban home was dehumanizing, being commonly based on an open floor plan centered around a television set on a swivel that came "at the expense of space for the individual, whose bedroom in the suburban development is often smaller than in city tenements."[36] Riesman's critique practically depicted the suburb as a conscious entity in its own right, working to imprison suburbanites in its midst, erode their individual space, and encourage like-mindedness.

Intellectuals attributed to American popular culture abilities similar to those of suburbs and corporations to influence the American psyche. One of the most noted critics of popular culture during the period, Dwight MacDonald, pronounced that an intellectually bankrupt and mass-produced middlebrow culture was threatening "to engulf everything in its spreading ooze."[37] Since it was produced for a mass audience, it had merged the "child and grown-up audience" to horrific effect. Pointing specifically to comic books, newspaper strips, movies, radio, and TV, MacDonald opined that they were all leading to the "infantile regression of the latter [adults], who, unable to cope with the strains and complexities of modern life, escape via *kitsch*" and to "'overstimulation' of the former [children], who grow up too fast."[38] Beyond the fact that it contained no inherent artistic value, the main problem with mass culture, according to MacDonald, was that it treated its audience as a collective mass, which not only ensured that its quality would inevitably fall to the level of the most unrefined members of its audience, but also encouraged Americans to identify with the mass audience until they lost their own "human identity and quality."[39] Like many other critics of the period, MacDonald perceived internal forces operating within the country that infantilized, manipulated, and dehumanized the American public until it finally shaped their identities. And like other critics as well, MacDonald argued that at least in this respect there was no discernible difference between the United States and the Soviet Union.[40]

Although by and large most of this scholarship converged on men, in the early 1960s Betty Friedan recognized similar forces preying on the female psyche. In *The Feminine Mystique,* published in 1963, Friedan argued that since the end of the Second World War American women had been subjected to a "propaganda campaign" that had led them to believe being a housewife was a prestigious, fulfilling occupation. Calling this the feminine mystique, Friedan argued that it had brainwashed two successive generations of American women and compelled them to conform to society's expectations instead of seeking a career outside the home. Trapped in their suburban homes, which Friedan directly likened to Nazi concentration camps, American women were suffering "a slow death of mind and spirit," stunting their intellectual growth in childhood, and turning away from "individual identity to become an anonymous biological robot in a docile mass."[41] The result of this campaign was essentially a feminized version of Whyte's organization man, and Friedan asserted that "by choosing femininity over the painful growth to full identity, by never achieving the hard core of self that comes not from fantasy but from mastering reality, these girls are doomed to suffer ultimately that bored, diffuse feeling of purposelessness, non-existence, non-involvement with the world that can be called *anomie,* or lack of identity, or merely felt as the problem that has no name."[42]

The aforementioned texts by no means represent an exhaustive survey, but they illustrate a trend that was becoming relatively commonplace in American intellectual culture in the years after the Korean War, namely, that the rhetoric and logic of the brainwashing discourse, which initially had been applied only to the Communist enemy, was starting to inform how American intellectuals described and conceptualized the built environment of suburbia and domestic economic, political, and cultural institutions. Whether the scholars in question were describing the organization, social institutions, or popular culture, they all identified forces operating within the United States that employed methods akin to psychological warfare to inhibit individuality and create a new breed of docile Americans who were as mass-produced as the "new Soviet man" or the standard suburban ranch house.

The frequent use of terms such as *indoctrination* and *propaganda* was not merely a rhetorical overlap but a sign of two significant facts. First, throughout the fifties and sixties many intellectuals had common assumptions about the American mind and believed it was vulnerable to attack and could be subconsciously influenced or manipulated. Second, starting around the end of the Korean War, intellectuals working independently of each other began identifying psychologically invasive forces operating within American society and argued that Americans were under attack by processes similar to brainwashing while they were at work, at leisure, and at home. As the historian James Gilbert pointed out in his analysis of this school of social criticism, "Much of this social psychology found its way into popular expressions, so much so that by the end of the 1950s, it passed for common knowledge."[43] Although Gilbert was specifically addressing the gendered implications of this criticism, its stress on the limits of individuality in postwar America also ran deep in popular culture. In this respect, the mainstream media, popular movies, and literature further publicized the perception that a number of dehumanizing forces existed in contemporary American society.

Attack of the Gray Flannel Suits

Two newspaper articles published in the *New York Times* in the spring of 1958 demonstrate how far the critique of American conformity had extended outside of academia. The first, published on March 20 and titled "Indians Beat Noncomformist Giant," profiled Peter Burnside, a left-handed pitcher for the San Francisco Giants. The preceding winter Burnside, a Dartmouth alumnus, had worked for an investment banking house in Chicago. In an era when professional athletes frequently sought additional employment in the off-season, it was not unusual for major league baseball players to complement their incomes during the winter months. For Burnside, finance had been an illuminating experience, but, as he told the press, he was grateful to leave his nine-to-five job in banking and return to baseball in the spring because it "enabled him to avoid mass conformity." Gay Talese, the journalist who wrote the article, noted that "without openly rebelling against anything, Burnside has tried to avoid what he calls the 'patterns' of his generation." These patterns, insisted Burnside, were difficult to escape, and he believed they were molding the character of his contemporaries outside of baseball: "We all go to grammar school, then to high school, then to college. Then we all get job interviews or join the Army. If we get the job, then we have a training program. Then we work our way up—and we're organization men." Burnside believed major league baseball was one of the rare institutions in American society that remained immune to these forces. He confided to Talese, "You know, I hope we do not get too many educated ball players in the game. Soon we would have organization men in baseball. They'd all be the same; do the same thing, think the same way."[44]

A little over a week later Talese wrote a second article addressing conformity in major league baseball. Apparently inspired by Burnside's comments, Talese had visited the spring training camps of four major league teams to examine the topic and arrived at a vastly different conclusion from that of the philosophical left-hander. Citing quotations from star players of earlier generations to bolster his argument, Talese wrote that a "new breed" of players was starting to appear in major league ballparks around the country, and, unlike their predecessors, they did not chew tobacco, partake in bench-clearing brawls, and antagonize their opponents. Talese was careful to note that major leaguers were still talented, skilled athletes and perhaps even stronger and faster than earlier generations. But something, he was quick to note, was missing. There was no showmanship anymore, and perhaps worst of all the new breed of ballplayer did not even "seem to be having any fun."[45] In Talese's view, baseball players had become organization men, and as a result the game was suffering from the "undeniably blighting effects of conformity" and had lost "its 'characters,' its nitwits, its boneheads and, what's worse, its unpredictability and sense of humor."[46] Unlike Burnside, who believed professional baseball was one of the few remaining bastions of nonconformity in the nation, Talese saw a game overrun by conformity and the organization ethic. Their contradictory points of view illustrate not only how divisive the issue of mass conformity could be, but how it was starting to be fretted about and spotted in communities and professions across the country.

The community that came in for the most intense scrutiny was the suburbs, and the mainstream media frequently explored their impact on American behavior. An article in the *New York Times* in 1954 addressing the suburbs' impact on children and "what parents can do about it" deals with many of the themes the media would routinely address in their treatments of the suburban landscape. The author of the piece, Simone D. Gruenberg, reckoned that the suburbs came with "a subtle psychological price." Since all the homes looked identical and were mass-produced, "the children growing up in New Suburbia run the danger of being homogenized."[47] Gruenberg gave suburban parents a blueprint for how to break free of the stultifying conformity of the suburbs and raise individualistic children. In retrospect, most of her advice appears quaint: introduce your children to a wide variety of people from different backgrounds, including "oldsters," who were practically nonexistent in the suburbs; take frequent trips to the city and country so children can become acquainted with the world outside of suburbia; arrange for your children to spend some time in your neighbor's home so you can reflect on your life and the "agencies and institutions" influencing it; and work on creating a community through study groups, public meetings, and recreational activities such as community theater. An illustration by Roy Doty appeared above Gruenberg's article and complemented her vision of the suburb. Depicting a typical suburban neighborhood from an aerial perspective, the illustration featured identical ranch houses lining interconnected streets, with a few sparse trees dotting the backyards. In the corner of the illustration was a stamp with a husband, wife, and two children engraved into it, and their image had been stamped across the entire neighborhood. A fitting illustration for the piece, its imagery was representative of a common critique of the suburbs that portrayed them as a potentially dehumanizing aspect of American life.

Although many of these themes were routinely reflected in popular and academic literature, many writers and suburbanites were not so quick to completely deride life in the suburbs. An article by Anne Kelley in the *New York Times Magazine* in 1958 offers an interesting counterpoint to the arguments of the experts who claimed that the suburbs were "homogenized like peanut butter." Kelley rattled off a long list of the most common criticisms of the suburbs in the 1950s: "Suburban life, for children, is over-organized; the father has little time at home because of commuting demands; the mother becomes sole disciplinarian and 24-hour chauffer; population turnover is great, with a resulting lack of stability; materialism is glorified, with sports cars, patios, hi-fi and country clubs set upon an altar and cocktail parties celebrated as a sort of social low mass; despite the dedication to the child's interests, children in the suburbs do not distinguish themselves in tests designed to measure mental-health."[48] In the remainder of the article Kelley contended that many of these worries were overblown and detailed a number of practical reasons people moved to the suburbs, stressing some of the benefits of suburban life. However, later in the article she acknowledged that if there was any truth to the pointed criticism of suburbia, it was not necessarily an indictment on suburban life but reflective of "the swing our total American culture has taken in recent years to conformity, conservatism, group adjustment and a balanced budget."[49] The admission is interesting and implies that even supporters of suburbia were beginning to believe there was a degree of validity in the notion that suburbia had some darker, perhaps subconscious, effects on American behavior.

A mother of two named Joan Sadur who lived in the suburban community of Lincolnwood, Illinois, wrote a letter to the *Chicago Daily Tribune* in 1959 that betrays a nascent internalization among some Americans of the antisuburbia ethos. Sadur was worried about the suburb's potential impact on her young children, especially after taking them "downtown and observing their startled reactions to city living." A photo accompanying the article illustrated just how sheltered suburban children had become: a man is driving an automobile with its top down and the woman sitting next to him, presumably his wife, is smiling and looking into the back seat, where seven youngsters are literally stuffed into the car. The photo caption read, "Many kids don't know what it is to walk; they expect to be driven everywhere." In addition to Sadur's unease about her children's stunned reaction to the city and their relatively sheltered existence in the suburbs, she was afraid she might not be preparing her children for the rigors of adulthood, a gap she mainly blamed on the suburban environment they lived in. Her anxieties about the long-term ramifications of the suburbs on her children echoed familiar themes:

> In our suburban area the family is missing the important social experience of mixing with people from all walks of life and all income brackets. Here in suburbia the fathers make about the same amount of money and have jobs that allow them to wear suits every day. Families keep two cars in every garage, and permanent maids or baby sitters are customary. Will these suburban kids, when they become adults, seek only those with the same social and economic background as themselves? If so, what kind of generation of social snobs are we raising? Hadn't we better do something to stop it while they are young, before it is too late?[50]

Sadur ended by saying that, even though she was "disturbed by the conformity in our lives," for the time being she would make the most of life in the suburbs and essentially hope for the best.

Like many parents, Sadur had misgivings about life in the suburbs but did not see many practical alternatives to living there. Many members of the middle class shared her doubts about the suburban environment's impact on their children and its potential to mold their character. Even parents who felt no cause for alarm recognized the need to assert their individuality and downplay the conformity in their particular communities. In an interview with a reporter, for example, another midwestern suburban mother of two told an interviewer, "We're not peas in a pod. I thought it would be like that, especially because incomes are nearly the same. But it's amazing how different and varied people are."[51] Other suburbanites responded to the criticism of the conformity and lack of individuality in their communities in a variety of ways. As the historian Clifford E. Clark Jr. has noted, they frequently customized their homes, having them placed at different angles on the lot before they were built or focusing on making their interior decoration unique.[52] A whole industry sprang up around suburbanites' desire to personalize their homes, a movement promoted by popular magazines like *Good Housekeeping* and *Better Homes and Gardens* and which ironically led many suburban homeowners to buy mass-produced furniture and other assorted knickknacks to demonstrate their individuality. Others took this a step further and put a great deal of time and effort into the civic and artistic life of their communities in order to invest their community with creativity and an independent spirit.

Many of these trends can be construed simply as a sort of instinctual push-back on some of the more authoritarian aspects of life in the early postwar suburbs, such as the rules in William Levitt's early housing developments regarding how often the lawn needed to be mowed and when the laundry could be put outside to dry.[53] But they also represented a highly conscious attempt to remake the suburban landscape into an individualistic utopia where Americans could simultaneously reap the benefits of mass-production and assert their individuality. A salient preoccupation of people was their perception that their behavior or, worse yet, that of their children, was being subconsciously fashioned by their life in the suburbs. One sociologist discussing the issue in 1959 noted that the common "urge to be different at home" could be attributed to Americans' newfound obsession with "themselves and their own inner psychology."[54] By the 1960s these ideas had started having an effect even on new suburban developments, which began attempting to break the monotony of the typical suburb by creating more orderly and distinct neighborhoods.

Two specific proposals for new development, the "cluster development" and "New Town," were publicly encouraged by LBJ in his housing message in January 1964, and he proposed new legislation to regulate suburban growth. Reporting on these new proposals in the *New York Times,* the architecture critic Ada Louise Huxtable stated that some form of action needed to be taken to end the damage suburbs were wreaking on American life, which was "social, cultural, psychological and emotional, as well as esthetic." In one particularly overwrought passage she described suburbia in overwhelmingly negative terms: "Suburban Christmas is a cheap plastic Santa Claus in a shopping-center parking lot surrounded by asphalt and a sea of cars. Suburban spring is not a walk in the awakening woods, but mud in the poorly built roads. Suburban life is no voyage of discovery or private exploration of the world's wonders, natural and man-made; it is cliché conformity as far as the eye can see, with no stimulation of the spirit through quality of environment."[55] Huxtable's description perfectly captures how the suburbs were frequently portrayed in popular culture as cheap, conformist, and potentially soul crushing.

Although perhaps not quite so overblown, such imagery was evident throughout popular culture from the early 1950s on. In one of the most popular fictional critiques of the new suburban and corporate order, Sloan Wilson's novel *The Man in the Gray Flannel Suit* (1955), the problem with the suburbs is their overriding dullness, which has started to slowly affect Tom and Betsy Rath's marriage and leads to their general state of weariness with life and with each other. When Tom sets out on a new career as a public relations man in a national campaign promoting mental health, it seems as though they might have an opportunity to move out of their decaying suburban house into a higher income bracket, which they initially believe will resolve all of their problems. But over time Tom realizes he is not willing to make the sacrifices necessary to become successful in the corporation he is employed by, especially when he compares himself to his boss, Ralph Hopkins, who is "a regular *machine* for work" and had sacrificed his family, his happiness, and the majority of his life to rise to the top of the corporate ladder.

By the end of the novel Tom opens up to his wife about the guilt he is still carrying from having served in the Second World War and the pressures he felt to conform once he had returned to the United States: "I really don't know what I was looking for when I got back from the war, but it seemed as though all I could see was a lot of bright young men in gray flannel suits rushing around New York in a frantic parade to nowhere. They seemed to me to be pursuing neither ideals nor happiness—they were pursuing a routine. For a long while I thought I was on the side lines watching that parade, and it was quite a shock to glance down and see that I too was wearing a gray flannel suit."[56] Once he finally learns how to assert his own convictions, everything ends up working out in Tom's favor. He explains to Hopkins that he is not willing to make the same sacrifices he had made to get ahead, and Hopkins, appreciating his honesty, gives him a less demanding position in the company. Betsy graciously forgives Tom for his infidelity during the war, and they renew their commitment to each other. Tom then inherits a large mansion and plot of land from his grandmother, which he ironically plans to turn into his very own suburban development.

Other sources that touched on the plight of Organization Men gave the American public less reason for optimism. *Patterns,* a film released in 1956 and based on a television drama produced by Rod Serling the previous year, corroborates that life in the corporate world not only deprives men of their autonomy but can potentially be hazardous to their mental and physical well-being. After Fred Staples is recruited to work for a firm in New York, he quickly discovers that the corporation controls the minutiae of his life, from where he sits in meetings to the furnishings in his new home to his diet. Over time it becomes clear that the head of the corporation, William Ramsey, had recruited Staples to replace Bill Briggs, who was second in command at the company and had worked there for nearly forty years. Briggs is on the verge of a nervous breakdown after a contentious dispute with Ramsey about purchasing a small plant and laying off half of its workers, and throughout the film Ramsey wages a drawn-out campaign against Briggs to undermine his authority and force him to resign. He starts by engaging in subtle acts of disrespect, such as reassigning Briggs's secretary to Staples. In the film's climactic scene, he delivers the knockout blow, giving Staples sole credit for an important joint report that Briggs had also worked on. Although Briggs secretly wants to confront Ramsey and stand up for himself, he can never summon the courage to do so, and after he meekly walks out of the conference room he suffers a fatal heart attack. Hardly missing a beat, Ramsey asks Staples to assume Briggs's responsibilities. Initially refusing, Staples, after confronting Ramsey and brokering a deal with him on his own terms, finally sells out and resigns himself to life at the firm. With heavy-handed symbolism the film portrays Briggs as the corporate everyman whose individuality and authority are attacked by the company, which drives him to drink, leads to his declining health, and ultimately pushes him to the brink of a nervous breakdown until he drops dead as his coworkers look on. Meanwhile, Ramsey is the inhuman face of the corporation, whose cold business sense has divorced him from his humanity. When Staples accuses him of driving his workers into the grave for the sake of his business, Ramsey angrily clarifies, "It's no one's business. It belongs only to the best. To those who can control it, sustain it, nurture it, keep it growing. Right now it belongs to us because we're producing, but in the future it belongs to whoever has the brains, the nerve and the skill to take it away from us." The corporation itself is ultimately the true villain in *Patterns*, and the film hints that once Staples and Ramsey are no longer producing for it they might be in store for a fate similar to Briggs's. In the film's bleak vision of postwar corporate America, humans no longer control corporations but the corporations control them, and the consequences can be fatal.

Around the same time as the theatrical release of *Patterns*, the terms *organization men* and its fictional counterpart *the man in the gray flannel suit* began appearing more and more regularly in American popular culture to denote a new "breed" of Americans who worked for the organization and lived in the suburbs. Years later Wilson reflected on how the title of his book entered the cultural idiom and became a sort of national punch line, specifically reminiscing about an episode of the TV show *The Honeymooners* "in which Art Carney climbed out of a sewer in dirty overalls and said to Jackie Gleason, 'What did you expect, the man in the gray flannel suit?' "[57] Behind the sarcastic front, the use of the terms often signaled a great deal of apprehension about new encroachments upon American individuality.

Not surprisingly, a good deal of that apprehension was spurred on by critics' affirmations that the real source of the problem was the unnatural gender dynamics of postwar America. For example, Leonard J. Duhl, a public health service psychiatrist, warned a meeting of community planners in 1955 that they needed "to try to save the mental health of suburban 'matriarchal society.'" Duhl believed that because men were working further and further from home, the suburbs had become sexually segregated and were ruled by women, which "may leave an imprint on the minds and health of men."[58] Writing in the *New York Times* in 1957, Margaret Mead elaborated on these concerns in an article titled "American Man in a Woman's World," arguing that new social expectations that infringed on women's opportunities to work outside the home had also impacted male behavior. Most notably, the propaganda that had sold the homemaker ethos to women was beginning to influence men, and in Mead's estimation it had an even stronger hold on their psyche than the corporate world. As men began to become subconsciously anchored in domesticity, they began wearing "their gray flannel suits to the P.T.A. rather than the executive meeting."[59] In the process they started to sacrifice their careers for the comforts of suburban life, which, in Mead's opinion, would eventually lead them to lose the devotion and competitive drive necessary to truly flourish in the corporate world. Although Mead admitted that these trends had some positive benefits, she averred that they made Americans' identities so dependent on their home life that they were losing any sort of identity outside of it. Ultimately, Mead concluded, "when we stopped short of treating women as people, after providing them with all of the paraphernalia of education and rights, we set up a condition whereby men also became less than full human beings."[60]

The article was accompanied by two illustrations by Abner Dean that would have helped readers further visualize Mead's argument. The first depicts a row of identical suburban homes stretching into the distance, each with an identical woman and two children standing on the front steps and waving goodbye to a man as he leaves the house. All of the men in the illustration are also identical, wearing a suit and hat, carrying a briefcase, and, most notably, wearing a rope tied around their waist that runs back into the house. In addition to criticizing suburban conformity, the image touched on Mead's assertion that American men were becoming subconsciously tied down by domesticity. The second illustration addresses the feminizing qualities of suburbia more directly by depicting the skewed gender dynamics of a typical suburban family of four. In the illustration a young girl and a woman are standing with their arms crossed and snidely glaring down at a man who is seated and cradling an infant in his arms. The man has a sheepish, downcast look on his face and his feet are positioned at an odd angle so that his toes are facing inward toward each other. The cartoon implies that he is not only out of his element, but being ruled by the women in his home and emasculated by his surroundings, as evidenced by his feminine body language and the fact that he has taken on stereotypically female responsibilities. Both illustrations exemplified Mead's point that postwar American men were constricted by the suburban environment and strongly hinted that new trends that tied men to their home lives—to such extremes that they might actually be caring for newborns no less—was a potentially harrowing development.

If these aspects of suburbia were beginning to trouble some Americans, there was a great deal more apprehension as well as mixed opinion about the corporate world. After being put on the defensive, many corporate leaders began publicly denying that subconscious or enforced conformity was an issue plaguing their workforce. For example, W. V. Merrihue, the chief of community relations for General Electric, told an audience at Rensselaer Polytechnic Institute's School of Humanities and Social Science in 1960 that misleading rhetoric had clouded Americans' views of big corporations, specifically citing the terms "the organization man, the power elite, and the status seeker."[61] Merrihue argued that since firms depended on creativity in order to succeed they actually fostered individuality, and he directly blamed the public's poor opinion of corporations on "the pseudo-psychology of a host of exposé artists."[62] In a speech at Princeton University in 1961 the president of DuPont, Crawford H. Greenewalt, went a step further, claiming that the entire body of social criticism aimed at corporations was flawed. Greenewalt began his speech by directly referencing Whyte, sarcastically noting, "If you believe Mr. Whyte of the 'Organization Man,' you will have the idea that my role is to convert my colleagues into a carbon copy of myself." Over the course of his talk Greenewalt attempted to explain why Whyte's critique of corporate conformity was misguided, pointing to the necessity of creativity in the corporate marketplace and underscoring his company's emphasis on "fresh and original ideas."

Like Merrihue, Greenewalt was attempting to rebrand corporations, portraying them as safe havens for individualistic expression instead of opponents to it. However, far from denying the existence of corporate conformity, Greenewalt turned the social criticism of corporate America on its head, asserting that in reality, "instead of the individual becoming the victim of pressures within the organization, it is the organization that falls prey to organization men." According to Greenewalt, the central "problem of our present society . . . is how best to preserve the creative power of the individual in the face of organizational necessity," and he emphasized that it was a problem that existed in almost every type of enterprise in the country, whether it was "the DuPont Company, Princeton University,

Illustrations by Abner Dean satirize suburban conformity and the feminization of the American men living there. Originally published in Margaret Mead, "American Man in a Woman's World," *New York Times Magazine,* February 10, 1957, 11 and 20.

the U.S. Marine Corps, the Church of Latter-Day Saints, or Tammany Hall." Given this scenario, corporate organizations were not the root cause of conformity but one institution among many that were threatened by social and economic forces curbing individuality in the United States. Moreover, Greenewalt indicated that social pressures to conform were undermining Americans' democratic values and entrepreneurial spirit, in large part because there was "confusion between the voluntary conformity of behavior which we call good manners and the enforced conformity of thought which represents an invasion of personal rights and a brake upon our capacity to follow our own destinies."[63]

Other voices from the corporate world had been calling for increased individuality and independent thought in similar terms since at least the mid-1950s. For example, at an American Management Conference in New York in 1957 personnel leaders from around the country deplored "yes-man-ship" in big business and discussed the portrayal of business leaders in popular culture, specifically addressing *The Man in the Gray Flannel Suit.* The most contentious moment of the three-day conference occurred during Lawrence A. Appley's introduction of the guest speaker, Melvin H. Baker, the chairman of National Gypsum Co. Appley was the president of the American Management Association and during his introduction of Baker he said that the collected assembly's primary mission was "to help others think as we think." After taking the floor, Baker proceeded to tear into Appley, attacking the "drift toward conformity" and predicting that "unless the current trend toward national conformity is reversed, we will be a race of thought-controlled robots."[64] At least publicly many corporate leaders would have sided with Baker, and by the mid-1950s it appeared that a sea change was beginning to take place in corporate culture around the country. A manager of a midwestern machine tool company attending the conference stated that the cultural focus on conformity had changed his company's hiring practices. His hiring department, he said, was consciously abstaining from uttering terms like "company man," "organization man," and "company patriotism" when interviewing job applicants, a sign that firms were conscious of the fact that workers were beginning to favor jobs that afforded opportunities for individual expression and creativity. A representative of the American Management Association, remarking upon perhaps the most ridiculous sign that change was in the air, commented "There's not nearly as many men with gray flannel suits here as you used to see."[65]

Although the suburbs and the corporate world were two of the most frequent targets of social critics, conformity, subconscious or otherwise, was primarily viewed as a larger, societal issue plaguing many facets of postwar American society. It was also such a frequent topic of debate that Americans were becoming self-conscious about their individuality as well as about the subconscious assaults on their psyches that were supposedly occurring at the office and in their living rooms. A number of parties took the organization man thesis and ran with it. William J. Kroll, a metallurgist who had done pioneering work in the titanium industry, called for more "lone-wolf researchers" and warned that, given the current emphasis on "team workers and conformity," the scientific geniuses of yesteryear "would probably be turned down at the plant doors as an eccentric, since he would not fit the pattern of the psychologist's organization man."[66] Advertisers began promoting a nonconformist aesthetic in print and radio ads, such as a Carlsberg beer ad in 1960 that announced, "In this age of the organization man, the Status Seeker, the beat generation—the Modern Quaffer stands alone as a bold individual force."[67] In 1959 the journalist Russell Baker, fearing that organization men might have infiltrated the nation's highest levels of government, wrote that there were indications that "the United States Senate, that exasperating, cantankerous, noble bastion of American individualism, has fallen to the men in the gray flannel suits."[68]

Organization men, it appeared, were everywhere. The debate finally came full circle when a number of writers and journalists began identifying organization men in the Soviet Union and Red China, starting with an article in the *New York Times* in 1957 titled "The Organization Man—Soviet Style." In the years to follow, the press would apply the organization man tag to members of the Twenty-first Congress of the Soviet Communist Party, all 8.7 million "elite" members of the Communist Party, the chief of the Soviet secret police, and the Chinese Head of State.[69] A full-length study titled *The Red Executive: A Study of the Organization Man in Russian Industry* was published. An article published in 1960 claimed that the Communist organization man was practically enslaved to the Communist Party, and although "his superiors, his orders, the theory or the line may change; the member's unquestioning loyalty, obedience and enthusiasm may not. The Communist goes where he is sent, does what he is told, and is judged by how well he does it. He is the world's first—and most capable—Organization Man."[70] Communist Party members—so frequently depicted as completely alien to American life earlier in the decade—were beginning to be portrayed in the same light as white-collar workers in the United States, and although they may have served a different master, a broad swath of American popular and intellectual culture saw them as suffering from very similar pressures on their individuality. If astute observers took this debate at face value, and many Americans clearly did, they may have reasonably concluded that the United States was beginning to resemble Communist society, only with money, after all.

A Democracy of Individual Participation

The practical implications of the debate over subconscious and enforced conformity in the United States in the 1950s can be a little difficult to gauge. Did it, for example, have any effect on where Americans actually chose to work and live in the 1950s and early 1960s? Who exactly was inside this discourse, who was outside of it, and what type of American was most likely to be influenced by concerns over individuality in the nation? And, finally, was it a top-down phenomenon, spurred on by the likes of Whyte and Wilson, or was it mainly driven from the bottom up and reflective of the larger populace? By some measures it would appear that ordinary Americans were hardly affected by the ongoing debate. For all the talk of the symbolism of gray flannel suits, for example, a dozen manufacturers attempted to cross-promote their merchandise with the film adaptation of Wilson's novel, purposely identifying "their products as essential parts of the wardrobe of every Man in the Gray Flannel Suit." The "tie-in advertising" featured nearly every type of men's clothing and accessory imaginable, including "Cavalier neckties, Dobbs hats, Excelio shirts, Revere sportswear, MurMil hosiery, Shields jewelry, Weldon pajamas, Pioneer belts and accessories, Gruen watches, Cooper's underwear, Regal shoes and Eagle suits."[71] Eagle Clothes even introduced a new light-gray color for its flannel suits, which it called Gregory Gray after the star of the film adaptation of the novel, Gregory Peck. These manufacturers were apparently not reluctant to associate their products with a fictional character derided for conforming to the status quo. Their gambit paid off, and gray flannel suits remained one of the best-selling styles of men's formal wear in 1955 and 1956.[72]

The majority of Americans appeared not to heed Whyte's or Wilson's warnings on more substantial matters either, and, most significantly, the two most heavily criticized hotbeds of conformity in the late fifties and early sixties remained relatively unscathed, as organizations and suburbs continued to grow exponentially. In many respects the anxieties Americans harbored about individuality are similar to those held about nuclear warfare during the same period, since they both informed Americans' beliefs and attitudes about numerous facets of domestic society but did not necessarily leave them paralyzed in fear. Americans continued to live in suburbs and work at corporations as well as buy gray flannel suits, for that matter, but a wealth of evidence attests that the seeds of a social rebellion had indeed been planted. Conformity, "belongingness," and groupthink were out. A postmodern strain of rugged individualism was in. Many factors contributed to this shift in ideology, which witnessed the emergence of much more critical attitudes about values that were in large part born out of necessity in the Great Depression and the Second World War. One factor was that some of the more invasive practices of earlier periods had continued evolving in business and suburban communities to the point that they had started to become borderline oppressive by the 1950s. Additionally, Americans may have been more willing to sacrifice their own identity in the midst of depression and a more immediate hot war, as evidenced by the countless Americans who eagerly applied for the most soul-crushing of jobs throughout the late 1920s and 1930s out of economic necessity and the millions of American men and women who answered the call to duty during the Second World War and marched into industrial factories throughout the country and into combat in the battlefields of Europe and the Pacific. The economic and political context of the Great Depression and the Second World War produced powerful incentives to sacrifice one's individuality for the sake of one's family, community, and nation. It also made an imprint on the social conditions that placed a priority on normality, which was one of the overriding features of the early postwar era, what Anna G. Creadick has called "a post-traumatic response to World War II, with Cold War consequences."[73]

By the 1950s, in the face of a booming economy and a new war that never actually touched down on American soil and did not require nearly as much manpower, many of the factors that had necessitated self-sacrifice in the previous generation simply no longer existed. But the rhetoric of the postwar period reveals that at the time Americans were framing their new convictions about individuality along different lines. Whenever the subject of individuality came up in American society, the domestic institutions that supposedly threatened it were routinely equated with similar practices within Communist society. The continuous referral to Communist psychological warfare not only illustrates that numerous Americans interpreted practices in domestic and corporate society within a broader Cold War framework, but also explains why those practices appeared so menacing. Conformity in the United States, both in the suburbs and at the workplace, was frequently portrayed as a form of psychological invasion and equated with the practices of indoctrination, propaganda, and brainwashing. Far from being a simple issue of personal behavior, the discourse on individuality divulged that larger societal institutions were subconsciously influencing Americans' behavior and could potentially undermine American democracy. As a result, the societal emphasis on normality and conformity during the Great Depression and the Second World War lost much of its traction and even appeared threatening.

Although historians have associated the anxieties surrounding individuality with white, middle-class men, they extended beyond the corporate and suburban world and the men who inhabited it. An individual's perception of any of the "anxieties of affluence" popularly ascribed to the suburban and corporate landscape of postwar American society would almost certainly have been colored by their social status, race, and class background.[74] For many minority groups and working-class ethnic whites, for example, the suburbs were just as likely to represent an alluring vehicle to middle-class respectability as an oppressive, dehumanizing force. In this context, the strong sales of gray flannel suits in the mid-1950s speak to the diverse messages the suit conveyed to different people, and just as some middle- and upper-class men were jettisoning gray flannel suits from their wardrobe to signal their individuality, other groups were embracing the attire of Peck's character in *The Man in the Gray Flannel Suit* to denote their middle-class status. Commenting on this aspect of postwar culture, Creadick noted that to businesswomen and minorities the gray flannel suit "remained a necessary mark of inclusion," which led to an ironic turn of events by the end of the 1950s, when "the freedom *not* to don a suit would come to signify one as solidly middle class."[75] For some Americans in the fifties a gray flannel suit remained a luxury, something that they were working toward, not running from.

Although interpretations of the trappings of a middle-class lifestyle varied, almost every sector of the nation expressed some degree of anxiety about individuality and conformity during the early postwar period. In a speech he gave in 1962 the associate executive director of the National Urban League, Alexander J. Allen, averred that conformity was detrimental to African Americans' campaign for civil rights, describing it as "at best a hopeless sedative. At worst . . . a fatal position to the progress of race relations in these critical times." Extolling the virtues of individuality, Allen encouraged the audience to avoid all "conformity to outmoded patterns of second-class citizenship" and indicated that African Americans could break the cycle of racism only by living as individuals and communities that stopped conforming to segregation and the stereotypes that had been projected upon them.[76] Women were given similar advice about how to gain their rights as individuals. Commenting on the plight of the typical suburban housewife, Friedan wrote that by conforming to social expectations women had become "less than human, preyed upon by outside pressures, and herself preying upon her husband and children."[77] Friedan's path to female self-fulfillment echoed the platitudes offered to middle-class men and African Americans: "Refuse to be nameless, depersonalized, manipulated."[78] In short, be an individual.

In 1961 the playwright Arthur Miller said that the most profound struggle for postwar Americans was not the Cold War but the inherently dehumanizing nature of living in a "massively industrialized society." In light of this, the central question Americans faced, Miller declared, was, "Can people remain human beings when every human quality is being suppressed except the thing we need to have in order to fit into the industrial scheme efficiently?"[79] Miller's comments prompted a minister from Chicago to assert, "The task we face in an era of the overstandardized mass is to illustrate, explain, and dramatize the meaning of being a person in our overstandardized society."[80] As the nation stood on the brink of the 1960s, many Americans appear to have agreed with this sentiment, and they weighed in on the best ways to reinvigorate the nation with individuality and avoid the dangers of dehumanization.

Some advocated a fairly conservative approach, one which was perfectly captured in a questionnaire titled "Are You a Conformist or a Rebel?" printed in the *Los Angeles Times* in 1959. The lead-in paragraph to the questionnaire outlined its basic position: "'Conformity' has become a bad word lately. Many people are concerned that they're 'running with the crowd' too much and losing their individuality. Actually, every well-adjusted person should conform to our accepted customs. There's no point in being a rebel unless you have a cause. The intelligent conformist observes the rules of society yet maintains his individuality. The 'bad' type of conformist may conform too much. Which kind of conformist are you?"[81] The quiz that followed featured a number of questions supposedly designed to teach the *Times* readership how to conform sensibly, with such insightful gems as "[Question] Every matchbook cover tells you to 'close cover before striking.' Do you? [Answer] The warning to close the matchbook is issued to prevent the entire pack from lighting and burning your hand. Rebelling is just foolish." Although the questionnaire was lighthearted in tone, it weighed in on the debate about individuality by championing a personal style for Americans predicated on the assumption that at least some level of conformity was unavoidable.

Other groups were in favor of a more serious reimagining of American democracy that combined the essentially personal issue of individuality with large-scale national politics. In the Port Huron Statement, released in 1962, the Students for a Democratic Society (SDS) offered a generational statement for the first group of Americans to come of age in the postwar era. Declaring that they had "matured in complacency," in large part because they had been deceived by the nation's high-sounding principles, lived in comfort amidst a booming postwar economy, and been misled by the paradoxes of the government's stated humanitarian aims and its actual policy in both foreign and domestic matters, they had reached adulthood only to discover they had inherited a "democratic system apathetic and manipulated rather than 'of, by, and for the people.'" In addition to identifying social injustices at home, such as racial bigotry, they accused the U.S. military and the political class of being psychologically coercive and of employing propaganda and motivational research to manipulate public opinion, practices that were threatening to further erode the role of the individual in the democratic system. Their solution to the disillusionment they felt with the current state of American society was to chart a new path forward based on "the establishment of a democracy of individual participation," one which was "an effort rooted in the ancient, still unfulfilled conception of man attaining determining influence over the circumstances of his life."

The SDS's vision for the future of the country can be completely understood only in light of the nearly decade-long debate over the state of American individuality that preceded it. By 1962 individuality had become a loaded term, a fact certainly not lost on a generation of Americans that had grown up in the midst of recurring angst over the psychological and mental invasion of the American psyche. In this sense the Port Huron Statement was not only an attempt to shake a new generation out of their political and social complacency but also an unequivocal rejection of all the existing forces within the United States that treated each citizen like "he is a thing to be manipulated, and that he is inherently incapable of directing his own affairs."

In its attempt to lay the foundation for a new American society, the SDS stood at the forefront of a number of emerging voices on the political left and right that rejected the limits placed on individuality in the early postwar era. These groups often shared some of the same Cold War principles that had driven Americans to the heights of the second Red Scare, but their perception of the United States had clearly evolved. American individuality was no longer threatened simply by a Communist bogeyman. Instead, American mass media, advertisers, politicians, corporations, and social institutions had all joined its ranks, employing the same mind-bending techniques to subsume the American individual into a mass, unthinking collective that had lost control over what they purchased, whom they voted for, and their public and personal lives in organizations and the suburbs. With these potential threats to their selfhood looming in the background, many Americans began to move beyond the Cold War politics that had pitted the United States against the Communist Party in a simplistic us versus them competition and started to adopt new, increasingly critical attitudes toward their own social institutions and to endorse a new social ethic that practically deified individualism. As the "me generation" came of age, current events and recurring debates about a variety of institutions that threatened to intrude on their behavior and thoughts would push many of them to take this ethic to heart.

7
The Legacy of Brain Warfare

The man who coined the term *brainwashing,* Edward Hunter, continued to resurface periodically in the national spotlight until the early 1960s. An appearance before members of the House Committee on Un-American Activities in 1958 outlined how his thinking on brainwashing had evolved since he had first published on the topic, and he frankly told the assembled congressmen that "the Communist hierarchy well knows that its brainwashing is only skin deep in the overwhelming number of cases." The admission represented a stark departure from many of his earlier comments about the long-lasting effects of brainwashing. Despite his reversal, Hunter still viewed Communist psychological warfare as a serious threat, and he spent the bulk of his testimony warning the committee members that the Communist Party was beginning to successfully deploy psychological warfare against the American people in order to weaken the United States. In order to defeat international Communism and protect Americans from their sinister psychological weaponry, Hunter advised the committee that Americans needed to develop "mental survival stamina," and he emphasized the necessity of reexamining the nation's social values. According to Hunter, the dilemmas raised by Communist psychological warfare called for a return to the values of his childhood:

> I remember when I was a young man, every personnel department was looking for leadership qualities. What was sought was a man's capacity as an individual to achieve new things. Today that is not even considered by personnel departments in their employment policies. They ask, instead, if the man "gets along" with everybody. They do not ask what is his individuality; they ask how he conforms. When we raise a young man to believe that at all costs he must get on with everyone, we have put him into a state of mind that almost guarantees, if he falls into the hands of an enemy such as the Communists, that he will react as he

> had been raised, to try "to get on," because he must not be "antisocial." Being "antisocial" has become the cardinal sin in our society. We have to again go back to characteristics of ours which made us, as individuals, say that what is right is right, and whether or not it is antisocial makes no difference.[1]

In its direct reference to the entrenched conformity of domestic American society, Hunter's testimony illustrates how the debates over Communist psychological warfare and American individuality were beginning to fold in on each other.

Hunter's last public statements to capture national attention came in a headline-grabbing appearance before a Senate Internal Security subcommittee in 1961. At the time of his appearance the Senate was embroiled in a tense debate over military sponsored anticommunist education seminars and training courses that were being given to troops, a debate that had largely been spurred on by a public scandal surrounding Maj. Gen. Edwin A. Walker, a high-ranking military official in command of the Twenty-fourth U.S. Infantry Division stationed in West Germany. In April an independent German newspaper, the *Overseas Weekly,* reported that Walker had been indoctrinating his troops with literature from the John Birch Society, anticommunist classics such as J. Edgar Hoover's *Masters of Deceit,* and, incidentally, one of Hunter's books on brainwashing. Walker said the purpose of his "pro-blue" campaign was to present troops with "a positive approach toward the defeat of open communist subversion of the American way of life."[2] Walker had also allegedly made disparaging remarks about a number of leading figures in American politics and entertainment, including former president Harry Truman, former secretary of state Dean Acheson and former first lady Eleanor Roosevelt, who, he claimed, were "definitely pinks"; in addition, he had said the newspaper columnist Walter Lippman, the director of the USIA, Edward R. Murrow, and Eric Sevareid, a news commentator for the Columbia Broadcasting System, were all "confirmed Communists."[3] There were also reports that Walker had been attempting to influence how his troops voted in the elections of 1960. Shortly after the allegations surfaced, rumors began to circulate that Walker was mentally unbalanced and may have been suffering from a brain tumor (a charge an army doctor later denied). Although the rumors may have been less than credible, many members of the administration of John F. Kennedy felt that Walker's political extremism disqualified him from serving in a command post in the army, and only three days after the allegations against him appeared he was temporarily relieved of his command and an official inquiry was launched.[4]

The fallout from the case was immense. Walker, a highly decorated

Edward Hunter on Capitol Hill in 1961 after testifying before the Senate Internal Security Committee. By coining the term, Hunter played a pivotal role in the brainwashing scare of the 1950s and 1960s, although he could have hardly surmised just how ubiquitous the concept would become. (AP Images)

veteran of the Second World War and Korea, had garnered a great deal of good will over his career and was not without his share of supporters. In addition, many conservatives in Congress agreed with Walker in principle and used the case to attack the Kennedy administration for being weak on Communism. The debate reached a fever pitch in August 1961, when an additional fourteen high-ranking military officials were named in an official government document, called the Fulbright Memorandum after Chairman J. W. Fulbright of the Senate Foreign Relations Committee, for suspicion of being "right-wing radicals" and engaging in propaganda activities. The memo was revealed in dramatic fashion when Sen. Strom Thurmond of South Carolina placed it into the *Congressional Record* to publicize it. He said it represented an attempt to gag the military and silence military leaders whose only objective was to alert the nation about the dangers of internal communism. Fulbright immediately responded by placing an identical copy of the memo into the record and then took to the Senate floor to defend his position and explain that his intent was to ensure that military leaders did not use their positions of authority to push their personal political agendas.

In his testimony to the Senate Internal Security subcommittee Hunter jumped head first into the debate, stating that the government's decision to silence anticommunists like Maj. Gen. Walker was evidence of a Communist conspiracy "to push this Administration, the press and public into a trap that would eliminate the anti-Communist program in the United States."[5] Hunter saw evidence of Communist influence nearly everywhere, specifically citing "anti-anti-communist" articles in over half a dozen major American publications (which he later submitted to the committee as evidence) and the recent decision by the U.S. Post Office to phase out its "Champions of Liberty" postage stamp series. Largely on the basis of this evidence, which he believed amounted to brazen Communist propaganda, Hunter jumped to the conclusion that a Communist conspiracy reached into the highest levels of American government and that Communist agents had infiltrated even the White House. As he explained to the subcommittee, "Moscow simply acquired agents who mingled with the new, intellectual elite at the top on terms of equality, were sometimes members of it themselves. They infiltrated the White House and other topmost government offices."[6] Hunter concluded that the efforts to censor the anticommunist military training programs were potentially disastrous and could lead the United States "to the condition of mental disarmament we were in when the Reds struck in Korea."[7]

After Hunter's testimony was made public, Sen. Thomas J. Dodd of Connecticut and Sen. Kenneth B. Keating of New York issued a joint statement calling his remarks "untrue and irresponsible."[8] It is perhaps ironic that Hunter, who had spent part of his career attempting to alert Americans to the dangers of Communist propaganda and psychological warfare, lost credibility by coming to the defense of an army general who was primarily being accused of indoctrinating his troops. Only a few months later Secretary of Defense Robert McNamara effectively ended the controversy by banning civil and military defense officials from making politically partisan statements at meetings sponsored by civic groups and forbidding the use of military facilities for public education programs.[9]

Meanwhile, the central figure of the debate, Maj. Gen. Walker, submitted his letter of resignation in November, bemoaning the "little men" who ruined his military career and defending his education program, aggressively asserting that it was "not possible to make a soldier of a man who has not first become a dedicated American."[10] Two weeks after Walker resigned, President Kennedy attempted to inject a voice of reason into the controversy that had unfolded over the previous seven months in a speech at a one-hundred-dollar-a-plate dinner at the Hollywood Palladium in Los Angeles. In his comments Kennedy warned the nation to ignore those voices that occupied the "fringes of our society" and trafficked in extremist fantasies and conspiracy theories. With twenty-five hundred supporters looking on, he declared,

> Under the strains and frustrations imposed by constant tension and harassment, the discordant voices of extremism are heard once again in the land. Men who are unwilling to face up to the danger from without are convinced that the real danger comes from within. They look suspiciously at their neighbors and their leaders. They call for a "man on horseback" because they do not trust the people. They find treason in our finest churches, in our highest court, and even in the treatment of our water. They equate the Democratic Party with the welfare state, the welfare state with socialism and socialism with communism. They object quite rightly to politics' intruding on the military—but they are anxious for the military to engage in politics. But you and I and most Americans take a different view of our peril. We know that it comes from without, not within. It must be met by quiet preparedness, not provocative speeches. . . . Let our patriotism be reflected in the creation of confidence rather than crusades of suspicion. Let us prove we think our country great by striving to make it greater. And, above all, let us remember that, however serious the outlook, the one great irreversible trend in world history is on the side of liberty—and so, for all time to come, are we.[11]

In the span of a few sentences Kennedy had redrawn the lines of mainstream American political discourse and in the process placed cold warriors like Hunter well outside of it.[12] Hunter, whose accusations about Communist infiltration in the U.S. government would have placed him at the center of the American political consensus only a decade earlier, was relegated to the margins of American political life by the early 1960s.

Hunter's books would remain central in right-wing circles, and conservative groups continued to list his works as recommended reading material and occasionally enlisted him as a guest speaker well into the mid-1960s. However, brainwashing had always been bigger than the man who actually invented (or translated) the term, having outgrown Hunter in influence and reach nearly from the time his first article on the subject had appeared in the *Miami News*. Unlike Hunter, who largely faded into obscurity, brainwashing remained relevant and was periodically thrust back into mainstream political debate, especially during times of war.

Déjà vu in Vietnam?

Brainwashing was revived and slightly reimagined during the Vietnam War when the media began speculating that the Viet Cong and the North Vietnamese Army had started utilizing the technique again. Such speculation was apparently confirmed in December 1965, when SSgt. George E. Smith and Spec. 5 Claude D. McClure reappeared at a Cambodian border post after spending two years in captivity. At their first news conference they praised their captors and adamantly denied they had ever been tortured while in captivity. They also released an antiwar statement to the press which asserted, "The United States has nothing to gain from the war in Vietnam, for the Viet cong are the people."[13] After additional questioning several days later, Smith acknowledged that "in a way" they had been brainwashed while held captive, and he told reporters he could not recall the pledge he had made at his initial press conference to lead an antiwar campaign once he returned to the United States.[14] Afterward, a Marine Corps commandment told reporters, "I'd say they've been brainwashed."[15] Once released into military authority, Smith and McClure were flown to an air force base in Thailand, given medical and psychiatric evaluations, and quietly sent back to the United States with less-than-honorable discharges.[16]

Echoes of Korea abounded. An antiwar statement allegedly written by an American POW was broadcast over a Viet Cong radio channel in 1967. It contained subtle clues of forced indoctrination, including mention of a camp where the POW had "learned the truth about the dirty, immoral, and illegal war that our government is carrying on here in Viet Nam."[17] Later in the year a Viet Cong interrogator who defected to the South Vietnamese government told military authorities that American POWs were the focus of a reeducation campaign behind enemy lines, although he reported it was not very successful.[18] The U.S. government largely refused to address the POW situation, which only fueled speculation about the plight of American soldiers being held in captivity. In 1968, when the crew of the USS *Pueblo* was captured by North Korean patrol boats in international waters, it became evident that America's old Communist foe was still utilizing psychological torture against enemy combatants. For the next eleven months the ship's crew was held in North Korea, where they were forced to make confessions about their war crimes and participate in propaganda activities while being subjected to physical torture and indoctrination.

The treatment of POWs in North Vietnam and the case of the USS *Pueblo* seemed to give the American public good reason to believe that brainwashing was still one of the primary weapons in the Communists' psychological arsenal. However, owing to a variety of factors brainwashing never inspired the same amount of public anxiety during the Vietnam era that it had a decade earlier. This time around the U.S. military simply seemed better prepared to wage war on a psychological battlefield. Only a week after the story of Smith's and McClure's apparent brainwashing first broke, the Associated Press reported that the Marine Corps had instituted a survival school that was successfully training thousands of marines to withstand Communist psychological torture. The school had actually been created during the Korean War as a direct response to the techniques the Communists were using in North Korean prison camps and had similar counterparts in other branches of the military. The marine course consisted of six days of escape training in the Sierra Nevada mountains, where trainees were dropped into the wilderness with no supplies and instructed to evade capture, and then another week of training at a mock prison camp, where they were instructed in enemy psychological warfare. According to one of the sergeants who taught at the school, "Marines have to be in good shape before they come here. But after they leave, they could run uphill and fight a bear."[19] When a Special Forces officer named James N. Rowe escaped from the Viet Cong and was rescued by an American helicopter in 1968 after spending nearly five years in captivity, the military had definitive proof that soldiers could withstand Communist psychological pressure and live to tell about it. In light of the rumors about what was occurring behind enemy lines, the military's vigorous efforts to train its soldiers to withstand Communist psychological warfare and reports about the bravery of men like Rowe offered the public compelling evidence that America's latest crop of fighting men were better trained and perhaps tougher and more disciplined than their predecessors in North Korea.

In addition, the very concept of brainwashing had lost some of its cultural cachet, and by the start of the Vietnam War a growing number of critics were questioning its legitimacy and effectiveness. An article in the *Los Angeles Times* in 1965 titled "The Myth of Brainwashing Revived" addressed the speculation circulating around the treatment of American POWs in North Vietnam and captured much of the skepticism surrounding the technique. One of the article's primary sources was Henry Segal, who had played a major role in the army's initial interviews of POWs at the end of the Korean War. Segal now attested that the furor over brainwashing in the early and mid-1950s was "a kind of neurotic projected guilt that we neatly foisted on our POWs, only to wash them (and us) clean again by crying foul over the supposedly uncommon powers of the enemy."[20] The article concurred and determined that the primary lesson the nation should have learned from the Korean War experience was that "the idea of exotic brainwashing techniques is so much nonsense—and dangerous nonsense at that."[21] As more time passed after the Korean War and in the face of little additional evidence beyond hearsay of brainwashing's validity, an increasingly skeptical outlook on the concept was beginning to gain traction.

That explains in part why reporters and military officials were generally more inclined to attribute the behavior of American POWs in North Vietnam to torture rather than to any "exotic brainwashing techniques."

Despite these changes in popular and public discourse, brainwashing continued to retain a strong grip on the nation's collective imagination throughout the Vietnam era. The concept's continuing authority was highly evident in the uproar surrounding comments made by George Romney, the governor of Michigan, in the fall of 1967. In a pretaped television interview that aired on September 4, the commentator Lou Gordon asked Romney why he had changed his position on the Vietnam War. Romney's response would dominate the news cycle for the next week and essentially derailed his undeclared bid for the presidential election in 1968. Romney said his initial support for the war had been influenced by a tour he had taken of Vietnam with a group of governors in 1965, during which he had received "the greatest brainwashing that anybody can get. . . . Not only by the generals, but also by the diplomatic corps over there, and they do a very thorough job."[22] Romney had employed the term *brainwashing* in what had become its most common colloquial usage and was clearly implying that government and military authorities had misled him about the true nature of Vietnam. Nonetheless, the comment sparked a firestorm of media scrutiny and a backlash from Romney's political opponents.

The Democratic national chairman, John M. Bailey, was one of the first to criticize Romney's allegations, calling them an insult to Ambassador Henry Cabot Lodge and Gen. William C. Westmoreland, who had been in charge of the briefings. Bailey demanded that Romney publicly apologize for questioning "the integrity of two honorable and dedicated men."[23] Several of Romney's companions on the trip in 1965 also went public. The former governor of Georgia, Carl Sanders, stated, "As far as I'm concerned, I was neither brainwashed, nor intimidated, nor influenced, nor coerced by any diplomatic or military official."[24] The other nine governors who had gone on the trip echoed Sanders's comments. The most critical member of the group, Philip H. Hoff of Vermont, stated, "It is outrageous that he would lead us to believe he was that naïve or that he was brainwashed . . . to say he hasn't enough ability to make a judgment on his own as a presidential contender. It's the old McCarthy tactic of guilt by innuendo. I think it's kind of stinking."[25]

Cabot Lodge attempted to make light of Romney's accusations when reporters pressed him for a response, asserting that he had "never brainwashed anybody in my life," before playfully adding, "You usually brainwash me."[26] Members of President Lyndon B. Johnson's administration were less coy about Romney's inflammatory rhetoric, especially after

Romney doubled down on his initial claims. When members of the press informed Romney about Bailey's demands for a public apology at a committee meeting at the National Governors' Conference in Washington, D.C., Romney took a newspaper clipping out of his coat pocket which contained quotes that Secretary McNamara had made the previous year about draft quotas. Romney proceeded to tell the reporters, "If you want to get into a discussion of who's been brainwashing who, I suggest you take a look at what the Administration has been telling the American people. The information has not been adequate."[27] The next day McNamara dismissed Romney's allegations in a press conference: "He appears to be blind to the truth. I don't think he can recognize the truth when he sees it or when he hears it."[28] Romney's opponents in the Republican and Democratic parties, perhaps smelling blood in the water, quickly piled on. Nixon's campaign chairman, the former Oklahoma governor Henry Bellmon, told reporters he would not comment directly on Romney's brainwashing notion, but he said that as a candidate Romney "show[ed] weakness" that could be "very damaging" to the Republican Party in the upcoming presidential election.[29] Sen. Everett Dirksen of Illinois echoed Bellmon's sentiment, telling reporters, "When a fellow says, 'I've been brainwashed,' the first thing that occurs to someone is that your background is such that you can't resist brainwashing."[30]

After several days of negative publicity Romney attempted to walk back his comments from earlier in the week, clarifying that he had not been the victim of the "Russian type" of brainwashing but the "L.B.J. type," which he defined as "a snow job, hogwash, credibility gap, and manipulation of the news."[31] Unfortunately for Romney's political ambitions, he had lost control of his political narrative, and his critics repeatedly used his brainwashing gaffe to undermine his credibility. A profile of him that appeared in *Time* a week after the Gordon interview referred to him as "The Brainwashed Candidate," an allusion to the Richard Condon novel that foreshadowed how Romney would be portrayed by the national media for the remainder of the election cycle.[32] Less than a week after his statement the *Detroit News*, the largest newspaper in Romney's home state and one of his biggest supporters, called on him to abandon his bid for the presidency and withdrew its support for his campaign. Romney's statement had also struck a nerve with the public. An angry citizen writing to the *Chicago Tribune* argued that Romney's words ultimately "revealed that he may have a brain."[33] Even after Romney attempted to shift attention from his remark by going on a tour of the nation's inner cities later in the month, the brainwashing meme continued to resurface. At a meeting with civic leaders in Indianapolis, for example, Romney was being

The stigma of brainwashing still lingered well into the 1960s. Gov. George Romney's assertion that he had been brainwashed by the U.S. military and diplomatic corps on American strategy in Vietnam effectively ended his bid for the presidency in 1968. (Conrad, "Governor Romney's preparing another speech on Vietnam!," *Los Angeles Times*, September 8, 1967. Used with permission of the Conrad Estate. Paul Conrad Cartoons, Special Collections Research Center, Syracuse University Libraries)

briefed on anticrime and antipoverty efforts in the city when an African American man in attendance, Jack D. Clark, stood up and proclaimed that all the programs were "shams" and accused the local authorities of giving Romney "his second brainwashing."[34] But by far the biggest sign of the damage Romney had incurred came in the polls: in August he was the highest-ranking Republican in the field, but a mere week and a half after his interview with Gordon aired he had fallen to fourth.[35]

In a last-ditch effort to save his campaign, Romney went on another trip to Vietnam in December. Before leaving he confidently told a group of reporters in his office that this time "nobody's going to brainwash me," and then he offered a bizarre analogy comparing his current mental state to a piece of metal that had been broken and then welded back together or a bone that had broken and then healed and was stronger as a result.[36] The trip, and Romney's remarks about it, hardly inspired confidence in voters, and he withdrew his bid for the Republican nomination a few months later. Political commentators who assessed his campaign at the time of his resignation pointed to the brainwashing gaffe as a turning point in Romney's candidacy, which demonstrates how the concept continued to have a powerful effect on public discourse and even on the fate of a presidential election. For Romney, an off-the-cuff remark made in an interview on local television in Detroit ultimately brought about his political downfall because brainwashing carried the weight of nearly a decade and a half of Americans' anxieties over mind control and individuality. By raising the specter of brainwashing, Romney had called his leadership qualities, masculinity, and mental tenacity into question. As some of his opponents pointed out, echoing earlier critiques of the manhood of American POWs during the Korean War, the admission demonstrated Romney's weakness. In essence, many of Romney's critics believed that any man weak enough to be brainwashed was not strong enough to lead the American people.

An article published in the *Chicago Tribune* succinctly captured why Romney's claims had been so damaging within the larger context of 1967:

> An important question that develops with Romney's admission that he can be brainwashed is whether the country can afford the risk of having a man in the White House who says he can be brainwashed. If Romney can be brainwashed by his fellow American diplomats and military men, why can't he be brainwashed just as easily by the Russians or the Red Chinese or Ho Chi Minh[?] When Romney makes his 19-day tour of urban America later this month, is he going to be brainwashed everywhere he goes or will he be able to evaluate clearly what he sees and hears?[37]

Not only Romney's manhood had been called into question, but his judgment and mental fortitude as well. If Romney had admitted to being brainwashed by American diplomats in the past, did it not stand to reason that he could be brainwashed by them or anybody else in the future? Despite Romney's attempts to go on the offensive and turn his faux pas into a pointed critique of the Johnson administration's policy in Vietnam, it critically undermined his credibility.

Beyond the fact that the Romney incident shows that brainwashing still held sway over public opinion, what stands out most about it is that Romney attributed his brainwashing to the U.S. military and diplomatic corps. In fact, Romney had gone out of his way to clarify that he had not been the victim of the "Russian type" of brainwashing. By doing so, he had taken a technique once closely associated with the Communist enemy and relocated it within the U.S. government. This aspect of his declaration was certainly not lost on the public. In a letter to the *New York Times*, for example, a concerned citizen asked, "How many other public officials, especially Congressmen who vote the appropriations to continue the war, have been similarly brainwashed? Also, since the news media are more or less controlled by our Saigon officials, how many American people have been brainwashed?"[38]

In the postwar era brainwashing had been variously identified as a sinister form of Communist mind control, a weapon employed by American cultural, political, and economic institutions, and a tool of the U.S. military. In large part, brainwashing's metamorphosis over the course of the 1950s and 1960s can be attributed to the fact that it had been so ill-defined from the start, and its vague qualities allowed it to be associated with a variety of techniques and incidents. By the time Romney accused the military and diplomatic corps of brainwashing him, that ambiguity granted the term a certain degree of open-endedness, and it could mean different things to different people. A journalist commenting on the term's flexibility in the mid-1960s described it as "a popular catch-phrase, loosed as easily at the former friend who switches political party as against the assassin in 'The Manchurian Candidate.'"[39] In this view, brainwashing had simply slipped into the postwar vernacular, a concept divorced from its original time and place. As the Romney incident illustrates, however, this view is not entirely accurate: the technique still could frighten, shock, and disgust Americans because it brought old wounds to the surface and because of what it implied about life in the postwar world.

Postscript: *Hsi Nao* in the Twenty-First Century

Today, notwithstanding his lengthy career as a foreign correspondent, writer, and political activist, Edward Hunter is best known for contributing the word *brainwashing* to the English language. In 1961 he donated the bulk of his primary research on propaganda in Red China to the University of Wisconsin-Madison. It currently resides in the Center for Research Libraries, and it has become one of the largest digital collections of Communist propaganda from the 1950s on the Internet.[40] Every few years the group that almost single-handedly pushed Hunter's concept into the spotlight, the POWs who refused repatriation, becomes a matter of renewed interest. By 1966 most of them had returned to the United States. One opened a chop suey restaurant. Two wrote memoirs. A few came home with Chinese wives and children. Only two of the POWs who did not come back were confirmed to have spent the rest of their lives in China, and one of them died shortly after the Korean War.[41] Judging by these statistics, the brainwashing appears to have been a pretty ineffective process. So what truly motivated twenty-one American men to refuse repatriation to the United States in 1954? If the men themselves are to be believed, it was a mixture of the Communists' promises of material and sexual riches, disillusionment with American class and racial inequality, and some effective Communist propaganda. Decades later, the Associated Press published a "Where are they now?" piece, and one of the former POWs they located refused to be interviewed because he did not want his friends and neighbors to discover his past, an indication that at least for this man the experience lingered even fifty years later.[42]

On returning to the United States, many of the former POWs discovered that their flirtation with Communism was hard to live down. Sen. John McCain, who had spent nearly five and a half years as a POW in North Vietnam and was arguably the most famous war prisoner in the last half of the twentieth century, recently claimed that an anti-American propaganda pseudo-confession he made while in captivity cast a long shadow over his subsequent career in politics. His comments reveal that some members of the public have continued to question the experience of any American POW who collaborated with the enemy, even long after they had returned home. In an interview with a historian of the Vietnam War, McCain said, "I still get a lot of mail attacking me for supporting the normalization of relations with Vietnam. These wacko people call me 'the Manchurian candidate.' They've got a Website. I'm evil incarnate. I cooperated with the Vietnamese. I'm a Vietnamese agent. Any moment I expect Angela Lansbury to come in and turn over the Red Queen."[43] Old anxieties about brainwashing die hard.

The most obvious legacy of the Korean-era POWs is the Code of Conduct they inspired. The code has been modified twice, and, with slightly updated, gender-neutral rhetoric, still requires all members of the U.S.

military to "never forget that I am an American, fighting for freedom, responsible for my actions, and dedicated to the principles which made my country free." Several sections of the code directly pertain to mental and physical torture and acknowledge the existence of "intense coercion," which some of America's enemies may use to elicit information. The most direct example of how the code attempts to prevent the type of behavior that was on display during the Korean War can be found in Code of Conduct V, which states, "Actions every POW should resist include making oral or written confessions and apologies, answering questionnaires, providing personal histories, creating propaganda recordings, broadcasting appeals to other prisoners of war, providing any other material readily usable for propaganda purposes, appealing for surrender or parole, furnishing self-criticisms and communicating on behalf of the enemy to the detriment of the United States, its allies, its armed forces or other POWs." It is evidence of the military's more proactive approach to American soldiers' behavior while in captivity and their intention to prevent them from ever succumbing to brainwashing again. The ideals that the Code of Conduct represents have trickled down through the branches of the military and their respective training programs, theoretically ensuring that today's fighting American men and women are prepared for the psychological facets of modern warfare.

As for the concept of brainwashing and the techniques associated with it, their legacy is all around us. Although the term *brainwashing* itself has almost completely lost its connection to the early Cold War, in the recent past the concept has seen something of a revival. Prior to 9/11, the notion of overt mind control was predominantly relegated to the margins of American political and popular culture and to the fever dreams of conspiracy theorists, although ideas about subtler forms of psychological manipulation remained prominent in apprehensions about mass culture and legal debates about cults and criminal behavior. Ben Stiller's *Zoolander,* a comedy he produced and wrote before 9/11 that was released shortly after the terrorist attacks on New York City and Washington, presented brainwashing at its most ludicrous. The film's protagonist, a male model named Zoolander played by Stiller, had been brainwashed and turned into a pawn in a conspiracy to assassinate the prime minister of Malaysia. In the over-the-top brainwashing scene reminiscent of *A Clockwork Orange*, Zoolander is strapped into a chair, subjected to electric shocks, and forced to watch a film starring Jacobin Mugatu (Will Ferrell) while a disc jockey plays his trigger mechanism, Frankie Goes to Hollywood's hit from 1983 "Relax." Mugatu's programming ranges from the assassination to the absurd, as Zoolander is instructed, "You learn martial arts," "Prime

Minister of Malaysia bad, martial arts good," "Obey my dog!," and "You're a super-hot Ninja machine!" Although *Zoolander* was obviously a comedy, the film's satirical take on the world of *The Manchurian Candidate* is indicative of how overt mind control was starting to be portrayed within a less ominous framework prior to the war on terror.

Since 9/11 the shift in tone in the popular portrayal of brainwashing has been pronounced, as the idea has been conceptualized in terms much more reminiscent of Cold War imagery and tensions. This was manifest in the remake of *The Manchurian Candidate* in 2004, an updated take on the classic film from 1962 that relocated the plight of the brainwashed assassin into a more modern political and cultural context. Since its premiere in 2011, the Emmy-award winning Showtime series *Homeland* has also dealt with brainwashing with considerable nuance, indicating that anxieties about individuality and free will are as timely as ever.[44] The series revolves around two characters with very distinct reasons for mistrusting their independence. Sgt. Nicholas Brody, played by Damian Lewis, is an Iraq War veteran who has returned home after eight years as a prisoner of al-Qaeda. He has been psychologically and physically tortured and eventually turned by Abu Nazir, the head of the al-Qaeda network. In stages the series unveils the extent to which Brody has changed as a result of his imprisonment. He has converted to Islam, a fact he takes pains to hide from his family. He has become a murderer, nearly pulling off a plot to assassinate a room full of American political leaders and shooting his former friend and partner, Tom Walker, in cold blood. He has become a terrorist, parlaying his reputation as a patriotic war hero into a congressional seat in order to destroy the United States from deep within its own political system. Throughout the series the viewer is left guessing about the extent of Brody's free will, as he demonstrates signs of post-traumatic stress disorder and inner turmoil about the terrorist plot he is party to.

Meanwhile, the show's main protagonist, the CIA officer Carrie Mathison, played by Claire Danes, suffers similar issues with her psychological sovereignty, although the source of her problems is wildly different from Brody's. Diagnosed with bipolar disorder in her early twenties, Mathison self-medicates with clozapine, a powerful antipsychotic. The lone CIA officer to suspect that Brody might be a sleeper agent, Mathison is increasingly marginalized at the agency as mounting evidence appears to vindicate him. In order to reveal his true nature and unravel the terrorist plot, Mathison takes it upon herself to bug his home, eventually make contact with him, and initiate an affair. By the end of the series' first season, Mathison has been betrayed by her complicated feelings for Brody as well as by her psychological disorder, and, having suffered a manic episode and lost all credibility when the terrorist plot she predicted fails to materialize, she becomes "unable to trust my own thoughts." Convinced that the entire plot was a figment of her imagination and that Brody is an innocent victim of her delusional mind, Mathison seeks electroconvulsive therapy (ECT) to treat her illness. A moment before electric pulses rush through her brain, she remembers that Brody had yelled the name Issa in his sleep, which, shortly before her procedure, her mentor at the CIA had informed her was the name of Abu Nazir's son. Mathison finally connects the dots, but it is too late. The ECT machine is turned on, and Mathison is "cured" of her illness as well as drained of her knowledge.

The brainwashed sleeper agent and the CIA agent attempting to capture him in *Homeland* are essentially interchangeable because they both lack autonomy, and the series ultimately indicates that free will is an illusion not only of the bad guys. What distinguishes Brody from earlier prototypes of the brainwashed assassin is that, although he is subjected to sensory deprivation, isolation, and psychological torture, his conversion is at least partially based on his ability to make his own choices. After Issa and dozens of other children are killed in an American drone attack sanctioned by the vice president, Brody chooses to work with Nazir to avenge Issa's death. All of the circumstances surrounding Brody's choice may have been carefully orchestrated by Nazir, but he is fully converted into an al-Qaeda operative only after he becomes convinced that the United States is morally culpable for the terrorists' actions. As a result, Nazir has created the perfect sleeper agent: one who can't be deprogrammed and whose reliability rests on the strength of his own moral convictions.

In the finale of the first season Brody has metamorphosed into a suicide bomber and is making preparations to assassinate the vice president and other high-ranking officials at the State Department. In a confessional videotape he records before carrying out the plot, he says:

> People will say I was broken. I was brainwashed. People will say that I was turned into a terrorist. Taught to hate my country. I love my country. What I am is a marine, like my father before me and his father before him. And as a marine, I swore an oath to defend the United States of America against enemies both foreign and domestic. My action this day is against such domestic enemies. The Vice President, and members of his national security team, who I know to be liars and war criminals, responsible for atrocities they were never held accountable for. This is about justice for eighty-two children, whose deaths were never acknowledged and whose murder is a stain on the soul of this nation.

Brody's confession perfectly encapsulates many of the complexities of the series. In a world in which the United States sanctions drone strikes on children and subjects its own prisoners to physical and psychological torture, the morality of the war on terror becomes a matter of perspective. Unlike the robotic, nearly catatonic brainwashed assassins of yesteryear, stretching from Raymond Shaw to Derek Zoolander, the main characters of *Homeland* are not programmed automatons. Nicholas Brody and Carrie Mathison are human beings simply trying to do what they think is right, and the series shows that although our choices may appear to be our own, in reality they are often beyond our control. Like Brody, we are products of our environment. His sense of honor, his experience in a war zone, and Nazir's shrewd program of psychological manipulation are what convert Brody from a patriot and father into a suicide bomber. Like Mathison, the series attests, we are products of our biology. Her relentless drive to discover the truth and her psychological makeup plunge her into a downward spiral, ultimately leaving her strapped on a gurney with electric current scrambling her mind. Within this cultural universe, the lone brainwashed assassin is obsolete because in one way or another we are all subjected to forces beyond our control. Situating brainwashing within a post–9/11 framework, the series reveals how it has been reimagined in popular culture and turned into an even more subtle and unnerving phenomenon than previously imagined.

As we find ourselves fighting another "war for men's [and women's] minds," paranoia about mind control and indoctrination has become more and more prevalent in some circles, especially fringe groups. In 2010, for example, an editor at a conservative think tank named Adrian Morgan wrote a blog post lamenting "the latest exercise in Muslim propaganda," a comic book titled "The Ninety-Nine" that was originally produced in Kuwait and featured superheroes based on the ninety-nine names of Allah. In addition to expressing his concern about the comic's distribution in the United States and the plans to turn it into a television cartoon, Morgan was especially irate about President Barack Obama's public approval of the comic at a summit meeting for Muslim business owners, opining, "It seems like indoctrination, an indoctrination made more blatant by Obama's totally inappropriate promotion." According to Morgan, the fact that American children were being indoctrinated with Muslim values was made all the more troublesome by the lack of comparable Christian role models in the mainstream media. He speculated that it was doubtful young Americans would ever read about the exploits of a trio of "ass-kicking Christian superhero nuns, called Faith, Hope and Charity, whooping sinner's butts and sending Satan into Hell."[45] Ironically, the creator of the comic book, Naif Al-Mutawa, maintained that his motivation for creating the comic in the first place was to counter the propaganda and indoctrination of extremist groups he saw in Muslim society. Writing about the purpose of his work, Al-Mutawa declared, "If we allow small-minded men to spout fear and hate in the name of our religion, we will enable them to brainwash another generation as they did our own. And soon, the next generation will fall into a pit of dissonance. To sit by silently makes us all complicit."[46]

Morgan's point of view, although extreme, is fairly representative of some of the alleged brainwashing conspiracy theories about the Obama administration that have been proliferating on the far right. In recent years such theories have been gaining exposure, and in 2010 two books featuring variations of these arguments appeared on the *New York Times* best-seller list.[47] What explains the resurgence of brainwashing conspiracies, which have largely occurred absent any credible evidence to support them? Today's brainwashing conspiracies, like yesteryear's, are a type of intellectual shortcut.[48] They hold great appeal because they appear to explain why some politicians and political parties gain followers and power, without actually necessitating a critical examination of their policies. Interestingly, many of these conspiracy theories also locate brainwashers deep in the heart of the American power structure. When Romney made similar allegations in 1967, he became a laughingstock. In today's political climate he might have been a best-selling author.

In the wake of 9/11, brainwashing has also resurfaced in the popular construction of radical Islamic terrorists. In 2009 the Pakistani military made international headlines when it reported the discovery of a Taliban brainwashing center in Nawaz Kot, Pakistan. The center purportedly recruited children ranging from twelve to eighteen years of age and trained them to become suicide bombers. The compound's walls were painted with brightly colored pictures depicting what awaited the young recruits in heaven, chiefly rivers of milk and honey lined with dozens of virgins. Commenting on the images, an expert on the Taliban named Zahid Hussein stated, "I have never seen such elaborate paintings about so-called heaven." According to Hussein, the Taliban's young recruits "are also led to believe that the Muslims who are killed in suicide bombings, they will go to heaven as well."[49] For young teenagers living in poverty and often struggling to survive in a war-torn country, these visions of heaven would serve as a powerful incentive to join the Taliban's cause. In the United States, centers like the one discovered in Nawaz Kot aided in the creation of a narrative about the war on terror that downplayed American complicity in the war and stressed how the terrorist enemy had deluded and brainwashed a generation to hate capitalist democracy and burn effigies of President George W. Bush in the streets of Baghdad.

Like other wars in the recent American past, the war on terror bears witness to the spectacle of American citizens fraternizing with the enemy. When a twenty-one-year-old American citizen, John Walker Lindh, was captured in the American invasion of Afghanistan in 2001, it became abundantly clear that some Americans had been influenced by radical Muslim tenets. Several aspects of Lindh's subsequent trial were reminiscent of the cases against the Korean POWs in the 1950s, although Lindh ultimately agreed to a plea deal and admitted to "knowingly and willingly" fighting for the Taliban. Significantly, after Lindh's case gained notoriety in the United States, his mother remained dumbstruck about her son's actions, finally asserting, "If he got involved in the Taliban, he must have been brainwashed."[50] Lindh is currently serving a twenty-year prison sentence at the Federal Correctional Institution in Terre Haute, Indiana, and his case highlights how the main objectives of the United States in the war on terror have not changed much from those of the Cold War. As the journalist Dean E. Murphy eloquently noted only a month after 9/11, "There is another war being waged by Americans, and it is nothing like the one unfolding on the pitted landscape of Afghanistan. America's retaliatory strikes, and the image of bullying power they represent for many in the Islamic world, are thrusting the United States into an urgent struggle for the hearts and minds of Muslims everywhere."[51]

Equally ominous signs of propaganda operating in domestic American society are also prevalent. In 2008 the *New York Times* reported that a group of prominent retired military officers who had appeared on national television and radio hundreds of times since 9/11, supposedly as objective military analysts, had been part of an intricately coordinated campaign emanating out of the Pentagon to sway public opinion on U.S. foreign policy. The extent of the ties between the analysts and the Bush administration was uncovered in literally thousands of e-mails, transcripts, and records that the *Times* gained access to after it sued the Defense Department for information. According to the journalist David Barstow, the treasure trove of documents described "years of private briefings, trips to Iraq and Guantánamo and an extensive Pentagon talking points operation. [The] records reveal a symbiotic relationship where the usual dividing lines between government and journalism have been obliterated."[52] The ethical implications of the campaign were further complicated when it was reported that many of these same military analysts had ties to military contractors and thus a financial incentive to promote the escalation of the Iraq War and military aggression abroad.

In addition, some of the analysts had ideological reasons for supporting the information campaign. As Barstow pointed out in his article on the "message machine," Paul E. Vallely, a retired army general who served as an analyst on Fox News from 2001 to 2007, had cowritten a paper in 1980 that argued that the United States had ultimately lost in Vietnam because they had been "out Psyoped." In order to prevent a similar scenario in the future, Vallely proposed a new approach to the government's and military's use of the media; he called it "MindWar." Its primary objective was to use "Psyops" on domestic audiences in order "strengthen our national will to victory."[53] In interviews with the *Times,* several other military experts acknowledged their misgivings about some of the information they were being force-fed by the Pentagon but never expressed them on air in order to avoid losing access to the administration. Some of the former officers associated with the campaign harbored regrets about their participation. For example, Robert S. Bevelacqua, a former Green Beret and analyst for Fox News, stated, "It was them saying, 'We need to stick our hands up your back and move your mouth for you.'"[54] Another general commented on the superficiality of some of the military briefings in question and recalled that he had told another member of the group that they were on "the George Romney memorial trip to Iraq."[55]

After the *Times* exposed the information network, members of the Bush administration and several of the military analysts publicly denied they had ever been involved in a propaganda campaign designed to influence American public opinion. However, a transcript of a meeting between Secretary of Defense Donald Rumsfeld, the chairman of the Joint Chiefs, Gen. Peter Pace, and seventeen military analysts indicates otherwise. During the meeting one of the analysts worried about how the public might perceive the relationship between the retired officers and the Pentagon. He said, "I'm an old intel guy. And I can sum all of this up, unfortunately, with one word. That is Psyops. Now most people may hear that and they think, 'Oh my God, they're trying to brainwash.'" Rumsfeld quickly interjected, "What are you, some kind of a nut?"[56] The comment reportedly drew laughter from those in attendance and points to how Rumsfeld effectively cut off critical analysis of the program. As one of the architects of the campaign, Rumsfeld was motivated to ridicule any criticism of the relationship between the Pentagon and the analysts. His defensive remarks aside, the campaign is proof that in the war on terror the Taliban has not been the only party attempting to manipulate public opinion.

Further evidence of brainwashing's legacy on contemporary military practices was discovered in the summer of 2008, when the Senate Armed Services Committee divulged that members of the military and the CIA stationed at the U.S. prison at Guantánamo Bay in Cuba had based an entire interrogation class on a chart documenting the effects of "coercive management techniques." The document had originally been published in 1957 in an air force study of Communist psychological torture during the Korean War. The original study had been written by none other than the sociologist Albert D. Biderman, who had attempted to refute the more negative interpretations of the Korean POWs' war record in the 1950s and early 1960s. An article by Scott Shane in the *New York Times* described the recycled chart as "the latest and most vivid evidence of the way Communist interrogation methods that the United States long described as torture became the basis for interrogations both by the military at the base at Guantánamo Bay, Cuba, and by the Central Intelligence Agency."[57] Several members of the Senate committee were shocked by the chart's lineage, and the chairman, Sen. Carl Levin of Michigan, questioned the validity of the practices it recommended, stating, "What makes this document doubly stunning is that these were techniques to get false confessions. People say we need intelligence, and we do. But we don't need false intelligence."[58]

In fact, the "coercive management" chart was just the tip of the iceberg, and it has been conclusively demonstrated that the contemporary use of "enhanced interrogation" in U.S. military prisons is a direct outgrowth of the CIA's and military's Cold War–era experiments in brainwashing and psychological torture. Addressing the links between U.S.-sanctioned torture during the war on terror and the CIA's behavioral research program, Alfred W. McCoy has determined that, after years of trial and error, the widespread failure of mind control experimentation to provide consistent results led to the development of new methods of torture based on sensory deprivation, isolation, and self-inflicted pain.[59] These new methods, based on research by prominent psychologists and behavioral scientists under the banner of the MKUltra program, ultimately produced the *Kubark Counterintelligence Interrogation* manual in 1963, which would remain in use for forty years and, according to McCoy, "define the agency's interrogation methods and training programs throughout the Third World."[60] The Cold War pedigree of enhanced interrogation methods in U.S. military prisons during the war on terror unearths the curious trajectory of brainwashing within the American intelligence community. Initially the source of acute anxiety about what Allen Dulles described as the Communists' "brain perversion techniques," brainwashing inspired the development of America's own "defensive behavioral research." However, as time wore on, the research funded by the CIA and the military revealed that Communist brainwashing was not a mysterious new method of mind control but an expansion of preexisting Russian police tactics and Chinese ideological reform. Nonetheless, research on mind-altering drugs, behavior modification, and interrogation continued in the United States, ultimately accounting for millions of dollars in funding and countless experiments on human subjects at universities and hospitals around the country.

Some participants in America's "brainwashing" program were conducting relatively benign research and were naïve about the sources of their funding. But there were also researchers like D. Ewen Cameron, an internationally renowned psychiatrist at McGill University whom the historian Rebecca Lemov has characterized as "Cold War brainwashing's real-life mad scientist."[61] Funded by the CIA in the middle of the fifties, Cameron conducted research in depatterning and psychic driving and subjected over a hundred of his patients to a regimen of illicit drugs, auditory feedback loops, imposed periods of sleep lasting up to three weeks, and, in some cases, electric shock treatment and prolonged sensory deprivation. The impact on his subjects was profound: many suffered psychological repercussions for years, and, driven to the brink of psychosis, they represent the human cost of the CIA's and military's futile quest for mind control. As Lemov notes, Cameron was not "a solitary mad doctor or CIA cipher," and the willingness of the military and the CIA to fund such inhumane research demonstrates their complicity in illegal and unethical covert activities designed to develop America's answer to Communist brainwashing.[62]

The fact that policymakers like Dulles were so desperate to secretly develop techniques to rival Communist brainwashing, while they publicly derided the Communist regime for its psychologically invasive practices against American POWs and Communist citizens, is a testament to the severe hypocrisy of the American Cold War state. For contemporary Americans that hypocrisy lingers. During the Cold War, the Communist enemy was portrayed as an inhumane, dehumanizing force, in large part because of its association with psychological warfare and brainwashing. During the war on terror, the United States has not only practiced methods of psychological torture and interrogation that emerged out of America's own covert research on brainwashing in the 1950s and 1960s, but also engaged in activities that were far more psychologically intrusive than the treatment American POWs were subjected to in Korea. Writing in the spring of 1953, when brainwashing was still in its relative infancy as a concept, a research consultant for the Psychological Strategy Board, the government agency responsible for coordinating national psychological operations, wrote a supplemental report on the technique that directly warned about the dangers of utilizing it on the behalf of the American state. The report unequivocally emphasized "the great importance of our total abstinence from anything remotely resembling these methods" and concluded, "There are few civilized people who, upon learning of the methods and techniques employed in brain-washing, would not view the process with loathing and thoroughly condemn the perpetrators of such inhuman methods."[63] Obviously, this warning went unheeded. By engaging in these practices the United States has become what it once feared and despised, turning into a contemporary version of the brainwashing monster of our national Cold War nightmare.

While some branches of the military and members of the U.S. intelligence community have been mining the past for techniques of psychological coercion, other groups have been calling for innovations in American psychological warfare. In 2008 the National Research Council released a report titled "Emerging Cognitive Neuroscience and Related Technologies" that was commissioned by the Defense Intelligence Agency. With regard to American soldiers, the report recommended exploring the use of brain-boosting drugs "to assist in maintaining the warfighting superiority of the United States." As far as enemy combatants were concerned, the report arrived at an even more troubling line of conjecture:

> Although conflict has many aspects, one that warfighters and policymakers often talk about is the motivation to fight, which undoubtedly has its origins in the brain and is reflected in peripheral neurophysiological processes. So one question would be, "How can we disrupt the enemy's motivation to fight?" Other questions raised by controlling the mind: "How can we make people trust us more?" "What if we could help the brain to remove fear or pain?" "Is there a way to make the enemy obey our commands?" . . . As cognitive neuroscience and related technologies become more pervasive, using technology for nefarious purposes becomes easier.[64]

Although the report openly admitted that some of its recommendations were highly speculative in nature, the fact that techniques potentially even worse than brainwashing may be possible in the not-too-distant future has already provoked legislators in eight states to ban the use of technologies associated with the surgical insertion of microchips into human beings.[65] Recent technological advancements, coupled with new developments in neuroscience, have made the potential for invasive, even diabolical, intrusions into the human psyche an unnerving possibility. Since there will always be the potential for new mind-bending technologies at some point further down the horizon, the anxieties surrounding brainwashing and mind control are not likely to subside any time soon.

Looking back, it is easy to overstate brainwashing's influence, but this book does not intend to imply that the concept was the sole factor in the widespread rise of cynicism in modern America or the only issue that led many Americans to dwell on the importance of individuality in the postwar era. To deny brainwashing's role in these historical processes, however, is to lose a crucial piece of the puzzle. In the first two and a half decades of the postwar era, Americans were repeatedly informed that their minds were under attack. Since brainwashing was initially defined as a Communist weapon, in the early 1950s Americans' distress over free will and individual autonomy were affected by the larger context of the Cold War. Crucially, as brainwashing gained cultural ascendancy it colored how Americans understood the Cold War itself. For the first time in the history of modern warfare an international struggle between two world powers was seemingly being waged over "human" territory, and the ultimate prize in the Cold War became capturing the minds and souls of the enemy and converting them to either Communism or American-style democracy. This new landscape was the basis for a tremendously powerful narrative, and by the middle of the 1950s the Cold War had largely been transformed in American popular discourse from a geopolitical struggle between competing economic systems to a literal battle over men's minds and the fate of humankind. More than any other single idea or issue in the fifties and early sixties, "brain warfare" and the techniques associated with it made American individuality a matter of national security and left many citizens with the impression that their individual psyches were a matter of crucial import. Once their individuality became infused with such dire meaningfulness, Americans became fierce guardians of their subconscious—and far more likely to view all manner of external influences in a critical light.

When the Cold War briefly thawed at the end of the 1950s, the mystery surrounding the Communist enemy slowly began to dissipate, and paranoia about the enemy's supposedly superhuman capabilities began to be replaced by more realistic attitudes. But once brainwashing was accepted as a legitimate weapon, the door was open to a host of new possibilities. If Communist brainwashing was possible—and in the early fifties many signs indicated that it was—wasn't it also possible that other groups could be employing similar forms of psychological treachery? At a critical period in the nation's history, brainwashing helped raise the issue of how modern Americans could retain their sense of self in a world overrun by large-scale political entities, mass media, and corporate and suburban institutions. It is an issue Americans still struggle with.

After being widely discredited by the scientific community, brainwashing and overt mind control are often relegated today to tinfoil hat territory and the margins of mainstream political discourse. Yet such forgetfulness obscures how profound the legacy of the technique is in contemporary American life. During the early postwar era, the backdrop of the Korean War and the uproar surrounding Communist brainwashing undoubtedly fueled Americans' anxieties about individuality, personal autonomy, and free will. Eventually, brain warfare prompted Americans to adopt increasingly suspicious attitudes about their own social and political institutions and to transform nonconformity and individuality into ideal character traits. As scientists race to unlock the remaining mysteries of the human mind, we find ourselves on somewhat similar ground as the postwar Americans of the 1950s and 1960s. What started as a uniquely Cold War state of mind has evolved into our contemporary perspective of the world and modern identity, a perspective frequently clouded by the suspicion that our own psyches may be under attack and marked by the belief that individuality is precious and merits safeguarding. Our common mission today, then, should be similar to that of Americans in the early postwar era: Not simply making the world safe for democracy but also ensuring the humanity of those living in it.

Notes

Introduction

1. Desson Thomson, "An Electable 'Manchurian Candidate,'" *Washington Post*, 30 July 2004.

2. In their book-length analysis of *The Manchurian Candidate*, Matthew Frye Jacobson and Gaspar González have analyzed the various versions of the film at length. Commenting on the remake, they concluded, "*The Manchurian Candidate* feels less like a vision of the Cold War than a waking, recurring dream." Matthew Frye Jacobson and Gaspar González, *What Have They Built You to Do? "The Manchurian Candidate" and Cold War America* (Minneapolis: University of Minnesota Press, 2006), 193.

3. After a congressional inquiry discovered the extent of CIA mind control experiments in the late 1970s, an entire literature sprang up addressing the sordid history of government-sponsored programs aimed at developing new methods of psychological torture and manipulation after the Second World War. Walter Bowart's *Operation Mind Control* (1978), Alan W. Scheflin Jr. and Edward M. Opton's *The Mind Manipulators* (1978), and John Marks's *The Search for a "Manchurian Candidate": The CIA and Mind Control* (1979) marked the first forays into this topic material. For a more recent analysis of the mind control experiments and their relationship to "enhanced interrogation" methods, see Alfred W. McCoy's *A Question of Torture: CIA Interrogation from the Cold War to the War on Terror* (New York: Metropolitan Books / Henry Holt, 2006).

4. "The POW in History," 3, folder Department of Defense, Code of Conduct Program, First Progress Report, Code of Conduct (Defense) (3), White House Office, Office of the Special Assistant for National Security Affairs: Records, 1952–1961, Special Assistant Series, Subject Series, box 2, Dwight D. Eisenhower Presidential Library.

5. Edward Hunter, *Brainwashing: The Story of Men Who Defied It* (New York: Farrar, Straus and Cudahy, 1956), 310.

6. Eugene Kinkead, *Why They Collaborated* (London: Lowe and Brydone Printers, 1959), 9.

7. Brainwashing was connected to several manipulative tendencies in domestic America society almost immediately after it was introduced, but the reciprocal development of grassroots protest against American popular and consumer culture and the publication of books like Fredric Wertham's *Seduction of the Innocent* (1954) and Vance Packard's *The Hidden Persuaders* (1957) brought these issues to national attention and laid the foundation for a series of congressional inquiries into American mass media and the advertising industry.

8. On the Kitchen Debates, Nixon, and American diplomacy, see Walter L. Hixson, *Parting the Curtain: Propaganda, Culture, and the Cold War, 1945–1961* (New York: St. Martin's Press, 1997), 151–83.

9. Andreas Killen and Stefan Andriopoulos, "Editors' Introduction on Brainwashing: Mind Control, Media, and Warfare," *Grey Room* 45 (Fall 2011): 8.

10. Ibid., 14.

11. The most notable academic studies of brainwashing include, in chronological order, Richard Severo and Lewis Milford, *The Wages of War: When America's Soldiers Come Home—From Valley Forge to Vietnam* (New York: Simon and Schuster, 1989); Abbott Gleason, *Totalitarianism: The Inner History of the Cold War* (New York: Oxford University Press, 1995); David Seed, "Brainwashing and Cold War Demonology," Prospects 22 (1997): 535–73; two articles in the *Historical Journal of Film, Radio, and Television* for March 1998: Susan L. Carruthers, " 'The Manchurian Candidate' (1962) and the Cold War Brainwashing Scare," and Charles S. Young, "Missing Action: POW Films, Brainwashing, and the Korean War, 1954–1968"; Susan L. Carruthers, "Redeeming the Captives: Hollywood and the Brainwashing of America's Prisoners of War in Korea," *Film History* 10.3 (1998): 275–94; Ron Robin, *The Making of the Cold War Enemy: Culture and Politics in the Military–Industrial Complex* (Princeton: Princeton University Press, 2001); David Seed, *Brainwashing: The Fictions of Mind Control: A Study of Novels and Films since World War II* (Kent: Kent State University Press, 2004); Jacobson and González, *What Have They Built You to Do?*; Timothy Melley, "Brainwashed! Conspiracy Theory and Ideology in the Postwar United States," *New German Critique* 103 (Winter 2008): 145–64; Susan L. Carruthers, *Cold War Captives: Imprisonment, Escape, and Brainwashing* (Berkeley: University of California Press, 2009); and articles by Timothy Melley, Andreas Killen, Rebecca Lemov, Stefan Andriopoulos, and Alison Winter in the journal *Grey Room* for Fall 2011.

12. William H. Whyte, *The Organization Man* (Philadelphia: University of Pennsylvania Press, 1956), 395.

1. The Origins of Brainwashing

1. There were two prisoner exchanges between North Korea and the United States during the Korean War, popularly known as Operation Little Switch and Operation Big Switch. Operation Little Switch was the first exchange and took place between April 20 and May 3, 1953. During Little Switch, 149 sick and wounded American soldiers were turned over to the U.S. military. Operation Big Switch took place between August 5 and December 23, 1953, and officially ended the Korean War. There were 3,597 prisoners returned to the United States during this period.

2. Allen W. Dulles, "Brain Warfare—Russia's Secret Weapon," *U.S. News & World Report,* 8 May 1953, 54.

3. Arthur Krock, "In The Nation: Allen W. Dulles Describes 'Warfare for the Brain,' " *New York Times,* 16 April 1953.

4. Dulles, "Brain Warfare," 54.

5. Krock, "In The Nation," 28.

6. It was not a coincidence that Dulles approved the Project MKUltra experiments on April 13, 1953, a mere three days after making his speech in Virginia. The purpose of the experiments was to provide American CIA operatives with brainwashing tactics and consisted of "mind-control" experiments that focused on the impact of drugs, hypnosis, and sensory deprivation in interrogation. Frequently the subjects of the experiments were unknowing participants.

7. Associated Press, "Converted GIs Give Reasons in 'Statement'—359 Sing Commie Anthem Arriving in Neutral Zone," *Long Beach Press Telegram,* 24 September 1953,.

8. "Korea: Twenty-Three Americans," *Time,* 5 October 1953, 35.

9. United Press, "'Go Home Yankee' Shout Balky U.S. Korea Prisoners," *Redlands Daily Facts*, 26 September 1953.

10. United Press, "'Red' GI Dilemma 'Very Important,'" *Edwardsville Intelligencer*, 3 November 1953.

11. "National Affairs: Flipflop at Panmunjom," *Time*, 11 January 1954, 13.

12. Ibid.

13. These campaigns are documented in Susan L. Carruthers, *Cold War Captives, Imprisonment, Escape, and Brainwashing* (Berkeley: University of California Press, 2009), 175.

14. "'We Got Everything You Wanted,'" *Life*, 19 October 1953, 45.

15. Virginia Pasley, *21 Stayed: The Story of the American GI's Who Chose Communist China—Who They Were and Why They Stayed* (New York: Farrar, Straus and Cudahy, 1955), 16.

16. Albert D. Biderman, *March to Calumny: The Story of American POW's in the Korean War* (New York: Macmillan, 1963), 200–201. Like many academics writing on brainwashing, Biderman had ties to the government. His initial research on the POWs was sponsored by the air force and was classified, including his "A Study for Development of Improved Interrogation Techniques" (1959).

17. "Fruits of Brainwashing," *New York Times*, 28 January 1954.

18. Abbott Gleason, *Totalitarianism: The Inner History of the Cold War* (New York: Oxford University Press, 1995), 92.

19. International News Service, "Germ Bombing Is Admitted by Yank Prisoners of Reds," *Charleston Gazette*, 6 May 1952.

20. Ibid.

21. There has been a minor debate among historians of the Cold War over North Korea's charges. In 1998 Indiana University Press published Stephen Endicott's and Edward Hagerman's *The United States and Biological Warfare: Secrets from the Early Cold War and Korea*, which concluded that the United States had indeed committed germ warfare during the Korean War. However, the *Journal of American History* for June 2000 described the book as "a prime example of shoddy scholarship masquerading as an objective examination of a controversial topic" and claimed that Endicott's and Hagerman's work never provided a "smoking gun" that supported their conclusions. In 1998 twelve documents from the Soviet Central Committee dating to the early 1950s were published, and some historians have pointed to them as definitive proof that the North Koreans' claims were fabricated. These documents were analyzed and published in an article by Kathryn Weathersby titled "Deceiving the Deceivers: Moscow, Beijing, Pyongyang, and the Allegations of Bacteriological Weapon Use in Korea," *Cold War International History Project, Bulletin 11* (Winter 1998), Woodrow Wilson Center for International Scholars.

22. Walter H. Waggoner, "Acheson Calls Germ Charge Soviet 'Crime,' Scouts Talks," *New York Times*, 8 May 1952.

23. Ibid.

24. Victor Riesel, "Red 'Brainwashing' of U.S. Prisoners Shown on Film," *Oakland Tribune*, 3 April 1953.

25. Ibid.

26. Ron Robin, *The Making of the Cold War Enemy: Culture and Politics in the Military-Intellectual Complex* (Princeton: Princeton University Press, 2001), 164.

27. Waggoner, "Acheson Calls Germ Charge Soviet 'Crime,'" 7.

28. Susan L. Carruthers, "'The Manchurian Candidate' (1962) and the Cold War Brainwashing Scare," *Historical Journal of Film, Radio and Television* 18.1 (1998), 78.

29. Memorandum for the Record, 12 May 1953, folder PSB 383.6 [Prisoners of War] (2), White House Office, National Security Council Staff: Papers, 1953–61, Psychological Strategy Board (PSB) Central Files Series, box 26, Dwight D. Eisenhower Presidential Library.

30. Associated Press, "Ten Repatriated Prisoners Deny Taking on Red Taint," *Long Beach Press-Telegram,* 4 May 1953.

31. United Press, "'Brainwashing' Breaking Down," *Traverse City Record-Eagle,* 20 October 1953.

32. "The World," *New York Times,* 18 October 1953.

33. Carruthers, *Cold War Captives,* 181.

34. Ibid.

35. A. Sabine Chase, chief of the Division of Research for the Far East, quoted in ibid., 183.

36. "Victims of Propaganda," *Washington Post,* 11 August 1953.

37. David Seed, *Brainwashing: The Fictions of Mind Control: A Study of Novels and Films since World War II* (Kent, Ohio: Kent State University Press, 2004), xxv.

38. J. A. C. Brown, *Techniques of Persuasion: From Propaganda to Brainwashing* (Baltimore: Penguin Books, 1963), 253.

39. Edward Hunter, *Brainwashing: The Story of Men Who Defied It* (New York: Farrar, Straus and Cudahy, 1956) 3.

40. Ibid., 4.

41. Edgar H. Schein, Inge Schneier, and Curtis H. Barker, *Coercive Persuasion: A Socio-psychological Analysis of the "Brainwashing" of American Civilian Prisoners by the Chinese Communists* (New York: W. W. Norton, 1961), 16.

42. Robert J. Lifton, *Thought Reform and the Psychology of Totalism: A Study of "Brainwashing" in China* (London: V. Gollanz, 1961,) 34, quoted in ibid.

43. Timothy Melley, "Brain Warfare: The Covert Sphere, Terrorism, and the Legacy of the Cold War," *Grey Room* 45 (Fall 2011): 28.

44. The distinction between Cold War policy and politics and the motivations behind the alarmist approach to Communism and to the "politics of insecurity" has been analyzed at length by Campbell Craig and Fredrik Logevall in *America's Cold War: The Politics of Insecurity* (Cambridge: Belknap Press of Harvard University Press, 2009). As their research indicates, there were practical and political reasons why members of the government played up the threat of Communism. In the case of brainwashing, it appears that some members of the government, like Hunter, were legitimately concerned about the technique. It is possible that other government officials had less reason to believe in the threat of brainwashing, especially after classified reports indicated that it was not as threatening as initially believed. Their motivation for continuing to promote anxieties surrounding the technique was almost certainly based on its usefulness in supporting the broader aims of the Cold War against Communism.

45. Edward Hunter, *Brain-washing in Red China: The Calculated Destruction of Men's Minds* (New York: Vanguard Press, 1951), 38.

46. Ibid., 4.

47. Ibid., 299.

48. United Press, "We Spied, Say Pair, Hailing 'Peaceful' China," *St. Petersburg Times,* 28 February 1955.

49. Associated Press, "Parents of Freed Yanks Skeptical of Opinions," *Los Angeles Times,* 28 February 1955.

50. "Faith His Only Weapon, Says Man Held by Reds," *Los Angeles Times,* 9 November 1954.

51. Associated Press, "Red Brainwashing Attempt Failed, Fliers Say," *Los Angeles Times,* 2 June 1955. For more on their experience, see Lt. Col. Edwin L. Heller, USAF, as told to Hugh Morrow, "I Thought I'd Never Get Home," *Saturday Evening Post,* 27 August 1955, 34–52.

52. "Missionary Jailed by Chinese Is Here," *New York Times,* 26 February 1956, 35.

53. Special to the *New York Times,* "335 Repatriates Return to Japan," *New York Times,* 4 July 1956, 3.

54. Robin, *The Making of the Cold War Enemy*, 167.

55. Joost Meerloo, *The Rape of the Mind: The Psychology of Thought Control, Menticide, and Brainwashing* (Cleveland: World, 1956), 27.

56. " 'Menticide' Is Listed as a New Crime: Broken Victims Another 'Human Right,' " *New York Times*, 11 March 1951.

57. Joost Meerloo, "The Crime of Menticide," *American Journal of Psychiatry* 107 (February 1951): 594.

58. This data was procured through two electronic databases: http://pqasb.pqarchiver.com and http://proquest.umi.com.

59. Hunter, *Brainwashing: The Story of Men Who Defied It*, 4.

60. Ibid.

61. Schein, Schneier, and Baker, *Coercive Persuasion*, 8.

62. C. E. Wilson to Walter E. Smith and Allen Dulles, 19 February 1953, folder PSB 702.5 (1), White House Office, National Security Council Staff: Papers, 1953–61, Psychological Strategy Board (PSB) Central Files Series, box 29, Dwight D. Eisenhower Presidential Library.

63. "Background Material," folder PSB 702.5 (1), White House Office, National Security Council Staff: Papers, 1953–61, Psychological Strategy Board (PSB) Central Files Series, box 29, Dwight D. Eisenhower Presidential Library.

64. Horace S. Craig to William H. Godel, folder PSB 702.5 (2) Brainwashing During Korean War, White House Office, National Security Council Staff: Papers, 1953–61, Psychological Strategy Board (PSB) Central Files Series, box 29, Dwight D. Eisenhower Presidential Library.

65. George A. Morgan to Allen Dulles, 5 March 1953, folder PSB 702.5 (1), White House Office, National Security Council Staff: Papers, 1953–61, Psychological Strategy Board (PSB) Central Files Series, box 29, Dwight D. Eisenhower Presidential Library.

66. Millard C. Young, "Memorandum for the Office of Psychological Policy, Office of the Security of Defense," 10 April 1953, folder PSB 702.5 (1) [Brainwashing During Korean War], White House Office, National Security Council Staff: Papers, 1953–61, Psychological Strategy Board (PSB) Central Files Series, box 29, Dwight D. Eisenhower Presidential Library.

67. Charles W. Mayo, Press Release No. 1786—Statement to the Political Committee on "The Question of Impartial Investigation of Charges of Use by United Nations Forces of Bacteriological Warfare," 26 October 1953, folder PSB 383.6 [Prisoners of War] (File #2) (5), White House Office, National Security Council Staff: Papers, 1953–61, Psychological Strategy Board (PSB) Central Files Series, box 26, Dwight D. Eisenhower Presidential Library.

68. United Press, "Ferndale GI Tells Senate Group about 'Do or Die' March as POW," *Holland, Michigan Evening Sentinel*, 3 December 1953.

69. Sgt. Eddie Davis, as told to James Lee, I.N.S. Staff, "3 Years in Red Hell: Sergeant Tells of Horrors Survived in Prison Camp," *Chronicle-Telegram*, 1 October 1953.

70. Associated Press, "Freed GIs Angry at Commie Label Hung on Them," *Greeley Tribune*, 4 May 1953.

71. Eugene Kinkead, *Why They Collaborated* (London: Lowe and Brydone, 1959), 22.

72. GIs' descriptions of the physical and mental torture they suffered during the war were not exaggerations meant to curry public favor. The fact that over 38 percent of American GIs captured during the war never lived to tell about it illustrates the severity of the POW experience in Korea.

73. "Freed Flier Cites Red 'Persuasion,' " *New York Times*, 7 August 1955.

74. "Ex-Prisoner Defines Red Brainwashing," *Washington Post*, 20 February 1954.

75. United Press, "Mom Still Hopes to See Pro-Red GI Son in Korea," *Ames Daily Tribune*, 9 December 1953.

76. United Press, "Sure He Signed Red Petition, He Says: New Englander Never a Communist But 'Brain Washing Was Rough,' " *Ada Weekly News*, 7 May 1953.

77. Ibid.

78. Forrest Edwards, "Indoctrinated GIs to Spread Communist Line: Others Overcome by Red 'Brainwashing' Remain in North Korea; Thousands Died in Prison Camps," *Frederick Post,* 11 August 1953.

79. Sgt. Eddie Davis, as told to James Lee, "POW 3 Years Tells How Red 'Brainwashing' Failed," *Mt. Pleasant News,* 3 October 1953.

80. Associated Press, "Freed GIs Angry at Commie Label Hung on Them," 7.

81. Ellen Schrecker, *Many Are the Crimes: McCarthyism in America* (Princeton: Princeton University Press, 1998), 42–46.

82. Elaine Tyler May, *Homeward Bound: American Families in the Cold War Era* (New York: Basic Books, 1988), 26.

83. Ron Robin has convincingly pointed out that the academic community's analysis of the concept was not without some faults of its own. According to Robin, "The behavioral scientists swept aside a host of challenging social and political issues associated with the POW experience. Their reports avoided the racial and ethnic composition of American POWs, and skirted the issue of social stratification in the armed forces and its impact on prison camps and battlefields." Robin, *The Making of the Cold War Enemy,* 163.

84. Albert D. Biderman, "The Image of 'Brainwashing,'" *Public Opinion Quarterly* 26.4 (Winter 1962): 547.

85. John Marks, *The Search for the "Manchurian Candidate": The CIA and Mind Control* (New York: W. W. Norton, 1991), 136. As John Marks first demonstrated in his seminal work *The Search for the "Manchurian Candidate,"* and Alfred W. McCoy has more recently documented in *A Question of Torture: CIA Interrogation, from the Cold War to the War on Terror,* the U.S. government sponsored a far-reaching research program of covert mind control experimentation stretching from the early 1950s until at least the 1970s that had an annual budget approaching a billion dollars and was carried out by dozens of universities, pharmaceutical companies, and some of the most highly respected behavioral scientists in the country. The research sponsored by the army, the CIA, and the air force on mind control in the 1950s, such as Hinkle's and Wolff's, was ostensibly geared toward studying the methods of psychological torture being employed by Communists, which hid the true motivation behind the government's inquiry into Communist brainwashing: to further develop their own techniques of psychological warfare. The extent of U.S. government–sanctioned mind control experimentation was first revealed to the public in 1975 after a series of government investigations unveiled the history of Project MKUltra. Based on how expensive and far-reaching these experiments were, McCoy has called them "a veritable Manhattan Project of the mind."

86. Lawrence E. Hinkle and Harold G. Wolff, "The Methods of Interrogation and Indoctrination Used by the Communist State Police," *Bulletin of the New York Academy of Medicine* 33.9 (September 1957): 609–10.

87. Associated Press, "Rip Military for Cruelties to GIs by Reds," *Chicago Sunday Tribune,* 30 December 1956.

88. Seed, *Brainwashing,* 46.

89. Among the most notable books from this period advocating a more scientific view of brainwashing, in order of their publication date, were William Sargent, *Battle for the Mind: A Physiology of Conversion and 'Brainwashing'* (Baltimore: Penguin Books, 1957); William L. White, *The Captives of Korea: An Unofficial White Paper* (New York: Scribner's, 1957); Eugene Kinkead, *In Every War but One* (New York: Norton, 1959); Lifton, *Thought Reform and the Psychology of Totalism* (1961); Schein, Schneier, and Barker, *Coercive Persuasion* (1961); and Biderman, *March to Calumny* (1963).

90. Some Cold War historians have claimed that while the more sensational interpretation of brainwashing initially caused a stir in popular culture, a more scientific interpretation of the concept eventually won out, and, at least according to Abbott Gleason, "as the term became somewhat better understood in the United States and Europe, it lost some

of the terror it originally inspired and became, in certain contexts, almost banal." Gleason, *Totalitarianism,* 93. This perception is due to the sources historians have focused on when studying the concept. The scientific interpretation certainly held sway among academics and members of the American intelligence community. However, to accept the notion that brainwashing had become "almost banal" in American culture would require one to ignore a multitude of cultural sources, from films to fiction, which heavily favored a sensational interpretation of the concept.

91. Seed, *Brainwashing,* 48–49.

92. Kinkead, *Why They Collaborated,* 32.

93. Hunter, *Brainwashing: The Story of Men Who Defied It,* 203.

94. Ibid., 309.

95. The historian Richard Hofstadter first alluded to the paranoid style of the McCarthy era in a lecture delivered at Oxford University in November 1963. For the modified print version of the lecture, see Richard Hofstadter, "The Paranoid Style in American Politics," *Harper's Magazine,* November 1964, 77–86.

96. During this period the *New York Times*'s coverage of brainwashing landed somewhere in between the threat of nuclear war and the threat of a communist takeover. The threat of a communist takeover was the topic of 85 articles in the *Times* during that decade, brainwashing was the topic of 231, and nuclear war was the topic of an astounding 5,391. The amount of newspaper coverage of brainwashing alludes to the fact that it was a common fear during the era.

97. The Redpath Bureau, "Brain Washing and What It Means to You: Forcefully Told by Edward Hunter," MSC0150, Chautauqua Brochures, Redpath Chautauqua Collection, University of Iowa, Libraries, Special Collections Dept.

98. For a detailed analysis of Mindszenty's and Vogeler's trials and confessions, see Carruthers, *Cold War Captives,* 136–73.

99. Marks, *The Search for the "Manchurian Candidate,"* 23.

100. Robert A. Vogeler and Leigh White, *I Was Stalin's Prisoner* (New York: Harcourt, Brace, 1951), 212.

101. Koestler was reportedly influenced by firsthand knowledge of victims of the Soviet purge trials of the late 1930s and early 1940s. This would imply that there was some degree of continuity in communist imprisonment techniques.

102. Robert A. Vogeler with Leigh White, "I Was Stalin's Prisoner," *Saturday Evening Post,* 10 November 1951, 136.

103. Biderman, *March to Calumny,* 200.

104. Joost A. M. Meerloo, "Pavlov's Dog and Communist Brainwashers," *New York Times Magazine,* 9 May 1954, 33, 31.

105. Walter L. Hixson, *Parting the Curtain: Propaganda, Culture, and the Cold War, 1945–1961* (New York: St. Martin's Press, 1997), 2.

106. Ibid., 3.

107. C. D. Jackson to Sam Anderson, 15 January 1954, Eisenhower, Dwight D.: Papers as President of the United States, 1953–1961 (Ann Whitman File), Administration Series, box 22, Dwight D. Eisenhower Presidential Library.

108. Federal Bureau of Investigation, "Communist Propaganda in the United States Part II Target Groups May 1957," ii, White House Office, Office of the Special Assistant for National Security Affairs: Records, 1952–1961, FBI Series, box 9, Dwight D. Eisenhower Presidential Library.

109. For the relationship between the Cold War and the civil rights movement, see Mary Dudziak, *Cold War Civil Rights: Race and the Image of American Democracy* (Princeton: Princeton University Press, 2002). For policymakers' concerns that Communists would exploit the use of nuclear weapons by the United States in the Second World War, see Naoko Shibusawa, *America's Geisha Ally: Reimagining the Japanese Enemy* (Cambridge: Harvard University Press, 2006), 231–34.

110. Alison Winter, *Mesmerized: Powers of Mind in Victorian Britain* (Chicago: University of Chicago Press, 1998), 2.

111. Ibid., 3.

112. Elizabeth Janeway, "Why They Become Communists," *New York Times Magazine*, 14 June 1953, 28.

113. Ibid.

114. Robert Genter, "'Hypnotizzy' in the Cold War: The American Fascination with Hypnotism in the 1950s," *Journal of American Culture* 29.2 (June 2006): 156.

115. Ibid., 159. The CIA recognized the potential for hypnosis as an interrogation technique in the late 1940s and, as John Marks has indicated, was "contemplating the operational use of hypnosis" in the early years of the Cold War.

116. Commenting on the recurring medical and scientific displays of hypnosis, Stefan Andriopoulos has demonstrated that the scientific and medical "performance" of hypnosis was influenced by the interplay between legal, medical, and cultural sources, effectively blurring the lines between the reality of the technique and widespread fantasies about its potential to influence human behavior. For his full analysis, see Stefan Andriopoulos, "The Sleeper Effect: Hypnotism, Mind Control, Terrorism," *Grey Room* 45 (Fall 2011): 90–94.

117. G. H. Estabrooks with Leslie Lieber, "Hypnosis: Its Tremendous Potential as a War Weapon Is Revealed Here for the First Time," *Argosy*, February 1950, 27.

118. Seed, *Brainwashing*, xxii.

119. In 1958 Huxley returned to these themes in *Brave New World Revisited*, claiming he was revisiting his earlier book in response to concerns that recent events were turning his nightmarish vision of the future into a reality. In the introduction, Huxley wrote that the book was meant to be read with the image of "those endless columns of uniformed boys, white, black, brown, yellow, marching obediently toward the common grave" in one's mind. Aldous Huxley, *Brave New World Revisited* (New York: Harper and Row, 1958), x.

120. Stefan Andriopoulos and Timothy Melley have noted the instrumental role fictional accounts of mind control played in the popular and academic discussion of brainwashing. Largely because there was an absence of clear, empirical proof validating the existence of the technique, some so-called authorities on brainwashing fell back on fiction. For example, as Andriopoulos notes, "William Sargent's *Battle for the Mind* (1957) . . . quotes literary texts by George Orwell and Aldous Huxley as if these novels constituted scientific accounts of real-life experiments." Andriopoulos, "The Sleeper Effect," 95. For more on the role fiction played in the popular and academic brainwashing narratives, see Melley, "Brain Warfare," 19–41, and Andriopoulos, "The Sleeper Effect," 89–105.

121. Arthur C. Clarke, *Profiles of the Future: An Inquiry into the Limits of the Possible* (New York: Harper and Row, 1958), xiv.

122. Ernest Havemann, "The Age of Psychology in the US," *Life*, 42.1 (1957), 68, as quoted in Genter, "Hypnotizzy," 158.

123. Ward Cannel and Leonard A. Paris, "Hypnotism Is Dynamite," *Los Angeles Times*, 23 November 1952.

124. Ibid.

125. Hunter, *Brainwashing: The Story of Men Who Defied It*, 249.

126. "Asia Sees Korea as Victory for China, Says Red Expert," *Long Beach Independent*, 3 September 1953.

127. Seed, *Brainwashing*, 34.

128. Hannah Arendt, *The Origins of Totalitarianism* (Orlando: Harcourt, 1951), 588.

129. Lifton, *Thought Reform and the Psychology of Totalism*, 4–5.

130. See Andreas Killen and Stefan Andriopoulos, "Editors' Introduction on Brainwashing: Mind Control, Media, and Warfare," *Grey Room* 45 (Fall 2011): 7–17. Timothy Melley uses similar terminology in "Brain Warfare," 19–41.

131. Melley, "Brain Warfare," 27.

132. The Secretary of Defense's Advisory Committee on Prisoners of War, "POW . . . the fight continues after the battle . . . ," 31, folder Code of Conduct Program (Defense) (1), White House Office, Office of the Special Assistant for National Security Affairs: Records, 1952–1961, Special Assistant Series, Subject Series, box 2, Dwight D. Eisenhower Presidential Library.

2. The Many Faces of the Communist Enemy

1. Associated Press, "Text of Eisenhower's Address on the Boston Common," *New York Times,* 22 October 1952.

2. Eisenhower was the first Republican to carry Massachusetts in a general election since Calvin Coolidge carried it in 1924 and the first Republican elected president since Herbert Hoover in 1928.

3. Ellen Schrecker, *Many Are the Crimes: McCarthyism in America* (New Jersey: Princeton University Press, 1998), 120.

4. Interestingly, the historian Michael Kackman has demonstrated how the televised image of the American spy working on behalf of the United States was an oddly inverted version of the Communist spy. While the Communist spy was a devious and sinister turncoat, the American spy was the "ideal citizen-subject." As Kackman notes, however, this portrayal was not without its complications, as "the spy was both the ultimate 'freeman' and a symbol of the wrenching anonymity of life as a corporatized postwar American 'organization man.'" Michael Kackman, *Citizen Spy: Television, Espionage, and Cold War Culture* (Minneapolis: University of Minnesota Press, 2005), xviii.

5. Associated Press, "Text of Eisenhower Speech Delivered in Cow Palace at San Francisco," *Washington Post,* 9 October 1952.

6. Cecilia Elizabeth O'Leary, *To Die For: The Paradox of American Patriotism* (Princeton: Princeton University Press, 1999), 61.

7. Susan L. Carruthers, *Cold War Captives: Imprisonment, Escape, and Brainwashing* (Berkeley: University of California Press, 2009), 135.

8. NSC-68 was one of the most influential policy papers of the Cold War. Issued in 1950, it promoted an arms race mentality and established military containment as official U.S. policy, which would have a dramatic effect on U.S. foreign policy for decades. NSC-68 reproduced in Thomas H. Etzold and John Lewis Gaddis, *Containment: Documents on American Policy and Strategy, 1945–50* (New York: Columbia University Press, 1978), 396.

9. Hannah Arendt, *The Origins of Totalitarianism* (Orlando: Harcourt, 1951), 591.

10. Ibid., 586–87.

11. Edward Hunter, *Brain-washing in Red China: The Calculated Destruction of Men's Minds* (New York: Vanguard Press, 1951).

12. Hanson W. Baldwin, "The Road to Total War," *New York Times,* 13 September 1953.

13. Ibid.

14. Edward Hunter, *Brainwashing: The Story of Men Who Defied It* (New York: Farrar, Straus and Cudahy, 1956), 22.

15. Ibid.

16. "Crusade for Freedom," *New York Times,* 24 January 1955.

17. Ibid.

18. H.T., "Why the Reds Want All Prisoners," *Chicago Daily Tribune,* 2 June 1953.

19. J. Edgar Hoover, *Masters of Deceit: The Story of Communism in America and How to Fight It* (New York: Holt, 1958), 78. On May 4, 1958, Hoover's book appeared on the New York Times best-seller list. For the next thirty-two weeks it retained the number one position on the nonfiction best-seller list and was the fourth best-selling work of nonfiction in 1958.

20. C. L. Sulzberger, "World Reds Enlist in Drive to Turn Stalin into a Deity," *New York Times,* 27 October 1952.

21. Quoted in Nora Sayre, *Running Time: Films of the Cold War* (New York: Dial Press, 1978), 207.

22. Some of the most prominent images of a benign Communist ally during the Second World War were produced by Hollywood. Films such as Warner Brothers' faux-documentary *Mission to Moscow* (1943), MGM's *Song of Russia* (1944), and RKO Radio Pictures' *The North Star* (1943) all presented an extremely favorable picture of Soviet Russia. All three films would later be cited by the House Committee on Un-American Activities as examples of Communist influence in Hollywood.

23. Quoted in Frank Costigliola, "'Unceasing Pressure for Penetration': Gender, Pathology, and Emotion in George Kennan's Formation of the Cold War," *Journal of American History* 83.4 (March 1997): 1310.

24. Ibid.

25. Mickey Spillane, *One Lonely Night* (New York: New American Library, 2001), 170. In his analysis of Detective Mike Hammer's rhetoric, the historian Stephen J. Whitfield wrote, "The explanation for the appeal of Communism is, apparently, insanity."

26. "Text of Conclusions of the U.S. Report on Soviet Education," *New York Times,* 11 November 1957.

27. Ibid.

28. Drew Middleton, "The New Soviet Man—in Diplomacy," *New York Times Magazine,* 7 December 1958, 107.

29. Ibid.

30. Ibid., 109.

31. Bill Ball, "Inside Czechoslovakia the People Wait, and Hope," *Chicago Tribune Sunday Magazine,* 27 September 1959, 40.

32. Ibid, 41.

33. Robert Hartmann, "Russ Ruled by Control over Mind," *Los Angeles Times,* 18 August 1959.

34. Ibid.

35. President Dwight D. Eisenhower, Memorandum for the Secretary of State, 21 July 1959, folder Coordination of Informational & Public Opinion, White House Office, Office of the Special Assistant for National Security Affairs: Records, 1952–1961, OCB, Subject Series, box 1, Dwight D. Eisenhower Presidential Library.

36. "A Strategy for Peace," 20 July 1959, Coordination of Informational & Public Opinion, White House Office, Office of the Special Assistant for National Security Affairs: Records, 1952–1961, OCB, Subject Series, box 1, Dwight D. Eisenhower Presidential Library.

37. *The Mikado* page of the Gilbert and Sullivan web archive: http://math.boisestate.edu/gas/mikado/html/index.html, quoted in Naoko Shibusawa, *America's Geisha Ally: Reimagining the Japanese Enemy* (Cambridge: Harvard University Press, 2006), 109.

38. John Dower, *War without Mercy* (New York: Pantheon Books, 1993), 9.

39. In his seminal work *Orientalism: Western Conceptions of the Orient,* Edward Said has argued that the long European discourse of Orientalism was fully appropriated by the United States after the Second World War, and the American media commonly portrayed Asians as blatantly inferior, animalistic, and inhuman. A number of historians and literary scholars have built on Said's study since its publication, including Christina Klein, who has argued that the image of Asia in the United States during the Cold War was even more complex than Said's study indicated. For her analysis, see Christina Klein, *Cold War Orientalism: Asia in the Middlebrow Imagination, 1945–1961* (Berkeley: University of California Press, 2003).

40. David Seed, *Brainwashing: The Fictions of Mind Control: A Study of Novels and Films since World War II* (Kent, Ohio: Kent State University Press, 2001), 10. Matthew

Frye Jacobson and Gaspar González arrive at similar conclusions, claiming "the 'Manchurian' of *The Manchurian Candidate* is rich in its significations." For their chapter-length analysis, see "Like Fu Manchu: Mapping Manchuria," in *What Have They Built You to Do? The Manchurian Candidate and Cold War America* (Minnesota: University of Minnesota Press, 2006), 100–129.

41. W. H. Lawrence, "Stevenson Advises Rival That 'Root' of Korea Is Russia," *New York Times,* 26 October 1952.

42. "Peiping and Moscow," New York Times, 15 February 1952.

43. The historian James Peck has noted that this interpretation was not confined to popular culture and is also evident in policy debates and classified NSC documents. For his analysis, see the chapter "China as Puppet," in James Peck, *Washington's China: The National Security World, the Cold War, and the Origins of Globalism* (Amherst: University of Massachusetts Press, 2006).

44. Kurt Vonnegut, Welcome to the Monkeyhouse (New York: Dell, 1970), 89.

45. As Peck notes, during the early Cold War the viewpoints espoused by government officials who saw Asian communism outside of this framework "were swept away in the rapidly escalating ideological war." Peck, *Washington's China,* 82.

46. "Four Years of Red China," *New York Times,* 3 October 1953.

47. William Henry Chamberlin, "The Silent People: Communists Brainwash the Once-Individualistic Chinese into Gloomy Conformity, Fear and Mental Atrophy," *Wall Street Journal,* 9 April 1956.

48. Kingsley Martin, "Peking's Brain Laundry," *Nation,* 28 May 1955, 458.

49. A. Doak Barnett, "Mao's Aim: To Capture 600 Million Minds," *New York Times Magazine,* 9 September 1956, 11.

50. Ibid., 76.

51. Ibid., 11.

52. "Mao's Flowers Bloom for Communists Only," *Saturday Evening Post,* 31 August 1957, 10.

53. Reuters, "China Reds Face Brain Washing," *New York Times,* 8 May 1957.

54. "Charges Castro Uses Brainwashing to Control Cubans," *Chicago Daily Tribune,* 13 November 1959.

55. Holmes Alexander, "Are Communists 'Human'? Writer Back from Moscow Raises Doubt," *Los Angeles Times,* 30 Jun 1959.

56. Peter Biskind, *Seeing Is Believing: How Hollywood Taught Us to Stop Worrying and Love the Fifties* (New York: Henry Holt, 2000), 141.

57. Sayre, *Running Time,* 193.

58. The Psychological Strategy Board's plans surrounding Stalin were outlined in a policy paper titled, PSB D-40, "Plan for Psychological Exploitation of Stalin's Death." For the OCB's plans on a satellite, see Memorandum for the Operations Coordinating Board, 1957 November 12, Weapons & Technological Field (3), White House Office, Office of the Special Assistant for National Security Affairs: Records, 1952–1961, OCB Subject Series, box 8, Dwight D. Eisenhower Presidential Library.

59. "A Strategy for Peace," 20 July 1959, Coordination of Informational & Public Opinion, White House Office, Office of the Special Assistant for National Security Affairs: Records, 1952–1961, OCB, Subject Series, box 1, Dwight D. Eisenhower Presidential Library.

60. Elizabeth Janeway, "Why They Become Communists," *New York Times Magazine,* 14 June 1953, 13.

61. Howard Fast, *The Naked God: The Writer and the Communist Party* (New York: Frederick A. Praeger, 1957), 24.

62. Hoover, *Masters of Deceit,* 102.

63. Ibid., 107.

64. By the time Hunter saw the film it was already several decades old. Andreas Killen

has written about the film's "complicated history" in detail, and it appears to have been originally created in 1925–26 as part of a Soviet cultural program, with various edited versions being shown to different audiences. For Killen's analysis of the film and its history, see Andreas Killen, "*Homo pavlovius:* Cinema, Conditioning, and the Cold War Subject," *Grey Room* 45 (Fall 2011): 45–46.

65. Hunter, *Brainwashing: The Story of Men Who Defied It,* 24.

66. Federal Bureau of Investigation, "Communist Propaganda in the United States—Part V Press and Publications August 1957," ii, White House Office, Office of the Special Assistant for National Security Affairs: Records, 1952–1961, FBI Series, box 8, Dwight D. Eisenhower Presidential Library.

67. For an analysis of the role of censorship in the racial politics of the 1950s, see Louise S. Robbins, *The Dismissal of Miss Ruth Brown: Civil Rights, Censorship, and the American Library* (Norman: University of Oklahoma Press, 2000). The best analysis of the role of big business interests in the Hollywood blacklist can be found in Lary May, ed., *Recasting America: Culture and Politics in the Age of Cold War* (Chicago: University of Chicago Press, 1989), 125–49.

68. United Press, "Books Burned in Oklahoma Town as Not Fit for High School Library," *New York Times,* 12 February 1952.

69. Quoted in Jonathan Zimmerman, *Whose America? Culture Wars in the Public Schools* (Cambridge: Harvard University Press, 2002), 82.

70. Benjamin Fine, "Textbook Censors Alarm Educators," *New York Times,* 25 May 1952, 1.

71. Ibid., 58.

72. "The Texts of Eisenhower Speeches at Dartmouth and Oyster Bay," *New York Times,* 15 June 1953.

73. Anthony Leviero, "Eisenhower Backs Ban on Some Books by U.S. Overseas," *New York Times,* 18 June 1953. As some senators at the time had pointed out, Eisenhower's comments at Dartmouth stood in stark contrast to the State Department's policy of banning books with Communist content in its Overseas Libraries, which is why he was asked to clarify his remarks at his next press conference. For an analysis of this controversy, see Louise S. Robbins, "The Overseas Libraries Controversy and the Freedom to Read: U.S. Librarians and Publishers Confront Joseph McCarthy," *Libraries & Culture* 36.1 (Winter 2001): 27–39.

74. Virginia Pasley, *21 Stayed: The Story of the American GI's Who Chose Communist China—Who They Were and Why They Stayed* (New York: Farrar, Straus and Cudahy, 1955), 58.

75. Ibid., 242.

76. Addressing this point of view, Carruthers has concluded that their recommendations about how to best prepare the public for the threat of Communist psychological manipulation was based on the assumption that "by becoming more like the cold war adversary—more cohesive, better regimented, more thoroughly indoctrinated in right-think—the United States would improve the odds on victory." For her analysis on the debate, see Carruthers, *Cold War Captives,* 210–13.

77. Sayre, *Running Time,* 204.

78. Hunter, *Brainwashing: The Story of Men Who Defied It,* 268–69.

3. Korean War POWs and a Reevaluation of the National Character

1. Describing the evolution of public opinion of American POWs, Susan L. Carruthers has written that their behavior became reinterpreted as "less a testament to communist brutality than an index of national collapse." Quoted in Susan L. Carruthers, *Cold War Captives: Imprisonment, Escape, and Brainwashing* (Berkeley: University of California Press, 2009), 201.

2. In *Totalitarianism: The Inner History of the Cold War,* the historian Abbott Gleason has gone so far as to proclaim that "the returned Korean POWs became, for a time, one of the most extensively studied groups in United States history." Abbott Gleason, *Totalitarianism: The Inner History of the Cold War* (Oxford: Oxford University Press, 1995), 101.

3. Albert D. Biderman, *March to Calumny: The Story of American POW's in the Korean War* (New York: Macmillan, 1963), 1–2.

4. Associated Press, "'Babes in the Woods': Ex-POW Tells Editors American Troops Weren't Trained to Fight 'Brainwashing,'" *Charleston Gazette,* 6 November 1953.

5. Eugene Kinkead, *Why They Collaborated* (London: Lowe and Brydone Printers, 1959), 10.

6. Ibid., 155–56.

7. Ibid., 156.

8. Ibid., 9–10.

9. "POW 'Traitor' Gets Army Back Pay: Major Gets Mad," *Chicago Daily Tribune,* 21 March 1954.

10. In an article about Hollywood's treatment of the Korean POWs, Susan L. Carruthers wrote, "The captives' experiences were scrutinized for what they revealed both of Communist techniques and of Americans' capacity for withstanding them." For her analysis, see Susan L. Carruthers, "Redeeming the Captives: Hollywood and the Brainwashing of America's Prisoners of War in Korea," *Film History* 10.3 (1998): 275–94.

11. Collier's Comment, "The Roots of Courage," *Collier's,* 30 September 1955, 106, Department of Defense, Code of Conduct, First Progress Report, Code of Conduct (Defense) (3), White House Office, Office of the Special Assistant for National Security Affairs: Records, 1952–1961, Special Assistant Series, Subject Series, box 2, Dwight D. Eisenhower Presidential Library.

12. Quoted in Virginia Pasley, *21 Stayed: The Story of the American GI's Who Chose Communist China—Who They Were and Why They Stayed* (New York: Farrar, Straus and Cudahy, 1955), 206.

13. C. D. Jackson to General Wilton B. Persons, folder PSB 383.6 [Prisoners of War] (2), White House Office, National Security Council Staff: Papers, 1953–61, Psychological Strategy Board (PSB) Central Files Series, box 26, Dwight D. Eisenhower Presidential Library.

14. Elie Abel, "Eisenhower Urges Tolerance for G.I.: Mentions Lesson of Prodigal Son in Case of Corporal Who Quit Korea Reds," *New York Times,* 28 January 1954.

15. "Victims of Propaganda," *Washington Post,* 11 August 1953.

16. Col. John J. Driscoll, "Commies Tortured US Flyers to Stage Germ Warfare Hoax: American Airmen Not to Blame for Forced Confessions Emanating from Their Prison Cells," *Lowell Sun,* 2 November 1952.

17. "GIs Outshine Eggheads in Resisting Reds," *Saturday Evening Post,* 31 October 1953, 10.

18. Associated Press, "POW Turncoats Are Sick Men, Says Expert: Author of Book on Brainwashing, Says Men Sick, Need Aid," *Bedford Gazette,* 1 September 1953.

19. United Press International, "U.S. Decides Not to Segregate Freed POWs Who Might Be Reds," *Panama City News,* 25 May 1953.

20. George Sokolsky, "These Days," *Marion Star,* 10 September 1953.

21. "Letters to the Tribune Forum," *Oakland Tribune,* 16 September 1953.

22. "Letters to the Tribune Forum," *Oakland Tribune,* 27 September 1953.

23. Anthony Leviero, "For the Brainwashed: Pity or Punishment?," *New York Times Magazine,* 14 August 1955, 12.

24. Carruthers, *Cold War Captives,* 191.

25. Forrest Edwards, "Indoctrinated GIS to Spread Communist Line: Others Overcome by Red 'Brainwashing' Remain in North Korea; Thousands Died in Prison Camps," *Frederick Post,* 11 August 1953.

26. Greg MacGregor, "Reds' Germ Propaganda Backfired When G. I. Captive Ate the Evidence," *New York Times,* 7 August 1953.

27. Robert Alden, "'Hostile' Captives Had a Rough Time," *New York Times,* 12 August 1953.

28. For a discussion of the POWs' "agency" and the distinctions between progressives and reactionaries, see Carruthers, *Cold War Captives,* 194–96.

29. Andrew Huebner, *The Warrior Image: Soldiers in American Culture from the Second World War to the Vietnam Era* (Chapel Hill: University of North Carolina Press, 2008), 105.

30. "City Takes the Korean Truce Step Quietly: Feelings of Anti-Climax and Doubt Evident," *New York Times,* 27 July 1953.

31. Special to the *New York Times,* "Red Methods Used on G.I.'s Effective: Foe Worked on Minds of Men Already Weak Physically and Deprived of Leaders," *New York Times,* 16 August 1953.

32. Edwards, "Indoctrinated GIS to Spread Communist Line," 1.

33. United Press International, "Some Released Americans Suspected of Being Red Agents," *Charleston Daily Mail,* 9 August 1953.

34. Ibid.

35. Edwards, "Indoctrinated GIS to Spread Communist Line," 1.

36. As Susan L. Carruthers has pointed out, U.S. intelligence officers estimated that 66 percent of the 149 American POWs in Operation Little Switch were "politically reindoctrinated." See Carruthers, *Cold War Captives,* 187.

37. Kinkead, *Why They Collaborated,* 48.

38. Lt. Col. Paul Liles, USA, Transcripts, Ia:224, quoted in Raymond B. Lech, *Broken Soldiers* (Chicago: University of Illinois Press, 2000), 204.

39. Cpl. Thomas Bayes, USA, Transcripts, 4:1138–39, quoted ibid.

40. Kinkead, *Why They Collaborated,* 44.

41. Gleason, *Totalitarianism,* 101.

42. According to the historian Raymond B. Lech, Segal's psychiatric task force was made up of thirty-six psychiatrists, nine psychologists, and thirty-six enlisted technicians.

43. Special to the New York Times, "More Ex-P.O.W.'s Still Face Courts: Others May Also Be Punished Administratively for Acts as Captives in Korea," *New York Times,* 25 September 1954.

44. United Press International, "Army Trial Hears 2 Psychiatrists," *New York Times,* 29 April 1954. For more on Dean's experience as a POW, see his autobiography, William F. Dean with William L. Worden, *General Dean's Story* (New York: Viking Press, 1954).

45. United Press International, "Army Trial Hears 2 Psychiatrists."

46. Associated Press, "Accuser Confused in Dickenson Case," *New York Times,* 28 April 1954.

47. "National Affairs: Flipflop at Panmunjom," *Time,* 11 January 1954, 13.

48. United Press International, "Brainwash Plea Lost by Ex-P.O. W.," *New York Times,* 16 September 1954.

49. Associated Press, "Ex-P.O.W. Held Normal," *New York Times,* 29 September 1954.

50. Associated Press, "Batchelor Awaits Review of Sentence," *New York Times,* 12 October 1954.

51. Robert Young, "Ex-POWs Tell Strange Acts of Schwable," *Chicago Daily Tribune,* 20 February 1954.

52. Associated Press, "Psychiatrist Aids 'Germ' Confessor," *New York Times,* 10 March 1954.

53. Ibid.

54. Elie Abel, "Schwable Case Shows How Communist Torture Works," *New York Times,* 14 March 1954.

55. Associated Press, "EX-P. O. W. Describes Red Brain Washing," *New York Times*, 26 February 1954.

56. Ibid.

57. While the Marine Corps did publicly condemn Schwable, they also awarded him a Legion of Merit in a private ceremony in July 1954 for his actions in Korea prior to his capture. The mixed message illustrates the military's general bewilderment over how to handle the returning POWs.

58. Special to the *New York Times*, "Schwable Freed, But Is Criticized," *New York Times*, 28 April 1954.

59. Dickenson and Batchelor had both belonged to the group of twenty-three American soldiers who refused repatriation to the United States. They were the only two members of the group who had a change of heart and returned to the United States, and some Americans felt they should be forgiven for their temporary lapse in judgment. For example, in Hattiesburg, Mississippi, Albert L. White of the Perry County Draft Board resigned in protest over the Dickenson verdict.

60. Elie Abel, "Army Convicts Dickenson of Collaborating with Reds," *New York Times*, 5 May 1954.

61. Elie Abel, "Eisenhower Gives View on Schwable," *New York Times*, 11 March 1954.

62. Leviero, "For the Brainwashed."

63. Gleason, *Totalitarianism*, 100. The exact number of American POWs who were captured during the war is hard to pin down because of the high number of soldiers who went missing in action. Recent government estimates put the numbers at approximately 7,140 American POWs and 2,701 deaths in captivity.

64. Kinkead, *Why They Collaborated*, 65. The court-martials led to eleven convictions and three acquittals.

65. Advisory Committee to the Secretary of Defense on Prisoner of War, quoted in Biderman, *March to Calumny*, 3–4.

66. Special to the *New York Times*, "Marine Corps Honors Five Ex-P.O.W.'s Who Defied Reds in the Face of Torture," *New York Times*, 12 January 1954, as quoted in Richard Severo and Lewis Milford, *The Wages of War: When America's Soldiers Came Home—From Valley Forge to Vietnam* (New York: Simon and Schuster, 1989), 332.

67. A. E. Hotchner, "They Were Not Brainwashed!," *Los Angeles Times This Week Magazine*, 17 July 1955, 7.

68. Kinkead, *Why They Collaborated*, 26–27.

69. Ibid., 17.

70. Ibid., 34, 17–18.

71. Biderman, *March to Calumny*, 4. Commenting on these activities, Carruthers has noted, "Mayer toured the country during the late 1950s and early 1960s, making a handsome livelihood from delivering the same talk approximately twice a week on the POWs' traitorous conduct and what it indicated about the 'rottenness of American character.'" For an analysis of Kinkead and Mayer, see Carruthers, *Cold War Captives*, 205–7.

72. Robert Trumbull, "G.I.'s in Far East Get Captive Code: Program Strives to Make Prisoners Tougher While in Hands of the Reds," *New York Times*, 12 August 1956. According to Abbott Gleason, the true number of American prisoners of war who collaborated with the enemy may have been closer to 10 to 15 percent. See his comments on this topic, and several sources that broach it, in Gleason, *Totalitarianism*, 251, note 88.

73. Gleason, *Totalitarianism*, 100.

74. "Why Did Many GI Captives Cave In?," *U.S. News & World Report*, 24 February 956, 57, in Code of Conduct Program (Defense) (4), White House Office, Office of the Special Assistant for National Security Affairs: Records, 1952–1961, Special Assistant Series, Subject Subseries, box 2, Dwight D. Eisenhower Presidential Library.

75. Kinkead, *Why They Collaborated,* 15.

76. Trumbull, "G.I.'s in Far East Get Captive Code," 19.

77. Ibid.

78. Philip Deane, *I Was a Captive in Korea* (New York: W. W. Norton, 1953), 89.

79. Roughly 38 percent of all American soldiers who were captured in North Korea died in captivity.

80. Kinkead, *Why They Collaborated,* 148.

81. Biderman, *March to Calumny,* 14.

82. Ibid., 16.

83. Ibid., 10.

84. George Barrett, "Portrait of the Korean Veteran," *New York Times,* 9 August 1953, as quoted in Severo and Milford, *The Wages of War,* 327.

85. Sokolsky, "These Days," 11.

86. Robert Cutler to C. D. Jackson, 5 August 1957, folder W—General (2) [1957–1958], White House Office, Office of the Special Assistant for National Security Affairs: Records, 1952–1961, Special Assistant Series, Name Subseries, box 4, Dwight D. Eisenhower Presidential Library.

87. Biderman, *March to Calumny,* 3.

88. One of the most in-depth analyses of Kinkead's and Mayer's arguments in the historiography of the Korean War can be found in Lewis H. Carlson, *Remembered Prisoners of a Forgotten War: An Oral History of Korean War POWs* (New York: St. Martin's Press, 2002), 4–10. Carlson convincingly demonstrates that the American POWs' behavior was decidedly not "something new in history," and that Kinkead's and Mayer's arguments overlooked extenuating circumstances that helped contextualize what had occurred in the prison camps.

89. This timeline of events has been adapted from Biderman, *March to Calumny* and Lech, *Broken Soldiers.*

90. Biderman, *March to Calumny,* 105.

91. Ibid., 106.

92. Ward M. Millar, *Valley of the Shadow* (New York: David McKay, 1955), ix–x.

93. Herblock, "I'd have said to those Reds, 'Now see Here!,'" *Washington Post,* in Code of Conduct Program (Defense) (4), White House Office, Office of the Special Assistant for National Security Affairs: Records, 1952–1961, Special Assistant Series, Subject Subseries, box 2, Dwight D. Eisenhower Presidential Library.

94. Bosley Crowther, "The Screen: Two New Films Arrive," *New York Times,* 2 July 1953. At the Academy Awards in 1954 the film was nominated for three awards, including Best Actor in a Leading Role, Best Actor in a Supporting Role, and Best Director. Only William Holden won, garnering the award for Best Actor in a Leading Role for his portrayal of Sergeant J. J. Sefton.

95. Bosley Crowther, "Prisoners of War: A Sharp Look at Men in the Film 'Stalag 17,'" *New York Times,* 5 July 1953.

96. The five American-made POW films set in the Second World War released during this period were *Stalag 17* (1953), *The Bridge on the River Kwai* (1957), *The Great Escape* (1963), *King Rat* (1965), and *Von Ryan's Express* (1965).

97. Charles S. Young, "Missing Action: POW Films, Brainwashing, and the Korean War, 1954–1968," *Historical Journal of Film, Radio and Television* 18.1 (March 1998): 49–50.

98. There were five films produced during this period that touched on the topic of Korean POWs: *Prisoner of War* (1954), *The Bamboo Prison* (1954), *The Rack* (1956), *Time Limit* (1957), and *The Manchurian Candidate* (1962). In addition to the original version of *The Rack* (1955), there were several television dramas that highlighted the experience of American POWs in Korea, including the *NBC Fireside Theatre* drama "The Traitor" (1953) and the *U.S. Steel Hour*'s "POW" (1953).

99. Carruthers, "Redeeming the Captives," 275–94.

100. The original version of *The Rack* was written by Rod Serling and appeared on 12 April 1955, on *The United States Steel Hour,* a live dramatic television series that featured hour-long plays. The film version was a remake and, aside from Wendell Corey, who played the prosecuting attorney, was completely recast.

101. Young, "Missing Action," 62.

102. Biderman, *March to Calumny,* 12.

103. Carruthers, *Cold War Captives,* 179.

104. After an initial exposé on the base by Peter Wyden appeared in *Newsweek,* the Associated Press picked up the story, and it garnered national headlines in September 1955. The air force later downplayed these initial reports, claiming that only instructors and volunteer trainees had actually been subjected to torture methods, but by December the course had been temporarily suspended.

105. Rear Admiral D. V. Gallery, USN, "We Can Baffle the Brainwashers!," *Saturday Evening Post,* 22 January 1955, 94.

106. Edward Hunter, *Brainwashing: The Story of Men Who Defied It* (New York: Farrar, Straus and Cudahy, 1956), 267.

107. "Charges Reds Hold Back Yank Prisoners in Korea," *Chicago Daily Tribune,* 3 February 1954.

108. Harold Walsh, "Legion Head Makes Americanism Plea," *Los Angeles Times,* 11 September 1952.

109. "Mildred Younger Backs Teacher Loyalty Check," *Los Angeles Times,* 23 May 1954.

110. Memorandum, "Report on the second day of hearings on s. 1689 before the Senate Internal Security Committee," 18 June 1959, folder Freedom Academy, White House Office, Office of the Special Assistant for National Security Affairs: Records, 1952–1961, OCB Series, Subject Series, box 2, Dwight D. Eisenhower Presidential Library.

4. Motherhood and Male Autonomy during the Cold War

1. United Press, "Mother Pleads with POW Son by Recording," *Los Angeles Times,* 27 September 1953, 12.

2. "A Journey for Richard," Life, 21 December 1953, 19.

3. Associated Press, "POW Jeers at U.S. in Letter to His Mother," *Chicago Daily Tribune,* 14 December 1953.

4. "Turncoat GI Says He May Face Court," *Los Angeles Times,* 14 December 1955.

5. William V. Jorden, "Case of P.O.W. Tenneson: His Mother's Explanation," *New York Times,* 20 December 1953.

6. United Press, "Editor Says Letters Were Not Religious," *Los Angeles Times,* 20 December 1953.

7. Greg MacGregor, "Pro-Red G. I. Asks to See His Mother: Propaganda-Laden Letter Says It Will Not Help Much—Captive Calls for Wife," *New York Times,* 15 December 1953.

8. Testimony of Lieutenant Colonel William E. Mayer to the Special Preparedness Subcommittee, Senate Armed Services Committee Hearings, 14 March 1962, quoted in Albert D. Biderman, *March to Calumny: The Story of American POW's in the Korean War* (New York: Macmillan, 1963), 8–9.

9. Quoted in Abbott Gleason, *Totalitarianism: The Inner History of the Cold War* (Oxford: Oxford University Press, 1995), 100.

10. Alonzo M. Mercer, "The Daily Brainwashing," *Chicago Defender,* 24 October 1953.

11. Although the group had a very high percentage of men from working-class or lower-middle-class backgrounds, these numbers are not representative of the class diversity in the army at the time. In his analysis of the predominantly working-class army of the Vietnam era, the historian Christian Appy has written that "the Korean War was not quite as

class skewed as the Vietnam War." Quoting an earlier study on draft policy and Vietnam, Appy points out that during the Korean era "the Selective Service System was commonly criticized not because it offered too many deferments to the privileged but because 'the under-privileged were too often barred from the benefits of military service by unrealistically high mental and physical standards.'" The study Appy quotes is Lawrence M. Baskir and William A. Strauss, *Chance and Circumstance: The Draft, the War, and the Vietnam Generation* (New York: Knopf, 1978), 20–21. Appy's analysis of class issues related to the Korean War can be found in Christian Appy, *Working-Class War: American Combat Soldiers and Vietnam* (Chapel Hill: University of North Carolina Press, 1993), 30.

12. Chalmers M. Roberts, "The GIs Who Went Red? A Portrait of Poverty, Ignorance, Strife," *Washington Post,* 29 December 1953.

13. Virginia Pasley, *21 Stayed: The Story of the American GI's Who Chose Communist China—Who They Were and Why They Stayed* (New York: Farrar, Straus and Cudahy, 1955), 227.

14. Ibid., 227–28.

15. William Worthy, "Red Bid to Negro PWs Muffed," *Christian Science Monitor,* 8 July 1955.

16. Robert Young, "Couldn't Stand Brainwashing, Gen. Dean Says," *Chicago Daily Tribune,* 9 March 1954.

17. Warren Unna, "Area Ex-POW Splits 'Pros' into 2 Groups," *Washington Post,* 26 December 1953.

18. Noting the inherent irony of blaming members of the working class for the indulgences of the middle and upper classes, Lewis H. Carlson stated, "In truth, the overwhelming majority of these men had come from hard-scrabble backgrounds where conditions were so hopeless they enlisted in the military as teenagers, many of them as young as fifteen or sixteen. As products of the Great Depression, they were arguably the least spoiled generation of the twentieth century." Lewis H. Carlson, *Remembered Prisoners of a Forgotten War: An Oral History of Korean War POWs* (New York: St. Martin's Press, 2002), 14.

19. Eugene Kinkead, *Why They Collaborated* (London: Lowe and Brydone, 1959), 148. According to Kinkead, the majority of soldiers who had contracted "give-up-it is" were the youngest men in the prison camps.

20. The court-marital of Fleming marked the first time since the Civil War that an American officer faced a trial for collaborating with the enemy.

21. John H. Thompson, "The Ordeal of Colonel Fleming," *Chicago Tribune Magazine,* 14 November 1954, 21.

22. Ibid., 49.

23. Kinkead, *Why They Collaborated,* 18.

24. Maj. William Erwin Mayer, quoted in Richard Severo and Lewis Milford, *The Wages of War: When America's Soldiers Came Home—From Valley Forge to Vietnam* (New York: Simon and Schuster, 1989), 335.

25. Kinkead, *Why They Collaborated,* 156.

26. As the historian K. A. Cuordileone has argued, the focus on "softness" and the frequency of hard and soft imagery in the rhetoric and political discourse of the late 1940s and 1950s was a symbolic expression of the gendered anxieties of the period. According to Cuordileone, in the face of the Communist enemy, American political culture "put a new premium on hard masculine toughness and rendered anything less than that soft, timid, feminine, and as such a real or potential threat to the security of the nation." K. A. Cuordileone, *Manhood and American Political Culture in the Cold War* (New York: Routledge, 2005), viii.

27. Special to the New York Times, "Marine Corps Honors Five Ex-P.O.W's Who Defied Reds in the Face of Torture," *New York Times,* 12 January 1954.

28. Cuordileone, *Manhood and American Political Culture,* xx.

29. Ibid., 37.

30. In 1950 Richard Nixon would play upon this theme when he claimed his opponent for U.S. Senate in California, Helen Gahagan Douglas, "was pink right down to her underwear," reminding voters of both her femininity and her supposed pro-Communist politics.

31. Addressing these "right-wing charges," Cuordileone argues that "since these accumulated failures and betrayals were implied by critics to be the work of an effeminate eastern establishment entrenched in the White House and the State Department, the patrician ideal of manhood would counteract those charges." Cuordileone, *Manhood and American Political Culture,* 23.

32. Associated Press, "U.S. Suspends Defiant Judge, Replaces Him," *Chicago Daily Tribune,* 10 December 1953.

33. Robert D. Dean, *Imperial Brotherhood: Gender and the Making of Cold War Foreign Policy* (Amherst: University of Massachusetts Press, 2001), 65.

34. K. A. Cuordileone and Robert D. Dean have both made this point explicit in their analysis of the gendered anxieties of the era. Cuordileone argues that the practical consequence to various affronts to liberal masculinity in the 1950s was that they began to harbor "an almost desperate need to prove their militancy in foreign affairs." Dean pushes the point even further, arguing that the Lavender Scare destroyed the careers of the "China Hands" and other prominent liberal diplomats and "encouraged adherence to a hard-line imperial anticommunism devoid of nuance." See Cuordileone, *Manhood and American Political Culture,* 23, and Dean, *Imperial Brotherhood,* 167.

35. For an analysis of Schlesinger's writings on the subject, see K. A. Cuordileone, " 'Politics in an Age of Anxiety': Cold War Political Culture and the Crisis in American Masculinity, 1949–1960," *Journal of American History* 87.2 (September 2000): 515–45.

36. James Gilbert, *Men in the Middle: Searching for Masculinity in the 1950s* (Chicago: University of Chicago Press, 2005), 32–33.

37. "Korea: The Sorriest Bunch," *Newsweek,* 8 February 1954, 40, as quoted in Cuordileone, *Manhood and American Political Culture,* 81.

38. Roberts, "The GIs Who Went Red?," 11. With regard to the Associated Press report, Roberts was misleading. The original Associated Press report indicated that the POWs had been acting out a "traditional Korean harvest dance." For the original report, see Associated Press, "POWs Defy Final 'Come Home' Plea," *Los Angeles Times,* 29 December 1953. Commenting on these reports, Susan Carruthers noted they accompanied stories that some POWs had fallen in love with Chinese women, concluding "curtain crossing and cross-dressing were, it seemed, all of a piece." For her analysis, see Carruthers, *Cold War Captives,* 176–77.

39. Associated Press, "21 Americans Tell Why They Joined Reds," *Los Angeles Times,* 27 January 1954.

40. John D'Emilio, *Sexual Politics, Sexual Communities: The Making of a Homosexual Minority in the United States, 1940–1970* (Chicago: University of Chicago Press, 1983), 42–43.

41. D'Emilio and David K. Johnson have both analyzed the emergence of a homosexual subculture in the periods they discuss in their respective works. See D' Emilio, *Sexual Politics,* and David K. Johnson, *The Lavender Scare: The Cold War Persecution of Gays and Lesbians in the Federal Government* (Chicago: University of Chicago Press, 2004).

42. Quoted in Cuordileone, *Manhood and American Political Culture,* 50.

43. D'Emilio, *Sexual Politics,* 44.

44. For more on Christine Jorgensen as a media celebrity and her role in shifting attitudes about sexuality, see Joanne Meyerowitz, "Transforming Sex: Christine Jorgensen in the Postwar U.S.," *OAH Magazine of History* 20.2 (March 2006): 16–20.

45. Associated Press, "U.S. Demands Reds Free 375 More Disabled Prisoners," *Chicago Daily Tribune,* 1 May 1953.

46. Associated Press, "Revolution in U.S.!," *Chicago Daily Tribune,* 26 October 1953.

47. Cuordileone, *Manhood and American Political Culture,* 79.

48. Sidney Herschel Small, "The Brainwashed Pilot," *Saturday Evening Post,* 19 March 1955, 31–73.

49. Elaine Tyler May, *Homeward Bound: American Families in the Cold War Era* (New York: Basic Books, 1988), 95.

50. Among others, the historian Mari Jo Buhle has demonstrated this to superb effect in her analysis of American intellectual culture in the 1940s, when scholars influenced by Freud and ego psychology concluded that mothers "shape not only their children's individual characters but collectively the personality structure of their entire society." See Mari Jo Buhle, *Feminism and Its Discontents: A Century of Struggle with Psychoanalysis* (Cambridge: Harvard University Press, 1998), 141. For more on similar topics, see Rebecca Jo Plant, *Mom: The Transformation of Motherhood in Modern America* (Chicago: University of Chicago Press, 2010), 19–54; Ruth Feldstein, *Motherhood in Black and White: Race and Sex in American Liberalism, 1930–1965* (Ithaca: Cornell University Press, 2000), 40–85; and Molly Ladd-Taylor and Laurie Umansky, eds., *"Bad" Mothers: The Politics of Blame in Twentieth-Century America* (New York: New York University Press, 1998).

51. Edward Strecker's *Their Mothers' Sons,* published in 1946, was the most notable academic study from the period that supported the "momism" theory, and it helped further engrain the concept in popular and intellectual culture.

52. For more on Philip Wylie and "momism," see Buhle, *Feminism and Its Discontents,* 125–64; Dean, *Imperial Brotherhood,* 171; and Jacobson and González, *What Have They Built You to Do? The Manchurian Candidate and Cold War America* (Minneapolis: University of Minnesota Press, 2006) 132.

53. A revised edition of *Generation of Vipers* appeared in 1955, serving as a timely reminder of Wylie's argument.

54. Addressing the roots of this critique, the historian Lewis H. Carlson has noted that although popular culture vilified Korean War vets and glorified Second World War vets, "those willing to blame overprotective moms for weakening the moral fiber of their Korean War sons conveniently ignored the fact that both Wylie and Strecker initially were writing about young men who served in World War II." Carlson, *Remembered Prisoners of a Forgotten War,* 3.

55. "The Reader Writes," *Christian Science Monitor,* 12 October 1955.

56. Quoted in Ron Robin, *The Making of the Cold War Enemy: Culture and Politics in the Military–Intellectual Complex* (Princeton: Princeton University Press, 2001), 165.

57. William A. Ulman, "The GI's Who Fell for the Reds," *Saturday Evening Post,* 6 March 1954, 64, as quoted in Adam J. Zweiback, "The 21 'Turncoat GIs': Nonrepatriations and the Political Culture of the Korean War," Historian 60.2 (Winter 1998), 350.

58. William A. Ulman, "The GI's Who Fell for the Reds," *Saturday Evening Post,* 6 March 1954, 64.

59. Although the shift from "parent-centered" to "child-centered" child-rearing practices was pushed into mainstream discourse by the publication of Spock's book, as the historian William Tuttle Jr. indicates, the shift from obedience to permissiveness was already well under way before Spock entered the public eye. According to Tuttle, this shift was the product of numerous cultural and social factors, including concerns about raising children in the midst of the Great Depression and the Second World War and new research in child development that offered alternatives to earlier models of parenthood. For his analysis, see William Tuttle Jr., "America's Children in an Era of War, Hot and Cold: The Holocaust, the Bomb, and Child Rearing in the 1940s," in *Rethinking Cold War Culture,* ed. Peter J. Kuznick and James Gilbert, 14–34 (Washington: Smithsonian Institution Press, 2001).

60. Benjamin Spock, *The Problems of Parents* (Boston: Houghton Mifflin, 1962), 275.

61. Betty Friedan, *The Feminine Mystique* (1963; repr. New York: W. W. Norton, 1997), 395, 399.

62. Ibid., 275. In their analysis of Friedan's discussion of American POWs, the historians Ron Robin and Lewis H. Carlson both point out that she relied heavily on the work of Kinkead and Mayer, or at least on the same reports they had based their analysis on. It was not a coincidence that she arrived at equally dire conclusions. For their analysis, see Robin, *The Making of the Cold War Enemy*, 165, and Carlson, *Remembered Prisoners of a Forgotten War*, 9.

63. "Opinions of Other Newspapers: It's Catching, Portland Oregonian," *Los Angeles Times*, 19 September 1953.

64. "Says She's a Mom, Defends the Name," *Washington Post*, 21 May 1953.

65. "She Expects to Earn Her Medals," *Washington Post*, 1 July 1953.

66. Hans Kraus and Ruth P. Hirschland, "Muscular Fitness and Health," *Journal of Health, Physical Recreation, and Education* (December 1953): 18.

67. United Press, "Draft Rejections Rise to 42 Per Cent," *New York Times*, 6 October 1952.

68. International News Service, "Americans Found Last in Fitness," *Chicago Daily Defender*, 10 May 1956.

69. Leonard Lerner, "British Girls Beat U.S. Boys," *Boston Globe*, 18 December 1960.

70. YMCA, "Fitness for Living," folder Youth Fitness, President's Council on 1956, Files of Special Assistant Relating to the Office of Coordinator of Government Public Service Advertising (James M. Lambie, Jr.) Savings Bonds, Misc. Printed—1956, box 36, Dwight D. Eisenhower Presidential Library.

71. Dwight D. Eisenhower to Robert Montgomery, 16 March 1954, folder Montgomery, Robert, Eisenhower, Dwight D.: Papers as President of the United States, 1953–1961 (Ann Whitman File), Administration Series, box 26, Dwight D. Eisenhower Presidential Library.

72. "Is American Youth Physically Fit? Today's Children Are Bigger, Softer, but Harden Up Fast," *U.S. News & World Report*, 2 August 1957, 66, in folder 156-A-6, Official Files 156-A-6 (2), box 844, Central Files, Dwight D. Eisenhower Presidential Library.

73. Bill Armstrong, "President's Conference on American Youth," *Amateur Athlete* 77.7 (July 1956): 6, in folder 156-A-6 (2), Official Files 156-A-6 (2), box 844, Central Files, Dwight D. Eisenhower Presidential Library.

74. Commenting on this aspect of the media's and government's focus on physical fitness, the historian Robert L. Griswold has noted that women were not the object of as much attention "because flabby boys—and ultimately a blabby, defenseless, 'woman-like' manhood—was the target of cultural concern." For his analysis of the Eisenhower and Kennedy administrations' fitness campaigns, see Robert L. Griswold, "The 'Flabby American,' the Body, and the Cold War," in *A Shared Experience: Men, Women, and the History of Gender*, ed. Laura McCall and Donald Yacovone, 325 (New York: New York University Press, 1998).

75. Anxieties about physical fitness and the nation's soldiers were not entirely unprecedented. They had also been prevalent during the Second World War, when the term *4-F*, the military classification for soldiers who were deemed physically, mentally, or morally unfit to serve, entered colloquial usage. At the time, it was reported that around 30 percent of American men were rejected for military service.

76. "Is American Youth Physically Fit? Today's Children are Bigger, Softer, but Harden Up Fast," *U.S. News & World Report*, 2 August 1957, 70, in folder 156-A-6, Official Files 156-A-6 (2), box 844, Central Files, Dwight D. Eisenhower Presidential Library.

77. Associated Press, "Eisenhower Appeals for Youth Fitness," *Los Angeles Times*, 18 September 1955.

78. "Is American Youth Physically Fit: Today's Children Are Bigger, Softer, but Harden Up Fast," *U.S. News & World Report*, 2 August 1957, 70–71, in folder 156-A-6, Official Files 156-A-6 (2), box 844, Central Files, Dwight D. Eisenhower Presidential Library.

79. Armstrong, "President's Conference on American Youth," 6. Eisenhower's emphasis on home and local institutions was common, and the family, church, and local community were frequently cited as a salve for all manner of societal and national ills. As James Gilbert has demonstrated in his analysis of juvenile delinquency in the 1950s, prominent public figures made similar pronouncements about crime, communism, and juvenile delinquency, "and at base, the counterattack was always similar—refurbished and strengthened family, home, church, and local community institutions." James Gilbert, *A Cycle of Outrage: America's Reaction to the Juvenile Delinquent in the 1950s* (Oxford: Oxford University Press, 1986), 72.

80. Dorothy Barclay, "Problems of the 'Overprivileged Child,'" *New York Times Magazine*, 24 January 1954, 44.

81. Marcia Winn, "Why Is Johnny Always Tired?," *Chicago Daily Tribune*, 20 October 1957.

82. Barclay, "Problems of the 'Overprivileged Child,'" 44.

83. Ibid.

84. Folder 156-A-6, folder 156-A-6 (2), Central Files, Official File, box no. 844, Dwight D. Eisenhower Presidential Library.

85. Mary Ann Callan, "U.S.—Nation of Softies?," *Los Angeles Times*, 13 April 1959.

86. Mary Ann Callan, "U.S.—Nation of Softies? Today's Recruit Less Fit Than Predecessor," *Los Angeles Times*, 14 April 1959.

87. Callan, "U.S.—Nation of Softies?," 13 April 1959.

88. "Parents Attend Trinity Classes," *Washington Post*, 15 February 1960, B4.

89. Several historians and film scholars have analyzed *The Manchurian Candidate*, midcentury American gender norms, and motherhood. They include Susan L. Carruthers, "'The Manchurian Candidate' (1962) and the Cold War Brainwashing Scare," *Historical Journal of Film, Radio, and Television* 18 (March 1998); Margot A. Henriksen, *Dr. Strangelove's America: Society and Culture in the Atomic Age* (Berkeley: University of California Press, 1997), 265–68; Tony Jackson, "The Manchurian Candidate and the Gender of the Cold War," *Literature-Film Quarterly* 28.1 (2000): 34–40; Matthew Frye Jacobson and Gaspar González, *What Have They Built You to Do?*; and Michael Rogin, "Kiss Me Deadly: Communism, Motherhood, and Cold War Movies," *Representations*, no. 6 (Spring, 1984): 1–36.

90. "Books: Pantless at Armageddon," *Time*, 6 July 1959, 80.

91. Analyzing the character of Mrs. Iselin, Carruthers concluded that by "making mom—and, by extrapolation, the whole school of suffocating momism for which she stood—the arch villain of the piece, the film again chimed with a striking contemporary mood and one which was owed in no little part to the Korean POW's presumed 'sad and singular record.'" For her full analysis, see Susan L. Carruthers, "The Manchurian Candidate (1962) and the Cold War Brainwashing Scare," 81.

92. Tyler May, *Homeward Bound*, 75.

93. Richard Condon, *The Manchurian Candidate* (New York: McGraw-Hill, 1959), 290.

94. Jacobson and González, *What Have They Built You to Do?*, 143. May's *Homeward Bound* and Enloe's *The Morning After: Sexual Politics at the End of the Cold War* (Berkeley: University of California Press, 1993) are seminal works in the historiography of the Cold War, and their research addresses how the family, domesticity, and gender roles became engulfed in the politics of foreign policy and national security.

95. Condon, *The Manchurian Candidate*, 70.

96. The historian Michael Rogin has also pointed out that Philip Wylie made an explicit connection between "momism" and rape in *Generation of Vipers* (1942), writing, "America was a matriarchy in fact if not in declaration [in which] the women of America raped the men." Quoted in Rogin, "Kiss Me Deadly," 6.

97. Commenting on anxieties about "authoritarian parents" and motherhood, Susan L. Carruthers has argued, "While indulgent stay-at-home mothers produced suggestible

'momma's boys,' independent working women were suspected of sapping their sons' manliness—as though a zero-sum Oedipal equation precluded the possibility that strong women might raise strong sons." Carruthers, *Cold War Captives*, 209–10.

98. Kinkead, *Why They Collaborated*, 179.

99. Ibid., 186.

100. Associated Press, "Army Going Back to Tough Training," *New York Times*, 15 August 1954.

101. The members of the panel were Brig. Gen. T. W. Dunn, Col. J. C. Hayden, Col. Glenn F. Rogers, Col. Roy E. Moore, Col. Joseph E. Buyes, Col. James J. Tolson, and Col. Louis F. Hamele.

102. Associated Press, "Army Going Back to Tough Training."

103. Ibid.

104. Malvina Lindsay, "Basic 'Toughening' Is Need of Army," *Washington Post and Times Herald*, 2 September 1954.

105. AMVETS Auxiliary, "Code of an American Mother," folder Code of Conduct Program (Defense) (5), White House Office, Office of the Special Assistant for National Security Affairs: Records, 1952–1961, Special Assistant Series, Subject Series, box 2, Dwight D. Eisenhower Presidential Library.

106. President Kennedy's policies and commentary on physical fitness were clearly indebted to the perception of the so-called epidemic during the Eisenhower era and channeled preexisting concerns about physicality, intellect and mental tenacity, consumer culture, and the state of the Cold War into a broad critique of the nation. The best illustration of this is an article written by Kennedy titled "The Soft American," which was published in *Sports Illustrated* in 1960 and cited Kraus's research, the rejection rate of the Selective Service, and the behavior of American soldiers during the early stages of the Korean War as part of a growing body of evidence that indicated "there is . . . an increasingly large number of young Americans who are neglecting their bodies—whose physical fitness is not what it should be—who are getting soft." Like Kraus and other critics, Kennedy largely blamed these soft bodies on the excesses of consumerism and materialism and the communities and parents that failed to prevent them. Like the critics who linked physicality to intellect, Kennedy wrote, "We do know what the Greeks knew: that intelligence and skill can only function at the peak of their capacity when the body is healthy and strong; that hardy spirits and tough minds usually inhabit sound bodies." For the article, see President-elect John F. Kennedy, "The Soft American," *Sports Illustrated*, 26 December 1960.

107. Austin C. Wehrwein, "Johnson Doubts 'Cold War' Thaws," *New York Times*, 28 August 1959.

108. Two distinct interpretations of the nature of "gender crises" have emerged in the historiography of American manhood. Michael Kimmel has argued that concerns about the declining state of masculine toughness have been a recurring theme in American life since at least the nineteenth century; he writes that panics over masculinity "occur at specific historical junctures, when structural changes transform the institutions of personal life such as marriage and the family." James Gilbert, on the other hand, has called the "crisis and response" interpretation into question, pointing out that some of the earlier gender crises in American history were actually first identified in the 1950s, which means that "the subject and object of study . . . [had] been combined and projected upon each other." In the context of this debate, brainwashing is useful because it highlights how recurring preoccupations about masculinity can be pushed into completely uncharted terrain by new developments in technology, warfare, and science. For Kimmel's and Gilbert's arguments, see Michael Kimmel, "The Contemporary 'Crisis' of Masculinity in Historical Perspective," in *The Making of Masculinities: The New Men's Studies*, ed. Harry Brod, 121–54 (Boston: Allen and Unwin, 1987); and Gilbert, *Men in the Middle*, 15–33.

5. Hidden Persuaders on the Home Front

1. Charles Stinson, "'Fearmakers' Treats an Off-Beat Subject," *Los Angeles Times,* 30 January 1959.

2. Timothy Melley, "Brain Warfare: The Covert Sphere, Terrorism, and the Legacy of the Cold War," *Grey Room* 45 (Fall 2011): 26.

3. Richard Condon, *The Manchurian Candidate* (New York: McGraw-Hill, 1959), 40–41.

4. The most extensive academic treatment of the debate over fluoridation can be found in Ann Gretchen Reilly, "'This Poisoning of Our Drinking Water': The American Fluoridation Controversy in Historical Context, 1950–1990" (Ph.D. diss., George Washington University, 2001).

5. Donald R. McNeil, "Fluoridation, Pro and Con," *New York Times Magazine,* 3 March 1957, 36.

6. In his book-length analysis of Wertham, Bart Beaty has analyzed Wertham's role in the Rosenberg and *Brown v. Board of Education* cases in further detail, which he argues would ultimately "lay the groundwork for his critique of mass culture." See Bart Beaty, *Fredric Wertham and the Critique of Mass Culture* (Jackson: University Press of Mississippi, 2005), 82–97.

7. Quoted in David Hajdu, *The Ten-Cent Plague: The Great Comic-Book Scare and How It Changed America* (New York: Farrar, Straus and Giroux, 2008), 102.

8. "Puddles of Blood," *Time,* 29 March 1948, 68.

9. "Urges Comic Book Ban," *New York Times,* 4 September 1948.

10. "Health Law Urged to Combat Comics," *New York Times,* 4 December 1951.

11. For more on some of these early critics of the comic book industry, including Sterling North and Rev. Robert E. Southard, see Hajdu, *The Ten-Cent Plague,* 39–45, 79–82; and Beaty, *Fredric Wertham and the Critique of Mass Culture,* 104–15.

12. Sterling North, Chicago Daily News, 8 May 1940, as quoted in Bradford W. Wright, *Comic Book Nation: The Transformation of Youth Culture in America* (Baltimore: Johns Hopkins University Press, 2003), 27.

13. Hajdu, *The Ten-Cent Plague,* 98.

14. Ibid., 114–26, 148–50.

15. The case that brought the issue before the Supreme Court was *Winters v. New York.* For more on the initial wave of anticomics legislation and the case, see ibid., 93–97.

16. Beaty, *Fredric Wertham and the Critique of Mass Culture,* 119–24.

17. Fredric Wertham, *Seduction of the Innocent* (New York: Rinehart, 1953), v.

18. Ibid., 85.

19. Ibid., 26.

20. Ibid.

21. Ibid., 101.

22. Ibid.

23. Ibid., 174.

24. Ibid., 179.

25. Ibid., 185.

26. Ibid., 190.

27. Ibid., 34.

28. Agnes Maxwell Peters to Fredric Wertham, 7 September 1948, Wertham MS, as quoted in James Gilbert, *A Cycle of Outrage: America's Reaction to the Juvenile Delinquent in the 1950s* (New York: Oxford University Press, 1986), 105.

29. Wertham, *Seduction of the Innocent,* 118.

30. Special to the *New York Times,* "Senators to Hold Teen Age Hearings," *New York Times,* 19 September 1953.

31. "Comic Book Hearing Is Set," *New York Times,* 21 February 1954, as quoted in Hajdu, *The Ten-Cent Plague,* 251.

32. It is not entirely clear if the entire investigation was driven by the publicity surrounding Wertham's book or if the timing of the hearing and the publication of the book were simply a coincidence, but, as Bart Beaty has noted, "That the subcommittee's hearings on comic books virtually coincided with the publication of the book [*Seduction of the Innocent*] ensured a high visibility for both." Beaty, *Fredric Wertham and the Critique of Mass Culture*, 155.

33. U.S. Senate, Committee on the Judiciary, *Hearings Before the Subcommittee to Investigate Juvenile Delinquency (Comic Books)*, 83d Cong., 2d sess., 21 April 1954, as quoted in Hajdu, *The Ten-Cent Plague*, 264.

34. U.S. Senate, Committee on the Judiciary, *Hearings Before the Subcommittee to Investigate Juvenile Delinquency (Comic Books)*, 83d Cong., 2d sess., 21 April 1954, 103, as quoted in Wright, *Comic Book Nation*, 168.

35. Beaty, *Fredric Wertham and the Critique of Mass Culture*, 159.

36. Scholars who have addressed the subcommittee's hearing on comic books in detail include Beaty, *Fredric Wertham and the Critique of Mass Culture*, 156–61; Hajdu, *The Ten-Cent Plague*, 250–73; Gilbert, *A Cycle of Outrage*, 143–61; and Wright, *Comic Book Nation*, 165–72.

37. Irving M. Kravsow, "Senate Comic Book Probers Learn Publisher Attempt at Cleanup Failed," *Hartford Courant*, 22 April 1954.

38. Mary Lou Downer, "Fight Urged on Unsuitable Comic Books, TV Programs," *Los Angeles Times*, 6 June 1954.

39. T. E. Murphy, "For the Kiddies to Read," *Reader's Digest*, June 1954, 6.

40. Gilbert, *A Cycle of Outrage*, 7.

41. Hajdu, *The Ten-Cent Plague*, 272.

42. Appendix to the *Congressional Record*, 82nd Cong., 1st sess., 1951, A3742, as quoted in Keisha L. Hoerrner, "The Forgotten Battles: Congressional Hearings on Television Violence in the 1950s," *Web Journal of Mass Communication Research* 2.3 (June 1999).

43. Willard Edwards, "Morals Suffer from TV Shows, Probers Told," *Chicago Daily Tribune*, 4 June 1952.

44. Josephine Ripley, "TV Link to Youth Crime Sought—Attack on Delinquency Mapped," *Christian Science Monitor*, 20 October 1954.

45. Thomas M. Pryor, "Impact of Movies on Youth Argued," *New York Times*, 17 June 1955. The major topic of debate that day was the film *Blackboard Jungle*, which had been released in March 1955 and focused on a rowdy high school filled with juvenile delinquents.

46. Addressing some of the apprehensions about television in the 1950s, David Greenberg has identified the presidential election of 1952 as a turning point. Both Eisenhower's and Adlai Stevenson's campaigns hired ad men and television producers, moves which received much public scrutiny. As Greenberg notes, the role of television advertising in presidential politics would bring new worries to the surface of American political culture, especially about the potential for public manipulation and for turning presidential candidates into hollow, "fabricated candidates." Of at least equal significance, Eisenhower and the Republican Party were more receptive to the ad men and created a series of twenty- and sixty-second televised political ads, which ultimately created "a new way of campaigning." For his entire analysis of television advertising and the election of 1952, see David Greenberg, "A New Way of Campaigning: Eisenhower, Stevenson, and the Anxieties of Television Politics," in *Liberty and Justice for All? Rethinking Politics in Cold War America*, ed. Kathleen G. Donohue, 185–212 (Amherst: University of Massachusetts Press, 2012).

47. Charles Sutton, "Effects of TV Violence Subtle and Long-Range," *Los Angeles Times*, 31 May 1960.

48. For a contemporary discussion on this topic between several prominent psychologists, see ibid.

49. Quoted in Gilbert, *A Cycle of Outrage,* 155.

50. Aldous Huxley, *The Devils of Loudon* (New York: Harper and Row, 1952), 351–52.

51. Stanley A. Rudin, "Letters," *New York Times Magazine,* 12 July 1959, 4.

52. Edith Evans Asbury, "Rock 'n' Roll Teen-Agers Tie Up the Times Square Area," *New York Times,* 23 February 1957.

53. Edith Evans Asbury, "Times SQ. Rocks for Second Day," *New York Times,* 24 February 1957.

54. Harold Hutchings, "Rock 'n' Roll Addicts Take Over Times Sq.," *Chicago Daily Tribune,* 23 February 1957.

55. Milton Bracker, "Experts Propose Study of 'Craze,'" *New York Times,* 23 February 1957.

56. Mill Whistle, "Pepper . . . and Salt," *Wall Street Journal,* 13 September 1957.

57. "Shepilov Assails Music of the U.S.," *New York Times,* 4 April 1957.

58. The most extensive analysis of this issue can be found in Penny Von Eschen, *Satchmo Blows Up the World: Jazz Ambassadors Play the Cold War* (Cambridge: Harvard University Press, 2006).

59. Arch Napier, "Pepper . . . and Salt," *Wall Street Journal,* 28 October 1957.

60. See, for example, Stefan Andriopoulos's analysis of early German cinema, *Possessed: Hypnotic Crimes, Corporate Fiction, and the Invention of Cinema* (Chicago: University of Chicago Press, 2008).

61. James Gilbert has labeled the debates over juvenile delinquency in the fifties an "episodic notion" because, in his words, it "rested on a history of controversy practically as ancient as the misbehavior of youth." Gilbert, *A Cycle of Outrage,* 4.

62. Gay Talese, "Most Hidden Hidden Persuasion," *New York Times Magazine,* 12 January 1958, 22.

63. Ibid., 60.

64. Robert R. Kirsch, "The Book Report," *Los Angeles Times,* 8 May 1957.

65. Vance Packard, *The Hidden Persuaders* (New York: David McKay, 1957), 3.

66. Ibid., 4–5.

67. Ibid.

68. One notable precursor was Marshall McLuhan, *The Mechanical Bride,* published in 1951. McLuhan defined the advertising industry in terms similar to those of Packard and, in the book's prologue, averred that their intent was to "manipulate, exploit, control."

69. Packard, *Hidden Persuaders,* 139.

70. Ibid., 6.

71. Ibid., 265.

72. Henry Greene, "Selling Your Subconscious," *Chicago Daily Tribune,* 12 May 1957.

73. B. Gough, "Is Psychology Too Much with Us?," *Hartford Courant,* 19 May 1957.

74. Jerome Spingarn, "The Manipulation of Buyers, Voters," *Washington Post and Times Herald,* 28 April 1957.

75. A. C. Spectorsky, "The MR Boys Are Out to Make You Buy and Buy and Buy," *New York Times,* 28 April 1957.

76. Everett G. Martin, "Beware of Background Music on TV Ads: The Tunes May Be 'Fixed,'" *Wall Street Journal,* 13 November 1959.

77. June Owen, "Food: Did I Buy That?," *New York Times,* 31 May 1957. Owen was likely reacting to Packard's accusation that supermarkets deliberately manipulated women by luring them into the store with sights, aromas, and sounds that placed them in a "hypnoidal trance" and encouraged impulsive shopping.

78. Vance Packard, "Resurvey of 'Hidden Persuaders,'" *New York Times Magazine,* 11 May 1958, 20.

79. John Crosby, "Invisible Commercials for the Subconscious," *Hartford Courant,* 29 September 1957. Vicary's findings have been questioned since the early 1960s. In an interview in 1962, he admitted that he had publicized his findings to secure interest in

his market research firm and that they were not based on sound science. According to the marketing professor Stuart Rogers, Vicary disappeared in the 1960s after receiving millions of dollars in consulting fees from some of the nation's largest advertising companies, and his "subliminal message" experiment was nothing more than an elaborate hoax. For more on the strange history of James Vicary, see Stuart Rogers, "How a Publicity Blitz Created the Myth of Subliminal Advertising," *Public Relations Quarterly* 37.4 (Winter 1992–93): 12–17, and Cynthia Crossen, "For a Time in the '50s, a Huckster Fanned Fears of Ad 'Hypnosis,'" *Wall Street Journal*, 5 November 2007.

80. Donald Craig, "Threat of the Hidden Persuader," *Los Angeles Times*, 24 February 1958.

81. Phyllis Battelle, "'Invisible Commercials' Stir the Subconscious," *Washington Post and Times Herald*, 18 September 1957.

82. Crosby, "Invisible Commercials," 31.

83. Larry Wolters, "Psychologist Creates New Ad Technique," *Chicago Daily Tribune*, 22 September 1957.

84. Carter Henderson, "A Blessing or a Bane? TV Ads You'd See without Knowing It," *Wall Street Journal*, 13 September 1957.

85. Jack Gould, "A State of Mind: Subliminal Advertising, Invisible to Viewer, Stirs Doubt and Debate," *New York Times*, 8 December 1957.

86. Carter Henderson, "The Phantom Sell: 'Subliminal' Salesmen Stalk Consumers via TV, Radio and Movies," *Wall Street Journal*, 8 March 1958.

87. Larry Wolters, "Where to Dial Today: 'Flash' Ads Vetoed by Networks," *Chicago Daily Tribune*, 10 December 1957.

88. Betty Friedan, *The Feminine Mystique* (1963; repr. New York: W. W. Norton, 1997), 206–7.

89. Ibid., 208.

90. Ibid., 228.

91. There were other reason's Friedan's article might not have sat well with her readership. When an excerpt from *The Feminine Mystique* was published in the popular women's magazine *McCall's*, hundreds of readers wrote letters to the publication vehemently disagreeing with Friedan's assertion that they sacrificed their individuality when they decided to become homemakers. For more on this topic, see Jessica Weiss, "'Fraud of Femininity': Domesticity, Selflessness, and Individualism in Responses to Betty Friedan," in *Liberty and Justice for All? Rethinking Politics in Cold War America*, ed. Kathleen G. Donohue (Amherst: University of Massachusetts Press, 2012), 124–53.

92. Henderson, "The Phantom Sell," 1, 12.

93. "New Concept of Advertising Demonstrated," *Los Angeles Times*, 15 January 1958.

94. Val Adams, "Subliminal Ads Shown in Capital," *New York Times*, 14 January 1958.

95. Oscar Godbout, "Subliminal Ads Blocked on Coast," *New York Times*, 7 March 1958.

96. Michael D. Reagan, "The Mind at Bay," *Nation*, 29 June 1957, 570.

97. Eric Dean, "Letters to the Times," *Los Angeles Times*, 25 November 1959.

98. Florence King, "Letters to the Editor," *Washington Post*, 31 May 1961.

99. Tirzah Stuart King, "The Reader Writes," *Christian Science Monitor*, 18 October 1957.

100. Gerald F. Smith, "Letters," *New York Times Magazine*, 1 June 1958, 4.

6. The Limits of Individuality in Postwar America

1. Adlai Stevenson, Smith College Commencement, June 6, 1955. Class of 1955. Commencement Speaker, AES, box 2199, Smith College Archives.

2. Associated Press, "Stevenson Deplores Hazard of Conformity," *Los Angeles Times*, 15 June 1954, 17.

3. K. A. Cuordileone, *Manhood and American Political Culture in the Cold War* (New York: Routledge, 2005), 97. Cuordileone provides a laundry list of books, novels, and films that touch on this theme, including "David Riesman's *The Lonely Crowd* (1950), William Whyte's *The Organization Man* (1956), Leslie Fiedler's *An End to Innocence* (1955), Paul Tillich's *The Courage to Be* (1952), Erich Fromm's *Escape from Freedom* (1941) and *Man for Himself* (1947), Arthur Schlesinger Jr.'s The *Vital Center* (1949), and Sloan Wilson's *The Man in the Gray Flannel Suit* (1955); books by popular psychiatrists and psychoanalysts: Edward Strecker's *Their Mothers' Sons* (1946), Robert Lindner's *Prescription for Rebellion* (1952) and *Must You Conform?* (1956), and Abraham Kardiner's *Sex and Morality* (1954); and films such as *12 Angry Men* (1957) and *Rebel Without a Cause* (1955)."

4. See Barbara Ehrenreich, *The Hearts of Men: Americans' Dreams and the Flight from Commitment* (New York: Anchor Press/Doubleday, 1984), 29–33; Timothy Melley, *The Empire of Conspiracy: The Culture of Paranoia in Postwar America* (Ithaca: Cornell University Press, 2000), 48–54; James Gilbert, *Men in the Middle: Searching for Masculinity in the 1950s* (Chicago: University of Chicago Press, 2005), 34–61; and Cuordileone, *Manhood and American Political Culture*, 98–99.

5. Cuordileone, *Manhood and American Political Culture*, 6–9.

6. David Riesman, with Nathan Glazer and Reuel Denney, *The Lonely Crowd: A Study of the Changing American Character* (New Haven: Yale University Press, 1950), 325.

7. Ibid., 349.

8. One of the clearest examples of this can be found in Arthur Schlesinger Jr.'s *The Vital Center* (1949), which attempted to chart a new path for postwar liberalism and largely attributed the rise of Communism to modern men's lack of mental tenacity and their desire "to flee choice, to flee anxiety, to flee freedom." Arthur Schlesinger Jr., *The Vital Center: The Politics of Freedom* (1949; repr. New Brunswick, NJ: Transaction Publishers, 1998), 52. On Schlesinger's analysis and the "crisis of liberal masculinity," see Cuordileone, *Manhood and American Political Culture*, 1–36; and K. A. Cuordileone, "'Politics in an Age of Anxiety': Cold War Political Culture and the Crisis in American Masculinity, 1949–1960," *Journal of American History* 87.2 (September 2000): 515–45.

9. William H. Whyte, *The Organization Man* (Philadelphia: University of Pennsylvania Press, 1956), 7.

10. Ibid., 3.

11. Ibid., 212.

12. Ibid., 105.

13. Ibid., 100.

14. Ibid., 173.

15. Ibid., 198.

16. An appendix to the book, titled "How to Cheat on Personality Tests," went into even more detail about how to beat the Organization's personality tests. The main trick, according to Whyte, was to "try to answer as if you were like everybody else is supposed to be."

17. Ibid., 179.

18. Ibid., 201.

19. Ibid., 365.

20. Jackson Lears, "A Matter of Taste: Corporate Cultural Hegemony in a Mass-Consumption Society," in *Recasting America: Culture and Politics in the Age of Cold War*, ed. Larry May (Chicago: University of Chicago Press, 1989), 44.

21. Ehrenreich, *The Hearts of Men*, 33; Cuordileone, *Manhood and American Political Culture*, 120; David Seed, *Brainwashing: The Fictions of Mind Control: A Study of Novels and Films since World War II*, (Kent, Ohio: Kent State University Press, 2004), 12.

22. Whyte, *The Organization Man*, 397.

23. Ibid., 394.

24. Ibid., 395.

25. Ibid., 262–63.

26. Lindner's notoriety was in part due to his study *Rebel without a Cause: The Hypnoanalysis of a Criminal Psychopath* (1944), which would famously become the title of the 1955 film of the same name starring James Dean. Besides lending the title of his study to the film, Lindner had nothing to do with the production of the movie.

27. Robert Lindner, *Must You Conform?* (New York: Rinehart, 1956), 23.

28. Ibid., 26–27.

29. Ibid., 167–68.

30. Ibid., 168.

31. Ibid., 174.

32. As Cuordileone has pointed out, there were some matters—notably sexuality—on which Lindner prescribed rigid conformity. For her analysis on the gendered implications of *Must You Conform?*, see Cuordileone, *Manhood and American Political Culture*, 159–63.

33. David Riesman, "The Suburban Sadness," in *The Suburban Community*, ed. William M. Dobriner (New York: G. P. Putnam's Sons, 1958), 376.

34. Ibid., 383.

35. Ibid., 387.

36. Ibid., 398.

37. Dwight MacDonald, "A Theory of Mass Culture," in *Mass Culture: The Popular Arts in America*, ed. Bernard Rosenberg and David Manning White, 63–64 (Glencoe, Ill.: Free Press, 1957). MacDonald's article originally appeared in the journal *Diogenes* in 1953.

38. Ibid., 66.

39. Ibid., 69.

40. MacDonald pointed out that the key distinction between mass culture in the Soviet Union and the United States was the primary motivating factors behind each: in the Soviet Union the main goals of popular culture were political, while in the United States they were commercial. In the approach to their respective audiences, however, they were practically identical.

41. Betty Friedan, *The Feminine Mystique* (New York: W. W. Norton, 1963), 307–8.

42. Ibid., 181.

43. Gilbert, *Men in the Middle*, 73.

44. Gay Talese, "Indians Beat Nonconformist Giant," *New York Times*, 20 March 1958.

45. Gay Talese, "Gray-Flannel-Suit Men at Bat," *New York Times Magazine*, 30 March 1958, 21.

46. Ibid., 19.

47. Simone D. Gruenberg, "Homogenized Children of New Suburbia," *New York Times Magazine*, 19 September 1954, 14.

48. Anne Kelley, "Suburbia—Is It a Child's Utopia?," *New York Times Magazine*, 2 February 1958, 22.

49. Ibid., 35.

50. Joan Sadur, "Do I Owe City Life to My Children?," *Chicago Daily Tribune*, 27 December 1959.

51. Housing and Home Finance Agency, "What People Want," 54, quoted in Clifford E. Clark Jr., "Ranch-House Suburbia: Ideals and Realities," in *Recasting America: Culture and Politics in the Age of Cold War*, ed. Lary May, 186–87 (Chicago: University of Chicago Press, 1989).

52. Clark, "Ranch-House Suburbia: Ideals and Realities," 187.

53. Ibid., 184.

54. "The American Home: Taking It Personally," *New York Times Magazine*, 20 September 1959, 38.

55. Ada Louise Huxtable, "'Clusters' Instead of 'Slurbs,'" *New York Times Magazine*, 9 February 1964, 37.

56. Sloan Wilson, *Man in the Gray Flannel Suit* (New York: Four Walls Eight Windows, 1955), 272.

57. Ibid., "Afterword."

58. Eugene Griffin, "Cites Danger of Matriarchy in Suburbia," *Chicago Daily Tribune,* 29 September 1955, C8.

59. Margaret Mead, "American Man in a Woman's World," *New York Times Magazine,* 10 February 1957, 11.

60. Ibid., 23.

61. "Sidelights, Conformist Held Business Rarity," *New York Times,* 12 February 1960, 38. The terms were the titles of William H. Whyte's 1956 book as well as C. Wright Mills's *The Power Elite* (1956) and Vance Packard's *The Status Seekers* (1959).

62. Ibid.

63. "Individuals and Organizations," *Wall Street Journal,* 27 March 1961, 14.

64. "Too Much 'Yes-Man-Ship' in Business, Not Enough Individuality, Personnel Men Say," *Wall Street Journal,* 26 September 1957, 7.

65. Ibid.

66. "Scientist Pleads for Lone Wolves," *New York Times,* 11 January 1958, 10.

67. Robert Alden, "Advertising: Fomenting a Beer Revolution," *New York Times,* 8 May 1960.

68. Russell Baker, "Has the Senate Gone Gray Flannel?," *New York Times Magazine,* 19 July 1959, 11.

69. See Thomas P. Whitney, "Organization Man—Russian Style," *New York Times Magazine,* 25 January 1959, 15; Max Frankel, "The 8,708,000 'Elite' of Russia," *New York Times Magazine,* 29 May 1960, 9; "Soviet Organization Man," *New York Times,* 10 August 1960; and Richard Hughes, "Most Likely to Succeed in Red China," *New York Times,* 21 October 1962.

70. Frankel, "The 8,708,000 'Elite' of Russia," 9.

71. Dan Corditz, "Man in Gray Flannel Gets a New Tie with Merchandizing Weave," *Wall Street Journal,* 8 March 1956.

72. For evidence of the continued popularity of the gray flannel suit, see Jim Bascom, "Man in Gray Flannel Suit—He's in Style!," *Chicago Daily Tribune,* 15 February 1956.

73. Anna G. Creadick, *Perfectly Average: The Pursuit of Normality in Postwar America* (Amherst: University of Massachusetts Press, 2010), 2.

74. For more on the "anxieties of affluence" and social criticism in the postwar era, see Daniel Horowitz, *Anxieties of Affluence: Critiques of American Consumer Culture, 1939–1979* (Amherst: University of Massachusetts Press, 2005).

75. Ibid., 86.

76. "Break from Conformity, UL Leader Urges Negroes," *Chicago Daily Defender,* 12 March 1962.

77. Friedan, *The Feminine Mystique,* 308.

78. Ibid., 309.

79. Miller is quoted in Harold Blake Walker, "Uniformity Threatens Our Personal Values," *Chicago Daily Tribune Sunday Magazine,* 23 April 1961, 47.

80. Ibid.

81. Lester David, "Are You a Conformist or a Rebel?," *Los Angeles Times This Week Magazine,* 11 October 1959, 11.

7. The Legacy of Brain Warfare

1. Committee on Un-American Activities, House of Representatives, 85th Cong., 2nd Sess., 13 March 1958, Printed for the Use of the Committee on Un-American Activities, United States Government Printing Office, Washington, 1958.

2. Sydney Gruson, "Birch Unit Ideas Put to U.S. Troops," *New York Times*, 14 April 1961.

3. Ibid., 19.

4. In his analysis of modern American conservatism, the historian Jonathan M. Schoenwald has argued that the case of Maj. Gen. Edward A. Walker exemplifies the growing disparity between different sanctions of the conservative party, especially with regard to the far and moderate Right, who interpreted the case in very different ways. For his analysis of the Walker case, see Jonathan M. Schoenwald, *Time for Choosing: The Rise of Modern American Conservatism* (Oxford: Oxford University Press, 2001), 103–23.

5. Associated Press, " 'Frontal Attack' on Anti-Reds Seen," *New York Times*, 27 August 1961, 48.

6. Ibid.

7. Willard Edwards, "Testifies Red Order Starts Pentagon Gag," *Chicago Daily Tribune*, 27 August 1961, 9.

8. James E. Clayton, "Writer Says Soviet Directs Drive on Anti-Reds in U.S.," *Washington Post and Times Herald*, 27 August 1961, A2.

9. Jack Raymond, "M'Namara Bans Partisan Talks," *New York Times*, 6 October 1961, 1.

10. "Excerpts from Walker Statement to Senators on Resignation," *New York Times*, 3 November 1961, 22.

11. Special to the *New York Times*, "Kennedy's Speech, in Part," *New York Times*, 19 November 1961, 54.

12. Kennedy's denunciation of "crusades of suspicion" is slightly complicated by the existence of a memo emanating from his office during the Cuban missile crisis of 1962 which asked, "Is there a plan to brief and brainwash key press within 12 hours or so?" Several historians have attributed the memo to Kennedy, although it has also been credited to his military aide, Chester V. Clifton. No matter who wrote it, the memo highlights how the concept of brainwashing had become ingrained in the cultural fabric of the nation and illustrates that the propagandistic impulses of high-ranking policymakers in the Kennedy administration actually may have legitimized the suspicious attitudes he denounced.

13. United Press International, "2 Freed Yanks Want to Lead Antiwar Drive," *Los Angeles Times*, 1 December 1965, 1.

14. "2 Freed POWs Will Undergo Medical Exam," *Chicago Tribune*, 6 December 1965.

15. Robert C. Toth, "Myth of Brainwashing Revived," *Los Angeles Times*, 5 December 1965.

16. For further analysis of how Smith and McClure fit into the larger history of the Vietnam POW experience and the "politics of loss," see Michael J. Allen, *Until the Last Man Comes Home: POWs, MIAs, and the Unending Vietnam War* (Chapel Hill: University of North Carolina Press, 2009), 13–14.

17. United Press International, "Letter of U.S. POW Hints of Brainwashing," *Chicago Tribune*, 30 May 1967.

18. William Tuohy, "Viet Red 'Reeducation' of U.S. Prisoners Fails," *Los Angeles Times*, 22 November 1967.

19. Associated Press, "Marine Survival School 'Brainwashes' Trainees," *Los Angeles Times*, 10 December 1965.

20. Toth, "Myth of Brainwashing Revived."

21. Ibid.

22. Associated Press, "Romney Claims He Was 'Brainwashed' on Vietnam Visit," *Los Angeles Times*, 5 September 1967.

23. Associated Press, "Raps Romney Charge of Viet Brainwashing," *Chicago Tribune*, 6 September 1967.

24. Associated Press, "Romney Stirs Viet Travel Companions," *Chicago Tribune*, 7 September 1967.

25. Robert J. Donovan, "Romney's Viet Remark Stirs Democratic Storm," *Los Angeles Times*, 7 September 1967.

26. Associated Press, "Romney Companions Voice Disagreement," *Los Angeles Times*, 7 September 1967.

27. John Herbers, "Romney Doubts Data about War," *New York Times*, 7 September 1967.

28. Fred Farrar, "McNamara Blasts Romney's Charges," *Chicago Tribune*, 8 September 1967.

29. Warren Weaver Jr., "Nixon Aide Doubts Romney's Ability," *New York Times*, 8 September 1967.

30. Aldo Beckman, "Romney 'Brainwash' Twitted by Dirksen," *Chicago Tribune*, 12 September 1967.

31. Russell Freeburg, "Romney Reply: No Regret, Still in the Running," *Chicago Tribune*, 10 September 1967.

32. "The Brainwashed Candidate," *Time*, 15 September 1967, 26.

33. Paul Clement, "Voice of the People: Romney," *Chicago Tribune*, 13 September 1967.

34. Thomas J. Foley, "GOP in Indianapolis Snubs Visiting Romney," *Los Angeles Times*, 19 September 1967.

35. These statistics are based on the Louis Harris survey, which was published in the *Washington Post–Times Herald* on September 18, 1967. The Gallup Poll also indicated that Romney had suffered a steep decline in support in September 1967, almost certainly a response to the publicity surrounding his brainwashing statement.

36. "Romney Will Resist a New 'Brainwash' on Visit to Vietnam," *New York Times*, 6 December 1967.

37. Chicago Tribune Press Service, "See Romney as His Own Worst Enemy," *Chicago Tribune*, 10 September 1967.

38. Roy P. Fairfield, "Letters to the Editor of the Times," *New York Times*, 20 September 1967.

39. Toth, "Myth of Brainwashing Revived."

40. The collection can be found at: http://ecollections.crl.edu/cdm4/about_hunters.php?CISOROOT=/hunters.

41. Susan L. Carruthers offers an interesting portrayal of the mixed experiences of several of the POWs who refused repatriation to the United States in the 1950s and 1960s. For her discussion of these subjects, see Susan L. Carruthers, *Cold War Captives: Imprisonment, Escape, and Brainwashing* (Berkeley: University of California Press, 2009), 217–20.

42. Associated Press, "Where Are They Now? New Lives, Old Secrets," *Seattle Times*, 2 April 2002, accessed July 15, 2011, http://community.seattletimes.nwsource.com/archive/?date=20020402&slug=roster02.

43. Sen. John McCain, as quoted in Christian G. Appy, *Patriots: The Vietnam War Remembered from All Sides* (New York: Penguin, 2003), 482–83.

44. Interestingly, the origins of the *Homeland* series lie in an Israeli television drama, *Hatufim*, which first aired in 2010 and focused on three Israeli POWs who were captured in Lebanon and held for seventeen years, further evidence that the brainwashing narrative has gone global.

45. Adrian Morgan, "Meet the Muslim Superheroes Who Are Ready to Indoctrinate American Kids," *Family Security Matters Blog*, 24 September 2010, accessed July 1, 2011, http://familysecuritymatters.org/publications/id.7470/pub_detail.asp.

46. Rachel Slajda, "Is Obama Trying to Indoctrinate Your Children with Muslim Comic Books?," *TPMmuckraker*, 28 September 2010, accessed July 10, 2011, http://tpmmuckraker.talkingpointsmemo.com/2010/09/is_obama_trying_to_indoctrinate_your_children_with.php.

47. The books were Aaron Klein's *The Manchurian President: Barack Obama's Ties to Communists, Socialist, and Other Anti-American Extremists* (Washington, D.C.: WND Books, 2010), which reached number ten on the list, and Jason Mattera's *Obama Zombies: How the Liberal Machine Brainwashed My Generation* (New York: Threshold Editions, 2010), which reached number fourteen on the list.

48. Commenting on the original historical context surrounding brainwashing's development as an ideological construct, Timothy Melley has observed how the continued growth of "mass society" and the new geopolitical reality of the early postwar era necessitated the emergence of a new "theory of social influence." As he has pointed out, "The Cold War ruled out the use of Marxist concepts or structural analysis. Brainwashing offered a solution to this conflict; it 'explained' ideological differences and conditioning as the result not of social institutions but of malevolent *intentions*—thus preserving a crucial feature of liberal individualism at a moment when it seemed threatened by both Communism and mass culture." Brainwashing has served a similar purpose in contemporary society, allowing contemporary Americans to "explain" terrorism and other foreign and domestic mediums of social influence in light of propaganda, indoctrination, and even mind control. For Melley's analysis, see Timothy Melley, "Brain Warfare: The Covert Sphere, Terrorism, and the Legacy of the Cold War," *Grey Room* 45 (Fall 2011): 27.

49. Zahid Hussein quoted in Arwa Damon, "Pakistan: Taliban Brainwashes Kids with Visions of Virgins," *CNN*, 6 January 2010, accessed July 20, 2011, www.cnn.com/2010/WORLD/asiapcf/01/05/pakistan.taliban.children/index.html.

50. Jack Hitt, "The Year in Ideas," *New York Times Magazine*, 15 December 2002, 116.

51. Dean E. Murphy, "A War Fought without Guns," *New York Times*, 14 October 2001.

52. David Barstow, "Behind TV Analysts, Pentagon's Hidden Hands," *New York Times*, 20 April 2008.

53. Quoted in ibid.

54. Ibid., 24.

55. Ibid., 25.

56. Ibid., 26.

57. Scott Shane, "China Inspired Interrogations at Guantánamo," *New York Times*, 2 July 2008.

58. Senator Levin quoted ibid.

59. Alfred W. McCoy, *A Question of Torture: CIA Interrogation, from the Cold War to the War on Terror* (New York: Metropolitan Books / Henry Holt, 2006), 31–33.

60. Ibid., 50.

61. Rebecca Lemov, "Brainwashing's Avatar: The Curious Career of Dr. Ewan Cameron," *Grey Room* 45 (Fall 2011): 63.

62. Ibid., 78.

63. Henry P. Laughlin, M.D., "Brain-Washing: A Supplemental Report," 11, 10, folder PSB 702.5 (2) Brainwashing during the Korean War, White House Office, National Security Council Staff: Papers, 1953–61, Psychological Strategy Board, (PSB) Central Files Series, box 29, Dwight D. Eisenhower Presidential Library.

64. National Research Council, "Emerging Cognitive Neuroscience and Related Technologies," quoted in Rick Weiss, "Minding Mental Minefields," *Science Progress blog*, 15 August 2008, accessed July 18, 2011, www.scienceprogress.org/2008/08/minding-mental-minefields/.

65. This figure is based on Eric Lach, "Health, Privacy and Judgement Day Concerns Spurring States' Microchip-Implant Ban Bills," *TPMlivewire*, 22 April 2010, accessed August 1, 2011, http://tpmlivewire.talkingpointsmemo.com/2010/04/concerns-spur-microchip-implant-ban-bills.php.

Index

NOTE: *Page numbers in italics indicate illustrations.*

Matthew Weaver Dunne was born and raised outside of Hartford, Connecticut. He received a Bachelor of Arts at Stonehill College and an A.M. and Ph.D. in history at Brown University. He has worked in higher education since 2008, and taught courses at Stonehill College and MCPHS University. He currently makes his home outside of Springfield, Massachusetts, with his wife, Teri, and their three young daughters.